S0-BYT-342

Divergent Realities

Divergent Realities

THE EMOTIONAL LIVES OF MOTHERS, FATHERS, AND ADOLESCENTS

Reed Larson and

Maryse H. Richards

 BasicBooks

A Division of HarperCollins*Publishers*

Copyright © 1994 by Reed Larson and Maryse H. Richards.
Published by BasicBooks, A Division of HarperCollins Publishers, Inc.

All rights reserved. Printed in the United States of America. No part of this book may be reproduced in any manner whatsoever without written permission except in the case of brief quotations embodied in critical articles and reviews. For information, address BasicBooks, 10 East 53rd Street, New York, NY 10022-5299.

Designed by Helene Berinsky

Library of Congress Cataloging-in-Publication Data

Larson, Reed, 1950–
    Divergent realities: the emotional lives of mothers, fathers, and adolescents / by Reed Larson & Maryse H. Richards.
        p.   cm.
    Includes bibliographical references and index.
    ISBN 0–465–01662–6
    1. Parent and teenager—United States. 2. Adolescent psychology—United States. 3. Family—United States—Psychological aspects. I. Richards, Maryse Heather, 1956–. II. Title.

HQ799.15.L37   1994   93–46394
306.874—dc20   CIP

94 95 96 97 ❖/RRD 9 8 7 6 5 4 3 2 1

Contents

Preface

Writing this book has been for us a personal journey. We put on new lenses and traveled into an intense, real, sometimes awe-inspiring, and sometimes troubling world—a world we have known not only as researchers, but as lifelong participants. Both of us have spent our lives in middle-class families like those we describe. In journeying into their inner worlds, we were obtaining fresh glimpses into our own at the same time.

What surprised us most in these families was how much feeling and animation surrounded their most basic transactions of daily life. Whether their members were getting out the door in the morning, dealing with obstacles at work or school, or quarreling with each other over kitchen tasks, we found their lives to be spontaneous and full of emotion. They did not live in "little boxes all the same." Their lives drew from cultural scripts that were familiar to us—yet their lives were also permeated with unexpected adversities, new excitements, improvisation, and challenge.

As we got deeper into the journey, we began to feel that this drama of daily experience is often more important than the abstractions and statistical trends that make up much research on families. The larger shape of people's lives often seems to emerge from these daily improvisations and raw feelings. Thus while most commentators look at children and parents from a level one step removed, this book focuses on their immediate lived experience. We examine the pains they suffer and pleasures they enjoy, and we attempt to understand how these pains and pleasures play off one another—within each person and within each family.

A tandem discovery was that each family member comes home each night to a different "family." Mother, father, and adolescent children experience dissimilar families—interacting, conflicting, tugging at each other.

The ups and downs in their emotions are not parallel. While they affect and are affected by each other, the daily lives of separate family members are often out of sync. In turn, we realized that the surrealness each of us has experienced in our own families stems from this situation in which interpretation of the most basic events may be contested. Our book, then, presents a postmodern image of family life composed of multiple, contending realities.

We have tried to tell this story in a way that is of interest to many audiences, including scholars, students, parents, therapists, policymakers, and other practitioners. In order to present a readable and "friendly" text, we have avoided complex statistical analyses and confined many of our technical points to the notes and appendixes. We also have not practiced the kind of continuous qualification that we would use in a professional journal; nonetheless, we hope readers will recognize the tentative and limited nature of our findings.

As with any book, our words invariably reflect our own values and biases. We write about our participants in the third person—as she's and he's—yet, unavoidably, we present their lives from our own viewpoint, colored by our own prejudices, beliefs, parochialism, and experiences as members of their culture. Both of us have spent our professional lives studying adolescents, and are newcomers to the study of families—thus we also are guilty, no doubt, of omissions and oversights that might have been avoided by authors with deeper knowledge of the hundreds of scholarly articles written each year on families.

This book, then, should be seen as the fallible travelogue of two apprentices. We hope that it is valued not for any answers it provides, but for the questions it poses. We do not claim to present any final truths, only some fleeting images that may suggest new ways of thinking about families.

We would like to acknowledge the contributions of many people who helped us on this journey. We extend our most bountiful thanks to the participants who gave generously of their time and graciously shared their experiences with us and with you the reader. They were our teachers and friends. And while we necessarily present only glimpses and fragments of their lives, we hope that the whole does justice to the underlying realities they encountered. We also give special thanks to all the wonderful school personnel who facilitated the research—to many administrators, teachers, counselors, secretaries, and custodians who helped us immeasurably.

Within our own staff there are several people without whom this study could not have been completed. Marcela Raffaelli and Mark Ham played invaluable roles in coordinating our study of young adolescents. Elena Duckett was vital in coordinating the study of families. Kathleen O'Donnell made crucial contributions to the background work for the text. Other people who provided valued assistance with data collection and processing include: Linda Asmussen, Steve Roller, Leslie Macomber, Alicia Joebgen, Daniel Kim, Jim Elison, Claudia Lampman-Petraitis, Carol Kirshnit, Imelda Catbagan, Michelle Mager, Ellen Stoltzfus, Meridith Foster, Meery Lee, Sandra Tenbrink, Shanna Brodie, Joseph Colletti, Carla Leone, Venette Cochiolo, and Karen Reitze, among others. We give our warmest thanks to all of these individuals.

A number of colleagues, friends, and students also played important roles in reading innumerable drafts of the text. A special thanks to Jo Ann Miller, our editor at Basic Books, and to Pauline Boss, who read through the manuscript from beginning to end. We also thank Paul Rosenblatt, Jeylan Mortimer, Maureen Perry-Jenkins, Harold Grotevant, Sharon Irish, Carol Spindel, Dale Blyth, Laurie Kramer, Marcelo Diversi, Sally Gillman-Hanz, and Suzanne Wilson-Shockley for reading parts of the text. These people provided valuable feedback but bear no responsibility for the many places in which we did not live up to their helpful suggestions.

We are also indebted to others who have in various ways contributed to the work of the book, including Bertram Cohler, Grayson Holmbeck, David Olson, Sonya Salamon, Mihaly Csikszentmihalyi, Robert Czeh, W. Andrew Collins, Anne Petersen, Daniel Offer, Anita Greene, Kay Michael Troust, Larry Chalip, Mary Kennedy, Jean Larson, Babette McNairy, Barbara Cain, and Ed Mascorro. Reed would also like to thank his wife, Sharon Irish, and his children, Miriam and Renner, for putting up with the daily stress on the family resulting from the work on this book. If the text is articulate in its image of fathers, it is partly from his observation of his own family behavior. Maryse would like to thank her parents for instilling a love of literature and ideas and Brandon Taylor for his devotion and support.

Major financial support for the study came from an eight-year grant from the National Institute of Mental Health to Reed Larson and Maryse Richards on "Stress, Coping, and Emotional Well-Being in Adolescence" (MH38324). Additional support came from another grant to Maryse Richards on "The Effects of Maternal Employment on Young Adolescents" (MH42618) and a Department of Agriculture grant to Reed Larson, "Divergent Family Realities" (ILLU-60-0332). Support also came from a one-year National Research Service Award (HD07513) to Reed Larson, which allowed him to spend a year writing at the Department of Family

Social Science and the Institute on Child Development at the University of Minnesota.

This book is the product of an amicable, productive, long-term collaboration between the coauthors. While we worked together at every stage of the project, Reed had primary responsibility for conducting the study of young adolescents, and he drafted and revised the text of the book. Maryse had primary responsibility for conducting the family study, and she contributed ideas and editorial feedback to the developing manuscript. Though we live in different cities, the fruits of our labors provide evidence that divergent realities can come together.

Divergent
Realities

CHAPTER 1

The Family:
A BREW OF EMOTIONS

H er family is the furthest thing from Natalie Vahn's mind as she struggles to pay attention to her sixth-grade science teacher. Only a few hours before, Natalie and her best friend, Sasha, had stood at their lockers joking about how cute their classmate Jake is. Then, just moments ago, Jake told her he would be coming to the track meet tonight to cheer for her in the 100-yard dash. Natalie is so excited she can think of nothing else.*

A few miles away, Natalie's mother, Madge Vahn, is also absorbed and animated, but by something quite different. An office manager in a medical supply firm, Madge is eagerly learning a new computer data system that, she sees, will make office operations more efficient. Her job has its ups and downs—just yesterday, her boss threw one of his fits—but she is invested in her career, and her income is important to the family; it allows them certain extras, like Jordache jeans for her four children.

In yet another part of the community, Natalie's father, Rusty Vahn, is up on a scaffold, laying the bricks of a fireplace for a new house. At the same moment that Natalie is jubilant and Madge is animated, Rusty is disgruntled because a high wind is blowing dust up into his face and eyes. To make matters worse, other members of his crew were called away this morning, so he has to work alone, and near his job site a school bus driver just had a heart attack, an event that is sending chills up his spine about the uncertainty of life and the vulnerability of his children.

*We have changed names and nonessential features of the people discussed in order to maintain their anonymity.

1

Excitement about a new romance, the stimulation of learning a new skill, vague worries about death—these three family members are living different emotional realities. That evening Madge's good mood falls apart when the alarm system at work malfunctions, forcing her to stay long beyond her usual quitting time. Rusty comes to Natalie's track meet and, unaware of Jake's presence, also cheers for her as she takes first in the 100-yard dash and two other events. Later all three family members arrive home and report feeling content, while Natalie washes out the kitchen sink, Madge vacuums, and Rusty showers off the grime of the day.

Yet even when Natalie, Madge, and Rusty are at home together, the convergence of their fast-paced lives is often more apparent than real. A few evenings later, for example, all are sitting at the table eating supper, but each has separate thoughts and feelings. Rusty has had another onerous day at work, and complains about the Thursday nights Madge spends taking a business management class. Madge is peeved about his male chauvinist griping and the fact that he slept Sunday while she and the children tackled a mountain of chores. Natalie is buoyant again, this time because she played well for her softball team that afternoon, but she also feels distant from her parents and frustrated with their bickering. The three of them—Natalie, Madge, and Rusty—are in the same room doing the same activity, but like many families today, they are in separate emotional worlds, which are often out of sync.

For decades commentators have been proclaiming a "crisis" in the contemporary American family. Skyrocketing divorce rates, the high incidence of spouse and child abuse, and increased adolescent violence and suicide suggest that something is not right in many families, especially as children move into the teenage years. These problems are partly attributable to worsening social and economic conditions: declining wages, deteriorating communities, and erosion of government support during the 1980s have had a direct adverse effect on many families.[1] Yet signs of dysfunction, from divorce to drug use, are also prevalent among families that seem to have everything going for them. Even in two-parent, middle-class families, day-to-day interactions often create conflict.

The immediate source of family dysfunction, we believe, lies in the emotional interior of families. Contemporary family life often breaks down because individuals do not understand and cannot negotiate the differing patterns of time and emotion that structure each of their lives. Busy parents have difficulty grasping what it is like to be an adolescent in the teenage world of MTV, rap music, and sex at fourteen. Husbands are confused about how to relate to their wives in an era when women's role models span from the 1950s housewife to the powerful business executive. And women do not know how much their husbands' inner lives are like Alan Alda's or Arnold Schwarzenegger's. Each family member lives in a separate, often fast-paced and highly charged emotional world. They are on different wavelengths; they experience excitement and strain in different parts of their lives.

This book investigates these divergent emotional realities and how they shape, and often disorder, the experience of two-parent European-American families like the Vahns. What do husbands, wives, and adolescents in these families feel as they go through the day? Where do their lives intersect? And how does emotional energy or conflict get transmitted from one to another? We examine the emotional interiors of these families and describe the dynamics of time and passion that structure family existence.

To accomplish this, we have employed a new research method—one never before used with families—to gather family members' ongoing accounts of their daily experience. While other researchers have probed attitudes, observed behaviors, and questioned beliefs, not until now has anyone obtained direct information on what individual family members actually feel as they go about their lives.

Compared to that of some families we'll meet, the friction in the Vahn family is mild. In others a girl threatens suicide to punish her mother, a father's alcoholism spreads anger through the whole family, and the raw contempt between one husband and wife spirals out of control until the wife kicks him out of the house. We shall also see families in which members are usually buoyant and maintain warm relationships. In this book we attempt to understand what is not working in many of today's families—as well as what is working in others.

A New Gold Standard

Of course, the lives of mothers, fathers, and children have always differed, but this divergence was less of a concern in the past. In the more rigid and authoritarian nineteenth century, each family member had a prescribed role. The success of a family depended not on how well the members related to each other, but on how well each member played his or her role: how productive the farm was, how many children a couple had, and how well a fixed set of moral injunctions was instilled in the children. It did not matter that men were emotionally isolated, children were unhappy, and women were exhausted—each person had his or her duty to perform.

As families have ceded many of their instrumental functions, such as economic production and in-home schooling, they have placed greater and greater importance on interpersonal functions, such as companionship, mutual support, and fostering the emotional development of their children. Family members now relate to one another less in terms of fixed roles and more as individuals.[2] As a result, getting along with one another has become much more important. In a sense, we have moved to a higher level on a Maslowian hierarchy of personal relationships, where cooking for, providing for, and obeying are no longer enough. In the contemporary "democratic family," having positive, close relationships is seen as the essence of a good family.[3]

In fact, close relationships have become the very purpose of families. Summarizing reports from a cross-section of the American population, one group of researchers concludes:

> The emotional quality of family relationships is [now] felt to be more important than the formal status of those relationships. Having a happy marriage is more highly valued than is being married. Respecting one's children ranks higher than does having children. The inner qualities of relationships are valued more than is the simple existence of the relationships."[4]

In another recent survey, three-quarters of American adults rejected the traditional definition of the family as a mother, father, and children, in favor of a definition based on the quality of relationships: "a group of people who love and care for each other."[5]

Interpersonal happiness has thus become the gold standard of a good family—and its Achilles' heel. Whereas in the past, marriage was often viewed as an economic arrangement, couples now embark an marriage with an expectation that they will be best friends, emotional intimates, and fulfilling sexual partners. Consequently, failure to sustain marital happiness is the most frequent reason for divorce. When couples divorce, they do so not because they are rejecting the institution of marriage, but because they feel that their marriage has not met the high ideal of a close, vital relationship to which they still aspire.[6]

Relationships between parents and children, likewise, are now judged by how well they live up to an ideal of closeness and warmth. In the not-too-distant past, the quality of feelings between parent and child was secondary. Parents were primarily concerned with a child's good behavior; physical and emotional abuse of children was tolerated, even promoted, as a means to this end.[7] Turn-of-the-century parents were encouraged to adopt a stern, authoritarian posture. They were even told not to play with their children, lest the relationship become too familiar. It was only in the middle of the century that child psychologists began advocating warmth, closeness, and having fun together.[8] Now the critical importance of a warm parent–child relationship is rarely questioned.

Of course, one might ask whether this new emphasis on family warmth is just another psychological fad. Are we just being taken in by another capricious twist of history? Research indicates that the answer is a definitive "no," at least for the families that are the focus of this book. By all evidence, these revolutionary changes in our family ideals are in the right direction. In our society, adults with warm and happy marriages have better mental and physical health; children who have close, trusting relationships with their parents do better in school, have higher self-esteem, and are better adjusted.[9] These new ideals are appropriate; they should be embraced. The problem is that we often do not know how to achieve them. We have raised our expectations, but we do not know how to live up to them.

Family values are a high priority with Americans, and interpersonal qualities such as support, mutual respect, and communication of feelings top the list of people's family values.[10] But in the bustle of contemporary life, well-meaning mothers, fathers, and children are often unable to bridge their differing realities.

THE ADOLESCENT GAUNTLET

At no time is the tension between family realities greater when children first enter adolescence. This is when the moorings of young people's lives begin to shift out of the family. In Western society we expect adolescents to become more emotionally independent of their families: psychologists recognize it to be one of the "developmental tasks" of this stage. Yet the age of this shift has been coming earlier and earlier, before parents and the children themselves are ready for it. Whereas adolescence used to correspond to the teenage years, now eleven-year-olds, like Natalie, are often midway through puberty and experiencing enticing lures to the world of peers and romantic relations. They begin listening to rock or rap music and spending more time alone and with their friends. As early as age ten or eleven, children begin to shift their center of gravity away from home, often with disruptive consequences for themselves and their families.

This early adolescent period subjects family relationships to their ultimate test. As a result of the many changes in adolescents' lives, communication between parent and child often diminishes, and conflict increases.[11] Parents lose touch with what is happening to their children at school and with friends. Even at home, parents and children often have discrepant views of the family. They have different perceptions of their family's rules and values; they may even disagree about whether the family is close or distant.[12] At this age, adolescents become less willing to automatically accept their parents' ways of seeing things, and parents are often slow to adjust. A breach opens between the generations, and when this breach is wide, it can have troubling consequences for both sides.[13]

This turmoil is not confined to the parent–adolescent relationship. For the parents as individuals, this can be a time of strain. Children's entry into this period of "sex, drugs, and rock 'n' roll" can throw a wrench into family life, putting everyone out of sorts. Interacting with a rebellious or questioning adolescent may force mothers and fathers to examine their own purpose and direction in life.[14] This is the time when a parent may change jobs, for example, or, like Madge, go back to school, requiring household readjustments that can bring out new tensions in the family. Or the conflict that one parent has with a teenager may spill over into interactions between spouses.

For some adults, their children's adolescence is a turning point in their marital relationship. They may find themselves arguing, in some cases for the first time, about how to manage their children. In fact, it is not until this period that some husbands and wives reach rock bottom and begin to recognize the emotional poverty of their marriage. They may start to admit that their lives do not match, that they enjoy different things, that their realities are discordant.

Like the pieces of a puzzle that just don't fit together, family life may suddenly seem out of joint: parents and children not getting along, husband and wife at odds. This divergence of realities makes the early adolescent years a particularly important window for observing why so many Americans families are not working well. It is a time when family relationships are tested. It is a time when the flaws and strengths of contemporary families come into full relief.

THE RHYTHM OF FAMILY RELATIONS

The Polanskys' Saturday morning starts out as though it is going to be a perfect illustration of the turmoil created by conflicting family realities. Eric, their husky thirteen-year-old son, gets up and puts on the comfortable clothes he has been wearing all week. But his mother, Ruth, an emotionally expressive woman who works part-time on an assembly line, thinks his clothes look too grubby for the lunch she is organizing with the in-laws.

Then his father, Burke, the owner of a small business who has just given up smoking, wakes up in a grouchy mood and reads the riot act to his son.

Despite this rocky start, things start to run smoothly for the Polanskys, once a compromise is found. Father and son go to the park and get absorbed in a competitive game of tennis, then Eric helps his mother put together her new exercise cycle. The lunch with the relatives is pleasant for all; in fact, Burke describes it as the high point of his week. Later that afternoon, Eric goes to spend the night at a friend's house and his parents go out to a party.

This family exhibits a sense of warmth and coordination that is absent in others, like the Vahns. On days Ruth works, Eric takes care of himself after school and performs a regular set of chores; Burke often gets home early and starts supper. On this Tuesday at noon, Ruth and Burke meet at a restaurant for lunch and discuss plans for redecorating the kitchen. Wednesday evening the family eats early and goes to Eric's school for the science fair, where they all express admiration for his exhibit.

The Polanskys are usually able to synchronize their day-to-day activities, but by no means do they have everything worked out. Burke can be overbearing with his son. Ruth is not satisfied with her menial factory job and, like Madge Vahn, reports unhappiness when doing housework. Eric falls in love with a girl, only to be crushed several hours later when he discovers she is going with someone else. Part of the challenge for the Polanskys and other contemporary families is just finding time for one another. Falling wages and rising costs require mothers and fathers to put in more hours of labor just to maintain their standard of living. Burke, for example, sometimes works fourteen- and sixteen-hour days. And children are more hurried than in the past: teens like Eric rush from school to a soccer match to a rendezvous with friends. As a result, families have become "time poor."[15] Family members sometimes cannot find time to sleep, let alone spend time and cultivate warm relations with each other.

Nonetheless, the Polanskys demonstrate that some families are able to get through the challenges of contemporary life with minimal tension and conflict. We believe they are able to do so by exercising a special wisdom that lies beyond traditional injunctions to love, trust, and honor each other. Some families appear to possess a combination of knowledge and art that allows them to coordinate family members' differing realities. Of course, attempting to define what makes for a "good" family is controversial, even taboo in some circles. We would be among the first to recognize that such attempts are fallible and culture-specific. Nonetheless, we strive in this book for insight into the processes whereby some of the families in our study negotiate daily activities and emotions in a way consistent with their members' separate and collective well-being.

Our goal in this book, then, is to examine the daily rhythms of contemporary family life in order to discover their role in family health. We believe that the minutes and hours of people's everyday lives are the arena in which family warmth is created—or family problems take shape and build steam. For families to be healthy, members must have daily interactions in which their emotional worlds come into meaningful contact: times when minds meet, when closeness is shared. To make families work, therefore, we begin with knowledge of their day-to-day patterns of time and emotion. By examining the daily stories of different families and identifying repeated patterns in their experiences, we illuminate how some families are successful in negotiating the difficult emotional terrain of modern life.

EXAMINING LAYERS

This book investigates three layers of existence in the families we studied. In part I we focus on the experience of *individual family members*: the lives of fathers, mothers, and young adolescents. Chapter 2 examines the daily experience of fathers, such as Rusty and Burke; we discover that their lives are structured by a pattern of stress and frustration at their jobs alternating with happier, recuperative time at home. By contrast, in chapter 3 we find that mothers like Madge and Ruth experience more stress in the family sphere and feel greater happiness away from home, even at their jobs. And in chapter 4 we show that young adolescents experience still another reality, characterized by widely fluctuating emotional states: feelings of loneliness, anger, happiness, and being in love. Each of these three individual realities—father, mother, adolescent—follows a unique psychological order or "emotional logic": family members experience joy, vulnerability, and distress in different domains.

The tension between these divergent realities is most acute when family members' lives intersect, and in part II we examine the overlap between the lives of each pair of family members. We are concerned here with the layer of family life involving *two-person, or "dyadic," relationships*. In chapter 5 we consider relations between husbands and wives, and find that day-to-day marital interactions are far from the gold standard of unbroken love and warmth. In chapter 6 we examine relations between mothers and young adolescents and uncover a mixture of daily closeness and conflict. And in chapter 7 we find that many fathers make the mistake of trying to be a recreational leader, trying to create "happy times" with their children, when emotional honesty, including acceptance of unhappiness, is more important to adolescents.

In part III we consider how family emotional systems, such as the Vahns and Polanskys, work as a whole. We examine how the lives of family members interrelate, with a goal of identifying the dynamics of daily life that differentiate healthy from distressed families. Chapter 8 examines a set of dysfunctional processes that we find in some families, including unchecked contagion of emotion from one family member to another. In chapter 9 we then ask what works in other families: what opportunities does the bustle of contemporary life provide for positive relationships? While we offer no simple formula for making families healthy, we conclude with insights about making family life run smoothly.

The rest of this chapter describes how we collected the data from which the book is derived.

A STUDY OF FAMILY REALITIES

The basis for this book is a unique study in which fifty-five Chicago-area families provided reports on random moments in their daily lives. They shared with us what they felt like when they got up in the morning, when they were at work or school, when they sat across the dinner table at the end of each day. We chose to focus on white middle- and working-class families because these are families that should be functioning well, yet often are not.[16] These families have everything going for them, yet they show surprisingly many signs of distress.

We also chose to focus on two-parent families, not because single-parent families are unimportant to study, but because of the question we wanted to ask. The great majority of American adults strongly believe in the two-parent family—96 percent in one survey.[17] The ideal of the happy, middle-class, two-parent family is what most people aspire to; it is their standard for family life. Thus we feel it is crucial to go inside such families to ask why so many of them are not functioning well, and what happens in those that are.

Sampling Daily Family Experience

Our interaction with the Vahns was typical of how we conducted the study. Our goal was to obtain an emotional photo album of their family life, a set of snapshots of what one young adolescent and her parents go through in an average week. We drove out to their suburban split-level home on a warm Tuesday night in April 1987. In a forty-minute instruction session we gave Natalie, Madge, and Rusty each an electronic pager and told them it would beep about eight random times between 7:30 A.M. and 9:30 P.M. for the next seven days.[18] Along with the pager, we gave each a self-report booklet. When the pager beeped, they were to complete one page in the booklet, providing information on what they were doing, thinking, and feeling just before the beep.

All three were a little excited to be in the study, and a little apprehensive. Rusty joked that the pager was sure to go off "the minute I sat down on the john." We assured him he could be forthright. Natalie was concerned about what to do with the pager during her athletic activities, so we discussed several options with her. We also told them that they should turn the pager off if they wanted to sleep during the target hours—we were not interested in sampling their dreams.

We wanted the research to be as "user friendly" as possible. All three family members would be signaled at the same time, but they were not to share what they recorded with one another or anyone else. To ensure privacy, we furnished stickers so that they could seal each page shut after writing their report. With Rusty and Madge we discussed how the procedure would work at their jobs; neither felt it would be a problem to stop what they were doing and complete the form at each signal. Since we had contacted the family through Natalie's school, her teachers already knew that her pager would signal her (by quiet vibration during class) and that she would take a minute out to write her report. Participants were also asked to fill out a short daily diary before going to bed to give an overview of the day.

This novel research procedure is called the experience sampling method, or ESM, and "sampling" experience is precisely what it does.[19] The objective was to obtain reports on random moments in family members' lives, including their time at work and school, at home and with each other. The value of the ESM is that it circumvents limitations of the laboratory and survey methods that are used in nearly all family research. The behavior of people in laboratory studies, researchers are learning, often differs from what goes on in real life. Studies of marriage, for example, show that a couple's behavior in a laboratory does not mirror how they behave at home.[20] Likewise, it is known that people are not good at remembering past experience, as survey studies require; what's worse, their memories are often systematically biased or distorted.[21] Therefore, even large survey studies employing thousands of respondents must be viewed with suspicion when they involve questions that people cannot answer accurately. If you are interested in families' daily lives, you need to gather data on their experience as it transpires, and this is what the ESM does. We have been employing the technique for fifteen years in studies of individuals, but this is the first time anyone has used it with families.

One week after giving the Vahns the pagers and booklets, we returned to their home to retrieve them and to conduct a separate interview with each family member about the week. We also had them complete questionnaires dealing with their well-being and features of the family.[22] We found that, like most families we worked with, everyone had been conscientious. Natalie had provided a nearly complete set of reports, except for one day when she had inadvertently left the pager at home. Madge had responded to nearly every signal she received. Rusty had turned off the pager during his Sunday nap and during a two-hour period when he was repairing a broken water main at his job, but otherwise provided a complete record. We estimate that participants in the study responded to about 90 percent of the signals we sent them. This means we obtained reports on their activities and feelings during the great majority of their typical daily lives.[23]

Appraising Emotional Realities

As we returned to our office with the completed ESM booklets, our objective was to try to learn what we could about each family's week. We wanted to be able to tell the story of Natalie's, Madge's, and Rusty's ups and downs during those seven days—to understand and be able to empathize with what they felt as the events of the week progressed.

We also wanted to uncover the emotional patterns in how a whole group of adolescents and their parents experienced the different parts of their lives. How did employed mothers and traditional homemakers spend their time? In what daily situations were fathers likely to be angry, irritable, or lonely? Because the reports occurred at random times, they provided a representative sample of people's experience. We found, for example, that Natalie and other adolescents were generally happy when with their friends and less happy when with their siblings. Such patterns are important because emotional states not only define people's internal feeling of health and well-being, they also determine how they behave toward each other, and how they work at their jobs or at school: people in better moods are more altruistic and productive.[24]

In order to capture these stories and these emotional patterns, we gave participants a series of standard questions on the ESM report form (see appendix 1.1). These included, first, questions about the participants' *objective situation* each time they were signaled: Where were they, who were they with, and what were they doing? From responses to these questions we were able to identify the daily contexts in which they spent their time and see the unfolding of important events in their lives. We also made a fundamental division between time in the "household sphere" and the "public sphere."[25]

We were equally interested in the participants' *subjective situation*: their internal experience. The ESM form posed a set of questions about what their emotions and other subjective states were just prior to each signal. In this book we employ a scale of overall "mood" or "emotion" to draw the main outlines of emotional states. This scale is derived from three questions that asked participants to rate the degree to which they felt happy to unhappy, cheerful to irritable, and friendly to angry at the time of each signal.[26] To paint a richer picture, we also report ratings for other "feeling states," including some that psychologists would not consider to be emotions, such as feeling hurried, tired, and competitive.

In asking participants to provide this varied range of information about their lives, we chose to buck the typical practice in our field of trying to reduce people's lives to a small number of dimensions. Rather, we sought to take a broad view of people's experience. We examine the participants' lives not by narrowing them down to a restrictive theoretical or statistical model, but rather by looking at them holistically—as the participants experience them. The picture we offer is, of necessity, partial and incomplete— people's lives have a complexity that can never be fully captured. Nonetheless, we have sought to present the lives of people like Natalie, Rusty, and Madge in their own terms.

Who Participated in the Study?

The procedures we followed with the Vahns were repeated again and again with other families. In the end we had fifty-five mother–father–young adolescent triads who had completed the study. In addition, we obtained ESM data from a large sample of 483 young adolescents (a number of whom were also in the family study), which we use in different places in the book. To fully understand our findings, the reader needs to know who these participants were and how they were selected.

We started with the large young adolescent sample. Fifth to ninth graders were invited from the student bodies of four elementary/junior high schools and the corresponding senior highs. Two of these schools were in a working-class suburb on the edge of Chicago; two were in a middle-

and upper-middle-class outlying suburb. Because of the rigid residential segregation of Chicago, both neighborhoods had populations that were almost exclusively of European or Eastern European ancestry.

We chose to focus on the age range of fifth to ninth grade because this allowed us to see the dramatic changes in daily life that come at the ages of puberty.[27] As the study progressed, we randomly selected equal numbers of students in each grade; we also selected equal numbers of boys and girls. Of course, some students were not willing to take part, a few lost their pagers or booklets, and a small number failed to complete all the procedures. In the end, our 483 students represented 70 percent of the randomly selected students we had invited to participate. A survey of all the students in two schools indicated that the sample was quite typical of the student bodies, both in demographic variables and mental health. It included jocks and burn-outs, kids who were doing well and kids having problems. Thus, though not fully inclusive, our sample encompasses the range of lives led by European-American young adolescents in middle America. Readers can obtain a complete account of this study elsewhere.[28]

The *family sample* came from a "piggyback" study on the young adolescent sample. As we were working with these students, many of the parents kept saying, "You think adolescents are going through a lot these days, you should study *us*." So we added them, and this book is the result.

Once a student agreed to be in the young adolescent study, we asked whether we might approach his or her parents about also carrying pagers. If the student said yes, we asked the parents to take part. Our participation rate for this study was about 45 percent, with approximately equal numbers of adolescents and fathers vetoing families' participation (mothers were usually enthusiastic). Toward the end, we solicited families more selectively in order to obtain approximately equal numbers of boys and girls spread across the fifth to eighth grades (we did not include ninth graders in this sample). We also attempted to include approximately equal numbers of families with mothers who were employed full-time, employed part-time, and full-time homemakers. We did not include single-parent families in the final family sample used for this book, but the sample does include four remarried families.

These fifty-five families closely resembled other two-parent families in their middle- and working-class suburban communities.[29] The average family had two children, with a range from one to ten. Nearly all mothers and fathers had graduated from high school; almost a quarter of mothers and over a third of fathers had completed college. Twenty-two mothers were employed part-time (eight to thirty-four hours a week) and fourteen were employed full-time. For both mothers and fathers, the number who had white-collar jobs was approximately equal to those with working-class jobs.[30] As you will see, there is an enormous range *within* the sample in family well-being, from those that were openly dysfunctional to those that appeared to be thriving.

In total, members of the family sample provided over 7,000 reports on their experience; the young adolescents provided about 18,500 reports. Taking into account the overlap between studies, the total pool includes about 24,000 snapshots of daily experience with which to investigate the daily lives of adolescents and their parents. Of course, these data were affected by all the foibles that go with any kind of research project, from pager malfunctions to families where one member's poor participation required us to exclude the whole family from the final sample. We make no claim that we succeeded in capturing every aspect of what goes on in family life, and we may have been hoodwinked once or twice.[31] But we believe that these thousands of reports provide an accurate sampling of the great majority of the participants' ordinary daily experience.

We turn now to examining what this rich set of daily snapshots tells us about life in two-parent European-American families.

PART ONE

Individuals

CHAPTER 2

Fathers:

CYCLES OF WORK AND LEISURE

MEN, ACCORDING TO STEREOTYPE, are calm and rational, rarely swayed by emotion. Many of our traditional images—as disparate as Ward Cleaver and John Wayne—present men who never demonstrate strong emotional states. As workers and public figures they are stolid; as fathers they are dispassionate, perhaps a little too dispassionate. Men's supposed lack of emotionality, in fact, was part of the justification for why they should be in charge, both of the family and the public world: they were thought to be in control of themselves; their decisions were ruled by reason, not by ephemeral feelings.[1]

These images, however, have been challenged by the psychologists Robert Levenson and John Gottman, who connected physiological sensors to husbands and wives in order to monitor their emotions during discussions of conflictual marital issues. Contrary to reputation, men registered as much emotion reactivity as women did. Men's hearts raced as fast; their blood pressure showed the same elevations. This emotional arousal was not conspicuous in what the men said: many were uncommunicative and "stonewalled" troublesome issues; men learn early not to express their feelings. But their emotional reactions clearly registered on the monitors. In fact, Gottman and Levenson marshal evidence that husbands may actually be *more* emotional than their wives and that men stonewall precisely because they are less able to handle emotional situations.[2]

In this chapter we'll see that men's strong emotional states occur not only during marital interactions, but across other domains as well. In fact, in our thousands of random snapshots the men reported more and stronger emotional states at work than with their families. These European American middle-aged married fathers got irritated by clients, PO'ed at their bosses, and swept away by the fascination of their jobs—just as they experienced occasions of anger, depression, and pleasure at home. True, these fathers were not as emotionally volatile as their adolescent children, as we shall see in a later chapter. But compared to their wives, the men's range of feeling states was at least as wide (see appendix 2.1).[3] Far from being unfeeling machines, men are passionately involved in their lives.

The important question is how fathers' passions are organized. Traditionally men were seen as heroes of the workplace who sacrificed their finite emotional energies to bring home a paycheck. But some critics argue that men's expenditure of emotion and energy is self-serving and sometimes has a net destructive effect on the family. Are men's strong daily passions compatible or at odds with the cultivation of warm family relations? Knowing the organization of fathers' emotional reality is an important first step to understanding how the family as a whole fits together.

FROM PODIUM TO PATIO

The luxuriant pleasure William found in doing chores on Saturday can only be understood by knowing what had transpired during the preceding week at his job. William is a high school chorus instructor who participated in our study during one of the last weeks of the school year, a time when the demands on him were intense. On Wednesday, his first day with the pager, signals found him in a flurry of different activities, from reviewing music holdings in the library to preparing for summer choral camp. Our graph of his moods, in figure 2.1, shows that he reported enjoyment when beeped while conducting. "This is what I do best," he wrote. But pressure got the best of him and he reported feelings of stress and irritability when setting up video equipment and dressing for a parent meeting that night.

Thursday was the day of the spring concert, and at 8:36 A.M. William indicated that he was "already a little nervous about tonight's performance." There was much to be done, and at 9:44 A.M. he felt "hardworking," but little else, as he reviewed his TTDT (Things To Do Today) list. At 2:30 P.M. he took a moment to talk with a colleague about river rafting in Wisconsin, but he also felt angry about taking time from his work and marked that he would rather be alone. Only when he and the colleague started working on music arrangements for the next year did his mood improve, though he still marked he would rather be alone. The concert weighed on him throughout the day. Unfortunately, but understandably, he turned the pager off in the evening, so we do not have a record of his experience that night, but in the daily diary he filled out before going to bed, he wrote that the concert was well received, and he was now much relieved. "There is still much to do, but the 'stress' of the performance is now over."

William got praise for the concert all day Friday, yet the many remaining tasks nullified any feelings of happiness or contentment. His emotions were controlled throughout the day, as he again burned the candle at both ends: preparing for student elections, setting up for rehearsal, recruiting new chorus members, and arranging for the awards banquet that night. The banquet turned out to be the highest point of his week, as the pager caught him while the audience was viewing a video about the history of the choral program he had built over the last fifteen years. He felt very happy, proud, strong, and "very much appreciated by students and parents." After months of frantic work, which had brought only limited immediate gratification, at last he got his due.

But it was only on the weekend, which he spent at home, that he really felt consistently happy. Our graph of his moods for the week shows that he was much happier on the weekend than during workdays (see figure 2.1). Like most fathers, as we shall see, William experienced his time at home as bringing more favorable emotional states. At his first beep on Saturday morning, he explained that his mood was positive because "I simply enjoy being with my family," and he expressed regret that he did not have more time to give them.

Over the weekend, William mixed leisure with chores as he recovers from the week. He helped out at home, dusting the basement, grilling dinner, cleaning the spa, and making his son's bed, among other chores. All these were done in a leisurely, enjoyable fashion and mixed with playing music with his son, watching TV, and reading *Lake Wobegone Days*. Monday was Memorial Day and he wrote, "This is lazy day. Plenty of small jobs to do and no real need to do them." He repeatedly marked that he felt "calm" and commented on how wonderful it was to have no pressure. Clearly the pleasure he got from doing chores was due to the contrast they provided to the hurriedness of work. On Monday night he wrote that his accomplishment for the day was "Rest!", something he would need for the upcoming week.

Then it all started again on Tuesday morning. At the first beep, he was back at school again and his emotional state was lower. He was working on his TTDT list and wrote that he had "another long day in store—I probably won't get home until 10 tonight." Even though William worked late into the night each evening, he, like most fathers, said his family was what

Figure 2.1

WILLIAM'S WEEK

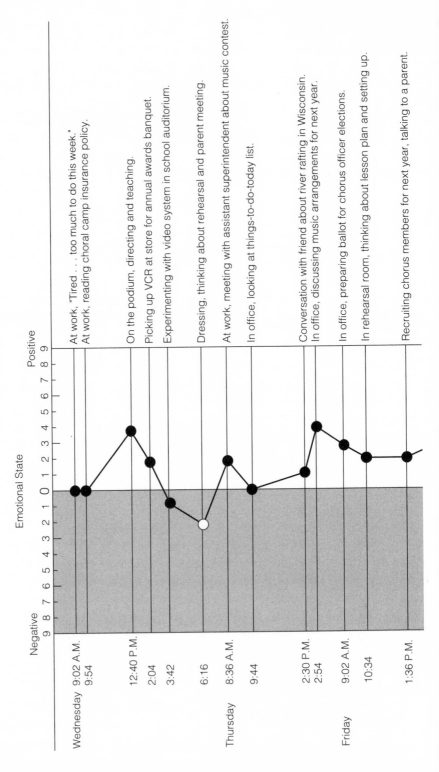

Emotional State

Negative 9 8 7 6 5 4 3 2 1 0 1 2 3 4 5 6 7 8 9 Positive

Wednesday 9:02 A.M.   At work, "Tired . . . too much to do this week."
9:54   At work, reading choral camp insurance policy.

12:40 P.M.   On the podium, directing and teaching.

2:04   Picking up VCR at store for annual awards banquet.

3:42   Experimenting with video system in school auditorium.

6:16   Dressing, thinking about rehearsal and parent meeting.

Thursday 8:36 A.M.   At work, meeting with assistant superintendent about music contest.

9:44   In office, looking at things-to-do-today list.

2:30 P.M.   Conversation with friend about river rafting in Wisconsin.
2:54   In office, discussing music arrangements for next year.

Friday 9:02 A.M.   In office, preparing ballot for chorus officer elections.

10:34   In rehearsal room, thinking about lesson plan and setting up.

1:36 P.M.   Recruiting chorus members for next year, talking to a parent.

WILLIAM'S WEEK (continued)

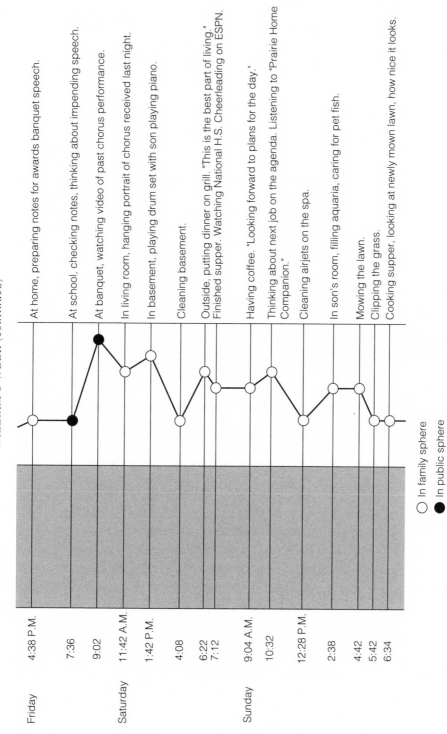

Friday

4:38 P.M. — At home, preparing notes for awards banquet speech.

7:36 — At school, checking notes, thinking about impending speech.

9:02 — At banquet, watching video of past chorus performance.

Saturday

11:42 A.M. — In living room, hanging portrait of chorus received last night.

1:42 P.M. — In basement, playing drum set with son playing piano.

4:08 — Cleaning basement.

6:22 — Outside, putting dinner on grill. "This is the best part of living."
7:12 — Finished supper. Watching National H.S. Cheerleading on ESPN.

Sunday

9:04 A.M. — Having coffee. "Looking forward to plans for the day."

10:32 — Thinking about next job on the agenda. Listening to "Prairie Home Companion."

12:28 P.M. — Cleaning airjets on the spa.

2:38 — In son's room, filling aquaria, caring for pet fish.

4:42 — Mowing the lawn.

5:42 — Clipping the grass.

6:34 — Cooking supper, looking at newly mown lawn, how nice it looks.

○ In family sphere
● In public sphere

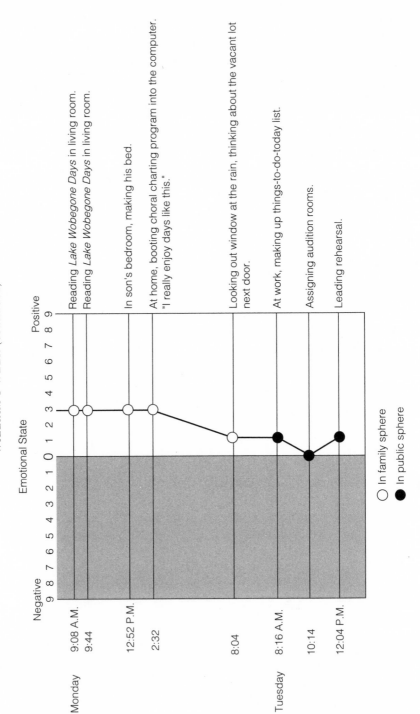

WILLIAM'S WEEK (continued)

was really important to him and these late work hours were a difficult emotional strain.[4]

MEN'S FAMILY ROLES

The emotional split in William's life between work and home is a product of historical forces that partly or wholly removed men from the daily lives of their families. Across the last two centuries, the declining viability of the small farm combined with hopes for a better life led family after family to what must have often been a painful decision to send fathers (and sometimes mothers) into the "satanic mills" or other income-producing employment. Fathers' withdrawal from homelife was a gradual process. Much nineteenth-century industry was not in large businesses. Production of shoes, cigars, and matchboxes, for example, often occurred in the home or in shops right next to the home, allowing fathers to maintain the level of direct involvement in the family that many had experienced as farmers.[5] And many nineteenth-century factories were more accommodating and supportive of families than is commonly thought.[6] But urbanization, the growth of larger, more depersonalized factories and offices, and ultimately the migration of families to suburbs in the early and mid-1900s moved fathers' place of work and home farther apart.

In effect, a deal was struck—or imposed—between men and women: husbands would contribute money and wives would contribute domestic labor to the family economy.[7] At the same time that fathers were moving into paid employment, a new ideology promoted women's place in the home as nurturer of children and guardian of a rarefied domestic sphere removed from the evils of the external world.[8] Parenting books of the nineteenth and early twentieth centuries virtually ignored fathers, while new ideas about child care and development expanded the mother's role into a skilled full-time nurturer.[9] For working-class families, this idealized division of labor was unobtainable and mothers also participated in wage labor. It was not until well into the twentieth century (and then only for a brief period) that a majority of blue-collar fathers were able to bring home enough to support the family alone.[10]

The result of these changes, according to the historian Elizabeth Pleck, was that "husbands and wives increasingly inhabited two different emotional worlds—the task-preoccupied husband taking a leisure-time interest in the family, his expressive wife providing all the love and nurturance."[11] Heir to this heritage, William put in fourteen-hour days at his job, while his wife, Alice, kept things running at home, as well as holding a part-time job. Like many wives, Alice also played a supporting role in her husband's career: she attended the parent meeting, the concert, and the banquet; she wooed parents, helped students with their costumes, and worried about his speech. In his words, she was "my best assistant."[12] In a separate interview, she commented: "He doesn't spend enough time with his family. On the other hand, he is an extremely dedicated teacher and I am proud of him."

For many fathers like William, their jobs have become not just a means to support the family, but an end in itself. In the Protestant culture that evolved during the eighteenth and nineteenth centuries, work came to be seen as virtuous and central to men's sense of self.[13] Within the religion of American individualism, a job became men's means of establishing their identity, of being men. In early adulthood, according to the psychologist Daniel Levinson, men discover a "dream" that drives their lives. Many fathers work late into the night in order to be the best sales agent, win a vice presidency, or build a choral program that brings adulation. The importance of work to men's identities is evident in their psychological devastation when unemployed.[14] As the sociologist Talcott Parsons stated in 1942, "Only in very exceptional cases can an adult man be genuinely self-respecting and enjoy a respected status in the eyes of others if he does not 'earn a living' in an appropriate occupational role."[15]

Whether coerced by economic demand or lured by a dream, across the last two centuries men have pursued their jobs as a separate and emotionally consuming part of their lives that pulls them away from their families. Jobs that required fifty, sixty, or seventy hours a week, plus a substantial commute, meant that Dad was simply not there much of the time. In 1900, *Harper's Bazaar* commented: "The suburban husband and father is almost entirely a Sunday institution."[16] Father became a distant figure who knew little of what was going on in the family. His role in child nurturance was downgraded, and his ignorance of the home sphere became a matter of occasional satire and ridicule.[17] As fathers moved out of the family, the family moved away from him.

The role of father, then, became depersonalized and redefined in the nineteenth and early twentieth centuries, as a provider, a laborer who brings home the paycheck the family depends on, rather than as an integral member of an emotional network. Researchers in the 1960s and 1970s found that most husbands and wives concurred in regarding the man's "provider role" as his most important contribution to the family, and recent data indicate that a majority still hold this view.[18] Even in families where both parents work, the father is still usually viewed as the "primary provider."[19] Bringing home a wage, not nurturing, has been and often still is men's entree to the family; in fact, men without jobs are seen as "unmarriageable."[20]

Since the turn of the century, many men have been able to win back some of the family time they lost in sixty-hour-a-week jobs. Saturday work is no longer expected in most employment; the coming of the forty-hour week meant that many men had some time with their families on weekday evenings.[21] The provider role now often takes less of men's time, and in many families it is shared with the wife. But are fathers still the outsider in the home, or have they become more emotionally involved than the stoical, remote breadwinners of the last few generations? Feminism and popular sentiment have encouraged men to become more involved in their families, and media ridicule of the father as a buffoon in the home has sharply decreased.[22] But how much time and emotional energy do contemporary fathers actually commit to their families?

HOW FATHERS DIVIDE THEIR TIME

By beeping men at random moments across the day, we obtained a large pool of information that can help us answer these questions. William and the fifty-four other fathers in the study provided reports on their activities and emotions at 2,268 representative moments during their waking hours.

The first thing we wanted to know was, simply, how did these fathers spend their time? To what activities did they devote their waking hours? We found that men's jobs, including transportation to and from work, accounted for an average of forty-six hours a week. This is far less than at the turn of the century, when workers organized unions to demand a tenhour day and a limit to their Saturday hours.[23] Of course, this segment of time also differed between individual men; some, like William, worked more, others less. Nearly all fathers we studied worked standard Monday-to-Friday hours and usually came home to their families between 5 and 7 P.M. As a result, their intervals at work and home had a fairly consistent daily and weekly rhythm that structured their time and emotional experience.

Overall, we found that these men's waking hours were almost equally divided between the job sphere and the household sphere. Men reported job-related activities for about half the times they were signaled and household-centered activities for the other half, with only a small sliver of time in the public realm apart from these two contexts (see appendix 2.2).[24] This means their time was evenly divided between their traditional provider role and their role as father and family member.

The really important question to ask is, What do men do and what do they experience in these two primary segments of their lives? What is their input of energy and emotion to each sphere and, ultimately, how does this shape what happens with the family as a whole? Some initial hints can be gleaned from how the men in our study divide their time within each sphere. We found that most of their time at their jobs was spent working. They took lunch, they stopped to chat, they used the bathroom, but 76 percent of their time at work was spent in labor. In contrast, only one-third of their time in the household sphere was spent in family work; the majority of their time in this sphere was passed in personal and regenerative activities such as leisure, talk, eating, and resting. The character of men's experience in these two spheres differed sharply, with important implications for the inner lives of their families.

MEN AT WORK

One father in our study, the owner of a boat store, lived, breathed, and probably dreamed his job. Nearly every time he was beeped, even on weekends, sailboats, speedboats, and other pleasure craft were on his mind. We found that men's jobs imposed a pattern of demands, stresses, and frustrations that structured their emotional lives. Whether a bricklayer or businessman, factory worker or FBI agent, their work ruled their daily emotional metabolism.

Challenge and Absorption

The key to understanding the impact of work on men's lives is to know the cognitive state they experience at their jobs. The fathers in our study reported that at work their minds were nearly always focused on the task at hand. In a capitalist society, workers are evaluated by the amount they produce, whether in goods or in services. As a result, the mental states these fathers reported at work were states of productive labor—not just physical labor, but mental labor as well. They reported significantly higher levels of "paying attention," feeling skilled, and being alert at work than at home. They also reported feeling strong and "in control" more often, and reported being "hardworking" 61 percent of the time, as compared to 28 percent when at home.

The psychologist Mihaly Csikszentmihalyi would say that this absorbed state is the experience of "flow," a condition of being wrapped up in what one is doing, of being totally engaged by an activity. Csikszentmihalyi has found that this special state occurs when people are personally challenged at a level just matched to their skills, becoming so engaged that awareness of time disappears and they lose consciousness of everything outside their current field of action.[25]

Most of us can think of a flow experience during leisure activities: while playing softball, skiing, or having a deep conversation with a friend. But Csikszentmihalyi has found that flow occurs most frequently in people's ordinary work.[26] One of the fathers in our study, a maintenance man at a nursing home, described flow while installing closet poles. He felt personally challenged to "hang them so they will hold heavy weight" and, as a result, got deeply engrossed. A dentist reported intense absorption while taking an impression for a bridge: "You have to do it just right or it won't turn out; you also have to be careful or you'll pinch the patient's cheek." Another instance of flow was related by an architect: when he started to sketch plans for a new building, he became so carried away that, when beeped, he reported feeling "in love."

Both fathers and mothers reported these absorption experiences at their jobs; however, fathers reported more of them: 41 percent of their time at work, as compared to 29 percent for mothers. Our findings do not imply that women are sloughing off—we have much to say about mothers' job experience in the next chapter. But they do suggest something about how the typical father relates to his job, and it is important to understand what controls this pattern, since it has consequences for the family.

Why are men so readily disposed to deep attention at work? Is it something about their jobs or something about men? One possibility, of course, is that men's absorption at work is related to the types of jobs they have. A history of gender segregation in the workplace means that men hold different kinds of jobs than women do. Our data, however, fail to show that absorption differed by job type. Men in blue-collar jobs, such as the maintenance man who installed the closet poles, were nearly as likely to report high attention at work as men in technical, sales, professional, and managerial jobs.[27] We also found that level of absorption did not differ substantially by the activity a person was engaged in at work: operating equipment, attending a meeting, and sales did not yield significant differences in rates of attention.[28]

Men's absorption, however, does relate to another aspect of the job. One of the items on the beeper sheet asked whether there was a leader in your current activity and, if so, who it was. Deep attention was strongly associated with reporting oneself to be the leader on this item, for both men and women, and men reported themselves the leader more often at their jobs than women (44 versus 31 percent). Being in charge requires attention, and, at this juncture in history, men are in charge in work settings more often.

But we think it is not simply the external structure of work activities that gets men absorbed, it is also what they bring to the situation. The fathers we studied reported more frequent deep attention at home than mothers did—one spent a whole weekend installing a barbecue, another was preoccupied with his son's Little League team. So the tendency to get absorbed may be partly men's cognitive style, irrespective of context. A University of Massachusetts researcher, Robert Weiss, documented this style in an extensive interview study of middle- and upper-middle-class men. He found that challenge was a central and highly valued part of these men's work experience. One of his interviewees described it as the "thrill that you can juggle fourteen balls in the air without dropping one of them."[29] Weiss discovered that men often go out of their way to create challenge at work when it is not there. Some, according to Weiss, bring to their work "fantasies of high adventure in which their courage or determination is tested."[30] While we did not ask about challenge, the men in our study reported feeling "competitive" more often at work than women did, and competitiveness for men is significantly correlated with greater attention.

Men's disposition to get absorbed in work—we might even call it a syndrome—showed itself when we examined the men who reported the highest attention at their jobs, relative to at home. These work-absorbed fathers manifested a whole profile of distinct psychological states when at work. In addition to identifying themselves as "the leader" more often and feeling more competitive at work, they appeared to be more intrinsically motivated. They reported greater excitement, interest, and choice over their activity when at their jobs.[31] Their jobs were where they got their adrenaline going.

Of course, this disposition to get caught up in one's job is not unique to men. Many of the correlations between attention at work and intrinsic motivation were suggested for the women in the study as well (see appendix 2.4). But most of these correlations were stronger for men, indicating that this syndrome had a more seductive pull for them. The work-absorbed fathers showed a greater imbalance in their lives, committing much more of their energy to work than to home. They reported being much more alert and less often tired at work than other fathers. Most significant is that, unlike work-absorbed mothers, they worked longer hours at their jobs and spent less time in the home sphere. These were fathers for whom the job had become an addictive and enthralling end in itself. Many of these "workaholics" stayed at their jobs into the evening and some went back on Saturdays.

William demonstrated a moderate case of this absorption syndrome. He was deeply invested in the goal of being a good choral instructor, with costs to his family. His long hours, however, were not fully a matter of choice, but rather were required by his job. A better example is the boat salesman, who worked six long days a week. When at work he almost always reported being interested and alert. On one report he declared, "I love selling boats"; on another he expressed exuberance because he had just sold a $30,000 yacht. For some other fathers, it is hard to separate whether they were driven by personal motivation, demands of the job, or the risk of losing it.

Men's absorption in their work, then, has multiple causes: more frequent leadership responsibility, commitment to the provider role, and a disposition to get caught up in competition and personal challenge. Because men's identity is typically anchored in their work, they may be easily susceptible to having their attention and energies captured by getting that closet pole just right or selling more boats than the other guy.

For Csikszentmihalyi, this is something to be celebrated: "If people admitted to themselves that work can be enjoyable [produce flow], they might work more effectively, achieve greater material success and in the process also improve the quality of their own lives."[32] However, our findings suggest that in addition to drawing men's time and energy away from the family sphere, their absorption in work has another undesirable side.

Emotional Consequences

The flip side of men's involvement in their jobs is their vulnerability to frustration and emotional distress. The deeply absorbed dentist got irritable when a patient became uncooperative. The maintenance man became angry when a boiler malfunctioned and his supervisor would not listen to his ideas on fixing it. The fathers in our study reported more frequent experiences of distress at work than at home. They also reported more frequent distress at work than employed women did.[33] But why is this?

As with men's absorption in their work, we are led to ask, Is men's distress at work due to something about their jobs, perhaps to harsher working conditions, or to something about men? Surprisingly, we found that blue- and white-collar fathers did not differ in their frequency of negative emotion at work: men wearing overalls reported a profile of typical emotional states similar to that of suit-and-tie employees. Equally surprising, we found that fathers felt greater distress than mothers did at work, regardless of the tasks they were performing.[34] Across most job activities, from computer work to sales, men reported more negative emotions than women did (see appendix 2.5). Together, these findings suggest it is not what you do at work that generates negative experience; rather, it is your gender or, more likely, factors related to your gender.

Men's greater average absorption in their work, of course, is one such factor. We found that men who were more absorbed in their jobs reported higher rates of frustration than other men did (see appendix 2.4). Robert Weiss's study also found that jobs with higher demand for attentiveness produce greater stress.[35] These high demands, we suspect, set men up for frustration. In fact Weiss asserts that the essence of stress is when people "mobilize their energies and attention to deal with challenge, but to no avail."[36]

We believe it is not just absorption, however, that feeds fathers' distress at work, it is also what they have at stake. Men are invested in their jobs as a source both of income to support their families and of personal identity.[37] Therefore, when things go wrong, men may be less able to distance themselves from the situation. The boat salesman, for example, became furious when an unhappy customer returned a Sunfish and demanded a refund. A post office mechanic became upset when the letter-sorting machine in his charge broke down, leaving a whole row of workers idle and impatient, "Then I get beeped on top of it!" The flip side of being invested in work is the experience of distress when one's investment is not rewarded.

The benefits of men's deep investment in work, then, come at an emotional cost, at least for some men. The middle-aged fathers in our study were at the peak of their careers and thus at the peak of their vulnerability to having this central identity threatened.[38] Middle-aged fathers also experience the peak of their family's demands for their income; hence threats to their role as a provider easily upset them. These pressures not only disturb their immediate calm but over the years they take a toll on some men's health and shorten their life span.[39] These pressures, too, have deleterious effects on the family, as we shall see later.

BETWEEN WORK AND HOME

As a result of their absorption and its emotional byproducts, men leave work with an emotional debt: both a feeling of exhaustion and the experience of happiness compromised. Many men view their work as a "sacrifice" they have made for their families, and this gives them a sense of entitlement.[40] Historians tell us that many nineteenth-century workers took the residual emotions from work to the local tavern.[41] The dehumanization they had endured at the factory was seen as justification for enjoying the company of friends and spending part of their paycheck on drink.

We found little evidence of this pattern of going to taverns and avoiding the family in the late-twentieth century American fathers we studied. Nearly all their waking time was spent at work or in the family sphere. Much of the small segment of men's time outside these two roles was spent in the car, and much of this driving was to and from work.

Emotional states during these in-between times were generally not distinctive. Emotions when driving for personal reasons were generally neutral. Driving home from work was associated with significantly higher boredom, competitiveness, and frustration. This pattern, we suspect, is attributable partly to spillover from work and partly to the congested conditions of Chicago's infamous Dan Ryan and Eisenhower freeways, which many of these men had to drive.

What is more interesting is these men's other time in public, outside their work and family roles, even though the amount of it was small. Was this "escape" from their roles an important and positive part of their lives? Did they come alive when separate from job and family? Our data suggest that the answer is generally no. Time outside the roles of worker, father, and husband was not associated with more pleasant, upbeat experience.

We were particularly interested in the segment of this public time that men spent with friends, because, as we will see, this is a particularly significant time for women. Men's time with friends away from work and family accounted for a comparatively small fraction of waking hours, constituting 2.7 percent of all self-reports. During this time they reported a greater "wish" to be in their current activity, positive attention, but a mean level of emotion that was typically neutral. Some men reported occasions with friends that generated strong positive feelings. One reported laughing and joking with a group of old friends about their high school escapades; another reported having a good time while driving to Indiana with a buddy; and another reported happiness while sitting in a cold camper by Lake Michigan fishing for smelt. But most of these interactions with friends elicited little extreme sentiment. Conversations dealt with sports, motorcycles, vacations, and work. They involved little self-disclosure and, as the psychologist Harry Reis has also found, were not especially satisfying.[42]

Researchers have discovered that deep personal friendship wanes for most men during adulthood and is replaced by companionate friendships, often shared with their wife.[43] Robert Weiss concludes that men do not need regular contact with friends to maintain their emotional well-being. Our data confirm that separate personal friendships are not a regular or emotionally significant part of most men's daily experience. Given the demands of their jobs and their families, most of the fathers we studied had limited time and energy for personal friendships. After work, nearly all fathers headed straight home.

MEN AT HOME

After a strenuous day at the office or factory, the fatigued father comes home to recover. The men in our study reported feeling more tired than usual in response to the first beep at home after returning from work.[44] Weiss suggests that a little "theater" is involved in this claim to be exhausted at the end of the day. He asserts that what men really feel is stressed, but a display of fatigue and weariness wins more credit than saying they feel "fried"; it communicates to others that they have had "a long hard day at work motivated by determination to provide for the family."[45]

According to the Victorian division of roles, home is Dad's sphere for recuperation and leisure. Having given of his energy in the cruel outside world, he claims a right to unwind. Many men resent the family pressures that require them to work; as a result, they feel home is their domain to do what they want.[46] In the past, some men expected other family members to meet the emotional needs created by their work, whether this meant being at the door with slippers and newspaper or even tolerating physical abuse. In the past, working-class wives and children sometimes denied themselves food, garments, and heat in order to sustain the breadwinner.[47] While the families in our study did not share these extreme interpretations of the breadwinner's privileges, they showed the same underlying assumption: home is Dad's place of leisure.

Leisure is defined by scholars who study it in at least two different ways, and men's time at home fits both. The first definition presents leisure as a *category of activities*: sports, entertainment, and recreation are termed "leisure activities" and are serviced by the "leisure industry." These are nonproductive, nonwork activities that are typically done for their own sake. The fathers in our study spent a larger portion of their homelife in these types of activities than the mothers did (34 percent versus 20 percent). If we include social activities and recuperative activities, such as personal care, eating, and resting, in these calculations, over 69 percent of the fathers' home time counts as leisure. In short, two-thirds of a father's time in this sphere is devoted to activities that serve his own interests and needs. When dads come home from work, they are more likely to engage in a leisure or recuperative activity than they are to take on family responsibilities.

The second definition of leisure portrays it as a *state of mind*, and fathers' experience of household time fits this definition as well. Researchers have found that people report "leisure" when they experience enjoyment, freedom of choice, intrinsic motivation, and lack of evaluation.[48] The experience at home of the fathers we studied differed from their experience at work along most of these dimensions. They felt happier and more cheerful; they reported feeling much less "hardworking" and hurried; and they experienced much greater choice over their current activity (see appendix 2.3).

To fully understand men's experience at home, however, we need to look separately at the different ways men spend time in this sphere. Do their leisure activities provide the rejuvenation they seek? Do men also experience a leisurely state when they perform housework? And what about the in-between activities like eating and personal care? The underlying question is how these different activities fit into the organization of men's lives and whether fathers' leisurely state at home draws them closer to, or apart from, the rest of the family.

Sedentary Leisure: Renewal Through Idleness?

Scholars who have theorized about the value of leisure have developed nearly mystic visions of its powers. John Neulinger's classic textbook on leisure defines it as doing "something which gives one pleasure and satisfaction, which involves one to the very core of one's being."[49] The theorist Sebastian de Grazia describes leisure as an ideal that few achieve: "Work may make a man stoop-shouldered or rich. It may even ennoble him. Leisure perfects him."[50] For these theorists, nearly all of them men themselves, leisure is not just an antidote to work, but an experience of self-fulfillment, of getting in touch with oneself in a higher realm.

One of the patriarchs of leisure studies, Joseph Pieper, argued that this idealized state is achieved through contemplation, through "idleness."[51] Curiously, we found contemplation to be extraordinarily rare in the lives of the fathers in our study, so rare and typically so *un*-uplifting that we put it in a category with idling and resting. Their largest quantity of leisure *was* in a physically passive activity, but one that would rarely be confused with contemplation: watching TV. These fathers identified television viewing as their main activity for 20 percent of all their homelife (as compared to 10 percent for mothers). And at certain times of the week, we can predict that

30 percent of all these fathers will be in front of the TV (see appendix 2.6). Our research is consistent with other studies in showing that fathers watch more television than mothers do, even when we include full-time homemakers who have extra opportunities to watch during weekdays.[52] The reason is that fathers spend much of the weekend watching sports.

On a typical Sunday afternoon, our data suggest, one-third of American men are watching sports on TV. The boat salesman in our study spent his entire Sunday, his one day away from work, watching TV and reading *Playboy*. The dentist watched TV part of Saturday, all day Sunday, and Monday night too. We will look first at their experience of sports, then more generally at TV watching.

In an adulatory book called *The Joy of Sports*, the sociologist Michael Novak claims that sports are an American religion, particularly for men. In his view, "Football is not entertainment. It is far more important than that."[53] Another scholar claims that sports often are central to the "life structure" of men, a locus for the expression of strong emotions they cannot express elsewhere.[54] This level of devotion is evident in one family in which the father (and mother) have made it understood that when the Chicago Bears are playing, no interruptions from the children will be tolerated. But is watching sports really a transcendent experience in men's lives? Is this a time when other family members should get out of their way and let them have their much deserved renewal experience?

We did not ask about religious feelings on the beeper form, so we cannot determine whether watching sports creates transcendental spiritual states. But we did ask about a wide range of other feelings and find that experience during sports viewing is far from distinctive. Events in the basketball or football game *did* affect these fathers' moods. On one occasion, four fathers—each at his own home—were watching the same moment of a football game in which the Bears were being trounced by the Minnesota Vikings. All four reported slightly negative emotion, and two wrote derogatory opinions on the Bears' performance. Yet across all sports viewing, the range of both positive and negative states was no greater than during other viewing and was less than in other domains of life. Excitement, happiness, even the wish to be doing what they were doing were not greater during sports viewing than during other moments in these men's lives. The men we studied felt more "competitive" during sports viewing than other TV viewing and reported greater "choice" over their current activity, but there was not a clue that sports generated religious ecstasy or transformed consciousness.

We found that all television viewing typically had a numbing effect on emotional states in our participants. Far from being contemplative, television viewing seems to have few of the cognitive qualities that leisure philosophers consider important. Average level of attention is low, excitement is rare, and drowsiness common. This same pattern of uninspired states occurred for the mothers and the young adolescents in the study. Other ESM studies have found a similar pattern across many different samples.[55] Although TV viewing is a voluntary leisure activity, it was not associated with positive emotional states; in fact, during TV viewing, our participants were *less likely* to feel cheerful, friendly, or proud than during any other home activity.

If TV doesn't generate a positive state, what is its place in the emotional ecology of men's lives? Why is this activity chosen so often? Our research suggests that it serves a different emotional function. First, in addition to experiencing fewer positive states during TV viewing, the fathers we studied also reported fewer negative states. They were less likely to report feeling irritable or unhappy than during most other activities. On our bipolar emotional items they often marked that they felt "neither" emotion during TV viewing. In short, they felt nothing, neither happiness nor sadness, friendliness nor anger, cheer nor irritability.

Could this be the function of TV: to make one feel emotionally empty? Perhaps after dealing with the stress of work, it is emotionally useful to drain oneself of all feeling. A mental health worker, for example, described liking TV at the end of the day because he could view someone's problems without having to try to solve them. Supporting this thesis is our finding that the fathers who reported the most TV viewing were those who experienced the highest rates of competitiveness, frustration, and worry at their jobs.[56] The theory that TV is sought as an emotional antidote to work is also borne out by another beeper study of adults by Robert Kubey and Mihaly Csikszentmihalyi, which found higher rates of TV viewing on days when people had been stressed at work. Furthermore, during TV viewing their participants reported feeling lower tension and challenge and greater relaxation than at other times. Similarly, our data show that TV viewing is characterized by extremely low rates of feeling hurried and hardworking. It is likely, then, that TV is chosen not as a means to feel positive emotion, but to relax, reduce tension, and avoid negative emotion.

As an antidote to stress, however, TV's effectiveness is limited. Although people feel relaxed when they watch it, Kubey and Csikszentmihalyi found that the longer people watch the less relaxed they feel. What's

more, *after* watching TV, their emotional state tends to be less favorable on
several dimensions than it was before watching. In a phenomenon the
researchers call "passive spillover," after watching TV people reported more
difficulty paying attention, less favorable emotion, and lower arousal. In
the late evening, this might be just what one needs to tune out from the
day: TV induces drowsiness and may be an effective means for getting to
sleep. But this sedative function serves little purpose during the weekend
afternoon viewing that constitutes much of the television time of the
fathers we studied.

In sum, it is questionable whether men's viewing of sports or other
programs on TV is emotionally restorative. While it meets the narrow
definition of leisure, in that people choose it, it has few of the positive
subjective qualities of leisure. The one redeeming feature of fathers' TV
time is that two-thirds of it takes place with at least one other family
member. TV brings family members together and may be particularly
valuable for family members who have little to say to each other, providing an opportunity to be together without awkward silence.[57] In one case
we encountered, a father and son would both watch football games in
their separate rooms and shout to each other when there was a touch-
down or fumble.

Fathers' other major media activity, reading, constituted 24 percent of
their media time in our study and produced psychological states that differed little from those for TV. The majority of this time was spent grazing
through newspapers, often on Sunday or other times between activities;
rarely did participants report reading magazines or books. Like TV viewing,
the kind of casual reading these fathers did elicited a frequent state of feeling nothing. Feelings of "skill" and interest were higher than average, but
there were few other distinctions to this experience. Reading may have provided these men with useful information—the weather for tomorrow, an
update on the Chicago mayoral race—but it did not have a significant
emotional impact on their lives. It was not an important segment of their
leisure.

Active Leisure, Active Renewal

The category of activities that most approximates the special qualities
lauded by leisure theorists is "active recreation." This is a relatively small
category, filling only 7 percent of the household time of the fathers we
studied, 3 percent of their time overall. But it was a portion of their lives
when they were in top form, at least from their point of view.

Active recreation includes everything from playing games to creative activities to family trips to the zoo.[58] Across these activities, fathers reported extremely favorable states: their attention was high; they were excited and interested; their cheerfulness and friendliness were at a peak.[59] A man lifting weights and listening to tapes in his basement reported buoyant moods. Another playing guitar in his room felt transported to another world.

Whereas television had a numbing effect, active recreation was experienced by these fathers as genuinely rejuvenating. This process of invigoration is evident when we evaluate the emotions fathers reported before, during, and after they participated (see appendix 2.8). For the beep occurring just before recreation, the men's emotional state was generally low; their positive mood did not precede taking part. It is beginning the recreational activity that elevates their state. What is most striking is that *the positive emotions created by recreation are sustained afterward.* Fathers reported feeling much better at the first beep after the activity than at other times, a finding exactly opposite to the negative spillover effect that Kubey and Csikszentmihalyi found for TV watching. Recreation not only raises your mood while you're doing it, it leaves you feeling better afterward.

Here, then, is Dad's chance to escape from the daily grind of his job, to have the positive restorative experience that wipes the slate clean from work and reinvigorates him. But recreation is rarely an escape from the family as well. To the contrary, for 88 percent of the time in this category, the men studied were with other family members, typically their children. These men experienced a very positive leisure state, with its restorative properties, at the same time they were interacting with, or at least in the presence of, family members.

This combination of joy and family companionship was reported by a father who was beeped while playing catch with his three children. Another man reported feeling happy while bowling with his wife. Recreational activities often allow fathers to fulfill a dual agenda: to be rejuvenated from work and be close to their families at the same time.

Recreation, then, might be part of the answer to our larger question of what makes some families run smoothly. It creates positive emotions in a shared activity. Thus far, however, we have looked only at fathers' experience of this time. The question of whether these occasions are also enjoyable for other family members remains to be answered; indeed, other findings raise doubts about whether they truly bring closeness between fathers and children.

But right now, we need to examine other segments of these fathers' time at home and how they fit into the organization of their emotional world. Even in traditional households, men were expected to do more during their home time than simply recoup and have fun.

Family Work: Another Leisure Activity for Men?

Joseph Pleck, a leading authority on gender roles, suggests that for men, housework is an unspeakable topic, which even the most "liberated" fathers will seek to avoid.[60] Housekeeping and child care have traditionally been the domain of women, their side of the bargain worked out between husbands and wives several generations ago. But as men's workweek has been shortened and more mothers have taken jobs outside the home, the expectation has grown that fathers should assume responsibility for more of these tasks, if not an equal share. What we see instead is that men's contribution to household work is often determined more by their inner emotional rhythms than by the needs of the family.

What proportion of a family's household work is actually done by fathers? Answering that question requires defining exactly what constitutes this work: Does watering the lawn count? How about installing a hoop so you can play basketball with your children? Yet whatever criteria researchers have used, mothers do more of it—usually two to three times more. Most striking is that the amount of time fathers contribute varies little with mothers' employment or other factors that affect demand, such as the size of the family or the number of hours the husband or wife works outside the home, though it is somewhat greater in homes with preschool children.[61] Fathers' input of time to family work does not appear to be particularly responsive to family needs.

The one factor that does affect fathers' contribution to household work is whether he sees himself as the "primary provider" for the family. Researchers Maureen Perry-Jenkins and Ann Crouter discovered that fathers who are most strongly identified with their role as provider do the fewest chores at home.[62] Because most men see their main contribution to the family to be financial, they claim a right to spend a majority of their home time on personal and recreational activities rather than housework—regardless of what needs to be done. Whether their wife is employed or not, most fathers assert that they "gave at the office" and that this is "their time."

What we find most interesting, however, is not how little time men devote to household tasks—a well-studied topic—but what they experience when they do them. Some feminists have argued that the household work traditionally done by women is degrading and enervating.[63] Simone de Beauvoir compared housework to "the torture of Sisyphus," because of the endless repetition of soiling and cleaning.[64] But is housework the same toil of Sisyphus for fathers? Do men avoid it because they find it noxious?

Surprisingly, men's experience of family work is much less aversive than women's. We included three general categories of activity in family work: housework, child care, and family transportation. The emotional states the fathers in our study reported during the first two were not particularly negative (see appendix 2.7). During housework, these men rarely reported feeling irritable or unhappy; positive states such as cheerfulness were common. To be sure, there were bad moments: One father trying to replace the barbecue grill accidentally broke the gas line, creating an enormous headache for himself. Yet when we compare these men's average emotion during household labor to that of their wives, it is significantly more positive. Men appear to enjoy household labor more, or at least are depressed by it less.

Likewise, during child care, the men we studied reported more positive emotion than their wives did. In fact, these men reported some of their most positive family experiences during this time, which included direct care of a child (including a younger or older child who was not the target child in our study) and helping a child with an activity. Fathers reported high rates of interest, attention, and excitement. They felt happy, friendly, proud, and kindly more often than in most other activities. Far from being a chore, child care was nearly as positive a pastime for these men as active recreation.

So men do less family work, but they enjoy it more. These findings suggest, perhaps, that it would not be hard for men to increase their contribution. A closer reading of what lies behind men's favorable emotions during family work needs to be taken, however. To begin with, these men reported greater happiness because they were doing a somewhat different mix of family work activities than women do. Within housework, fathers do more outdoor work and maintenance of possessions, activities that generate more favorable moods. Fathers do less laundry, kitchen cleanup, and housecleaning, chores that are less enjoyable for either spouse. Likewise, men's child care activities are more often pleasant tasks, like coaching or helping with a child's homework, while mothers do proportionally more direct care and grooming of children. Thus men's experience of family work is happier partly because they engage in more enjoyable tasks.

Even within identical activities, however, these fathers' emotional states tended to be more favorable than mothers'. When fathers did kitchen cleanup, laundry, and shopping, they reported more positive states than mothers did (see appendix 2.7). One father, for example, reported great delight in grocery shopping. Again, this suggests that fathers might be a valuable untapped source of motivated household labor. But another important variable lies behind fathers' positive experience of family work: the amount of choice they exercise.

Each time our participants were beeped, they were asked: "How much choice did you have about doing the current activity?" We found that during virtually all family work activities, fathers were much more likely to report that they'd had a choice than mothers were (see appendix 2.7). Furthermore, mothers reported the least choice precisely in the activities dads do less often: cooking, kitchen cleanup, laundry, and housecleaning. These findings suggest that fathers do these chores when they want to do them, whereas mothers perform them when they need to be done.[65]

Our finding that family work is a more voluntary activity for fathers is reinforced when we look at the time sequence of men's moods before and during child care activities. Rather than being a consequence of the activity, men's positive moods during child care actually preceded it (see appendix 2.9). *Their emotions were positive before they even started.* This finding suggests either that dads are so excited about the chance to care for their children that their moods rise in anticipation—which we doubt—or, more likely, that they choose to take care of children only when they are in a sufficiently positive mood.

These data imply that fathers have the luxury of choosing to do child care and other family work when they feel like it, that they relate to household work as an elective activity done as part of their leisurely experience of the family sphere.[66] They view their actions as "helping out," as a gift they are making to their wives and family—not as responsibilities they are committed to. Other research demonstrates that fathers take much less responsibility for what happens at home than mothers do. While they may watch the kids for a few hours so their wife gets a break, they rarely devote mental energy to worrying about the children's conflicts with friends or planning their birthday parties.[67] On days they feel good, they may volunteer to grill meat for supper and, like William on such an occasion, express great pride and satisfaction in this contribution. But on days when men are exhausted from their jobs, they do less family work; they act as though they have an escape clause in the marital contract that allows them to avoid family tasks when they're not in the mood for them.[68] Many fathers, like one who is switching on the TV say, "I should interact and do some jobs at home, but I'm too tired." Another tired man sips wine with his wife while she cooks dinner.

Other Household Activities: Talking and Personal Needs

Between the poles of leisure activities and household work lie two additional categories of home time—talking and personal needs—and the same themes apply. Instances when fathers in our study identified their activity as talking ran the gamut from one man's joking at a neighborhood party with his wife and friends about fishing to another talking with his daughter about a friend who kept hitting her. Some of this talk was clearly leisure, some was really family work, much was in between or hard to categorize. Talk can serve many functions, explicit and inexplicit. And though these men spent less time talking than their wives did, they usually experienced it as something they chose to do and they reported enjoying it, regardless of its function.

These men's emotional states during conversations with family were typically positive and the tone upbeat. There were certainly instances of anger, such as a husband discussing the possibility of a job move with his resistant wife, another distressed by his daughter's lack of sensitivity about a friend's death. But there were many more instances when fathers enjoyed conversations with their families. One dad reported joyous moods, for example, when discussing basketball with a daughter, another when chatting about women bodybuilders at a gathering of relatives, and another when teasing his wife about how her "bottom lip sticks out when she wants to get back." Fathers reported experiencing family members as being "friendly," and they responded in kind with friendly, often joking remarks.

The emotional states of these fathers during talk tended to be most positive when they were with a group of family and friends. We noted earlier that being with friends was not associated with particularly positive moods for these men, but here is the important exception. When these fathers got their family and friends together, they experienced some of their most positive moments. There was a kind of epiphany for them when they brought together these two segments of their lives. In this situation, they experienced others as much more "joking" than "serious," and this dimension had a strong relationship to their mood.[69] A typical situation was a machinist who reported feeling "very" cheerful, happy, and proud when family friends stopped by. He was beeped during a conversation about one of the friends' recovery from surgery. His wife reported a neutral mood and his daughter was bored; nonetheless, he was on top of the world.

Talking was experienced positively by these men because it combines personal gratification with family interaction. The same can be said for their experience of activities categorized as "personal needs." This label includes eating, self-care, and "resting and idling." All in various ways are restorative, and all are associated with a high degree of choice.[70] Yet these fathers spent two-thirds of their personal care time with family members. Fathers were taking care of their own needs, but at the same time they were available to their families. Again we see that household time combines family interaction with the personal goal of rejuvenation from work.

EMOTIONAL CARRYOVER FROM WORK TO HOME

Men's experience at home, then, is shaped by their jobs, as well as by the license they claim from them. We see the connection between the two spheres in the pattern of these men's states as they come home from work in the evening. During the 5–7 P.M. period, they reported peak levels of tiredness and other signs of this emotional carryover. At 7:30 P.M. one father reported feeling "still keyed up from work." In a study of air traffic controllers, the psychologist Rena Repetti concluded that people with stressful jobs bring home elevated sympathetic arousal, which can take hours to dissipate.[71]

This emotional carryover from work is most evident when we look at what happened after good and bad days. The correlation between the emotions the men in our study recorded at work and at home in the evening was remarkably high.[72] If a man had a positive day at work, he was more likely to come home in a positive mood. A father who landed a major contract, for example, came home all smiles.

Likewise, if a father developed a negative mood at work, he was likely to bring that negative mood in the door. One salesman got very upset when several cameras were stolen from the store. "Thieves drive me to distraction; I take it very personally," he wrote at the time; hours later, when he got home, he still felt angry and irritable. Another man described arriving home fuming: "On the way home from work, my car went out. Now what am I going to do. I have no money to fix it; maybe I should just die and get it over with."

For men who have unpleasant jobs, this carryover happens day after day, with cumulative consequences for their emotional well-being. We found that the amount of time a man spent at work and his degree of absorption were not related to his psychological health. But repeated experience of frustration and anger at work *was* correlated with his well-being. Research by others confirms that the amounts of distress and satisfaction men experience at work are major factors in their overall adjustment.[73] Fathers bring home the emotional residue of their jobs, good or bad.

Home as an Antidote

Whatever their experience at work, most men find home to be a welcome respite. It effects an incremental improvement in their mood: if they had a lousy day, they are likely to feel somewhat less distressed; if they had a good day, they often feel even better after they get home.

We can see this incremental improvement when we look at the overall pattern in the moods of the fathers in our study across the average weekday. Their typical emotional state during work hours was below average, reaching a low point around 4 P.M. But as they came home between 4 and 6 P.M., their average moods rose. Even though men reported extreme tiredness on their first beep at home, they usually also reported a substantial rise in their emotional state, which attenuated only as bedtime approached. (This pattern is graphed in chapter 3, figure 3.2.)

Homelife, then, is experienced by these men as an emotional antidote to their jobs. The reason for this, as we have discussed, is that fathers engage in leisure activities during their home time and, even when they do household work, they do it in a leisurely, unhurried way. For the same reasons, men's emotions are usually above average on the weekend too, despite the large amount of time spent in the emotion-numbing experience of watching TV.

The effectiveness of homelife in easing the stresses of work is suggested when we compare fathers whose experiences of home differ. Those fathers who reported the greatest choice over their activities at home showed more signs of well-being, as did those who reported greater happiness at home than at work. A man like William who can control and enjoy his time at home appears to benefit emotionally.[74] For many men, home is the remedy for the competitive fever of their jobs.

MEN'S DAILY PASSIONS

According to scholars of emotion, the feeling states experienced by a person or group provide a "royal road" to understanding their underlying values and ideology—they show what really matters for them.[75] The states experienced by the middle- and working-class fathers we studied reflected their sense of themselves as instrumental "doers." These men reported many occasions of deep attention, excitement, and feeling competitive. They also reported feeling quite or very "strong" twice as often as the women in our study (see appendix 2.1). These are states of action, of being absorbed and stirred by an instrumental goal.

But as a corollary to this action orientation, the men in our study also reported more negative emotions than the women did, especially at work. These fathers felt angry, irritable, and frustrated more often at their jobs than employed mothers. Some of this distress occurred when an instrumental venture was thwarted—for example, when a carpenter discovered his tools were locked up in someone's shop. Others were related to threats to the self-esteem men have invested in their jobs, such as when the boat salesman was sued for sex discrimination and went into a panic. These fathers also reported emotions that reflected feeling out of place—nervous, self-conscious, lonely—which can be linked to a masculine ideology that sees the self not in connection to others, but as separate and autonomous. The personal cost of men's orientation to action, then, is frequent frustration, anger, and feelings of isolation.

Flies in the Ointment

Viewed on its own, the daily emotional pattern of these fathers' lives has a certain rhythm or logic to it. The absorption and accompanying negative states they experience at work are compensated by their more leisurely time at home. For many fathers, recreation with children at the end of the day is the perfect balance to the draining expenditure of energy at work. Some may even feel that the availability of a pleasant refuge or cushion at home allows them to exceed their emotional threshold at work. They can run at full throttle during the day because they know they have their evenings and weekends for recuperation. These fathers' reality is organized around a cycle of exertion and rest, effort and leisure.

But there are several flaws in this logic. For one thing, our evidence that a leisurely experience of home benefits men is not entirely robust. We find no evidence, for example, that men feel better on Monday after a weekend of time for themselves. Furthermore, individual men who have less leisure and do more housework do not suffer poorer mental health; their emotional well-being is not markedly worse. In fact, the sociologist John Robinson actually found that *less* leisure, not more, is associated with greater life satisfaction.[76] Of course, it is possible that these flaws result from a failure to measure the right variables or that the phenomenon is more complex than we are able to determine. The reader should keep in mind that the sample size for this study is quite small, and while most of our findings are consistent with other research, some of these findings might come out differently, if the study were done again, even with a similar suburban white middle- and working-class sample.

But there is another weakness in this emotional logic. The balanced emotional order of men's lives presupposes a spouse who is willing and able to take primary responsibility for the home: someone to attend to the family's needs, including possibly the strong negative states and emotional needs fathers may sometimes bring home. This problem becomes particularly acute when a mother, either because of need or desire, decides to take outside employment. Does the wholesome balance between work and family apply to such mothers as well? Do they expend at work and recuperate at home as men do, and if so, who does the housework and child care when they need to be done?

As we shall see in the next chapter, the emotional order of mothers' lives follows a logic different from that of their husbands'. Making a family run smoothly is more complex than simply seeing that one person gets his needs met.

CHAPTER 3

Mothers:
INTERWEAVING WORK AND RELATIONSHIPS

THE LIVES LED BY the mothers in our study were diverse, much more so than the fathers'. Our pager found Anne, a full-time special education teacher, preparing the family's supper, then returning to school in the evening to judge science exhibits. Our pager found Sara, a full-time housemaker, spending the morning hemming her husband's new suit, then sharing a confidence with a friend over lunch. For the men we studied there is a single mold: They get up, go to work, and come home to their families; the essential structure of their lives is fixed. For women there are multiple templates, an array of competing and historically changing conceptions of how they should spend their time and energy.

Across cultures and historic periods, social norms have often restricted women's involvement in public life, limiting their activities to the home.[1] It was once argued that public life and wage labor were too coarse for women. In the 1960s, however, a new set of voices began attacking the home as a degrading prison for women. Betty Friedan painted the housewife role as one that inevitably results in alienation, exhaustion, and meaninglessness. She decried the "ludicrous consignment of millions of women to spend their days at work an eight-year-old can do."[2] Taking these sentiments to an extreme, Germaine Greer asserted that a housewife's life is not "real" and that raising children is "not a real occupation."[3]

Thus women's presence in both spheres—the workforce and domestic labor—has been challenged in public debate. Sara's decision to be a full-time housewife is held in low regard by some circles of our society, just as Anne's full-time employment is criticized in others. Yet such criticisms are often made with little concern for what women actually feel.

In this chapter we examine what women like Sara and Anne experience as they go about their lives. What are the emotions engendered by women's role as mothers and homemakers? Is it as bleak as Friedan and Greer described it, or can a full-time housewife like Sara have a buoyant life? And what type of emotional experience do women like Anne encounter in a full-time job? Does employment increase the negative emotion in their lives, or provide something that is missing from their existence at home?

Beneath these questions is the fundamental issue of how the two-parent family is organized. The traditional division of labor between mothers and fathers was based on the assumption that their labors were comparable: he "slaved" at his job; she "slaved" at home. But is this assumption valid, especially when she is employed? The family therapist Virginia Goldner suggests that if we found the balance of "suffering and pleasure" to be unequally distributed, it would challenge how our society constructs family life.[4]

The Evolution of Women's Family Role

The way the women in our study spend their time has been shaped by historically changing visions of "women's nature." Nineteenth-century farm mothers were a premodern version of "supermom." They worked in the fields, nurtured children, and often earned additional income for the family on the side. Life was often brutal; it was not uncommon for husbands to die prematurely or abandon the family, leaving women with full responsibility for the farm.[5]

In the late nineteenth century, however, our society developed a radically different image of women's nature and how women should spend their time. As husbands took wage-earning jobs, mothers—in theory, at least—became full-time guardians of the home sphere. The mother's job, according to popular writings, was to create a "happy home" for the rest of the family; professional home economists developed the conception of "mothercraft" into a scientific vocation.[6] Among the middle and upper classes emerged the ideal of the Victorian "lady," who was thought too genteel and pious to deal with the cruel and unseemly outside world.[7] This rationale and this image of women's nature became so powerful that the U.S. Supreme Court upheld laws barring women from certain occupations.[8]

But the "naturalness" of this new conception of how women should spend time was belied in a number of ways. To begin with, working-class mothers, whose families could not afford the middle-class ideal, functioned successfully as both workers and mothers. They labored in sweatshops or domestic service to keep children in school and, by their efforts, elevated a whole generation into the middle class.[9] Even many middle-class mothers participated behind the scenes in income-generating labor and brought in substantial income by taking boarders, sewing, or selling eggs.[10] It is estimated that 25 percent of a family's total income at the turn of the century came from these sources.[11] In very few cases were men really the sole financial providers.

Further, the conception that women did not fit in the public sphere was quickly set aside in wartime, when women readily took their place in the workforce. During World War II, women's employment rose dramatically, as "ladies" were asked to perform jobs such as welder and riveter, previously thought feasible only for men. Seemingly overnight, the war changed the public's attitude toward women working, from outright condemnation to tolerance.[12] The "nature of woman" had been redefined, at least temporarily. Suddenly she was capable and strong enough to hold the kind of job previously thought possible only for a man.

Despite women's demonstrated capability, after World War II "ultra-domesticity" once again became the ideal, and beliefs about women's "true nature" were revived. Returning soldiers needed jobs, so women were not only expected and urged to quit, but at times fired to make room for men. Reinforcing this ideal, magazines of the 1950s were filled with bright and smiling housewife/mothers, who cherished their "unique femininity."[13] Talcott Parsons and other social scientists of the 1950s sanctified the ideal types of the instrumental male who brings home the bacon and the expressive domestic female who is a "professional" at cooking it. Although many women continued in their jobs, Parsons wrote, "there can be no question of symmetry between the sexes, and there is no serious tendency in this direction."[14] Motherhood became glorified and home was deemed the proper place for a woman.

Yet from 1900 to today, more and more women, including married women, have sought work outside the home, and demographers project the employment rate for married women to surpass 80 percent by the year 2000.[15] In the early part of the century, this change was attributable to improved birth control and development of occupations related to women's roles as homemakers, such as nurse, secretary, and teacher. In the second half of the century, economic factors have fueled the dramatic acceleration of women's employment: Diminishing male wages since 1970 have confronted families with a declining standard of living and given many women little choice but to seek employment. Nearly eight in ten adults now believe that "it is getting to be impossible to support a family on just one income."[16]

These repeated historical changes, then, show that definitions of "women's nature" and associated injunctions about how women should spend their time shift as society's needs shift. If society needs extra factory workers, women are hired. If men need those jobs, women are told they should be at home. If the family needs more money, Mom goes to work. If the couple is getting divorced, the mother cares for the children *and* holds a job.

No Single Pattern

Because of this inconsistent legacy, the outward structure of contemporary women's lives varies greatly from person to person. Some women face enormous pressures on their time. All the mothers in our study were European-American, lived in working- and middle-class two-parent families, and only a handful had preschool children, yet we cannot describe a typical day for them as we did for their husbands. About a third were full-time homemakers, a third held part-time jobs, and a third held full-time jobs.

All these women reported at least a little time outside the household sphere: visiting friends, shopping, or going to the doctor. But for many full-time homemakers, like Sara, this amount was quite small. On the average, the full-time homemakers we studied spent a consuming 90 percent of their waking time in their role as wife and mother. One woman who provided forty-five random reports on her life was beeped only once outside her household role. She did go out—she drove the children places and went shopping—but it was always as a part of her role as a mother. For most full-time homemakers, the family role dominated their time.

In contrast, the full-time employed mothers, like Anne, divided their week equally between their domestic and public lives. Adding their time at work to other time away from their maternal role, they spent 46 percent of their waking hours in the public sphere. Because of their jobs, the employed women spent less time than the housewives in every category of family and household activity: less time in housework, family transportation, leisure, and talk. For Anne, who worked forty hours a week or more at her job, all these activities were packed into evenings and weekends.

Many commentators see an injustice in the number of hours that employed mothers work, especially compared to fathers'. When we consider total work time, including household work *and* paid work, the women employed full-time spent more of their waking hours laboring than their husbands did.[17] These mothers put in as many hours at their jobs as men, but household work accounted for 23 percent of these women's time and only 14 percent of the men's time.[18] What is striking is that husbands do not markedly increase their contribution to household work when their wives are employed, even when their wives earn as much pay as they do.[19] Employed women come home each evening to a pile-up of tasks—in the words of the sociologist Arlie Hochschild, to a "second shift."[20]

When the issue is total work time, then, employed mothers like Anne have the most arduous days, and homemakers like Sara have the least arduous. The full-time homemakers we studied spent more time than other women in household work, but this does not begin to equal the total time that employed women (and men) devoted to their jobs and household work.[21] Of course, such time estimates can be deceptive—we do not know, for example, whether some of the talking these mothers did should have been categorized as family management and how much of their seemingly leisurely day might be tied up by household obligations, such as waits between driving children from one activity to another. On the other hand, Betty Friedan cites findings that the typical housewife works inefficiently and that Parkinson's Law is in effect: her work expands to fill the available time.[22] If Friedan is right, then these assessments of time overestimate the actual amount of work homemakers accomplished.

Such assessments of time, however, get us only so far. To evaluate the magnitude of people's toil, we should consider not just the minutes and hours they clock in, but also the tribulations they endure. We must ask, What is the underlying emotional quality of women's daily experience? What balance of "suffering and pleasure" do they encounter in the different segments of their lives, and how does it compare to their husbands'?

WOMEN AT HOME

"I am the glue that keeps the house together," said one of the part-time-employed women we studied. "My primary responsibility is to be a wife and mother." Similar investment in the day-to-day care of their families is reported by Anne, Sara, and other women in the research. Tradition has assigned the sphere of children and home to mothers, and most women continue to take this assignment to heart. For nearly all the women in the study, home is the central context of their lives. Although employment reduces the number of hours women spend on domestic tasks, home and family remain a primary focus of their energy. No matter how time is examined, whether by the activities they did, where they spent time, or the thoughts they reported, all the mothers in our study were heavily involved with their families.

The fact that women are invested in their household activities, however, does not mean they enjoy them. Women are invested in part because they have been socialized from an early age to see household work as their responsibility. Indeed, we found that the teenage girls in our study reported more favorable experiences than boys when doing such work.[23] But have they been sold a bill of goods? Does women's homelife, with its mix of work and leisure activities, provide fulfilling hour-to-hour experiences, or is it depleting and empty, as Betty Friedan and Germaine Greer charged?

The Emotions of Child Care

Care of children is the traditional rationale linking women to the home sphere. Indeed, it is the reason many women stay home. "My kids need me," Sara explained. "You can't put the time and energy into this if you're not home." But what about her needs? What does she feel?

Sara was the mother of five children, ages four to eighteen, and while her family could benefit from the income if she were employed, she valued the flexibility she had. Our interviewer described Sara as an energetic and physically fit woman with short-cropped hair and an optimistic disposition. She had many happy moments caring for her children; for example, she described the pleasure she gets when her four-year-old says, "I need a hug." Her beeper reports, however, showed that her children kept her running and often brought her mood down. On Monday, for example, she was over-whelmed by a deluge of fast-breaking events and demands: her eldest daughter had just broken her foot; another daughter had a friend over; her son forgot his gym socks at home.

Our data show that for every happy moment taking care of children, mothers also experience an unhappy one.[24] The mothers in our study reported more frequent pride and cooperativeness during child care than during other activities, but also more frequent anger. This is true of employed mothers and homemakers equally. A part-time sales clerk, for example, reported several of her most positive moments talking with her son and driving him to school, but also three of her lowest times: once at his baseball game complaining to the umpire about a bad call and twice during discussions with him about his messy room. Another woman enjoyed tickling her eight-month-old daughter at one moment, then at another was furious because "I can't control my baby. The baby wants all the attention; she doesn't let me do anything."

Researcher Anne Wells has found that mothers' self-esteem often takes a beating when they are with their children.[25] Asked about the "worst time" of the week, many mothers in our study described stressful situations with their children: getting a resistant girl off to school, breaking up a fight between siblings, figuring out what to do about a son whose temper was creating a problem in the classroom.

When you add up all these negative and positive moments, mothers' average mood during child care was significantly lower than the consistently positive moods reported by fathers (see figure 3.1). The reason for the difference, of course, is that mothers experience less choice. Unlike fathers, who generally have to be in a good mood before they will take care of the children, mothers are not able to excuse themselves when things get more difficult. They cannot evade the whining, taunting, and defiance that kids sometimes dish out.

Sara often reported that she was doing something for her children not because she wanted to, but because it had to be done. Once she reported reading a children's book, *Wishes Come True,* to her four-year-old, but felt hurried and slightly angry because she'd been rushing all day and there was still much to be done. Ironically, while Sara read this optimistic story to her daughter, her own wishes counted for little. And the next day she drove through three inches of "treacherous" new snow to take her son his basketball socks. "The roads are terrible," she wrote, "but I can't tell him to play without socks." Then she added: "Why not?"

Figure 3.1

MOTHERS' AND FATHERS' EMOTION DURING
ACTIVITIES IN THE HOUSEHOLD SPHERE

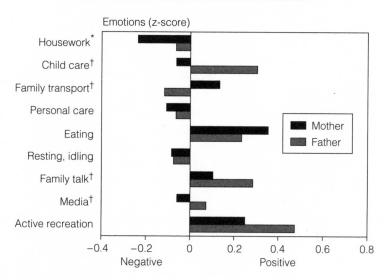

Figure displays average
emotions for each activity.
† p < .10; * p < .05

The answer to this rhetorical question, according to the family sociologist Arlene Skolnick, is that women have internalized care of children as a "moral enterprise."[26] Because it was part of their traditional role and part of their socialization, full-time homemakers like Sara, as well as employed mothers like Anne, feel a rock-bottom commitment to tending to their children's well-being, irrespective of their own needs. While men withdraw from child care when they want, for women there is no choice.[27] It is typically women who get up at 3 A.M. to deal with a child's illness, for example. Regardless of how difficult and unpleasant looking after a child might become, the task falls to the mother.

The Daily Grind of Housework

Along with child care, mothers acquired housework as part of the duties of their traditional role. Because housework is part of their "job," the low moods women reported during housework—states much lower than those that accompany child care—may be dismissed by some as part of the traditional exchange between women and men. We found that fathers' states at their jobs were not always pleasant; isn't housework comparable toil for mothers?

Our data indicate that women's experience of housework is bleaker than men's experience of their jobs. Women reported feeling less happy, cheerful, and strong during housework than their husbands felt at their jobs.[28] This is true of both employed and unemployed women: both Anne and Sara reported dull, empty moments doing laundry, washing dishes, and cleaning up after other people.[29]

More significant than their low moods, however, may be our finding that women reported less than half the rate of deep attention during housework that men reported at their jobs. They also reported much less frequent interest and less feeling of skill.[30] In discussing men's work, we introduced the concept of "flow," a rewarding psychological experience of getting caught up in and enjoying a task. Men frequently experience this state at their paid jobs, as do employed women at theirs. But women's low rates of attention and interest during housework suggest that flow is rare during their traditional "job." Indeed, when asked to describe an occasion of deep absorption during the week, only one woman mentioned a time when she was doing housework. A housewife who had spent the weekend cooking explained that it provided a "creative outlet," something that could hardly be said about most household chores.

The structure of housework simply does not lend itself to deep and engaging absorption. Flow requires a "channel" of novel challenges to pit one's skills against, according to Mihaly Csikszentmihalyi; however, most housework is extremely repetitive and one is hard-pressed to find such novelty or challenge in it. One researcher found that 65 percent of house-work tasks need to be done again the next day.[31] Thus a mother who described flow experiences during church work reported that it just does not happen at home: "It's harder to focus with family. There's too much functioning by rote." Most of women's household tasks are also short, tak-ing less than fifteen minutes, further precluding deep involvement. In fact, women often have to handle several of these tasks at once.[32] Sara complained on Monday that she could not even get lunch made because there were so much interruptions. While many men have the freedom to spend Saturday afternoon immersing themselves in the challenge of repairing the garage roof or building a playhouse, the tasks that mostly women do—laundry, cleaning the floor, picking up after children—do not allow immersion.

Instead of "flow," researcher Catherine Berheide describes the mental state of housework as vacant or "numb"; Friedan calls it "narcolepsy"; researchers Marie Allison and Margaret Duncan discover frequent "anti-flow."[33] It is not that women always feel unhappy, irritable, or angry when doing housework. They more often feel nothing; they feel tired and weak; they report little desire to be doing what they are doing.

Rather than being a personal challenge, much of women's housework is motivated by feelings of obligation. This sense of inescapable duty is evi-dent in one nurse's report that she felt tired and bored "because I don't really want to be cleaning house." This sense of obligation, of course, comes from without and within. On the one hand, children and husbands are uninhibited in making claims on mothers' time.[34] On the other hand, women are socialized to be invested in getting things done right and to experience housework as a test of their worth.[35] Whether the issue is the cleanliness of the house or the quality of the dinner, a mother is likely to view herself—and be viewed by others—as responsible. In the case of William's wife, Alice, it is simple: "I don't like housework, but feel guilty when I don't do it."

In comparison to men's jobs, then, housework provides a less satisfying kind of psychological experience. Women face frustrations like those in paying jobs, but not the rewards. To make matters worse, many women feel that their labors are rarely appreciated. One woman said it was only when she got a job that family members realized how much she did around the house. Society attaches little value to "women's work," diminishing a woman's sense of importance as a homemaker, wife, and mother. A full-time kindergarten teacher described the end of summer as one of her worst times of the year: "I felt like a maid. . . . Every year at this time in August I'm ready to go back to school. I get tired of waiting on everyone."

Housework is a black hole for women: it sucks up hours of dull, often solitary labor for which they get little back.[36] But do the other domestic activities interspersed with family work make up for this emotional drain?

Self-Care, Rest, and Eating

The time women spend in various personal-care activities might provide the opportunity for self-nurturance and the experience of a more positive state. Yet when we look at self-care activities, such as bathing, grooming, and dressing, we find they were second only to housework in the low emotional states they created for the mothers in our study (see figure 3.1). Certainly there were exceptions: One mother was beeped during a long, luxurious bath. In general, however, these activities were not relaxing; they more often produced feelings of frustration and weakness.

The reason for these negative states, we suspect, is that self-beautification, which accounts for a major segment of this time, is an activity that produces a sense of conflict and limited choice for women in our society. From early childhood, they learn that being physically attractive is a key to success and to pleasing others. In fact, studies confirm that a woman's attractiveness increases her likelihood of being promoted at her job, and it even affects qualities of her marital life.[37] One husband commented to his wife that he was tired of seeing her in the same dress—reinforcing the cultural message that looking attractive is part of women's role.

When women are putting on makeup or attempting to select the right outfit, they may be only too aware that society's idealized standards of youth and beauty—dictated by a multibillion-dollar cosmetic and fashion industry—are unattainable. In a culture where maintaining one's appearance is essential to feeling successful and confident, it is understandable that self-beautification activities would generate frustration and feelings of powerlessness.

Resting and idling are little more effective in raising women's mood in the home sphere (see figure 3.1). Anne had a pause at 4:10 P.M. Thursday, but she was preoccupied with figuring out what to make for supper. Likewise, Sara sat down for a moment on Monday at 1:44 P.M., but she was trying to think through finding a baby-sitter for her four-year-old.

Eating, however, stands out for these mothers as a consistent positive activity. When eating, women reported that they were content; in fact, they were slightly happier than men at these times. In between running all day and working all evening, Anne, for example, found eating dinner with her family to be one of her few chances to sit down and relax. In addition to eating, we might expect that women's leisure would compensate for the strain of family work.

Mothers' Household Leisure: An Oxymoron?

When we look at these women's TV watching, we see that this leisure activity has an even more emotionally numbing effect on them than it has on their husbands. The women reported fewer positive and fewer negative states during media than during other activities.[38] They may turn on the TV in hopes of finding an emotional antidote to the emptiness of housework, but TV is usually ineffective in lifting their mood.

These women did experience reading as more favorable. Several mentioned the value of getting away from it all and curling up with their current book. One reported feeling relaxed while reading a romance novel, explaining that "I was doing what I enjoy," and added a comment on how mean one of the characters always was to her sister.[39] Another noted how she considered the time between 9:30 and 10:30 P.M., after the kids were asleep, her "little vacation"—a time when she could sit in bed and read. But while women were more likely to report absorbed attention when reading and little desire to be doing anything else, their emotional state was not more positive than during TV.

Active recreation, in contrast, produced more pleasurable experiences for these women, although not to the same extent as for the men. Women reported the same activities as men—sports, games, family outings—but the emotional rewards for women weren't as strong. Furthermore, these activities do not appear to have had the lasting aftereffects on mood that we saw for men's recreation.

Thus, while providing some pleasure, mothers' household leisure appears to be less "leisurely" than fathers' (see figure 3.1). Indeed, several authors have questioned whether "leisure" is an accurate term for mothers' free time at home.[40] For one thing, household responsibilities often intrude into their minds or "lurk in a menacing way."[41] They may be watching TV, but they are thinking about what to prepare for tomorrow's picnic, or worrying about a child's Halloween costume. For another thing, mothers' leisure is more often sandwiched between other activities. While fathers have the luxury of getting deeply absorbed in TV or a game, mothers have to fit leisure activities into shorter, more unpredictable time periods.[42] The phone rings, the plumber arrives, a child needs attention—and Mother's leisure comes to an end.[43]

Because of their household responsibilities, women are less able to establish a boundary between work and leisure at home. They experience less control over their time in the home sphere.[44] While men see leisure as a "right" they earn by their work, many women believe they aren't entitled to take time off for themselves. Many housewives feel they have not earned it; employed women feel that if they have any additional time, they want to spend it with their children.[45]

Anne articulated the constraints on women's leisure at home. After a long day of teaching and dealing with the family's needs, she said, she enjoyed going off by herself to read. But frequently, "the children follow me. I sometimes ask them if I can please be alone. But sometimes I feel that their need to be with me is greater than my need to be alone."

Conversation: The Medium of Mothering

Talk with others, whether in person or by phone, accounts for the remaining large segment of women's household time. Full-time homemakers in our study reported twice as much time in "family talk" as employed women, but even employed mothers reported more talk than men.

Conversation was a major part of these women's household activity, yet their moods during it were less positive than men's (see figure 3.1). This contradiction—spending more time in a less pleasurable activity—is explained by the fact that this conversation often served a different function for women. Mothers are more often the family "kin-keeper," the person who maintains contacts with relatives, as well as friends and neighbors. Robinson found gender differences in husbands' and wives' topics of conversation. Women talked more about home-centered things, such as child care, personal needs, health concerns, and family and friends; men more about work and news events.[46] These same difference are suggested in our data. It is usually the wife who stays in touch with grandparents, plans gatherings with family friends, and arranges for neighbors to feed the cat during the family's summer vacation.

Thus less of women's family talk is pure leisure and more is care-giving, or cultivating the family's social ties. Compared to their husbands, the mothers in our study reported much more talk with neighbors and relatives, usually their mothers, sisters, and occasionally sisters-in-law. And in a crisis situation, it was usually the mother who sprang into action. This happened with Laura and Jay, a working-class couple. When they learned that his sister's husband, who was sick, had left home and had not returned, it was not Jay but Laura who got on the phone to help think the situation through.

Part of the reason women's talk is less pleasurable, then, is that it is often instrumental; indeed, it can be quite taxing. Women are called on to resolve family crises, as well as misunderstandings and hurt feelings. Rather than receiving gratitude for her efforts, Laura commented "families don't appreciate your help at times." In response to a different situation, she noted "how my mother gets so upset when I get anything. She gets so jealous. I'm tired of feeling guilty and trying to hide things." Women typically assume the role of trying to work through complex feelings in a family, and sometimes they find themselves in no-win situations.

Much of mothers' conversation with children is also care-giving. Many mothers have a chat with their children to check in after school. On Friday evening at 8:56 P.M., the beeper found Sara having discussions with her three teenage children about where each was going that night and who would be driving.

Mothers' talk, then, is central to their activities as mothers. It is through this medium that they become the glue that keeps the family together. Denigrations of women's household role, such as those made by Greer and Friedan, neglect this caring part of what they do. This is not "eight-year-old" stuff. Mothers' traditional household role involves much more than the material tasks of cleaning and cooking, it involves these important executive tasks of tending to the emotional and social needs of the family. DeVault (1991) demonstrated that even cooking involves much more than assembling a meal; women devote much thought and care to preparing food that family members like and, in some cases, a dinner experience that brings the family together. As Lopata (1971) wrote, "The important and difficult actions of mothers lie not so much in specific tasks or activities they perform, but in the thought they devote to managing a household."

The problem, however, is that this caring can be emotionally draining and unrewarding.

The Emotional Ecology of Women's Homelife: Paradox #1

As we look across all the women's time at home, we find that their average emotional states were less favorable than when they were away from the household sphere. And they were certainly less favorable than

fathers' states at home. The pleasures of meals and leisure do not counter-
balance the aggravations of housework, the stresses of child care, and the
insecurities associated with self-care.[47] This is true for employed women
and full-time homemakers equally.

The reason the home sphere is not pleasant for women is succinctly
captured by looking at where different family members feel "hurried" (see
appendix 3.1). Husbands reported frequently feeling hurried at work and
much less so with their families. Likewise, children reported feeling hurried
at school and much less hurried with their families. Mothers, however, felt
hurried *both* at home and away from home. There was no letup for them.
Whether they were brushing their hair or talking, they felt more rushed at
home than their husbands did.[48] Neither employed women nor full-time
housewives found home a place of rest and repose. There is always another
dish to wash or crisis to deal with.

The depleting effect of a mother's household activities is suggested
when we examine the mental health of those women who put the most
time into them. Our analyses looked at the women who reported the most
housework and those who reported spending the most time in the home
sphere. Statistical manipulations were used to adjust for their hours of
employment. The striking finding is that these women were more
depressed.[49] Irrespective of whether a woman was employed full-time,
part-time, or not at all, spending more time doing housework and in the
home sphere were associated with greater depression. Of course, this finding does not prove that one causes the other, but the suggestion is chill-
ing: that the traditional activities assigned to women are not good for their
mental health.

We thus come to the first major paradox, or trap, that defines the
structure of women's lives. On the one hand, they are strongly invested in
their family role. They recognize it to be important; they have been
socialized to see it as central to who they are.[50] But they discover it to be
lacking in immediate emotional gratification. Much of their labor, especially housework, is dull, repetitive, and unappreciated. Paradox #1 is
that they are invested in a role that is frequently draining. A mother's traditional role is to make the home "happy," yet she is not happy playing
that role.

Arlie Hochschild attributes this situation to a stalled revolution. As our
data show, men are hardly waiting with dustmops in hand to take over an
equal share of the housekeeping burden. Husbands do not increase their
contribution to housework when their wives are employed. Even when
fathers do contribute, Mom may have to supervise Dad's family work, and

in some cases he may do it so poorly that she has to do it over again.[51] Although there is some evidence that men are very gradually increasing their share of time in housework, they are clearly resistant.[52]

But simply to blame men is to miss part of the paradox. Many women are undecided about whether they want to sacrifice the power that more equitable sharing would entail, especially when they are not guaranteed equivalent power in the job sphere. In some cases they resist or even undercut their husband's efforts to share what they see as their domain.[53] One father described overseeing a young child's lunch, when his wife stepped in front of him and took over, as if he were not there. One survey found that only a quarter to a third of mothers say their husbands should be doing more housework.[54] Women are fundamentally invested in their role of mother and household manager, even though it is not a pleasant one.

Sara's World: The Life of a Housewife

The full-time homemakers in our study lived this paradox hourly. While family work is emotionally unrewarding, it was their main source of self-worth. They spent an average of 90 percent of their time in the household sphere, a substantial part of it doing family work. And despite the value many women place on social interaction, these women lived more solitary lives than women who were employed.[55]

As a result of this situation, some of the full-time housewives in the study led a pretty drab existence. On the average, we found that full-time homemakers reported feeling weak more often than employed women did. In chapters 6 and 8, we introduce you to a number of homemakers who have clearly suffered from being trapped by their role.

Nonetheless, some homemakers, like Sara, were doing quite well. We found that in spite of the depleting nature of family work, many of the full-time homemakers in the study spoke favorably about their situation. They liked the freedom they had to choose when to do certain chores and the time to do what they wanted when the chores were done. The greater time they spent in the noxious experience of housework was balanced by greater time in leisure or discretionary activities outside the home. In an extensive study of American housewives, the sociologist Helena Lopata found that, far from leading a unidimensional existence, many live rich, imaginative, and complex lives.[56]

Sara had dull and bleak experiences of household labor, as other women did, but she also seemed genuinely to enjoy caring for others. At the first beep she was eating out with her husband, helping him think about ways to lose weight. The next morning she was having coffee with a friend, discussing the destructive effects of alcoholism on the friend's marriage. That night, the beeper caught her in conversation with her husband about the medical treatment for her father, whom she thought was dying. And the next day she mobilized the family to help their eighteen-year-old daughter, who had broken her foot. Sara's life went on like this, full of personal problems and resolutions. Her mood dipped when she worried about her father's illness, but more often she felt cheerful when helping and added notes about how "courageous" or "resilient" people are in the face of adversity.

Sara enjoyed caring for others, but did not neglect her own needs—an occupational hazard of housewives. She said that she valued time by herself and recognized the calming effect it has on her. In between mopping the floor and tending to the dog, she snatched time to go off and work on a quilt or finish the Sarton novel she was reading. Like other homemakers, she spent much time alone, but she said, "I enjoy being alone."

The key to Sara's emotional buoyancy appears to be her activities outside the home. In addition to her informal counseling of friends, she spent a day volunteering at the high school cafeteria and taught a class on parenting skills on Monday nights; in the past she had done political work. She was also known in the neighborhood for her skill at designing decorative curtains and brought in some additional family income this way. "I enjoy the challenge of hanging curtains," she reported while doing it, and when it is completed, she expresses happiness at how "great it looks." Sara counteracted the emptiness of housework by involvement in these activities outside the home.

This introduces us to the second paradox in women's lives. Even for a mother who enjoys caring for her family, such as Sara, her best moods occur when she steps out of her role as mother and participates in the world beyond the home.

WOMEN AT WORK

On initial examination, Anne's life as a special education teacher looks much different from Sara's. It more closely resembles William's life as a high school choral instructor. At the first beep, this quiet and earnest woman was at school and wrote that she was "overwhelmed by the amount of things to do right now." At the next report she felt friendly while teaching synonyms and antonyms, explaining, "I like my class." And at the next report, she felt happy and cheerful leading a discussion on geometric shapes. By 1:48 P.M. she was tired and irritable, though her mood was more positive later that night when she returned to school to judge science exhibits. Like William's, her job kept her going from early in the morning until late at night.

On closer inspection, however, Anne's life is more similar to that of Sara and other women. In between her work at school, she rushes home to cook and take care of her family. On Wednesday, for example, she got home in time to meet her three daughters returning from school. Then she tended to the needs of her eight-year-old, who had been vomiting earlier in the week, supervised her eight-year-old's homework, and discussed with the fourteen-year-old the pluses and minuses of taking honors algebra next year.

Unlike William, Anne does not have her homelife as a place of respite. She cannot lounge on the patio when she gets home from work. Instead, she goes from her demanding job at school to her demanding job at home. When beeped at 4:10 P.M. on Wednesday, she was making supper and feeling grouchy, though her mood improved a little later when she and the children watched "Days of Our Lives." Then she reported a second dip in her mood after she came home from school again, at 7:52 P.M., to more family responsibilities. Even though he was unemployed at the time, her husband did little to help with child care or chores. Anne reported that he did not understand their daughters, and on Friday night when she needed him to stop and pick up something she needed at the store, he contended he could not, and she had to do it.

In spite of this hectic crunch, Anne said she liked being employed and liked her job. Most of the women in our study, like national samples of employed women, said they held jobs for economic reasons: with skyrocketing medical costs and rising prices for everything from housing to teenagers' tennis shoes, many families, including middle-class families, feel they simply cannot get by on one paycheck.[57] Even one very traditional woman, who found the public world "dirty and disgusting," said, "When we looked at our debts, we realized that if I didn't work, we'd be in debt for fifteen years."

Yet most working women, including those in menial jobs, said that they would choose to be employed even if they had no financial need.[58] Why? For Anne, we will see that her job played an important emotional function in her life and helped her endure a bitter dispute with her husband. The value of women's employment lies not only in the pay and the immediate experience at a job, but also in the role it plays within the overall emotional organization of their reality.

Emotional Strains

For the most part, the women in our study did not have exciting or glamorous jobs. One filled vending machines, another worked a switchboard, others were teachers, nurses, clerical workers, sales representatives, and junior-level managers. Many of these jobs were service-oriented and many could be described as low-paying, dead-end, and menial.

These jobs are as taxing as the jobs that generate so much frustration and negative emotion in the lives of the fathers we studied. In fact, these mothers spent a higher percentage of their time at their jobs working than their husbands did, and they rated themselves as "hardworking" just as often as the men did.[59] When we asked about the "worst time of the week," many mothers mentioned events at their jobs. They told of conflicts with coworkers, impossible time pressures, and fear of being fired. One nurse described feeling devastated when a critical-care patient died. There is little question that women encounter the same stress at their jobs as men do at theirs.[60]

Yet, surprisingly, the immediate emotional experience at work of the women we studied was not as negative as the men's. The women's average state at work was more favorable than their experience at home, and it was more favorable than men's experience at their jobs. Compared to at home, at work they were less likely to feel unhappy, drowsy, and lonely; not once did any woman report feeling guilty at work.[61] Although their jobs were stressful, they seemed to experience fewer of the negative emotional side effects we saw among men: they were less often irritable, frustrated, and angry.

Why didn't these women experience the negative emotions that the men did at their jobs? One explanation might be that the women felt less trapped at their jobs than the men. In chapter 2 we proposed that men's negative experience at work was partly related to their bearing the family role of "primary breadwinner." Women's wages are seen as important to families; nonetheless, women typically enjoy somewhat more freedom than their husbands to quit if the job is not going well.[62] By this argument, employment is women's domain of choice, just as home is men's domain of choice.

The flaw in this explanation, however, is that women do not experience choice when at work. In fact, women typically have jobs in which they have less autonomy and control over their immediate actions than men do. They are frequently taking orders from others and have limited task flexibility.[63] When beeped at work, the women in our study reported significantly less "freedom" and "choice" over their current activities than they experienced at home and than men reported at their jobs. Clearly, it is not a feeling of personal control that accounts for women's more favorable emotions at their jobs.[64] Work is not a context of personal liberation.

So why, then, did these women find their jobs less onerous than the men did, and than their experience at home?

Emotional Rewards

Hints of what women find emotionally rewarding at their jobs appear when we look at the social side of their work experience.

To begin with, the women in our study reported a more amicable disposition at their jobs. Whereas the men felt more "competitive" at work than the women, the women felt significantly more "cooperative" than the men (see appendix 3.2). The women also felt friendlier. Rather than working *against* other people with the kind of "take no prisoners" attitude some men seem to relish, women are oriented toward working *with* others. When one man reported that a coworker was fired, he commented, "I could give a shit"; a woman in a similar circumstance reported deep concern.

In turn, the happiness of these women at work was strongly related to the amiability they experienced in others. On each beeper sheet participants were asked, "Are the people you are with: friendly . . . versus unfriendly?" We found that many of these women experienced their colleagues at work to be as friendly as family members at home. Furthermore, those women who perceived their coworkers to be most friendly were happiest at their jobs.[65] In contrast, the friendliness of others was not related to the happiness of the men at their jobs.

These findings suggest that the social experience is what makes work emotionally valuable to women. One woman described feeling happy and relaxed at work because "the people I like best are here." A nurse cited a comradely lunch with her coworkers as the best time of her week. She said things were chaotic at the hospital, but they shared a positive feeling of togetherness and "punchiness." Anne described the social interaction with her special education students as a source of positive experience. "I like the children and all of their little quirks. They're so cute."

For many of these women, work provided social rewards they did not get at home. Their labor was not taken for granted; they got appreciation from others; many of them also received social support. Other research confirms that social aspects of work contribute heavily to women's well-being at their jobs.[66] By adopting a more congenial disposition, women have less negative experience at work than men do and gain emotional buoyancy.

But women do not fully escape the frustration and grief of the rat race. It catches up with them when they get home.

The 6 O'Clock Crash

For fathers, the period after work is a time when they are able to take off their shoes and claim "fatigue." Employed mothers also feel fatigued, but they get no such break.[67] Many would love the opportunity to relax, unwind, and regroup.[68] But they face the second shift. Supper has to be cooked; children's needs from the day must be addressed. "Everybody wants me," Anne said. Yet husbands of the employed women in our study were no more likely to help deal with these pressing demands than the men married to housewives were.

The result of this end-of-the-day crunch for women is an emotional scenario opposite the one that occurs for dads. If you will recall, the emotional state of the men in our study rose substantially around 6:00 P.M. when they came home to the family. In contrast, the employed women's emotional state tumbled. Figure 3.2 charts the average emotion experienced by the full-time employed mothers across the weekday and contrasts

Figure 3.2

EMPLOYED MOTHERS' AND FATHERS' EMOTION ACROSS THE DAY

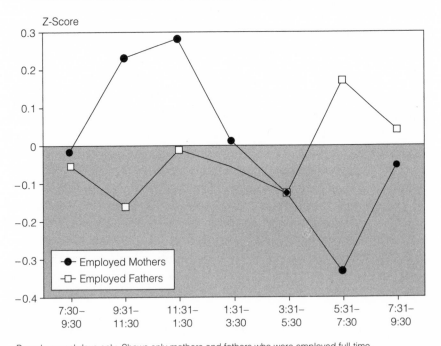

Based on weekdays only. Shows only mothers and fathers who were employed full-time.

it to the fathers'. The employed mothers' emotional state, you can see, is above average from 8 in the morning until mid-afternoon, during the time they are at work. But then we see the "6 o'clock crash." Their mood plummets to the lowest point of the day.

"I'm tired, I have a headache, I wish the day were over and I could go to bed," wrote one woman who was busily cleaning up the kitchen at 5:48 P.M. Another woman, whose husband had called to say he would be working until 10 P.M., was furious at him and wrote, "This is a rough time of day when I have to play both mom and dad."

We saw that fathers' good moods at work carried over to home, but this is not evident for women. Regardless of whether a woman's last mood at work was extremely positive or extremely negative, the outcome when she got home was identical: a deluge of demands on her time and an unhappy mood (see appendix 3.3). Positive emotion at work provided no buffer against what happened when she got home.[69]

The only time worse than the 6 o'clock period on weekdays for employed mothers was Saturday afternoon, when their mood plunged to the lowest point of the whole week. This was another time when performance of housework reached a peak. During the weekend, when she may have been hoping for some time off to relax, the full-time-employed mother played catch-up with housework.[70]

Work as an Antidote to Work: Paradox #2

The divergence between fathers' and mothers' reality is nowhere more apparent. The home functions as fathers' place of respite, it provides emotional compensation for the stress they experience at their jobs. But for women there is no comparable place of respite from their labor. This leads us to the second fundamental paradox that structures women's lives.

Women's primary alternative to the stress and exertion they experience in their traditional home sphere is more stress and exertion at a paid job. Their primary option for escape from drudgery at home is to take a job—where they do more work. "Instead of liberation," the sociologist Myra Ferree has written, "the double day of housewife and paid work appears to be creating a new form of exploitation."[71] Nowhere do employed women get the opportunity for the long expanses of relaxation and replenishment that men claim in the home sphere. The hurriedness at work is their primary antidote to the hurriedness of home.

As a result, the employed women in our study reported the feeling of being stretched, torn, pulled in two or three directions. In response to the question "What's the worst thing about working and raising a family at the same time?" they almost all responded with frustration about their lack of time and resources. One owner of a small business said: "I have a great job and I love making money, but it's difficult. You spread yourself thin. I get a feeling of satisfaction, independence from the job, being able to provide for my family, but my schedule is hectic. I never have time just for me, to do what *I* want. I feel pulled apart sometimes."

A kindergarten teacher said: "(There's) not enough time to do all the things I want to do. I don't have enough time to do everything one hundred percent. I feel very stretched a lot of the time. It's draining and difficult. I often make choices, give up one thing for another."

Not surprisingly, researchers find that the work–family juggling act is currently more stressful for women than for men.[72] Paradox #2, then, is that the positive experiences women enjoy at their jobs have a price. There are clear gains to be had from a job. In addition to a paycheck, it provides social and emotional benefits, as we have seen, and in many cases it offers valuable intellectual stimulation.[73] But the costs, given the current lack of support for employed women, include the constant feeling that there is not enough time to get everything done and the 6 o'clock crash at the end of each day.

Role Strain or Role Gain?

This uncertain balance of benefits and costs has led researchers (and many women, no doubt) to ask whether a job is worth it: do the emotional rewards of employment for mothers outweigh the stress it brings under current circumstances? Does employment have a net positive or negative effect on women's well-being? When we add together all the moments in each woman's life, we find that the overall frequency of anger and joy, excitement and boredom, even energy and exhaustion do not differ greatly between employed women and homemakers.

The net daily emotional experience of employed women in our sample was as positive as, if not slightly more positive than, that of the full-time homemakers. The low moods of the 6 o'clock crash and Saturday afternoons was more than compensated for by better moods at work and on Sundays. Employed women felt "accepted" more often than homemakers (68 percent versus 47 percent), because women feel accepted more frequently at work than at home. And they felt "weak" less often (1 percent versus 6 percent), partly because they spent less time in enervating housework.

This slight emotional advantage that employed women hold is not very great. Although the housewives in our study spent more time in the less-happy home sphere and in emotionally deadening housework, this was partly compensated for by more time talking with friends and in other leisure activities.

Much research with larger samples has come to similar conclusions about the relationship of employment to women's physical and mental health. Some, but not all, studies find employed women to have slightly better mental health, a greater sense of mastery, and higher self-esteem.[74] Even when one adjusts for the fact that healthier women are more likely to seek employment, the conclusion is still that the net emotional effect of work on women's well being is neutral, or perhaps slightly positive.[75]

Conclusions about effects of women's employment, however, need to be qualified by all the contingency factors we have already discussed. If their jobs put lots of pressure on women's time, they may harm their well-being. We found that the women who were often "hurried" at work were less happy.[76] Because of their non-negotiable household obligations, mothers are more vulnerable to time demands at work; indeed, other researchers have found that the frequency of overtime work, evening shifts, and longer hours are associated with greater physical and mental strain on mothers than fathers.[77] Work is a positive experience for mothers as long as it does not become too frantic.

Likewise, if housework puts a lot of pressure on a woman's time, it may also adversely affect her well-being. If she has a larger family and a husband who is unhelpful and highly involved in his career, the demands on her time increase and her well-being may be compromised. Conversely, if she has a husband who is supportive, contributing to child care and housework, the balance may tilt in the "gains" direction.[78]

Anne had a husband who was anything but supportive; nonetheless, we can see that her job played an important role in buffering her against the difficult events that occurred in her family life during the week of the study.

Anne's Employment as an Emotional Refuge

Arriving home from a trip on Friday night, Anne's husband announced that he wanted to take a new job in Cleveland. This would be the seventh move in eighteen years of marriage and Anne was extremely upset at the prospect. She was especially concerned about the disruptive effects of a move on their children

This situation made Anne's time at home much more difficult than it would otherwise have been. The effects on her are evident in the graph of her emotional states over the week, presented in figure 3.3. "The day is

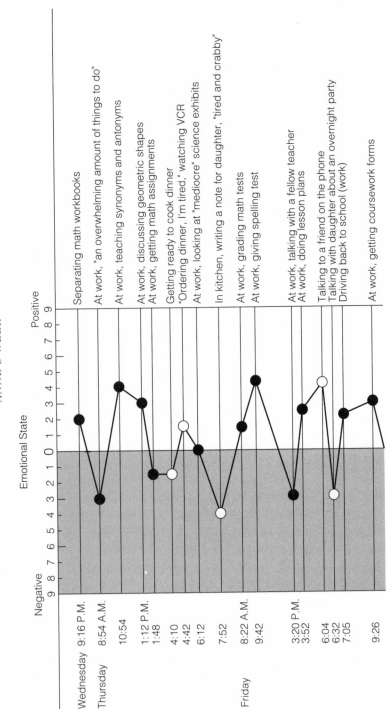

Figure 3.3

ANNE'S WEEK

ANNE'S WEEK (continued)

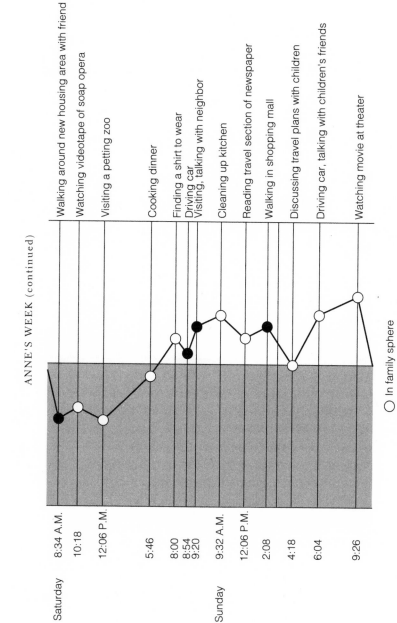

Saturday

8:34 A.M. Walking around new housing area with friend

10:18 Watching videotape of soap opera

12:06 P.M. Visiting a petting zoo

5:46 Cooking dinner

8:00 Finding a shirt to wear
8:54 Driving car
9:20 Visiting, talking with neighbor

Sunday

9:32 A.M. Cleaning up kitchen

12:06 P.M. Reading travel section of newspaper

2:08 Walking in shopping mall

4:18 Discussing travel plans with children

6:04 Driving car, talking with children's friends

9:26 Watching movie at theater

○ In family sphere
● In public sphere

ANNE'S WEEK (continued)

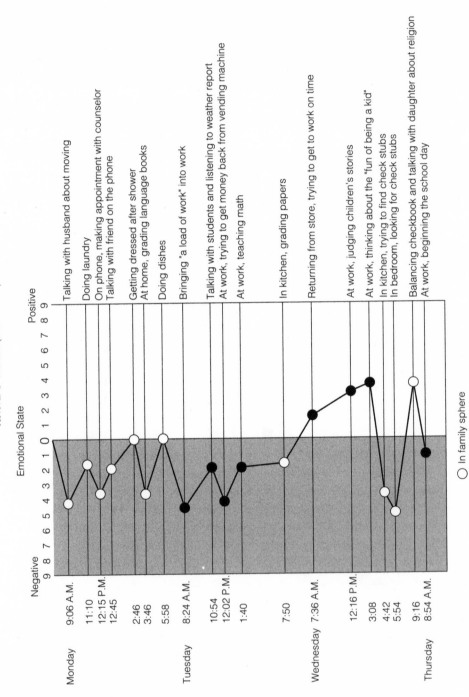

lost," Anne wrote Saturday. She brooded much of the morning and afternoon, and got nothing done. Saturday evening her mood came up when she and her husband went to a party, and Sunday she was cheered when a friend and her children came and stayed with them. But at other times her mood at home was despondent.

The unpleasantness of her homelife was prolonged because Monday was a holiday. Early that morning Anne confronted her husband about the move, but she found him rigid and unwilling to compromise. She argued, cried, and experienced heart palpitations. She wrote, "I feel like I'm being smashed to pieces." A depression set in that lasted until the next day, as can be seen in the graph.

But Anne's enjoyment of teaching rescued her from this constant brooding over the situation. Although her mood was still low Tuesday morning, she reported that it was "good to be back to work." And on Wednesday, absorption in teaching pulled her mood back up again, even though the conflict with her husband was not resolved. She wrote that her class was fun to be with, though the satisfaction she gained, of course, did not prevent her from experiencing the 6 o'clock crash when she returned home.

Anne's job provided her with an important separate emotional base—she described it as an "escape from the problems of home." Asked how she felt about holding a job and being a mother at the same time, Anne was fully aware of the costs. She complained about "not having enough time to fix proper meals, not enough time for my kids in the evening, and an untidy house." But she felt the gains were worth it. "It's a challenge, but I couldn't stay home all the time; I'm not the type. I would get dissatisfied if I weren't working; the kids would see it and it would rub off. The job makes me more interesting and makes me appreciate them more." Anne *wanted* to be working, and, whether employed or not, women have been found to be happiest when they are doing what they want to be doing.[79] During this week, her job gave her the strength to hold her own in the battle with her husband.

FREEDOM AND FRIENDSHIP

A segment of time that is a particularly important part of women's lives is time in the public domain away from work, when women step outside the roles of both mother and employee. It includes time in transit, taking classes, and meeting with friends. All the women in our study provided at least one report in this domain, and those who spent the most time in it, like Sara, reported the least depression.[80]

Lorraine, a reflective and spiritual full-time homemaker, said, "By stopping routines, whether by getting together with friends or just meditating, I don't feel weighted down or victimized." Another woman attributed the positive emotion of public time to "feeling completely removed from the aggravations of home: from children's schedules and husband's schedules."

Nearly all activities the women in our study engaged in away from the home sphere elicited more positive emotion for them than for the men. Figure 3.4 shows these comparisons. We already know that the women were happier than the men at their jobs. We see here that they were also happier in other public activities. Driving to work, for example, was associated with negative average emotion for the men, yet for the women there was no such negative taint. The women also felt happier than the men during other nonfamily driving.

Several mothers in the study were going to school and reported rewarding experiences during these times. Two identified the satisfaction of getting a good grade as the best time of their week. It was a heady experience for these housewives in school after many years at home to discover that they could excel in this foreign territory. Several also identified studying as

Figure 3.4

MOTHERS' AND FATHERS' EMOTION
DURING ACTIVITIES IN THE PUBLIC SPHERE

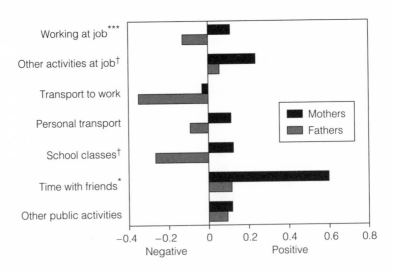

† p<.10; * p<.05; *** p<.001

their occasion of deep absorption and described particular relish in the quiet and freedom from interruption that came with digging into their coursework. Participation in clubs or organizations also seemed to be a chore for the men, but the women reported much more positive states.

The women's most frequent activity in the public domain was meeting with friends, and these occasions were most often described as the best times of the week. Lorraine, for example, took a whole day away from home to spend with friends, and this gave her a feeling of being tremendously "connected." She had lunch with a companion who was in a lot of pain from a personal crisis. Lorraine felt it important to "stand with her and give her some hope"; they had a deep exchange of feelings that both found very meaningful. In the evening Lorraine then had dinner with another friend and had a similar deep conversation about the ups and downs in their lives. Later she reflected that these interactions made her aware of all "the gifts that are around me"; they gave her a feeling that "life is rich."

Other women described similar uplifting moments from the experience of emotional communion with friends. One woman had the pleasant experience of feeling "competitive, excited and relaxed at the same time" while playing on a women's volleyball team with close friends. Sara described joy in "helping a friend through some things" over breakfast. Asked why it was a happy time, she said: "Because I was feeling her need and my response to it." Anne also described feeling happy and strengthened when she got away from home to talk with a friend about her marital situation.

Although their conversations with friends were often about personal crises, the emotion reported was the most positive of any regular situation in these women's lives. When we isolate times the women were in public with friends, we find a set of the most happy moments in their week. The linguist Deborah Tannen concludes that women's talk often embodies their concern for connectedness, their orientation that "life is a community, a struggle to preserve intimacy and avoid isolation." The feeling of connecting with someone else transforms pain and distress into an exhilarating experience of community.[81]

The specialness of this time with friends for the women in our study is suggested by its rarity among the men. The mothers felt significantly more calm, interested, and kindly during times with friends than the fathers did, and the content of interaction dealt with current, deeply meaningful events in their lives. Men's time with friends was more often devoted to sports than to talk, and the content of conversation, when it occurred, was more likely to be "motorcycles," "snipe hunting," or high school events that happened twenty years ago. As figure 3.4 shows, the average emotion that mothers experienced during times with friends was exceptionally high and dramatically above what their husbands typically experienced in this context. Regular sharing with friends was a special and emotionally rewarding part of women's lives that Lorraine cogently called "sacred ground."

THE EMOTIONAL PITFALLS OF MOTHERS' REALITY

What we have seen is that beneath the diversity in these women's external lives is an underlying similarity, a basic emotional structure that shapes their inner lives. Whereas we described the order of the men's daily experience in terms of a "rhythm" of work and recuperation, we find ourselves describing the structure of women's experience in terms of two paradoxes shaped by the historical evolution of their role. The fundamental constant with mothers is their commitment to caring for their families, yet the day-to-day activity of caring is depleting and often emotionally unsatisfying. Furthermore, the primary escape women have from the demands of this role is taking a job, where they face more demands.

Given these paradoxes, we find it remarkable that the women in our study reported daily levels of happiness that were comparable to the men's. The average woman reported no lesser rate of feeling happy or cheerful (see appendix 2.1). Writer Mary Catherine Bateson argues that one of women's greatest assets is their flexibility, "the ability to shift from one preoccupation to another, to divide one's attention, to improvise in new circumstances."[82] Thus Sara achieves buoyancy in her life by juggling care of her children and husband with vital involvements in civic activities. Anne survives the difficulties of her homelife by finding enjoyment with a classroom of special education students.

But the paradoxes of women's situation do take their toll. Anne endured distress during the week of the study and eventually caved in to her husband's demand, allowing the family to move yet another time for his career. The average mother in our study reported feeling tired and weak more often than her husband did (see appendix 2.1). Full-time homemakers are particularly susceptible, yet even the global well-being of employed women remains below that of men.[83] Thus the balance of pleasure and suffering in mothers' and fathers' lives appears to be tilted in favor of fathers.

Ultimately, we shall see that the imbalances between mother and father can create strains in the marriage that affect the rest of the family.

Mothers' daily experience, like fathers' daily experience, affects their relationships with other family members and the family system as a whole.

Before we discuss these interpersonal dynamics, however, we must examine the third emotional reality of the families we studied: that of the young adolescent. Although we have stressed the differences between the mother's and father's experience, in many ways their realities are similar: work dominates both their lives and both have achieved some degree of control over their daily emotions. When we contrast their daily lives with that of the young adolescent, we see a larger and more fundamental divergence. Anne's and Sara's children live in an emotional world much different from their parents'.

CHAPTER 4

Adolescents:
LIVES OF EMOTIONAL FLUX

A T THE SAME MOMENT that Sara is hemming her husband's new suit, her son Selman is angrily changing clothes in the school locker room. Selman's friend is denigrating his basketball ability, "he's saying stuff about me," and Selman is hurt. As a short, late-maturing seventh grader, Selman is particularly sensitive about such matters. Only minutes later, however, his anger is forgotten as he jokes and laughs with teammates about their upcoming game; and later that day he is ecstatic over an A he receives on a social studies exam. Selman's emotional state shifts frequently from extreme upset to extreme happiness and back again in a matter of a few hours.

Anne's stylishly dressed eighth-grade daughter, Amy, demonstrates similar emotional changeability. At one moment she is joyful while alone in her room doing her hair and listening to a song by Cyndi Lauper; at another, she is annoyed with her dad because "he is chewing too loudly; he's eating too much and needs to lose weight." Later she is happier watching a soap opera with her mother, but then gets intensely distressed talking with a friend about who will be at a party that night. Selman's life is usually upbeat, but Amy frequently worries about how others see her; in fact, she expresses a feeling of accomplishment one evening that "I went all day without becoming so anxious about fitting in."

Adolescents have a reputation for strong and changeable emotional states. According to stereotype, they are not quite in control of their passions, swinging between extremes of joy and anger, happiness and despair, abandon and acute self-consciousness. Believed to be prey to "raging hormones," adolescents are considered "unstable," "impulsive," and "wild."[1] Even Aristotle claimed that youth "are heated by Nature as drunken men by wine."[2]

Is this stereotype really true? There is indeed a lot happening in young adolescents' lives in our society. The period of youth covered by our study, ages ten to fourteen, is a transitional time, when the easy life of childhood comes to an end and formidable hazards begin to appear. The fifth graders in our study are sometimes identified as "preadolescent" or "latency"-aged, a comparatively calm period when children have achieved mastery over their limited social world. But within their bloodstreams, the hormonal changes of puberty have already begun to course. In late fifth grade or shortly there-after, girls' bodies start changing into those of women and, somewhat later, boys' bodies start becoming those of men. On top of these physical changes come a whole set of other transitions, such as entry to junior high school, growing independence from family, and greater exposure to the darker side of life, which make their world more complicated and challenging.

Although the major problems of adolescence—delinquency, drug use, suicide, and pregnancy—do not reach their peak until the high school years, more and more scholars are recognizing that these problems have their roots in how kids respond to these many changes of early adolescence. It is in early adolescence that a child establishes a healthy orientation to life, or begins a downward spiral leading to these difficulties.[3]

Which path children take, we believe, is determined by how they sur-vive day to day. Their emotional well-being is shaped by how they fare in the competitive environment of school, the highly charged world of friends, and the reconfigured terrain of the contemporary family. Getting through the day is often the biggest challenge. As a young person passes from home to class to lunch period, do his or her emotions career out of control, or can some kind of rhythm and order be maintained? The answer to this question shapes adolescents' well-being, which in turn affects the emotional lives of their families.

THE EMOTIONAL TEENAGER

Before looking at the specific organization of adolescents' daily reality, let us address the issue of adolescent emotionality or "moodiness." The reports we gathered on adolescents' hour-to-hour feelings provide an opportunity to look closely at this age-old issue. Do teenagers experience wider emotional swings than adults? Than children? Do they experience their lives as out of control? And if so, why?

Selman's Highs and Lows

Selman's emotional experience on Saturday provides a dramatic pic-ture of what it feels like to be a twelve-year-old. Eating breakfast with the family at 9:06 A.M., Selman reported feeling glum and fat. He felt left out at times and had a lisp that reflected his wavering self-confidence. But only a little while later, at 10:58, he was very happy and cheerful, playing catch with his four-year-old brother. In this situation his insecurity was forgotten; he was the leader and felt proud. "I am having fun," he wrote.

Selman's emotions rarely stayed in one place for very long. At 1:13 P.M. he felt very irritable and "grouchy" because "my older brother made me play football." His fifteen-year-old brother drafted Selman as a much needed extra player, then kept him in his place with teasing and ridicule. "He makes fun of my lisp," Selman complained. An hour later, they were still playing football, but Selman was happy again, just because he had been included.

Fluctuating relations with his father filled out the rest of Selman's day. At 3:42 he was happy cheering the Michigan football team with his dad. But at 6:12 he was angry and upset at his imperious father. "I joke around with him a lot. He doesn't like that." Later that night, his mom and dad went out to visit friends, leaving Selman to baby-sit. Selman felt happier watching *To Kill a Mockingbird* on the VCR, but had residual feelings of anger toward his father. This roller coaster of emotions continued through-out his week, at home and at school, with friends and with family.[4]

But the question is, Are Selman's emotional fluctuations really differ-ent from those experienced by his parents? Selman's mother, Sara, you may recall, also had ups and downs: she was despondent discussing her father's illness and in high spirits when sharing personal experiences with close friends. Are teens really more emotional and out of control than adults, or is this just a convenient stereotype?

We can begin to investigate this question by comparing how Selman and his parents reacted to a common sequence of family events. On Sun-day evening the family held a discussion about the fate of their elderly cat, Chestnut, who was dearly loved by all family members. Chestnut was limp-ing badly from an injury and the family reached the decision that Chestnut needed to be put to sleep. The decision was painful for Selman's mother and father; Sara wrote, "I will miss her, she's been *my* cat." However, the emotions they reported were nowhere near as extreme as Selman's: he was devastated. Similarly, the next day, when the veterinarian determined that Chestnut did *not* need to die, Selman's report of euphoria far outstripped his mother's and father's.

Both Selman and his parents were reacting to the same events regard-ing a cat they all loved, yet Selman reacted more extremely. This suggests that adolescents like Selman may be more emotional; that they react more intensely to daily events. But might adults like Sara and her husband have *different* events in their lives that elicit equally strong feelings, perhaps events at work or with friends?

Our research indicates that adolescents *are* more emotional than their parents. Across the thousands of times they recorded their feelings, our sample of adolescents reported many more extreme emotional states than their parents did. They reported many more euphoric highs than their parents; in fact, they felt "very happy" *five times* more often. Likewise, they reported many more extreme lows than their parents; they felt "very unhappy" *three times* more often (see figure 4.1). Additional evidence leads us to believe that this is not just what psychologists call a "response set"—a tendency of adolescents to use more superlative language about everything.[5] Rather, teenagers genuinely experience their internal lives as swinging between greater extremes of joy and distress.

This emotionality is also apparent when we look at adolescents' reports for a wider palette of psychological states (see appendix 2.1). They reported

Figure 4.1

HOW OFTEN FAMILY MEMBERS FEEL GRADATIONS
OF HAPPINESS AND UNHAPPINESS

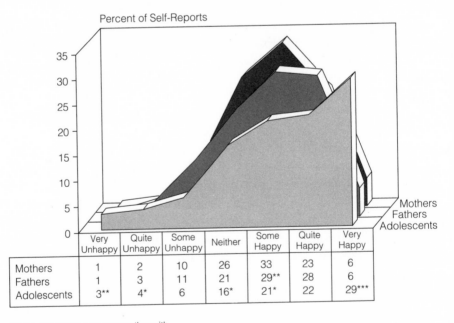

	Very Unhappy	Quite Unhappy	Some Unhappy	Neither	Some Happy	Quite Happy	Very Happy
Mothers	1	2	10	26	33	23	6
Fathers	1	3	11	21	29**	28	6
Adolescents	3**	4*	6	16*	21*	22	29***

Significance tests compare mother with
father and child with same-sex parent.
* p<.05; ** p<.01; *** p<.001

feeling "self-conscious" and "embarrassed" two to three times more often than their parents did; they more often reported social discomfort on a wide range of dimensions: awkward, lonely, nervous, and ignored—a whole array of painful feelings that remind us adults why we never want to be adolescents again.

These teenagers, however, were not more intense on all psychological states. Adolescents like Selman felt "in control" much less often than their parents did. They also reported feeling strongly "interested" less frequently, and they more often said they wished they were doing something else. These teens appeared to experience themselves as less in command and less invested in their immediate lives than their parents did. Perhaps for this reason, they reported feeling bored much more often; they also felt tired, weak, and drowsy more frequently than their parents did.[6] In spite of their youthful bodies and their less harried lives, these adolescents went through the day with more lapses in energy and motivation.

We can conclude, then, that young adolescents live in an emotional reality that differs greatly from their parents'. As adolescents look back on the last twenty-four hours, or anticipate the next, they see themselves hurtling through a more rugged emotional terrain. Teens experienced themselves ascending higher peaks of rapture and tumbling into deeper crevasses of dejection; the adults traversed a more moderate and controlled set of hills and valleys. Given these differences, it is easy to envision why adolescents and parents often misunderstand each other—they are on different wavelengths. But now we need to look at how adolescents' emotionality is related to their immediate lives. Why are they more emotional?

The Evolution of Adolescents' Family Role

The daily emotional experience of teens in our society, no less than that of their mothers and fathers, has been shaped by cultural and historic forces. In the agrarian life of the past, the time and energies of young people were much more tied up with their families. Young people assumed major responsibilities on the farm or were apprenticed in a trade, with the family receiving much of their income. In fact, laws in many states committed the wages of children under twenty-one to their parents.[7]

The introduction of secondary education, however, changed what we expect of young people, and how they spend their time. High schools marked off a separate category of minors, more privileged and worldly than children but with none of the obligations young people previously had assumed on the farm. They were now bound by fewer norms and responsibilities, especially within the family; as early as 1943, Talcott Parsons commented on adolescents' "roleless role." They also spent less time with the family, or with other adults. The channeling of adolescents into junior and senior high schools meant they spent much of their day with same-age peers, and this led to the emergence of the peer group as an important element in teens' lives. As we will see, it has become a major focus of their emotional energy, as well as a major counterweight to their allegiance to their families.

Unfortunately, at the same time that history has been establishing adolescence as a unique stage of life, this stage has been arriving earlier and earlier for each new generation. Because of improved nutrition, puberty, which used to occur at fifteen or even seventeen, now begins as young as nine or ten for girls and eleven or twelve for boys. Since World War II we have also seen the development of a separate "youth culture" which inducts younger and younger children into styles and values distinct from, and sometimes antagonistic to, those of adult society. Other markers of adolescence—questioning of identity, conflicts with parents, and sexual intercourse—are occurring earlier than they did even a generation ago. While Tom Sawyer and Huck Finn were unquestionably children, today they would be five-and-a-half-foot adolescents, with blaring Walkmen and sexual interests.

The result of this evolution has been the compression of multiple life changes within the early adolescent years. Kids from ten to fourteen now experience a concentrated set of personal transitions, often before they are developmentally ready. In addition to normal, expected life changes, such as puberty and the move from elementary to junior high school, they are more likely to encounter a set of idiosyncratic personal crises that can come with adolescence, such as trouble in school, worry about AIDS, and encounters with gangs. This pileup of change is evident among the 483 young people in our larger sample.[8]

This recent compression of stressful changes, of course, affects some teens more than others. Some youths, like Selman, are lucky—events are spaced out, allowing them time to adjust to each one, then get ready for the next. Other teens, like Anne's daughter Amy, however, experience a deluge of stressful events and life changes all at once. Amy, an intelligent and resourceful fourteen-year-old, was coping not only with the uncertainty and conflict surrounding her family's potential move: she had just had a falling-out with her group of friends; she had recently had a major illness; and she was distraught about the new body puberty had just given her. Research shows that teens like Amy, who encounter a pileup of life changes, are much more at risk for psychological problems.[9]

The paradox is that during the same historical period when adolescents are free from the responsibilities assigned to young people of the previous era, they are now burdened with an unpredictable array of major life changes at an earlier age. Young adolescents have more freedom, but also more stress. They have less defined responsibility, yet face increased undefined responsibility—for dealing with these indeterminate personal crises. Not surprisingly, this situation is a crucial factor in their emotional lives.

THE FALL FROM GRACE

Prior to adolescence, before this pileup of changes, many children actually have quite enjoyable lives. The elementary-age youngsters in our study basked in a kind of naive happiness. For a remarkable 28 percent of the random times they were signaled, they reported feeling "very happy." One mother expressed astonishment at how exuberant her sixth grader seemed to be when he came home from school; in fact, she even asked us whether she shouldn't "pop his bubble" sometimes.

Part of the reason for these preadolescents' joie de vivre is that their emotional lives were quite simple. When we asked them in the interview whether they ever felt two different things at once, the fifth graders were much more likely than the older youths to say no. They also claimed to know nearly always the reason *why* they were feeling happy or sad: they suffered few of the amorphous, free-floating moods that were more common among the older students. Life was uncomplicated. On the beeper reports, their principal explanation for their negative emotions was concrete immediate events, like getting scolded by parents or losing a game, events that quickly pass and are forgotten.[10]

By seventh grade, however, daily life gets more difficult. The mother of a seventh grader lamented, "She used to be such a happy person. She's become more depressed and intense. It's like someone turned up the volume." These older students felt "great" and "proud" much less often; the ninth graders felt "very happy" only 14 percent of the time, a substantial drop from the 28 percent rate for the fifth graders.[11] This deflation of childhood happiness occurs for both boys and girls.[12] The older students of both sexes also felt "in control" much less than the fifth graders did, and they reported a level of motivation that appeared to be a low point for the entire life span.[13]

Lest the picture seem too bleak, we must emphasize that these adolescents reported feeling happy for the majority of time, and their average mood state was not worse than their parents'. Nonetheless, from their point of view, their experience of negative emotions had increased substantially from just a few short years before. Parents of older students said more often that their children got sulky, raised their voices, and acted violent than parents of younger students reported. Daily life in the middle-school years brings more worry and anger than in the elementary years.

According to the stereotype, these strong adolescent emotions are due to puberty, to "raging hormones." But our findings suggest a more complex set of causes. Contrary to folk wisdom, we found little relationship between pubertal stage and negative emotion or variability in emotion.[14] Rather, we found that adolescents' negative states were related to the pileup of transitions and life events they encountered. Those who were inundated by the most transitions and stressful life events were most likely to be "moody adolescents." Individuals like Amy who encountered multiple, simultaneous personal crises were more likely to report high rates of anger, worry, and sadness.[15] While her parents may dismiss her moods as a product of puberty, they are more likely attributable to the many changes she is trying to cope with.

But it is not just *what* adolescents experience, it is also *how* they interpret these experiences that accounts for their increased emotionality. This is an age when young people develop abstract and critical reasoning skills, described by Jean Piaget and others. And, although these skills represent psychological growth, they actually heighten children's sensitivity to difficult circumstances. These advanced reasoning skills allow them to see beneath the surface of situations and envision hidden and more long-lasting threats to their well-being.[16] As a consequence, adolescents are often troubled by nuances and implications of daily life that do not enter the minds of preadolescents.[17]

We can witness this heightened vulnerability in adolescents' relationships with friends. David Elkind, a student of Piaget, argues convincingly that adolescents' new reasoning skills allow them to imagine what their peers think of them, and this becomes a source of distress. Before adolescence, friends' thoughts and feelings were opaque; teens become able to conjecture what they might be. The result in Amy's case was that she was continually and painfully self-conscious about how others viewed her. The capacity for deeper analysis of her relationships undermined her self-confidence.

Elkind also proposes that these new skills create a growing awareness of the politics of peer relationships, which also makes teenagers more vulnerable to being hurt.[18] One eighth-grade girl in our study reported feeling worried because "I don't want Stacey to know I like Greg." A boy felt torn apart because a girl he liked preferred his friend. Such anxieties over triangular relationships were never reported by the preadolescents in our study. Only in adolescence do children begin to conceive a complex political world in which a network of peers exchange good and bad feelings about each other.

These new reasoning skills, then, magnify adolescents' sensitivity to events at home as well as with friends and at school. Teens begin to form theories about what their parents feel, and they speculate on how these feelings may play out over time. When a fight raged between the parents of Roger, a fifth grader, his emotional states were unaffected by it. When Amy's parents' fought, however, she was acutely aware of what was happening and responded with gloom and depression. Whereas Roger experienced his parents' fight as an isolated event, Amy perceived the long-lasting implications of her parents' quarrel.

Thus not only do adolescents encounter more stressful events, they are also more likely to be deeply affected by them.

Consequences of Negative Emotions

Of course, a certain amount of anger, worry, and hurt in adolescence is to be expected. It is normal for an adolescent like Selman to react strongly to insults from a peer and the potential death of a loved pet. We probably cannot prevent adolescents from losing some of their naive childhood happiness and finding life a little harder.

Above a certain rate, however, this negative emotion becomes chronic distress and a breeding ground for psychological problems. The adolescent who is regularly unhappy may turn to drugs or alcohol in hopes of increasing pleasure, or anesthetizing pain. We find that those seventh to ninth graders who report more negative emotion are more likely to report symptoms of depression, to do poorly in school, and, among girls, to show warning signs of eating disorders.[19] We suspect that the current epidemic of adolescent problems partly reflects individual teenagers' desperate attempts to deal with feelings they cannot control.

These persistent negative emotions also affect the family. If a teenager is repeatedly reacting to events with anger, bitterness, or despair, it can unhinge the family's internal sense of well-being. Given that some increase in negative emotion is inevitable with this age period, the important issue becomes not how to stop it, but how to cope with it. How do adolescents manage this distress on a day-to-day basis? In the face of multiple changes and difficult events, how can they maintain an internal sense of equilibrium? To answer this, we need to understand how their daily reality is organized.

ADOLESCENTS' PUBLIC EXPERIENCE

The sociologists Roberta Simmons and Dale Blyth propose that all adolescents need to have some part of their lives that is an "arena of comfort," a segment of daily experience where they are able to relax, feel at one with themselves, regroup, and regain a sense of control.[20] Fathers, we noted, have this arena of comfort at home; and if we look solely at how young adolescents spend their time, their lives look much like their fathers'. The amount of time teens spend at school is almost as much as their fathers spend at their jobs (though adolescents devote less time to actual work); they spend similar amounts of time in the household sphere, with a majority of it in leisure and recuperative activities (see appendix 2.2).

As we look more closely, however, we see that adolescents' lives do not have the rhythm of exertion and recuperation that fathers' lives have. The emotional order of their daily reality is more complex than that of either parent, involving four distinct experiential contexts: classes, friends, family, and solitude. To understand their lives, we need to ask how daily experience in each of these contexts contributes to their emotionality and which are potential arenas of comfort that help them modulate their emotional swings.

Life in the Classroom

We asked in the interview: "In your daily life, what is the biggest problem for you? What is it that most often makes you feel bad?" The adolescents' most frequent response was schoolwork and school grades.[21] Likewise, in the beeper reports, teens cited school circumstances as the most common reason for their negative emotions.[22] An extreme illustration is an eighth-grade girl who reported feeling so anxious about her oral report in science that she blanked out in front of the class, then panicked and ran out of the room. A ninth-grade boy felt angry because "the teacher is using me as an example and getting on my nerves." Many reported anxiety over grades and boredom with having to sit in class.

Going to school may be painful at times, but shouldn't it be considered an adolescent's job? Its purpose is not to make teens happy in the immediate moment, but to plant the seed of longer-term benefits, to improve their well-being (and society's) in the future. Fathers reported frequent frustration and other negative emotions at their jobs; shouldn't we accept teens' negative feelings at school as part of a similar emotional cost?

Some scholars argue that schools take a toll on adolescents' well-being that is too consequential to be dismissed lightly. Since the 1950s, critics have charged that the competitive environment of secondary schools progressively erodes many students' sense of self-worth. More recently, the psychologists Jacquelynne Eccles and Carol Midgley have asserted that young adolescents experience junior high school as an unfriendly environment, and that this experience is a powerful contributor to many of the psychological problems that begin to occur at this time.[23] Eccles and Midgley demonstrate that just at an age when children are becoming acutely self-conscious, they endure much more public, whole-class evaluation of their work. These researchers also present evidence that compared to elementary school teachers, junior high teachers adopt a less personal and more adversarial relationship with students. Junior high students rarely feel close to their teachers. At a time when young people are facing a pileup of life changes and their self-confidence is wavering, they get teachers who are more critical and less supportive of their abilities. The argument is that the junior high environment is fundamentally out of sync with the needs of young adolescents.

Our findings support these criticisms and suggest that school is a different kind of stress than parents' jobs. We would like to emphasize that compared to many junior high or middle schools, the institutions our sample of students attended were small, friendly, and caring. Indeed, for most of these students, their typical emotional state during class was not terribly pained. They were less happy than mothers at their jobs, but not worse than fathers. These adolescents reported feeling frustrated and nervous more frequently during class than at other times.[24] But they were not typically in a state of distress like that of Japanese and Korean adolescents, for example, cramming for their do-or-die college entrance exams.[25] In fact, these adolescents reported many happy moments in school. Teens' most positive moments tended to come during active, participatory classes, such as music, shop, and gym.[26]

What sets classroom experience apart from parents' work experience is not adolescents' emotional states, but their motivational and cognitive states. When in class, the teens in our study often indicated that they wished they were doing something else; they reported "paying attention" less often than elsewhere.[27] They were not invested or engaged in what they were doing. The most striking finding is that these adolescents reported boredom for 32 percent of the times they were beeped during class.[28] Even Natalie Vahn, who said she enjoyed school, frequently marked that she was bored during social studies and science class; her mind would wander, then she would get upset because "my teacher didn't tell us about a test."

These adolescents' experience during schoolwork was markedly worse on these dimensions than the men's experience at their jobs. The adolescents reported significantly lower average motivation, interest, and skill during class than their fathers did at work. And they were more likely to be bored and less likely to feel "in control"—to feel that they governed their own actions.[29]

We find, then, that adolescents' experience in class sometimes produces intense emotional stress but more often creates an alienated state. Beeped during class, one fifth-grade girl drew two pictures of flowers: one flower marked "before school" is a well-formed daisy with a bright smile; the other marked "after school" is wilted and unhappy. Later she drew a graveyard, titled "School Kills," shown in figure 4.2. Many of these signs of alienation increase from fifth to eighth grade, suggesting that the bad fit between students and the school environment gets worse as they move into the teenage years.

Figure 4.2

A PREADOLESCENT'S DRAWING OF A GRAVEYARD SCENE

We must emphasize that some teens reported little distress or alienation in class. Selman, for example, was nearly always happy and motivated during class. In this setting, he was not disadvantaged by his small size and lisp, as he was elsewhere. Even when he was beeped in the middle of a science test, he reported feeling calm, in control, and quite happy.

At the other extreme, however, is Wayne, an eighth grader who was always bored, unhappy, and unmotivated in school. He wrote "I hate school" when beeped during class. His teachers deplored his lack of effort, but their harangues only made him more alienated. While he managed to get B's in eighth grade, two years later when we conducted a follow-up of many of the adolescents, Wayne was getting D's and was heavily involved in drugs. Our data suggest that an adolescent like Wayne may turn to drugs as a deliberate antidote to the deadened state he experiences in school.[30]

Quite often this bad fit between school and an adolescent like Wayne starts with experience at home. Wayne did not receive support from his parents for his classwork. Regardless of its source, distress or alienation in class can be a contributing factor to a range of problems. We found that students who reported the most negative emotional states in school were more likely to have later declines in grade-point average and increases in depression and deviant behavior.[31] Eccles and Midgley have demonstrated that the experience of a hostile classroom environment is correlated with deteriorating attitudes and performance. Other researchers have shown boredom is a factor that leads students to drop out.[32] For some students, school is a tormenting part of their daily lives that accentuates dysfunctional patterns of adaptation.

Secondary education, we should recognize, is a historically new institution, and we have not yet learned to make it fit well for many adolescents. Indeed, for most teenagers, while they may be doing their "job" as a student, school is a source of regular boredom and periodic distress they must cope with.

The Enthralling World of Friends

Interaction with friends is the most frequent immediate remedy to the stress of class. After school, between classes, at moments when the teacher's head is turned, teens check in with friends and usually experience an immediate uplift in their moods. The large amount of time teens spend with the peer group is also a historically recent development, which has grown along with schooling. And American adolescents spend more time with peers than their counterparts in most other cultures do.

On the surface, friends seem like the perfect solution to the teenagers' negative moods. But if David Elkind is correct, adolescents' new reasoning skills increase their vulnerability to being hurt by friends. This leads us to ask, Are friendships really an arena of comfort that stabilizes teenagers' emotional swings, or, beneath the positive moods, might they be another source of disequilibrium? To answer this question, we first need to understand why the world of peers is so enticing.

Friends were a much larger and emotionally fundamental segment of the experience of the adolescents in our study than for either parent; they filled more than twice as much of the teens' time. The number of friends a teenager has peaks in early adolescence, when peer influence reaches what is probably its highest point in the life span.[33]

The adolescents also reported their most positive emotions with their friends. Selman's happiest moment of the week was eating pizza at a restaurant with friends. Amy's was talking and playing basketball with three chums. Teens felt happier, more cheerful, and friendlier when they were with peers than during other segments of their lives, and these positive feelings increase from fifth to ninth grade.[34] They also reported their highest rates of paying attention with friends and their greatest desire to be doing what they were doing.[35]

Why is being with friends so enthralling? We believe there are a number of reasons. First, the cognitive changes we discussed earlier allow teens to experience their friends as mirror images of themselves. These new reasoning skills enable them to recognize that their friends are centers of thought and feeling—like themselves—and this is a very heady discovery.[36] For example, a seventh-grade girl said of her friend: "She feels the same about the same things, and she understands what I mean. Mostly, she is feeling the same things, depending on what it is. And if she doesn't, she'll say, 'Yeah, I understand what you're talking about.' And like, if each of us has a problem or something that you can't figure out, I'll try and help her, or she'll try to help me." This girl and her friend took part in the study at the same time, and when they were together their moods were positive and highly correlated—they were constantly attuned to each other's feelings. At an age when one's sense of self is fragile, knowing that a friend understands and feels what one feels is profoundly reassuring.

This sharing of confidences increases in adolescence, especially among girls, and it becomes a source of deep gratification.[37] Boys experience closeness through shared activities, girls through comparing their private thoughts.[38] Remarkably, the amount of time the girls in our study spent talking with friends nearly *tripled* between fifth and ninth grade.[39] Furthermore, their talk was increasingly focused on themselves and each other, representing 75 percent of all conversation by ninth grade. These girls' emotional states during this frequent conferencing also rose, suggesting that, like their mothers, they were developing a capacity for rewarding communion.

But it is not just self-disclosure that makes friends enjoyable. Boys report happiness with their friends too, even though they share less of their private selves. A second reason for the pleasure of friends, we believe, is the special cascading positive-feedback dynamic that animates their interactions.[40] Teens egg each other on: one says or does something, then the other will continue and elaborate in the same mode. The result is often great fun. This happened, for example, when boys hanging around a back yard started spraying one another with the hose, taunting and laughing. It happened when girls at a sleepover started dancing on the ping-pong table, giggling and hugging each other.

Adolescents feel free and open with close friends in a way they do not feel with anyone else. They experience each other as responding positively to nearly anything they say or do. Sometimes it involves being rowdy, joking, or improvising on whatever "crazy" thing their friends do. Other times it takes the form of giving support and reinforcing each other's deep feelings, including, quite often, feelings about the other sex.

Love, romance, sexuality is the third reason the world of peers becomes so entrancing. Preadolescents find the freedom and pleasure of peers only with same-sex companions. Fifth graders rarely spend time with children of the other sex, and when they do, they tend to feel ill at ease. With age, however, relations with the opposite sex become a larger and more comfortable part of peer interactions. Older students spend more time thinking about and interacting with the other sex, and they report enjoying those experiences more.[41] The beeper caught several older students while they were "making out"—most reported positive states—and found one eighth-grade boy in bed with his girlfriend, in love and enthralled. Teenagers become more skilled at joking, teasing, talking with, and even making love with these creatures who are not quite like them. The effect on their emotions can be forceful—though not always positive.

Amy's Troubles with Peers

The overt themes of peer interaction are pleasure, self-reinforcement, and fulfillment of romantic desire. But there is a subtext that is more painful. The wish to be liked and participate in this fun is strong, but not always readily fulfilled. The same qualities that make peers enthralling also make them a source of anger, frustration, and hurt.

Friends were second only to school as the reason the teens in our study gave for their negative emotions.[42] Just as reinforcement from peers was a source of positive moods, failure to obtain it was a major source of distress. During time with friends, these adolescents reported more frequent self-consciousness and embarrassment than during their other waking hours.[43]

This dark side lurked continually in Amy's private thoughts and feelings over the week. After school on Thursday the beeper found her at her friend Lonnie's house, talking with two boys. She reported being in a "great mood" but also feeling self-conscious, because "I get uptight and think I look terrible; or I can't say the right thing when I talk to boys. But I like it."

The painful side of Amy's ambivalent sentiment won out at a party on Friday evening where most of the people were strangers. Beeped at the party, she reported feeling scared and very unhappy. "I get nervous when I go anywhere or do anything with people I don't know too well." In the diary she filled out later that night, she wrote, "I wish I was like some of the other girls at the party that could talk to boys."

During the subsequent days, while her father and mother were battling about his job offer in Cleveland, making home life unbearable, Amy brooded continually about her looks and her failures in romance. Saturday at noon she sat in her bedroom, doing her hair and listening to "Brand New Lover" on the radio. She was in a terrible mood, wondering, "Why can't I be more popular. I want people to see me as they see the ones that don't worry. I want them to see me as a fun, happy-go-lucky person, NOT a goody goody or a bore." Sunday she reported feeling cheerful because "I sat next to Sam." But then Monday, she felt unhappy and ugly, because "My hair and makeup is wrong. I just feel gross."

Precisely the same cognitive changes that make peers a source of powerful understanding and pleasure also make them a source of anxiety and distress. Amy's ability to imagine how others feel about her made friends enthralling, but also made her intensely insecure. Because of these cognitive changes, early adolescence is a time of peak concern with fitting in, with being accepted.[44] Young adolescents are only too aware that others are judging them and that those judgments may be harsh. Triangles, misunderstandings, and conflicting alliances were a regular part of the social lives of the eighth and ninth graders we studied.

In some cases this sensitivity to others' thoughts is a vehicle of constructive change. For example, when a ninth-grade boy showed up an hour and a half late for a rendezvous with his friend, the friend was so angry that he avoided him for several days. The boy spent much of this time alone feeling guilty. "I'll just think about it and I'll get upset; I'll listen to music and not worry about what I can do now, but okay, next time, don't do that." As a result of this soul-searching, he approached his friend and they had a good talk about their relationship. Subsequently their moods when together were more positive again. Conflicts such as this one can stimulate insight, discussion, and mutual growth.[45]

In other cases, however, the consternation created by this new capacity for self-reflection leads nowhere, except to depression and brooding. Amy's concerns about her looks and her lack of success with boys did not have an easy solution, and the helplessness she felt was accentuated by all the other things going wrong in her life. Tuesday she felt lonely because "everyone else has a boyfriend or someone likes them." In a despondent state later, she reported daydreaming about "getting married," an easy solution she fantasied would resolve both her romantic needs and her family problems.

Romantic relationships, in particular, resemble playing with fire at this age. Romantic incidents accounted for a large number of both happy and unhappy times in the lives of the eighth and ninth graders we studied.[46] Some of these incidents were at the fantasy level, such as the girl who reported feeling great "because my future boyfriend talked to me," or the boy who was intensely jealous because "Kerry has a girlfriend and I don't." It is important to realize that love and romantic hurt are common sources of negative feelings, even among those who never talk to the other sex. Yet frustration, anger, and fluctuating emotions due to romance are especially common among those who have a boyfriend or girlfriend.[47] Some of these relationships began, ended, and were replaced in the short week of our study, generating moments of bliss, but also frequent despair, such as those described in figure 4.3.

Adolescent friendships and romances can have all the positive and destructive features of adult close relationships, and more. The desire to be liked, to fit in, to have fun can lead to heart-wrenching feelings of rejection. Teenagers with troubled peer relationships typically report greater loneliness and poorer self-esteem than other teenagers do. They also do worse in school and are less resilient to other stresses in their lives.[48] One father watched his twelve-year-old daughter slide into a fourteen-month period of depression, and learned only later that she was suffering the consequences of her painful decision to separate herself from a peer group that had started using drugs.

For some teens, the world of peers is a place of enjoyment, perhaps at times even an arena of comfort. For others, like Amy, it is source of anxiety that more often adds to their distress. For most, like Selman, it is both. As these teens go through their day, the world of friendship is a wild card, usu-

---

Figure 4.3

MOMENTS OF JOY AND SORROW IN
EARLY ADOLESCENT ROMANCES

Jealous because my friend likes the same girl I do.

*Melanie is a super duper foxy momma. I'm crazy about Melanie
    Torance.*

I'm more in love with M.T. than I've ever been before.

Jealous because I saw Melanie walking with Don, her boyfriend.

I felt great because Sue was flirting.

Sue hugged me. I should have told her how I feel.

I felt sorry that I said anything to Darcy about him not Frenching me.

Darcy and I made up.

I'm going to dump Darcy.

I was in love because this guy asked me out.

What I have to do to break up with boyfriend.

*I was proud because I told my boyfriend I didn't want to go out with him
    anymore.*

In love—I walked home with the most popular boy in school.

I kissed my boyfriend but I was scared.

I still love Ward even though he upsets me.

Got close to girlfriend. Wish I had kissed her.

*Worried and nervous because Tom is supposed to ask me out. I hope I
    don't goof.*

*Frustrated that I said sorry to Jason and now he's (I think) trying to
    make me feel guilty of even other things.*

---

ally happy, but with an undercurrent of emotional hazards. Like the school
experience, time with peers can be rewarding or destabilizing. Teens arrive
home each day bringing happiness, excitement, and satisfaction, or raw dis-
appointment, worry, and anguish.

YOUNG ADOLESCENTS' HOMELIFE

Are teens' daily interactions with their families part of the solution or
part of the problem? Does the segment of the day teens spend at home
serve to stabilize their precarious moods or to fuel the flames?

In Amy's case, the answer to this question is not clear. Saturday morning after Amy's unhappy and unsettling party with too many strangers, she sat down to watch "Days of Our Lives" with her mother, hoping for a good talk and a little sympathy. But her mother, Anne, was unable to give it to her because she was furious about the bombshell her husband had just dropped on the family. Amy complained on our form that "no one understands me" and continued to feel glum. The raging war between Amy's parents hardly made the family an arena of comfort for her.

But what about other adolescents? We were dealing in this study with teenagers in what has traditionally been defined as optimal family circumstances: they lived with two parents in pleasant suburban communities. What did they feel in the portion of their waking lives they spent at home and with family members? Was home typically an arena of comfort or a theater of further tumult and stress, and how does this change with age?

In order to understand the emotional dynamics of the whole family, we need to be able to see what family life is like from each member's vantage point, including adolescents'.

Adolescents' Typical Experience with Their Families

Like parents who have jobs, adolescents arrive home each evening bringing the exhaustion and emotional detritus of the day. The fathers in our study used this weariness as an excuse to do their own thing: to relax, watch TV, whatever they chose. Though equally tired, the employed mothers in our study felt obligated to deal with all the family's pressing demands: getting supper ready, providing crisis counseling, whatever might need to be done. Most dads deal with their own needs; most moms must ignore theirs. Which pattern do adolescents follow?

Like their fathers, the adolescents in our study rarely pitched in to help out with the 6 o'clock crunch; indeed, they contributed half as much time as fathers did to housework. Amy, for example, reported cleaning her room several times but, despite the fact her mother worked full-time, the beeper never caught her doing any work for the family as a whole. Selman did better—he baby-sat, and the beeper found him assisting his little brother with a bath and helping his mother make her bed. In the interview, nearly all the adolescents in the study reported a few regular chores, but the amount of time they devoted to them was quite small, much less than that reported by young people in most other cultures.[49]

Rather than helping out, these adolescents claimed the largest amount of their home time for themselves. Recreational and personal activities, from TV viewing to hair styling, accounted for the great majority of their household time. They watched TV as often as their dads did and they spent much more time than their fathers in active recreation, such as playing sports and games and doing art, music, and craft activities.

Not surprisingly, girls and boys differed somewhat in how they spent this abundance of free time at home, showing patterns that may anticipate women's and men's use of free time. Like their mothers, the girls reported more time talking—they chatted with their siblings; they invited friends over or called them on the phone. The girls also reported more time in personal care than the boys did, a pattern that foreshadows the greater investment in grooming among their mothers. Selman's weekend was fairly typical of the pattern for boys, with more time spent in sports and somewhat more TV watching.[50] For both boys and girls, however, the underlying pattern was that of their fathers: they used their home time according to their own, not the family's, needs.

Where the teens differed from their fathers was in the moods they reported during this part of their lives. Despite spending the majority of their time in leisure activities, adolescents reported an emotional experience at home that does not stand out as distinctly positive, as it does for their dads (see appendix 4.1). Certainly there are pleasant moments. A boy reported enjoying teaching his mother to play baseball. A girl reported that the high point of her week was her dad's company picnic, where she went on rides and won a prize playing bingo. We could list dozens of other examples of adolescents' enjoying themselves with their families.

Most often, however, experience at home and with the family had the flavor of marking time or "hanging out." Active recreation in the family sphere, you may recall, was positive for the mothers in our study and particularly positive for the fathers. It did not yield consistently favorable moods for adolescents. An eighth-grade boy, for example, reported that he was throwing a ball against the wall and lamented that his sister did not want to play games. Likewise, the emotions these adolescents reported during TV viewing were neutral, not unlike the numb states reported by their fathers and mothers. An eighth-grade girl watching TV with her parents and brother said she did not know what show they were watching, then added in capital letters: "I WISH I HAD SOMETHING TO DO." These adolescents' home leisure activities were rarely planned and boredom was common.

These adolescents' experience of home time, then, differed from that of their parents'. Their activities were more leisureful, even more so than their dads', yet no segment of the adolescents' home time was consistently positive. Homework was typically reported as dull and unpleasant. Housework was not as noxious as for mothers, but it was not enjoyable either. And other leisure and personal activities did not bring dependably favorable moods (see appendix 4.1). When we average across all their domestic experience, these adolescents' highs and lows in this context canceled out to create an average that is neutral. This pattern of time and emotion is similar for young people in single-parent households.[51]

Family as an Arena of Comfort?

So is this neutral mix of family experience a source of solace, or stress? These adolescents' flat mood watching TV with the family, for example, might be hypothesized to be useful if it dampened their volatile states. But is emotional numbing what teens need? Is family experience an arena of comfort?

It is, and it isn't. If we look just at times when the adolescents were with family members, they felt more comfortable even than with peers on several dimensions: they reported feeling more important and calm and less nervous, embarrassed, and frustrated than in any other context. In the household sphere, they also experienced less variability in happiness and excitement. These findings suggest that even when dull, family experience may provide an important respite from the frenzied world of peers and the demands of school.

The calm and comfort of family is apparent in the report of a fifth-grade boy pleasurably sitting at the kitchen table sketching monsters, while his mother prepared food. Similarly, a ninth grader reported that the high point of her week was an evening spent singing and watching soap operas with her family. Eighty percent of the parents in our study said they actively helped their adolescents manage their emotions; we suspect that this support contributed to these adolescents' feelings of security and warmth at home.

But these adolescents' home time was also filled with repeated, often petty aggravations. Though chores were a small part of these teens' lives, they mentioned them frequently as a source of tension with their parents. One boy claimed to feel "horrible" because he had to help his dad cut wood. Another boy was happy taking care of his little brother until the child asked to go to a friend's house. "I wasn't supposed to let him go, so he got mad at me." The result was that he felt "terrible, guilty, and grouchy." These parents regularly asked their teens to share part of the burden of necessary household labor, but their kids often experienced this request as harassment. Many of these adolescents, especially boys, felt little responsibility for their family's needs, and were therefore annoyed when asked to do their part.[52]

Much of the irritation these teens experienced in the family arose from the inevitable conflicts of living with people who were different from them and could get on their nerves. One girl was mad because the whole family got up at 6 A.M. to watch a wedding in the British royal family (to which they claimed a distant relation). The only working TV was in her room, so they woke her up and everyone piled in, including her grandmother and uncle from next door. Hassles with siblings were another daily part of these teens' experience, as our collaborator Marcela Raffaelli has shown. Teens come into conflict with siblings over power, personal property, intrusions into personal space, acts of betrayal, and, sometimes, just for something to do.[53] Family life is often a dose of brutish reality.

In most cases, these daily irritations did not prevent home from also being an arena of comfort for these adolescents. These were not the kinds of stresses that kept them from getting out of bed in the morning. In fact, they reported far fewer negative daily experiences emanating from family than from the world of peers. It is a well-kept secret that the great majority of adolescents feel close to their parents and warm toward their families.[54]

In some cases, however, these daily irritations were more ominous and threatening. A ninth-grade girl reported that her drunk stepfather called her names and pushed her to the wall for no reason. A boy described how his parents fought all the time, and although he tried to ignore it or escape to his room, it made him terribly upset. Although small family hassles have little relationship to young adolescents' emotional well-being, we find that major family events take a toll on their daily emotions.

If young adolescents have an Achilles heel, it is their vulnerability to events that disrupt their experience of a stable family environment. Much research confirms the central importance of a secure family climate to adolescents' well-being, and this is true whether the child lives in a two-parent family, a one-parent family, or some other arrangement. If the family environment is tumultuous, it affects a teenager's mental health, not only at home but at school and with friends.[55]

The importance of a secure family environment is felt every day. Our data show that adolescents bring home whatever emotions they experience during the schoolday.[56] If their parents are unavailable or unresponsive to the negative feelings teens sometimes bring home, those feelings may persist and grow. Because Amy's mother was preoccupied and her father showed little understanding, we see Amy's anxiety running out of control during the week of the study. In contrast, although Selman fought with his brother, he felt supported by his mother, and that support helped him repeatedly rebound from the knocks life dealt him. Thus despite the many petty irritations most adolescents experience at home, their families are a crucial arena of comfort.

The irony is that during this same period that families are vitally important to adolescents, adolescents in our society are gradually withdrawing from them. Older youth in our study spend nearly as much time at home as younger ones, but the portion of household time teenagers spend in the company of their family members declines precipitately as they get older.[57] In fact, the amount of time children spend with their families is nearly cut in half between the fifth and ninth grade.

The Closing of the Bedroom Door

As teens spend less time with their families, they spend more time alone. Rather than flopping down on the living room couch, as they did a couple of years ago, they now disappear into their rooms. Even those who do not have their own bedroom find ways to be alone, spending long periods in the bathroom, or in some recess of the basement.[58] Suddenly they are closing or locking the door, and may become very touchy about parents or siblings violating their privacy.[59]

To many parents, such dramatic withdrawal feels like rejection or, worse, conjures up fears of depression or suicidal tendencies. Just at an age when young people's stress increases and they need more support, they are putting themselves out of reach, behind a firmly closed door. What is going on in there? Is this solitary time an arena of comfort or of disturbed brooding? Can time alone with Public Enemy or Madonna be healthy?

Adolescents in our research were quite forthright in reporting what they did and felt when alone in their rooms. They recorded a wide range of activities, from drawing to primping to lying on their beds. As they get older, adolescents do more of their homework, TV watching, and chores by themselves. What we found is that rather than coming alive in this secret sanctuary, they were more likely to shut down. Their moods when alone were anything but positive: they were more likely to feel weak, lonely, and sad.[60]

In spite of these negative states, however, we find much evidence that adolescents use this solitary time in a way that is emotionally restoring. Teens retreat to their bedrooms not so much because they are repelled by their families, but because they are drawn by certain opportunities they begin to perceive there.[61] In many cases when beeped, they reported that they were alone because they "enjoyed" being alone, or because it allowed them to focus on an activity or to think.[62] A sixth-grade girl, for example, described going to her room because her brother bothered her and she felt grouchy. Being alone, she thought, helped her feel better. Indeed, despite the low moods encountered during solitude, adolescents often reported an elevated mood after a period of being alone.[63]

Not surprisingly, the solitary activity that increases most dramatically in adolescence is listening to music; its potency is suggested by the posters of rock stars that begin to appear in teenagers' rooms, side by side with the cuddly stuffed animals of childhood. One girl reported a good experience lying in bed listening to "True Colors" by Cyndi Lauper and thinking about who she wanted to go to the dance with. A boy described the best time of his week as listening to a Led Zeppelin album in his room. He enjoyed it because "I don't really have that much time to relax." Teenagers begin to use music for "mood management"; in fact, they report that listening to music is their number one way of coping with daily stress.[64]

Lying on their beds or idling at their desks, adolescents also explore images of who they are and who they might become. These may include images of desirable selves as well as potential selves they revile and would like to avoid.[65] Early adolescence is a period when young people begin to question who they are, and when they begin to discover a "private self" that is different from the person they enact in public. A seventh-grade boy described this kind of Walter Mitty experience while home alone watching the World Series on TV. "Nobody was home. Nobody bugged me. I felt really into the game, like I was one of the players. I just watched somebody hit a home run and I felt really good." Solitude and its flights of fantasy provide an opportunity for exploring new and different selves.[66]

Amy reported being alone for eleven of her forty-three beeper reports, and her solitude included many of these elements. It was lonely time, but it also felt valuable to her. She brooded about her looks and how everyone else had a boyfriend, but then added "I like to be by myself. I don't have to be worried or aggravated by my parents. I have noticed that when I'm alone I feel better sometimes." Then her ambivalence came out, and she adds "!NOT ALWAYS!" The loneliness of these solitary times can be overwhelming.

Solitude is like a potent medicine for teens that is good in limited doses, but can be deleterious in larger ones. In this and two previous studies we have found that spending too much time alone is often a sign of trouble, a sign of an adolescent who cannot quite cope with the world. Teenagers who use their newly gained cognitive skills to endlessly brood and ruminate can make themselves unhappier.[67] Spending large amounts of time apart from others is correlated with depression, lower grades, and other signs of psychological problems. At the opposite extreme, however, we find that adolescents who are rarely alone are also less well adjusted. The teen who is always with someone tends to be less happy and do less well in school.[68] These findings indicate that spending an intermediate quantity of time in solitude may be optimal for an adolescent's well-being.

Solitude, then, is often "down time" for teenagers, but this can be healthy. After a long day in which their emotions are played upon by peers, teachers, and family members, a measured period of time by themselves, to reflect, regroup, and explore, may be just what they need.

GETTING THROUGH THE DAY

Compared to many young adolescents, those in our study were fortunate. Their lives were not constrained by the economic deprivation experienced by increasing numbers of American young people. They did not face the constant threat of violence that has become a daily reality for many adolescents; their future lives were not clouded by the racism that blocks opportunities for those who are not white. A few of their families had incomes near the poverty line and their neighborhoods had intermittent gang activity, but all of them lived in two-parent families and encountered little of the community disorder that puts many teenagers today at extreme risk.

In spite of this privilege, these students experienced a substantial downswing in their emotional states as they entered adolescence. They reported more instances of anger, irritability, and depression than children only a few years younger, and these emotions threatened to destabilize their overall well-being. Compared to their parents, they also reported much wider fluctuations in moods, including more extremes of both happiness and unhappiness.

What our findings suggest is that teens live life with less epidermis. Adults have had more opportunity to become hardened and desensitized to the slings and arrows of daily life; adolescents feel them directly. The emotions of adolescents like Amy and Selman are acutely responsive to events in the immediate moment. And as they grow they confront more challenging events: historical changes have created a pileup of stresses and transitions in early adolescence. As young people crawl out of bed in the morning, they face a gamut of potential demands from their teachers, misunderstandings with peers, hassles with parents, and private anxieties that can disrupt their mood.

Within their four-cornered emotional world of school, peers, family, and solitude, each adolescent seeks his or her own way of achieving personal balance. While parents' lives have a semblance of rhythm, the emotional order of adolescents' lives is more complex and varied from person to person. Each of the four corners can be a source of stress or a source of stability.

Selman was able to rebound from the tribulations of his life, such as the insults about his basketball playing, because he repeatedly returned to contexts where he felt competent and secure. He felt affirmed and able in class and he had a good relationship with his family, especially his mother. Both contexts were arenas of comfort.

For some kids, like Amy, however, there is no place where they feel consistently at ease. Getting through the day for Amy was a succession of hurdles, with no place of repose to stabilize her feelings. As she passed from hour to hour, distress in one context built on distress in another. Conflict at home fed her anxiety with peers, which affected her concentration in class; her experience in solitude sometimes magnified these anxieties. It is not surprising that Amy reported low self-esteem and a high level of clinical depression. Without a consistent arena of comfort, she was beginning to develop chronic feelings of worry and helplessness.

The Confluence of Lives

Adolescents' troubled and fluctuating emotions are an issue not only for them but for the family as a whole. Up to now we have treated each family member as though her or his emotional experience is independent of others'. Yet we know that adolescents', fathers', and mothers' lives interweave as they go through the day. An adolescent's emotional experience with friends or at school feeds back on interactions with his or her parents. Likewise, what happens at a father's or mother's job influences other family members.

As we turn to examining these interrelationships, we ask: How does the emotionally turbulent world of adolescents connect with the busy and controlled world of their mothers and fathers? How do husbands' cycles of exertion and recovery intersect with wives' lives of work and caring? The focus in part II of the book is on the relations between pairs of family members. We have seen wide differences in mothers', fathers', and adolescents' daily realities. How does each combination of individuals find common ground?

PART TWO

Relationships

CHAPTER 5

Fathers and Mothers:
MARRIAGE IN THE TRENCHES

JERRY AND GLENNA couldn't have felt closer and more in love on Friday night. It was his birthday, they had a small party, and everyone had a great time. In fact, since Wednesday, when they received their pagers, Jerry and Glenna had been using the extreme end of our scale to describe how close they felt toward each other. Despite the stresses in each of their lives, they both experienced their relationship as especially warm. But Saturday morning, when certain family chores came due, this close bond was fractured.

Marriage is typically constituted on a foundation of love, with a hope and prayer that the strength of this bond will carry you through. Premarital couples absorb scenarios from song and cinema of falling in love and living happily ever after. These hopes are reinforced because courting is enacted through leisure and social activities, which allow the couple repeated experience of pleasure in each other's company. It is not surprising, therefore, that at the moment of marriage, most couples hold extraordinarily high expectations for a life together of closeness and mutual enjoyment.

Yet, in the words of Erich Fromm, "There is hardly any activity, any enterprise, which is started with such tremendous hopes and expectations, and yet, which fails so regularly, as love."[1] Fifty percent of marriages in the United States end in divorce. Even among those couples that hang on, like the ones in our study, by the time their kids reach adolescence marital satisfaction hits an all-time low.[2] Over the last century, our society has increasingly emphasized companionship, warmth, and shared happiness as the central purposes of marriage, but many couples are unable to sustain these.

To comprehend what happens after the honeymoon period, one needs to consider the daily ecology of marital life. What a cold, bracing shock it can be when the recreational, premarital relationship must be enacted on the rugged terrain of domestic obligation, child-rearing stresses, and bone-deep fatigue. Marriage means enduring each other's unexpected demands, dirty laundry, and divergent emotional worlds. Whether a marriage survives or fails lies in how well a couple fares with the difficult exigencies of daily existence and how well they can negotiate the differences we have seen between husbands' and wives' emotional realities.

To understand marriage, then, we need to examine what life is like in the trenches. The fifty-five married couples in our study were mostly in marriages that had held together. All but four couples were in their first marriage, and the median length of the marriages was sixteen years. After this period of time, how often and under what conditions did these husbands and wives interact with each other? Does the electricity still flow, or has the dross of daily existence long since extinguished marital happiness? And what patterns of daily interaction distinguish warm from distressed marriages?

The answers to these questions will play a significant role in addressing the larger issues of the book, for as we will see, the quality of relations between husband and wife shapes a family's emotional life. Conflict or warmth between parents gets passed to children. Parents' tensions, such as those we will examine between Jerry and Glenna, affect not just them, but the whole family.

TIME TOGETHER

People get married, in part, because they want to spend time with each other. Companionship is often people's primary goal for marriage; many couples report that they got married because they were "having fun together."[3] Yet we know that rewarding activities such as conversation and shared leisure decline in the first year of marriage and fall off further with the arrival of children.[4] After sixteen years of marriage, what is left? How much "quality time" do husband and wife spend together?

The first discovery we made about the lives of the couples in our study is that wives and husbands often *did not agree on when they were together*. One partner would indicate being "with my spouse," but the other partner did not reciprocate. The distinguished sociologist Erving Goffman argued that in social life we usually communicate and clearly demarcate when we are "with" each other and when we are apart.[5] But this is not true among people married sixteen years. Being "together" is more shadowy and ambiguous; partners drift in and out of each other's penumbra. For example, a woman cooking dinner in the kitchen reported being with her husband, while the husband reported being alone watching TV in the next room. Their perceptions do not correspond. This "unmutual togetherness" occurred about a third of the time that either spouse indicated being with the other.

The next discovery we made is that even when these husbands and wives agreed they were together, they reported separate activities for about half this time. On Sunday afternoon, for example, both Jerry and Glenna reported being together in front of the TV, but he was absorbed in the Bears' football game, while she was folding laundry, stopping periodically to watch the replays. They were physically in the same room (and shared anger toward each other), but their attention was focused on different enterprises. Not surprisingly, during such shared time wives were more likely to be doing family work or talking with someone; husbands were more likely to be watching TV or engaged in other leisure activities.

As we attempt to zero in on how much quality time these couples actually spent together, we find ourselves looking at smaller and smaller concentric circles (see figure 5.1). If we restrict our focus to occasions when the hus-

Figure 5.1

HUSBANDS' AND WIVES' TIME TOGETHER AND APART

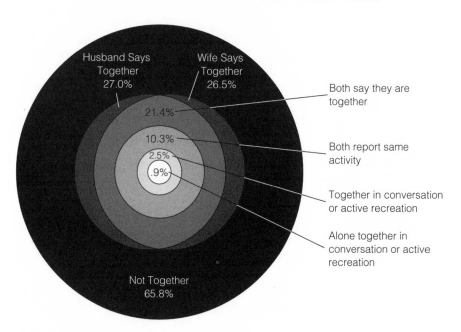

Figure gives the percentages for waking hours between 7:30 A.M. and 9:30 P.M.

bands and wives were together *and* doing the same activity, the average amount of joint time was about 10 percent of their waking hours. This is comparable to an hour and a half per day (an amount raised substantially by the inclusion of weekends).[6] Even then, the couples spent the great majority of this time not in rich, stimulating activities, but rather in mundane things, such as cleaning the humidifier, sorting clothes at the laundromat, or watching TV. Over two-thirds, 71 percent, of this time occurred at home. The most frequent shared activities were watching TV, eating, and housework, not likely to be the venue for rich, rewarding interactions.

By the time we narrow our focus to occasions when these husbands and wives shared interactive activities such as conversation and active recreation, the portion of time was only nineteen minutes a day. Of course, even this nineteen minutes included occasions when others—children, relatives, friends—were present and may have been taking part. If one is interested solely in these parents' times alone with each other in conversation or active recreation, our estimate becomes even smaller, though not infinitesimal: an average of seven minutes a day. Much of this private time was deliberately scheduled. Some couples arranged to have lunch during the week while the kids were in school; some phoned each other during the day.

The final truth, of course, is that even when the couples got this time alone with each other, they talked about family concerns. Topics of conversation when the couples were alone included where to send a son to college, child rearing and the stages kids go through, estimates on furnaces, and whether to buy a new car.[7] This private time together is not so much an escape from the duties of family life as a chance to plan and reflect on them.

As we look at these narrowing circles, the overwhelming majority of marital interaction is absorbed by ordinary everyday activities. Yes, people did report occasions of deep personal conversation, humor, and sexual intimacy. But such rich one-on-one time, which binds couples together during courtship, is rare at this stage of marriage, at least during the 7:30 A.M.–9:30 P.M. period covered by our study. One wife said, "As our children grow older, the time we have together, for just us, is smaller and smaller and later and later at night."[8] The great majority of daily contact between wives and husbands in our study was less direct, occurring in the presence of children, or while each was doing different activities—or when husband and wife did not even agree they were together.

EMOTIONS WHEN TOGETHER

To anyone who has been in or observed a marriage, it may not be surprising that nearly all daily marital interactions occur in mundane activities. What is more important, one might argue, is how these interactions are experienced, what partners feel together. Might not some couples find pleasure in sharing the routine tasks of everyday life—like Tolstoy's joy in scything wheat?

In one case, for example, a wife and husband both reported ebullient states while cleaning up dishes with their children after supper. She commented that "we are having a good time," and both reported feeling close to each other; in fact, they were talking about going for a walk to look for deer in the nearby forest preserve. In another instance, however, this wife and husband were at wit's end over a mistake in their insurance policy. Both reported extreme anger and distress about the error, and it affected how they felt toward each other.

The question is, Which is more typical of daily marital interactions? Is doing dishes together an activity that regularly evokes mutual pleasure? Or is it more common for the aggravations of everyday life to dominate shared time? The social psychologist Ellen Berscheid suggests that the sheer length of a relationship inevitably diminishes the experience of positive emotion.[9] Is it naive to think that after an average of sixteen years of marriage, being together would have a positive effect on partners' emotional state?

We were heartened to find that these wives' and husbands' shared time *was* associated with moods a notch above the rest of life. Their average emotional state when together was significantly above baseline. This positive effect is confirmed when we see that there was a change in emotional state when they entered each other's presence. For the beeper report just before being together, their emotions tended to be below average, but they jumped to above average once they were together.[10] One woman reported that "his being around puts me in a good mood, because we are close." Many others named situations in which their spouse's presence improved their emotional state.

Of course, certain situations are more likely to encourage shared positive feelings than others. If husband and wife did not agree they were together, their emotional state was *not* more positive. During this "unmutual togetherness," one partner's presence had little effect on the other's mood (see appendix 5.1). But if husband and wife agreed they were together, then their moods *did* tend to be more positive, whether they were sharing the same activity or not. As one might expect, the most positive emotion was reported when husband and wife were directly interacting, in talk or active recreation. In general, then, the narrowing concentric circles of figure 5.1 were associated with more favorable moods.

Thus even after sixteen years of marriage, husbands' and wives' interactions are not entirely stale. Certainly, moods when together are not wildly euphoric—we do not see the passionate states that a couple may have experienced during courting or at the beginning of marriage.[11] And certainly, behind these positive *average* moods is a wide range: some couples have more favorable experiences together than others. Also within any couple's week there are ups and downs; for example, the couple who was so ebullient washing dishes together reported negative states later in the week when sitting on the couch discussing how to get wax out of his ear. Nevertheless, the typical experience when these husbands and wives were together was above the norm for their lives. It appeared that the electricity still flowed.

But we need to understand this finding in context.

His and Her Marriage

As we look deeper, we discover different reasons why these husbands' and wives' average emotions were favorable in each other's presence. These reasons stem from the differences in their realities discussed in chapters 2 and 3. Most husbands came home from work claiming fatigue and entitlement to leisure. Most wives, in contrast, experienced the home and family environment as less pleasant and relaxed because they felt constant responsibility for household tasks.

These men, then, were happy in the presence of their wives because they were in a context that was typically relaxing and happy for them. In fact, if we employ statistical procedures to adjust for the effect of context and activity, the presence or absence of their wives had no additional relationship to their mood state, except when they were eating or in direct conversation.[12] Therefore, these husbands' happier state in their wives' presence was related more to release from the stresses of work. Of course, without the wife's stage management, home might be a much less pleasant place for the husband. She does much of the household labor that allows him to relax at home. Nonetheless, it is this setting and context more than her presence per se that appears to raise his moods.

But why, then, were these women happier in the presence of their husband? After all, home is the sphere where women's emotional experience is generally *less* positive. The setting and context did not raise their moods, nor were their favorable moods attributable to the activities they did in their husband's company.[13] Whether doing housework, resting, or in active recreation, these women reported more favorable states if their husband was present.

The happiness women reported in this situation suggests images of the depressed and lonely housewife who cheers up only when her family comes home. Yet this was not what was going on either. We found that employed women showed as strong an effect from the presence of their husband. A husband's presence did nothing to head off the 6 o'clock crash at the end of the workday, but at other times, including Saturday afternoons, his presence had a positive relationship to an employed wife's mood.[14] But why?

Two things appear to account for women's more positive mood with their husband. First, they appeared to slow down in their husband's company. They reported feeling less hurried and hardworking than at other times, irrespective of activity; this slowing down is associated with a more positive mood.[15] The frenetic pace of women's homelife was temporarily stilled.

A second reason is the companionship itself. These women reported more favorable emotions in their interactions with friends and coworkers, so their pleasure in their husband's company partly reflects their disposition to enjoy any adult company. Women tend to be more sensitive and invested in interpersonal relationships, and thus they get more emotional rewards from them.[16] With their husband, our data suggest, these women were more open to emotional give-and-take. They reported feeling less self-conscious and more accepted than usual when with their spouse (whereas the men did not). Other research confirms that marital interaction may be more important to women's well-being than men's.[17]

According to the sociologist Jessie Bernard, husbands and wives experience different marriages, and these differences are evident in our study.[18] Both the husbands and wives got happiness from their spouse, but they got it in different ways. When we asked what their wives did that raised their mood, many husbands mentioned instrumental activities, such as cooking a good meal. Bernard demonstrates that being married has a more positive effect on husbands' overall well-being than on wives'—because husbands' global happiness is boosted by the many household services their wives provide.[19] In these men's reality of exertion and recovery, this was what mattered to them.

The wives we studied, in contrast, appeared to get greater pleasure than husbands from spousal companionship. Asked what their husband did that made them happy, these women did mention instrumental actions but were more likely to report interpersonal things: "when he's considerate," or "when he asks me out for dinner." In these women's reality of unremitting care, it was this interpersonal validation that was most rewarding.

This difference creates an unspoken emotional exchange: his companionship for her labor. This asymmetric exchange can become a source of conflict when negotiated in the hour-to-hour flux of everyday life.

AN UNEASY EXCHANGE

Husbands and wives both try to get their needs met, but in the trenches of daily life, unequal exchange and misunderstanding happen easily. Because they are caught up in the fast pace and constant mundane demands of jobs and family, the asymmetric relationship between their worlds easily leads to imbalance and hurt feelings, as we see with Jerry and Glenna.

Birthday, Haircuts, and Football

Glenna, a sensitive and outspoken full-time homemaker, was strongly invested in the traditional role of wife and mother. Jerry, a relaxed and well-spoken insurance analyst, felt distressed by his job and was thinking about quitting during the week of the study. They lived in a pleasant split-level suburban home with their three children and two collies. They were interested in the study because they hoped it might reveal something about their youngest son, a quiet and stubborn ten-year-old boy. But it was their marriage that became the focus of the week.

By all appearances their marriage was happy. Between Tuesday evening, when they received their pagers, and Friday night, each separately reported the typical patterns of ups and downs in personal emotional states. Glenna's week was taken up by acts of caring, including a campaign to repair a rift between two of her friends, a visit to a beloved aunt who was dying, and a painful conversation with the school principal about their older daughter's behavior and attitude. Jerry experienced unhappiness about irresolvable problems at work and, like most men, he reported more positive moods at home with the family. Despite these stresses and the accompanying fluctuations in their personal moods, Glenna and Jerry reported unwavering warm feelings toward each other, as can be seen in figure 5.2. When beeped, they both reported feeling very "close to," "relaxed with," and "friendly toward" each other.

The pinnacle of their week was Friday night when they had Jerry's extended family over to celebrate his birthday. Both reported extremely positive feelings when beeped during this gathering. Glenna wrote that she felt lucky to have this "very good man" for her husband. Expressing a level of devotion that may seem anachronistic, she said: "He's my world. When he's happy, I'm happy." Jerry also reported enjoying himself, but added that he would prefer to be alone—with Glenna.

Then came Saturday morning. Jerry woke up feeling "crabby" and "pooped," and felt the kids were being a "real pain." But all three children needed haircuts, and there were other family needs that mobilized Glenna into her homemaker's role. On her beeper report she wondered "how anyone in this house gets by without me doing it." Later she explained that in her flurry of labor, Jerry "got lost in the shuffle. Sometimes my brain is going so fast that I forget a simple hug." A cold shoulder, a harsh word—they did not tell us exactly what was said—but suddenly Jerry and Glenna's closeness was shattered and both felt angry and distant from each other.

Jerry dealt with his anger at her by withdrawing. Like other men in our study, he claimed the right to do what he pleased at home. He went to his room and played the piano, leaving Glenna in charge of the kids and other family tasks. When beeped at 2:44 P.M. he was playing "The Girl I Left Behind" and wrote, "I'd like a few minutes of peace and quiet." *Five hours* after disappearing, he emerged, having had a "challenging, gratifying, and enjoyable" music session.

As a result of this "flow" experience, Jerry felt much better and once again reported feeling close to Glenna. At 6:42 P.M. the whole family was in Jerry and Glenna's bedroom watching *Jaws* on TV, and he wrote in his booklet, "I wonder what we are going to do tonight. TV? Company? Sex?" The problem was, there were unresolved issues for Glenna. At the end of the day she wrote that she "hates this attitude when he thinks he is being put upon."

The exchange between them had broken down. Jerry had gotten the respite from work that he wanted. But Glenna had put in a full Saturday of work with no recognition and little of the companionship and support she would have liked from her husband. And once the sense of reciprocity between husband and wife is disrupted, it can be difficult to restore.

Thus the conflict between them continued for several more days. On Sunday morning, Jerry approached Glenna and tried to make up, but was rebuffed. By his account, "I tried to open the door to communicate, but she slammed the door in my face." By Glenna's account, "I get bullheaded. I can make you into a piece of furniture until I let you be something else." On Saturday, Glenna was the angrier party in the dispute. As a result of this snub, Jerry was now the angrier person, and he continued to feel annoyed and distant from her during football on Sunday and through Monday morning. Then, as one can see in figure 5.2, their anger at each other flared up again Monday night and Tuesday morning.

Figure 5.2

THE EVOLUTION OF A MARITAL CONFLICT

Warmth Toward Each Other

Cool — Warm

Birthday party for Jerry.

Jerry feels ignored by Glenna and gets angry.

Jerry plays piano alone.

Family watches TV together.

Wednesday 8:24 A.M.
11:14
2:58 P.M.
4:58
5:46
6:46

Thursday 8:42 A.M.
11:16
1:18 P.M.
2:08
4:28
6:22
7:40
8:14

Friday 8:54 A.M.
10:06
11:54
2:44 P.M.

Saturday 11:00 A.M.
1:14 P.M.
2:44
6:12
6:42
8:10

THE EVOLUTION OF A MARITAL CONFLICT (continued)

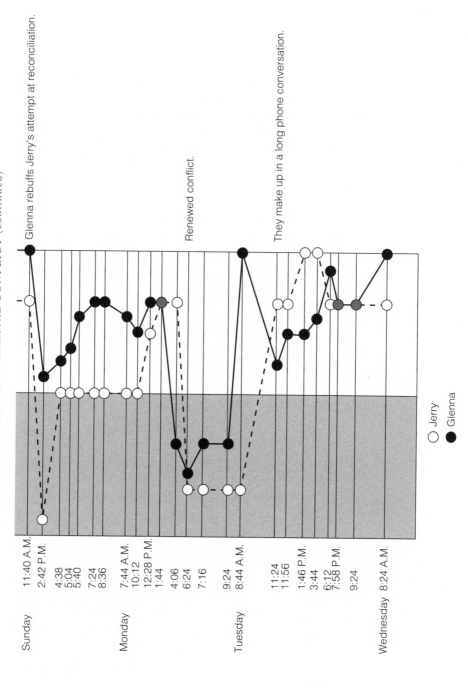

It was only late Tuesday morning, when they talked by phone, that the breach got repaired. "There is a light at the end of the tunnel," he wrote when beeped at 11:56 A.M. The interview with her on Wednesday night indicated that she had backed down. She admitted that she had let him "get lost in the shuffle" on Saturday, and she added, "I can't get caught up in the kids' needs. You can't lose sight of the fact that your husband comes first, then the children. I try to be independent, but he must come first." Faced with what appeared to be an interminable conflict, she reverted to a traditional interpretation of her role, and accepted blame in order to buy family harmony.

If we look back at the cause of their conflict, we can see it is rooted in the tension between Jerry's and Glenna's realities and their inability to mediate their asymmetric needs and expectations. Jerry's first priority for the weekend was getting relief from the distress of his job, and he had no qualms about doing what he needed to get it. Glenna's priority for the weekend was taking care of the children and enjoying some time with her husband, as well as, perhaps, enlisting some support for her labors. However, her traditional attitudes that "he is my life" and that "he comes first" put her in a situation where she could not speak up for her needs. So when his feeling "pooped" coincided with the Saturday morning haircuts, conflict was almost inevitable, and things did not get resolved until she backed down, denied her needs, and accepted blame as the one who did not fulfill her marital role.

Certainly both Jerry and Glenna contributed to their conflict, but an imbalance existed. It was not just that their realities were *different*: there was an inequality in what each expected from the other. Jerry expected Glenna to adjust to his needs, with no reciprocal consideration of her needs. Further, he held the trump card of withdrawal, a strategy men commonly use for dealing with marital conflict.[20] In the barter of daily realities, his needs were worth more.

Who Influences Whom?

We also see this imbalance between husband and wife when we examine how emotions get passed between them. We wanted to know whose emotional states most often influenced the other's. Did shared negative feelings, for example, more often start with his bad moods or hers? To answer this question, we examined times when either husband or wife had a strong mood, then looked at the next report to see whether the other spouse had picked up that mood.

Unsurprisingly, the husband's mood more often predicted the wife's subsequent moods. His emotional state was more dominant. If a husband reported a strong emotion at one point in time—either positive or negative—that emotion was likely to be evident in his wife's report of her mood at the next beep (see appendix 5.2).

This "emotional transmission" appeared to occur from Jerry to Glenna on both Friday night and Saturday morning. Jerry had a better than usual day at work Friday and his good mood seemed to lift Glenna's state; indeed, she said: "When he's happy, I'm happy." Then Saturday morning, Jerry woke up feeling "crabby," and shortly thereafter, Glenna, who had been feeling perfectly fine, also acquired a negative mood. While we cannot say for certain that Jerry's state affected Glenna's in these two specific situations, the pattern of husbands' prior mood predicting wives' subsequent mood occurred so often as to be unmistakable. Other research suggests this one-way path of transmission as well.[21]

This emotional transmission was most common when the husbands in our study came home from work. We described in chapter 2 how these men brought home emotional states from their jobs: if they ended their day at work in a good or a bad state, they were likely to be feeling that state when they got home. These moods often influenced their wives' state. The joy, anger, or distress a man reported at his last beep at work significantly predicted his wife's mood after he got home (see appendix 5.2).[22] Many men try to screen out bad news at work and just bring home the good.[23] Yet the reality is that both positive and negative emotions get transmitted to their families.

But don't wives also bring negative emotions home from work that affect their husbands? Quite rarely. We noted in chapter 3 that employed women's last-reported mood at work did not even predict their *own* emotional states upon returning home—these women tended to experience a crash at 6 o'clock regardless of what had happened at work. It is not surprising, therefore, that emotional events in wives' lives at their jobs—or at home, if they were not employed—were less likely to influence their husbands' emotional states in the evening.

The Politics of Receivers and Senders

Why do emotions mainly get transmitted one way? Let us consider another example. At 7:36 P.M. on a weekday evening, a full-time secretary and mother of two was in the living room enjoying a movie, *Killer Whale*. She reported feeling calm, in control, and cheerful. At that same moment, her husband, a policeman, was in the kitchen talking on the phone about operating a hot dog stand at a school function. He was angry and upset because he felt they were getting a "dirty deal." Sure enough, at the next beep at 9:03 P.M., the wife's mood had dropped; now both of them were in a funk talking about the school event.

What is going on here? One explanation for the asymmetry focuses on differences in the emotional receptivity of each spouse. The psychologist Karen Rook and her colleagues argue that mothers' greater receptivity to others' emotions reflects their assumption of the "burden of care."[24] By taking responsibility for the emotional well-being of the family, women open themselves to the ups and downs of those they care for. Women try to buffer their husband's stress and in the process are recipients of some of it.

Men, by contrast, are usually less tuned in to what is going on emotionally and thus less receptive. Confronted by a distressing situation, they are more likely to avoid it, stonewall, or issue peremptory advice.[25] Because caring is defined as part of women's traditional role, it is wives, not husbands, whom we find sharing their spouse's anger about a hot dog stand, massaging their spouse's back when he is sore from work, and cleaning wax out of his ear despite his negative disposition.

Another explanation focuses on the sender. Men assume a position of power in the family, and people in power easily influence the emotions of those with less power.[26] If they had a good day at work, some of the fathers in our study took their families out to eat or to a ballgame. If they had a bad day, they expected others to accommodate their mood, and were more likely to take their anger out on others; in some families this may take the form of physical abuse. Thus Jerry expected homelife to function on his terms, whereas Glenna could exercise power only by denying Jerry what he wanted.

The one-way emotional transmission between husbands and wives, then, is attributable to men's being both more impervious and imperious than their wives. She is more open and receptive; he is more stoic and domineering. The result is that in the hour-to-hour negotiation of family life, his emotional world more often dominates hers. His needs, his reality often take precedence over hers.

Of course, this varies from marriage to marriage.

DAILY LIFE IN HAPPY AND DISTRESSED MARRIAGES

Our sample covered a tremendous range of ways couples negotiated their separate realities, and a range of how they felt within the marriage. One husband and wife expressed open hatred of each other; another pair repeatedly commented on how much they were in love. Generally, if one spouse felt good about the marriage, the other tended to as well. The question is how patterns of daily interaction differ for people in happy and distressed marriages. Are feelings about the marriage related to the amount of time a couple shares or by the pattern of emotions partners experience when together? And are they related to how a couple arbitrate their daily realities?

We used two criteria to identify happy and distressed marriages. One was a frequently used scale, the Locke-Wallace Short Marital Adjustment Test, which asks each partner to provide an overall evaluation of marital functioning. It combines a global assessment of how happy each spouse is with the marriage with ratings of how much agreement there is between them. We refer to this as "marital adjustment." The other measure we used assessed hour-to-hour feelings of "warmth" versus "coolness" between spouses. It was obtained from the beeper sheets: at each report, participants rated whether they felt "close to," "relaxed with," and "friendly toward" their spouse. This scale obtained an assessment of the ongoing feelings toward the spouse. We would like to emphasize that conclusions based on these scales are relevant only to the limited cultural context studied here, since happiness, agreement, and warmth may be less relevant criteria for evaluating marriage in other cultural groups. Nonetheless, research suggests that these dimensions correspond with what most people in our society consider to be a "good" marriage.[27]

These two different measures, for the most part, tell us the same story about shared time and emotion in happy and distressed marriages.

Time Together and Apart

A major obstacle to happiness in marriage, we have suggested, is simply the demands of daily life: dirty laundry, children's needs, the enormous pressures on time in contemporary society. Some commentators have suggested that the hurriedness of modern life is a major stress on marriage because it prevents husbands and wives from spending time with each other. In this vein, we expected to find that partners in happy marriages would spend more minutes within the "narrowing circles" of joint time.

Indeed, we found that partners in cool marriages were less likely to be at home at the same time (see appendix 5.3). This tendency was not due to their working different shifts or longer hours at their jobs. Furthermore, when they were at home together, the partners in distressed marriages were more likely to be apart—to be in different rooms. He would be in the basement, she in the kitchen; he in the living room, she in the back yard. Their locations did not seem to be coordinated, or maybe they *were* coordinated—like repelling magnets.

Even when one partner said they were together, the other spouse in a distressed marriage was more likely to disagree. These marriages had more of what we call "unmutual togetherness." In one example, a husband and wife were both in the dining room, but he, absorbed in reading mail, did not acknowledge her presence. We suspect that warm couples are more likely to communicate a sense of connection when they want to spend time together, and there may be more understanding that when she curls up with a book, she wants to be alone. Conversely, in distressed couples, it may be more common for one partner not to acknowledge the other's presence, perhaps to freeze the other out, as we saw Glenna do to Jerry on Sunday morning.

The warm couples, then, reported more shared time. As shown in figure 5.3, the total amount of time that partners agreed they were together was nearly twice as high for them. This included times in parallel activities—for example, a husband fixing a light while his wife, in the same room, was setting her daughter's hair. And it included times they were

Figure 5.3

AMOUNT OF TIME TOGETHER AND APART
IN COOL AND WARM MARRIAGES

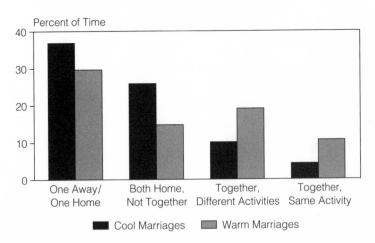

Cool marriages were those where both spouses had mean warmth scores below
the median (N = 17); warm marriages where both were above the median (N = 18).

doing the same thing, whether it was going shopping for their daughter's Easter outfit or preparing dinner together. Happy couples seem to make an extra effort to be together or do joint activities.[28] In one case, a man reported that he and his wife talked by phone five times a day in order to keep up on the breaking events in each other's lives.

As we get to the center of the narrowing circles, we find a difference between husbands and wives that should not be surprising by now. Marriage counselors advise that a healthy marriage requires spending time talking or in leisure together, but we find this to be true only for wives. The proportion of shared time in these activities is correlated only with wives' marital happiness (see appendix 5.3).[29] One unhappily married woman complained that they spent too much family time doing chores and not enough doing fun things. This finding repeats a theme that comes up again and again: that the social is more important for women. Men care less about how this time is spent, perhaps partly because they experience chores more as a leisure activity.

We now face a "chicken or egg" problem: Do couples avoid each other because the marriage is bad or is the marriage bad because they don't spend enough time together? The family researcher Paul Rosenblatt and his colleagues have taken the first position. They even argue that this avoidance is valuable to maintaining what shreds of good feeling remain in the marriage.[30] This interpretation is supported by our finding that distressed spouses spend more time in leisure apart from each other.[31] Since there is little reason to expect that separate leisure causes marital distress, it is more likely a symptom of the distress. Conversely, if you can enjoy your spouse enough to spend time with her or him, especially during your valued leisure time, your marriage must be good.

But there is evidence of an opposite path of causality, too. Martha Hill, a University of Michigan researcher, found in analyzing data from a very large and careful longitudinal study that even adjusting for marital satisfaction, the amount of time spent together predicted marital stability (versus dissolution) in the future. Couples who shared time were less likely to break up.[32] This suggests that shared time is not merely a symptom of marital quality, but that it also contributes to it. Shared time draws couples together. When life gets so hectic that shared time disappears, misunderstandings fester.

Of course, just spending time together is not enough. The feelings partners experience when together must also be considered.

Pleasure Together or Pain?

In the lyrics of popular song, a relationship is over when a couple has "lost that loving feeling." As we have noted, even after sixteen years of marriage the typical husband and wife in our study reported a slight average uplift in mood in each other's presence. Being together brought many couples a small notch above their quotidian experience. Does this increment of happiness define a happy marriage?

Needless to say, real life is always more complicated than song. Contrary to what one might expect, unhappy couples reported many occasions of feeling happy when together.[33] The beeper found them enjoying themselves watching their child's baseball game, having a barbecue with neighbors, even going out to a movie alone with each other. On some of these occasions mutual enjoyment even created feelings of closeness and warmth between them, however temporary. Numerous laboratory studies (though not all) have suggested that marital distress does not dampen positive marital interactions.[34] It does not reduce a couple's ability to exchange positive words or even have fun during the limited times they are together.

What really differentiates cool from warm couples is greater frequency of negative experiences, rather than fewer positive experiences when together. The distressed couples in our study reported twice as many times together that both were in negative moods. They reported a much higher rate of joint anger, irritability, and unhappiness in each other's presence.[35] Researchers have also observed greater shared negative emotion among distressed couples in laboratory studies; indeed, Levenson and Gottman verify that distressed couples get much more worked up physiologically than other couples.[36] In these laboratory studies, men's negative emotions were often expressed as anger and contempt, while women's negative emotions were expressed as fear, complaining, and sadness.[37]

Despite some occasions of mutual happiness, then, distressed couples are much more susceptible to things suddenly turning sour. This is partly because such marriages have an underlying climate of suspicion in which partners are ready to see the worst motives in their spouse's behavior.[38] Thus the most trivial misunderstanding can turn into a major incident. For example, one man in our study got upset because he was trying to be an involved father, making plans to take the children to karate on Sunday afternoon, but then discovered that his wife had made other plans for them. Rather than accepting the situation as a simple failure of communication, which was her version of events, he insisted: "My wife deliberately tried to embarrass me."

Mutual suspicion creates cycles of negative emotion. Three hours later, this man was still upset about being "embarrassed" by his wife and had developed other complaints: "When I try to talk to her she doesn't answer or explain what she feels or thinks." The anger of one spouse triggers anger in the other, which builds. The usual reciprocity of labor and love is replaced by cycles of animosity.

We found that these exchanges of negative feeling could go on for hours, or even days, as in the case of Jerry and Glenna; in some couples, they could spiral into violence, or at least the threat of it. One man wrote, "I want to punch my wife out." The irony is that it was in the marriages with high disagreement that the partners' emotions were more likely to be connected to each other's. Rather than being autonomous, their emotional lives were actually more intertwined than those of people in close marriages.

Not surprisingly, it was most often the husbands' negative emotions that triggered these cycles. In cool marriages, we found that the husbands' emotional states were more often transmitted to their wives.[39] It is also not surprising that the issue which triggered these conflicts most often was household work.

Frictional Realities

The origins of conflicts between husbands and wives are always complex. A couple's financial well-being and their attitudes and personality traits, even before marriage, influence the emotional climate of their relationship.[40] Every couple has an intricate history. Nonetheless, the incidents that spark daily animosity may be quite simple.

We can see the deep roots of marital conflict in the relationship between Bennett and Sandra. He is an ear, nose, and throat doctor. She works seventeen hours a week in his office and is going to school to develop her own career. In the interview, Sandra related how, when they were first married, she started doing all the household work because he was in medical school. But that pattern never got changed when medical school was over. Sandra complained, "He believes in women working and contributing to the income, but he does not take the modern view of men helping with housework." Overwhelmed with responsibilities, she was still trying to get him to contribute. Bennett complained, "She's usually telling me I don't do anything around here—every weekend she has a project for me."

Given their differing assumptions about who should do what, it is not surprising that the negative emotion in Sandra and Bennett's marriage was frequently sparked by household tasks. On Saturday morning he accepted the job of cleaning the filter on the furnace humidifier. But he could not do it alone and recruited Sandra to help him. When beeped in the midst of this task, Bennett wrote that he felt "hateful" because he hated the task. Sandra wrote that she was "getting more anxious to get homework (for school) done rather than wifely/motherly chores. My husband keeps distracting me from what needs to be done."

Again and again, the unhappy couples in our study reported household tasks and responsibilities as the provocation for negative emotion: a husband was angered by "what a lousy lunch my wife made"; a wife was incensed that her husband was unwilling to stop at the store and pick up needed grocery items. In families where husbands contributed less to household labor, wives' mood level was lower and the marital satisfaction of both partners was lower.[41] Other research confirms that husbands' contribution to household labor and a couple's satisfaction with their division of household labor are related to both partners' well-being and satisfaction with the marriage.[42] Even when husbands help with the housework, it can be a source of tension. One woman in our study complained that when her husband sweeps the floor, "everything goes into the garbage."

The finding that family work is a frequent flash point in marriage might suggest that conflict is greater for two-earner couples, who have less time. But this was not evident in our data. We found that partners in two-earner marriages did spend slightly less time together, particularly in cases where they worked different shifts, but their emotions during their shared time were as favorable as among single-earner couples.[43] Overall, we found that wives' hours of employment were not related to greater marital distress, lower warmth, or less marital adjustment.[44]

The critical time for the two-earner couples in our study was the 6 o'clock crunch. In couples where labor is shared during this time, marital quality was high, but if a wife got stuck with all the urgent labor of this time period, it became a major source of tension. Her emotions and the amount of labor she reported during this period were strong predictors of the health of the marriage.[45] Of course, this might also be a time when the husband was bringing home stress and anger from his job with an expectation that other family members adapt to his needs. The combination of her "second shift" and his traditional expectations becomes a formula for disaster.

A Happy Marriage: Del and Marlene

When we add up all the things that can make a marriage unhappy, we begin to see why more marriages in this society fail than succeed. Our culture has put a premium on interpersonal happiness, but happiness is a fickle thing. The most interesting question, then, may be how some marriages are able to beat the odds, rather than why so many fail. Del and Marlene's week illustrates how elements of distressed marriages are reversed in a warm and happy relationship.

Del and Marlene worked different shifts, he as a mechanic for a meat-packing factory, she as a part-time clerk in a trucking center. Research suggests that these "off-shift" couples are at risk for marital problems. In other ways, too, Del and Marlene are at risk: she was a victim of childhood sexual abuse, and both she and Del reported bringing a lot of unresolved personal issues ("anger and garbage") into their thirteen-year marriage. Yet they went out of their way to connect with each other, and their ability to communicate about their "garbage" reduced the cycles of negative emotion that we saw in other couples.

Marlene and Del's first beep was at noon on a Wednesday, a time when most couples are immersed in routine daily activities. Del and Marlene, though embarrassed to be "caught," reported being in bed making love. Both indicated extremely positive emotion, and he reported that they were talking about "feelings." It was her day off and he did not go to work until 3 P.M., so they spent much of this time together. At the next report, at 1:40 P.M., they were together at a home improvement store buying paint for the new addition to their house.

Del and Marlene made deliberate efforts to get time together on other days as well. Three days a week she met him in the parking lot of his factory, "because it's the only time we can talk." They were already planning a week that summer to go away by themselves while their kids would be at camp.

This shared time gave Marlene and Del the chance to dissipate tensions that might otherwise have worsened. Dennis Orthner, a family sociologist, suggests that such time may serve as a stabilizer and "shock absorber"; it allows partners to think creatively together and learn each other's views. Even noninteractive pastimes like watching TV may "anesthetize" negative feelings generated by conflict.[46] Other authors suggest that spending time together facilitates construction of a "joint marital reality."[47] Del and Marlene's plan to remodel and expand their kitchen is a focus of many of their interactions. Both reported being extremely invested in it—a country-style family kitchen with an eating nook and abundant counter-space for group cooking projects. She said she stayed up late many nights drawing plans. He described the addition and their home as an essential "refuge from the rat race." Through this shared project and other shared activities, they cultivated a sense of "we-ness."

Like other happy couples, Marlene and Del often experienced neutral and sometimes negative emotion during shared time. On Friday, they drove to the bank together and reported being extremely upset that they had to wait so long. But rather than turning against each other, they found humor in the situation. A half-hour later they were driving home and teasing. He said he was "aggravating her by commenting on how her lip sticks out when she wants to get back." She commented, "We really enjoy 'playing' with each other—it's fun and allows us to be 'childlike.'"

Del and Marlene had arguments, too, but their disputes were unlikely to get out of control. On Sunday afternoon they did not "see eye to eye" about some issue and got into a fight. Research indicates that "hot" marital conflict, by itself, is not destructive for a marriage.[48] We found it to occur in many of the happy marriages in our study. What is important is what follows a fight. Marlene said that during the fight, "I felt tense and angry, but close to him, too." In nondistressed couples, partners *do* yell back at each other, but neither loses touch with the underlying commitment to their marriage; suspicion does not take over. Partners' core conception of the marriage is less reactive to an immediate conflict.[49]

Because they were able to step back and look at themselves, Del and Marlene were able to break the cycle of negative emotion before it spiraled out of control. In healthy marriages, partners fight fair. They are less likely to say or do things that lead to negative escalations; their arguments include assent, empathy, humor, and constructive problem solving.[50] Partners listen to and validate each other.[51] Marlene wrote, "We argue like anyone else, but we always resolve our differences immediately. Both of us believe that this is one reason we have a very close, loving relationship."

Sunday night at work Del was still focused on his wife, but rather than dwelling on the anger, he reported that he was thinking of ways to improve his relationships with her and the family. In fact, he wrote that he "can't wait until I try my ideas for getting closer." In the interview, Marlene reflected on the fight and talked about her needing to work on her attitude. She said, "How you feel is how you decide to feel . . . I sulk for a while. I have a major self-pity party and nobody comes but me!" She recognized her contribution to the conflict and was trying to change. Despite occasional disagreements, people in satisfied marriages take more responsibility for problems and give their spouses more credit for contributing to the relationship.[52]

Del's willingness to engage in the emotional work of making up after the fight is one of the key factors that set this couple apart from many marriages. Men's tendency to disengage from discussion is a repeated obstacle to resolution of marital issues. In other ways, however, Del and Marlene were a fairly traditional couple: the daily exchange between them was asymmetric. He generally left housework to her and she reported valuing her dominion over most family responsibilities, sometimes in ways that made it hard for him to be involved. Nonetheless, on Monday, when Marlene had a bad cold, he took over getting the kids off to school and made her chicken soup while she rested in bed. He was not imperious or impervious; he demonstrated a sensitivity to her needs that affirmed her reality.

In other couples in our study, the husbands' willingness to discuss and contribute to household labor appeared to be related to marital contentment. One remarried professional woman, whose first marriage had been bitter, expressed amazement that when she had a list of things to do on Saturday morning, her new partner actually cared about it. "With my previous husband, my agenda was secondary; in fact, it didn't even count." In the new marriage, her reality was acknowledged and important; tasks that had to be done were negotiated. What is important is that both spouses feel empowered within the household sphere.[53]

MARITAL HAPPINESS IN THE TRENCHES

The marriages we have examined in this chapter are far from the cinematic ideal. We have talked about "happy" and "distressed" marriages as though they were clearly distinct from each other, but the reality is that a continuum exists between them, with all couples demonstrating features of both. After years of living together, even the happiest couples in our sample experienced conflict and negative emotions. Instead of accepting the idealized images of "living happily ever after" manufactured by the media, we would be wiser to recognize that marriage, like all systems, has an inherent tendency to decay. According to the second law of thermodynamics, everything in the universe is subject to processes of disintegration, or entropy.

In day-to-day experience, decay creeps into marriage in the form of a humidifier that has to be cleaned, a mistake in an insurance policy, a wife coming home to a husband who's in front of the TV when a pile of chores is waiting to be done. In our sample, husbands' job stress and limited participation in family work were frequent starting points for marital conflict. Small incidents would become incendiary and build into uncontrolled cycles of conflict and chronic marital distress.

The difficulties of daily life and the differences between realities, we find, make some friction in marriage unavoidable. But the pessimism of the second law has been amended by a new brand of physics that recognizes the capacity of living systems to grow and create order in spite of decay.[54] While the idealized romance of the first years of marriage may inevitably dissolve, couples have the potential to create a new marital reality. The family sociologist David Mace reports that successful couples are able to use conflicts as raw materials for growth.[55] Rather than allowing anger to breed more anger, they use it as feedback for reshaping their marital reality. Whereas some couples, like Glenna and Jerry, bickered over conflicts for days, others, like Del and Marlene, reflected on their disputes with the goal of making daily interactions work better. Rather than withdrawing, men in these families acknowledged their wives' realities. And shared time provided a forum for keeping in touch with each other's experience and cultivating joint understanding. People in happy marriages are continually renewing their relationship within the challenges posed by their daily interactions. Certainly these are not blithely happy newlyweds, but the electricity still flows.

As we turn now to examining relations between parents and adolescents, we might hope to carry some of these lessons with us. "What is true for marriage," suggests the psychologist Raymond Montemayor, "probably is true for parent–adolescent relationships as well."[56] We might hypothesize that a good parent–adolescent relationship involves spending time together, avoiding cycles of negative emotion, and negotiating household duties.

We shall see, however, that many of these features of daily interaction that make for a good marital relationship change for the worse in parent–child relationships as the child enters adolescence. The potential for friction and entropy between parent and adolescent is, in many ways, even greater than that between husband and wife.

CHAPTER 6

Mothers and Adolescents:
LOVE AND CONFLICT

BEGINNING AT BIRTH, it is typically a child's mother who is most attuned and responsive to the child's emotional needs. It is she to whom a child usually goes with hurts and heartbreaks, joys and triumphs. She probably spends more time with the child than anyone else, and she is most personally invested in the child's well-being. But having grown accustomed to a child whose feelings are usually transparent and happy, a mother suddenly finds herself caring for an adolescent who is more withholding, more prone to negative moods, and who sometimes directs the brunt of his or her displeasure at her.

Young adolescents in our society experience a pileup of personal changes that intensify their emotional lives. They are going through puberty; they are enduring an often stressful transition to middle school or junior high; they are finding relations with peers more enthralling yet difficult. They are also developing new cognitive skills that can make them more perceptive, more critical of their parents, and more emotionally vulnerable.

Mothers' reality is more stable than adolescents, but mothers are often stretched thin, with limited energy left over for adapting to radical changes. Mothers' lives are hurried. Along with attending to children, they are juggling obligations they feel to their husbands, their extended families, their friends, and, in many cases, to their jobs. We have seen that women value relationships and are sensitive to them. Mothers' daily interactions with friends, husbands, and coworkers influence and usually raise their moods. The question is, How does this sensitivity to others play out when the partner is an emotionally changeable, sometimes rebellious, adolescent child? Although child care books of the past avowed that mothers find deep pleasure and fulfillment in their role, in reality we know little about what mothers of teenagers really feel on a day-to-day basis.[1]

What we do know is that this stage of the mother–child relationship is typically experienced by both as the most difficult.[2] Teenagers' problems in school, disappointments in romance, boredom, restlessness, anger all usually register, in one way or another, on their daily interactions with their mothers. Adolescents experience more daily conflicts with their mothers than with their fathers, yet also feel closer to them.[3] But is this period invariably painful? Are mothers and teens inevitably at loggerheads?

DISPARATE "TASKS"

To some degree, societal expectations put mothers and adolescents on a collision course. Despite all the current talk about equal parenting with fathers, in most two-parent families, like the ones we studied, mothers are still the primary caregivers for children.[4] And whereas mothers of prior centuries saw their task as feeding, protecting, and training their children, contemporary mothers have inherited from the 1950s the burden of believing that their affection and attention are the crucial factors shaping their children's well-being.[5]

"Spock-oriented mothers," according to the psychologist Philip Slater, "believed, deep in their hearts, that if they did their job well enough all of their children would be creative, intelligent, kind, generous, happy, brave, spontaneous, and good—each, of course, in his or her own special way."[6] Child-care books in the 1950s created the impression that lapses in a mother's sensitivity could lead her offspring into a life of loneliness and delinquency, or even to suicide.[7] During this era, mothers of older children acquired the roles of den mother, chauffeur, teacher's aide, and especially personal confidante.

Although professional opinion has started to take some of this burden off mothers, most women continue to feel bound by these high expectations. Child-development experts now recognize that the mother is just one of many influences on a child's well-being—the child's father, teachers, community, and genetic inheritance are all part of the equation. Nonetheless, the kind of personal investment expressed by one woman is common: "My kids need me no matter what age they are. In the fall, my daughter had mumps. Her dad was here, but it wasn't the same. The best thing I can give my kids is a proper upbringing so they know they're safe so they can go out and face the world and be strong. This is my gift to them—my offering—which I hope will better their lives."

If anything, mothers' ideal of a high-quality personal relationship with their adolescent children has become stronger as our society has increasingly come to value relationships as important ends in themselves.[8] The mothers in our study wanted to be more, not less, engaged with their children: 67 percent wished their child would share more with them (as compared to 43 percent of fathers). In the words of Linda Thompson and Alexis Walker, "Mothers' sense of purpose is founded on feeling needed by and essential to their children."[9] They view mothering as a non-negotiable moral commitment.

But at the same time that mothers continue in their role of being close to and responsible for their children, young adolescents hear societal voices suggesting that their challenge is to break away, to become their own person. In traditional theories of adolescence, teens face the "developmental task" of becoming autonomous and independent from their parents. Though it is less true among other cultural groups, European-American adolescents are expected to become self-reliant and emotionally self-sufficient at an early age.[10]

Therefore teenage children begin spending more time with friends or by themselves. They may close their bedroom doors, expressing a desire for privacy that excludes parents. Girls will fill pages of a diary or spend hours conversing with a girlfriend as they dissect the intricacies of personal relations. Boys may absorb themselves in playing computer games alone or shooting baskets with friends. Such activities are a way for growing teenagers to establish a personal sense of who they are, a private self separate from parents and family.

Up until this age, parents could readily sense strong internal centripetal forces that pulled the child back to the family each night. There was no mistaking that the child needed and depended on what he or she received from the family. But with age, these forces loosen their hold, and mothers who used to punish children by sending them out of the house may now do the opposite: they ground them and make them stay home.

Two Encounters

The potential for conflict between the child-rearing "task" of mothers and the developmental "task" of adolescents is illustrated by a heated exchange between Rob and his mother, Rita. Rob was a tall, somewhat overweight eighth grader, whose shirt often hung out of his pants. Rita was a petite, thirty-two-year-old, full-time mother of two, who described herself as an inveterate Elvis Presley fan. They lived in a small, working-class home that Rita had decorated for Halloween with bats, skeletons, and black chains. Rita said Rob had his father's inclination for joking, which often made her laugh: "He comes up with some good stuff; he mimics and makes noises; he's a good comedian." But at times, his silliness got on her nerves and the joking took on a sarcastic edge that cut deep.

On Thursday at dinner Rita told Rob to stop acting silly, especially since his aunt was there. Rita was asserting her mother role and reported feeling pleased that "Rob acknowledged my discipline for a change." Then later, at 8:45, they were all playing cards and she again upbraided him because he was "trying to be the center of attention." She tried to explain to him that "he's not the only person who knows everything." But his sarcastic reply led her to think, "I am tired of Rob's smart mouth when someone tries to tell him something." At 10 P.M. when she filled out her daily diary, she was still upset about his insolence.

By Rita's account, she had attempted to perform her parental role of training her son to act like a mature adult; in fact, in the first instance she reported feeling quite close to him at the same time she was trying to discipline him.

But from Rob's perspective, the incident had a completely different meaning. To begin with, he had had a rough day; he'd had a falling-out with his friends earlier in the day, and it would have been nice if someone would have shown some understanding. Further, while Rita claimed she "explained" things to him, Rob said she "screamed at me." Beneath these issues, Rob said that his father was trying to transfer out to Oregon, which would be very disruptive to Rob's life. But his mother had a "thing about Oregon," so any time he said something negative about it, she got mad. From his point of view, the incident was not about his behavior but rather about her domineering attitude and his right to say what he thinks. Both occasions made him feel angry and distant toward her.

The divergence of experience between Rita and Rob exemplifies the inherent tension between the roles of mother and adolescent. She wanted him to be mature; he wanted a measure of autonomy. Both wanted control of the situation.

At the opposite extreme from this incident were the warm feelings Carol and her daughter Chloe reported on a Thursday evening as they sat in the kitchen discussing Chloe's social life. Carol was a part-time nurses' aide, often dressed in T-shirt and jeans. Chloe was an introspective drum majorette, in her final weeks of eighth grade. When beeped at 9:08 P.M. this Thursday, Carol said: "We are girl talking." Chloe said they were discussing a conversation she'd had that day with a girlfriend she really liked. Both mother and daughter reported feeling cheerful, happy, and close to each other.

Carol and Chloe seemed to be sharing the kind of "sacred ground" women experience with close friends. With teenagers' development of more adultlike reasoning abilities, deeper and more personal conversations with them become possible. But does this happen often? Or is it more common for adolescents to use these reasoning abilities in opposition to their mothers—as Rob does with Rita?

Before evaluating the emotional substance of mother–child interactions, we examine how often and under what conditions the daily lives of adolescents and mothers in our European-American two-parent sample came together.

TIME TOGETHER

Shared time is the fundamental medium of any relationship. As we did with daily marital relationships, we ask whether shared time between our mothers and their adolescent children occurs in situations that permit meaningful interchange.

The first thing we find is that the adolescents and mothers in our study agreed even less than husbands and wives about when they were together. For *half* the times that either mother or teenager said she was with the other, the other did not agree. Mothers were more likely to say they were together when the teen's did not (see appendix 6.1). This "unmutual togetherness" occurred most often when they were nearby but in separate rooms; even when adolescent and mother were in the same physical space, the question of whether they were "together" may be ambiguous, as in the case of a mother who reported driving five hours without exchanging a word with her headphone-clad sixth-grade daughter.

The mothers in our sample spent somewhat more time with their children than the fathers did, but the difference was largely in peripheral time. In addition to having more of this "unmutual togetherness" with their adolescents than the fathers did, the mothers had more time where both they and their children agreed they were together but their activities differed (see appendix 6.1). Often the mother was doing housework and the teen was watching TV, playing a game, or getting dressed. Because the fathers had longer work hours, the mothers spent more time with their children than the fathers did on weekdays, especially during the difficult transitional times when everyone was getting ready at the start of the day, or when supper had to be prepared at the end of the day.[11] Even the employed mothers left home later in the morning and returned earlier than their husbands; hence mothers shared more of this dicey time when multiple family tasks needed to be accomplished quickly.[12]

If we look at the amount of time these mothers reported doing the same activity with a child, the quantity was quite small: 7 percent of waking hours, or about one hour a day. This is about the same amount that the fathers reported; however, the mothers reported sharing more intimate and personal activities. The most frequent shared activity with either parent was watching TV, followed by eating, but talking was a more common shared activity with the mothers than it was with the fathers.[13] Mothers, as we have seen, are more attentive to interpersonal relationships; it is not surprising, therefore, that they were the parent who engaged in more talk with their children, even though the amount of time was quite small, an average of seven minutes a day.[14]

The greater intimacy with mothers, however limited, was also evident in the content of the conversations their adolescents had with them. These adolescents reported more conversations with their mothers than with their fathers about friends and family. Other research shows that mothers and adolescents communicate about a wider range of topics, including more personal issues.[15] The kind of confidence shared between Carol and Chloe was less common between fathers and adolescents. In the interview, 69 percent of the mothers reported talking about "feelings and emotions," at least weekly with the child (as compared to 40 percent of fathers). Adolescents typically perceive their mothers to be more empathic; they more often go to their mothers for social support.[16] Even boys feel their moms are more open to listening, though boys avoid the topic of sex and dating.[17]

Daily life, then, provides the average mother and adolescent a large amount of peripheral time together but only limited direct and personal interaction. In chapter 4 we reported the sobering statistic that the amount of time children spend with family declines by close to half between fifth and ninth grade. While fifth graders spend a large amount of time hanging out in the living room, kitchen, or family room, in the presence of family, older students are much more likely to disappear to their bedrooms.

The good news, however, is that though older kids spend much less time with mothers (and fathers) in group family situations, they spend as much time alone with them, as can be seen in figure 6.1. They also spend as many minutes in shared activities with their mothers, and just as much time talking with their mothers.[18] The decline with age is largely in peripheral time when they are in the same room but doing different activities.[19] Thus even though Chloe was probably spending much less time

Figure 6.1

AGE CHANGES IN ADOLESCENTS' AMOUNT
OF TIME SPENT WITH FAMILY MEMBERS

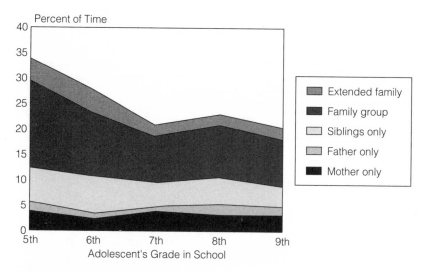

Based on reports from adolescents in two-parent
families from the young adolescent study.

lounging around in the kitchen or living room than she was a few years before, the amount of face-to-face, direct interaction with her mother was likely to be undiminished. For the average adolescent, one-on-one time holds constant.

What this means is that opportunities for direct personal access between mother and teenager do not diminish across this age period. The important issue, however, may not be the quantity of this access, but its typical emotional quality. And when we turn to examining the emotional quality of mother–adolescent interactions, we find that there are two sides to consider. There are really two relationships here: teens' experience of their mothers and mothers' experience of their teens.

How Teens Experience Their Mothers

Before adolescence, children's feelings toward their mother are usually positive and uncomplicated. This unambivalent warmth is illustrated by the feelings of Roger, the fifth-grade son of Glenna and Jerry, whose three-day marital conflict we related in chapter 5. Roger's parents described him as stubborn and periodically troublesome. Glenna said in the interview, "He's too bullheaded for his own good. We are talking about one donkey." But we did not see this intransigence in Roger's reports of his feelings toward her.

While Roger's parents were feuding with each other, he spent much of the time in the living room, kitchen, and back yard, seemingly oblivious to the tension in the house. Of the thirteen times the pager found him with Glenna across the week, he felt happy and warm toward her (as well as toward his father) in nearly all instances. Sunday morning, for example, while Glenna was making Jerry "into a piece of furniture," she helped Roger with his homework and he reported a positive mood and the greatest possible warmth toward her. Later in the afternoon, while Glenna folded laundry and watched the Bears game, Roger reported riding his bike outside and continued feelings of extreme warmth toward her.

Certainly there are moments when fifth graders get angry at their mothers. Roger was mad when Glenna asked him to turn off the TV to do a chore and on another day when she tried to get him to wear the new blue jeans that they had spent three hours shopping for. But rarely do these become anything but quickly resolved confrontations. Mothers get their way—Roger gave in and put on the jeans—and things are fine again. At bottom, children of this age accept their parents' right to wield authority over most domains.[20]

But as kids move into seventh and eighth grade, their feelings toward their parents become more complex and their emotional experience with them more mixed. Compared to Roger, the older students in our study reported fewer extreme positive and more negative emotions when with their mothers: they were less often exuberant and more often despondent, angry, or grouchy. These adolescents reported the majority of times with their mothers to be positive—talking, going out together, and sharing dinner were moderately pleasant. But occasions when the child felt "very happy" in the mother's company virtually disappeared, and occasions of unhappiness became much more frequent.[21]

What parents may not know is that this downward shift in adolescents' emotional states occurs in other parts of their lives as well. You may recall from chapter 4 that the transition to adolescence is associated with an overall decline in children's typical emotions. Careful analysis indicates that this drop is particularly great during adolescents' times with their parents. Their emotional experience with mothers and fathers does deteriorate even *relative to* each adolescent's average emotional state (see appendix 6.2). But why?

This decline in adolescents' emotional states with parents is partly due to increased competition from friends. Parents simply cannot offer the kind of cascading enjoyment adolescents are beginning to discover with peers, nor can they provide the captivating thrill of romantic encounters. Parents are becoming boring. They like different things. One mother reported that her daughter was becoming much more selective in the kinds of family activities she would take part in. In the past, anything with the family was fun for her, but now she was choosier—and taciturn if forced to take part in something she objected to.

This greater interest in peers can also create friction when it is at odds with what the mother thinks is good for the teen. During the week of the study, Becky, an eighth grader described by the interviewer as "feminine, sweet, and soft-spoken," was carried away by a burgeoning romance; in fact, she was moved to write "I love Art" on many of the beeper sheets. Hence this soft-spoken girl was enraged when her mother made her end a phone conversation with Art, and she was upset another time because her mother would not let her stay out late with him. Becky felt double-crossed because she thought her mother should understand what it is like to be in love. "I hate her," Becky wrote right after the phone incident, then added, "I love Art." Yet her mother felt responsible to set limits on the relationship.

Study after study has shown that conflict with mothers increases in adolescence, typically around the age of puberty.[22] When they were with their mothers, the seventh graders in our study reported feeling less friendly toward them than the fifth graders did, and the seventh graders felt their mothers were less friendly toward them. Conflict over potent issues, such as relationships, money, and access to the outside world, often increase at this age. And because mothers spend more time with their teens and are more involved in monitoring their lives, they are more likely than fathers to be on the front line of conflict over such issues.[23]

But it is not just that adolescents experience more tension between their desires and their mothers' rules. Their more advanced reasoning skills lead them to see parental regulation differently. Whereas Roger accepted his mother's authority, older kids in our society start to question it. They begin to assert that certain domains, such as the condition of their rooms, use of the phone, and homework, are outside their parents' jurisdiction. Becky got very upset because her mother woke her up at 1 P.M., when she hadn't gotten home from a field trip the night before until 2:30 A.M. She felt she was old enough to be able to sleep when she wanted. But most mothers do not experience parallel changes in their view of their jurisdiction; therefore large differences can open up between mothers and adolescents regarding who has say over many matters, and conflict increases.[24]

Young adolescents, like Becky, also begin to see some of their parents' rules as capricious and arbitrary.[25] They realize that there is no God-given reason why they need to be in by 9 or 10 P.M. A seventh grader in our study reported anger with his mother because she wouldn't extend his curfew. Such differences of opinion lead teens to see the issue as one of power and control. An eighth-grade girl complained repeatedly that her mother was "always making decisions for me," and a ninth-grade boy reported that his mother "tries to gain control of the whole situation over you, and just puts you down, saying, 'I'm older than you are and your elder, so do what I say.'"

In the eyes of teenagers, the authority of parents over some matters seems increasingly illegitimate. Mothers lose their halo of omnipotence and privileged power: they become just ordinary people, with faults of their own. Adolescents develop the critical skills to compare their mother to other mothers and to hold her accountable if she is overweight, alcoholic, or depressed. Thus an eighth-grade girl did not hesitate to comment on her mother's "stupidness" because "my dad and I had a hard time explaining the beeper study to her."

As a result of mothers' fall from grace, and adolescents' surer footing in the world of friends, teens in our study experienced a shift in their baseline perception of their relationship with their mothers. With age, their feelings of closeness to their mothers became more conditional, more situation-specific. Whereas for younger kids, being close was assumed, almost dogmatic, among older kids this feeling varied from hour to hour; it was up for grabs.

Even in a close relationship, such as that between Carol and Chloe, the adolescent reported significant fluctuations in warmth. As can be seen in figure 6.2, one moment Chloe felt warm to her mother, the next she felt cooler. On Thursday evening they had an intimate conversation about Chloe's close friend; on Saturday evening, Chloe was furious with her mother because of the chores she was asked to do.

With entry into adolescence, there are fewer occasions of unquestioned warmth. Across all the adolescents' beeper reports, feeling "very close" to their mother fell from 68 percent in the fifth grade to 28 percent in the eighth grade. Likewise, feeling "very distant" from her increased from 1 percent of all reports to 13 percent across the same period. Teens did not report feeling angry at her more often, just less consistently friendly and more often tense.

These mothers could no longer count on their adolescents to feel close and enjoy their company in the way they did in the past. One mother who delighted in how frequently her fifth grader came up to her and said "I need a hug" could expect to experience something much different a few years later. These teens swung between wanting their mother's special attention and being absorbed in a life that was separate from her. As the mother of an older girl said, "There are now more hills and valleys in our relationship."

The dilemma behind this is that just at an age when children need support to face the rocky changes in their lives, they are making it more difficult for the one who cares most about them to provide this support. Don't these changes put the adolescent at risk?

Mothers' Contribution to Adolescents' Well-Being

If we consider the features we saw in happy marital relationships— shared time with few negative emotions—then it appears these adolescents' relationships with their mothers were decaying, at least from the adolescents' point of view. Mothers and adolescents spent less total time together (although time in shared activities, including talk, did not decline), and the adolescents reported more negative emotions with their mothers than they did a few years earlier. If these were marriages, we might expect an unraveling of the relationship. And we might expect repercussions for the well-being of the child.

There is good news and bad news in what we find. The good news is that the amount and emotional quality of time these mothers and adolescents spent together were not related to the warmth or closeness in the relationship.[26] Kids who talked less with their mother or spent less time alone with her did not evaluate the relationship less favorably. In contrast with marital relationships, spending time together was not a major factor in the perceived strength of the bond between adolescent and mother.[27] Likewise, adolescents who experienced lesser happiness or unhappiness when with their mother (relative to the rest of their experience) did not differ in warmth or closeness to her.

The bad news, however, is that the amount and emotional quality of the time the adolescents spent with their mothers *were* related to the adolescents' well-being (see appendix 6.3). So even if the changes in teens' daily contact with mothers did not affect the relationship, they might put the child at greater risk for psychological problems.

For boys, it is the amount of interaction with their mothers that appears to be important. Boys who reported more time with their mothers, particularly time alone or talking, were rated as better adjusted by their

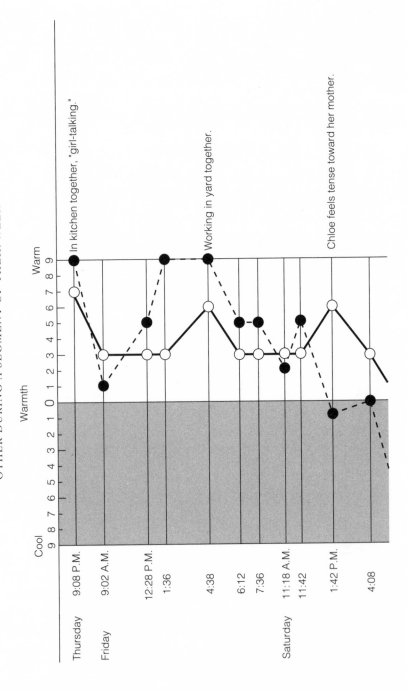

Figure 6.2

WARMTH CHLOE AND CAROL FEEL TOWARD EACH
OTHER DURING A SEGMENT OF THEIR WEEK

WARMTH CHLOE AND CAROL FEEL (continued)

Chloe is angry at her mother about chores;
Carol says Chloe is "short-tempered and ornery."

Watching TV together.

In church, singing together.

Chloe's friend is over, Carol going out.

At a christening together.

Saturday

6:22 P.M.

7:12

8:32

Sunday

9:04 A.M.

10:32

12:28 P.M.

2:38

4:42

6:34

9:12

○ Carol
● Chloe

teachers, were less depressed, and reported more positive daily emotions. Of course, there is a possibility of reverse causality here: a boy's maladjustment may deter interaction with his mother. But it is equally likely that spending time with his mother contributes to a boy's well-being. For example, we found that doing homework in the presence of parents was related to higher achievement in school.[28]

Among girls, it is not the amount of time they spend with their mother that counts. One very distressed girl, Roxanne, whom we will meet again in chapter 8, spent nearly all her nonschool time with her mother. What appears to be important is girls' emotional experience during this time. Girls who reported positive emotions with their mothers were less depressed and had healthier attitudes toward eating and body weight. Conversely, girls who experienced negative emotions with their mothers were more depressed and ill at ease with food and their bodies. Feeling consistently good in the presence of one's mother appears to be crucial to a girl's fundamental feelings about herself.

Our findings, then, suggest that adolescents' interactions with their mothers do make a difference in adolescents' negotiation of this volatile age period. The correlations here are not enormous, and clearly many other factors affect an adolescent's well-being. Nonetheless, these correlations affirm that mothers do have something to offer that can make a difference to their adolescents. Determining exactly what this "something" is, however, is a more difficult question and requires that we look first at mothers' experience of these interactions.

How Mothers Experience Their Teenagers

How do mothers feel interacting with a changeable adolescent who swings between avoiding and wanting her attention? Mothers come to the relationship from a different vantage point and thus have a different constellation of experiences. Becky's mother, Brenda, was a neat, well-spoken woman who juggled care of her two children with working three days a week as a sales clerk at K-mart. She expressed the strong commitment to caring for her two teenage daughters that is part of mothers' historic role, saying: "They need me now more than ever." But how did this credo shape her experience?

Caring has two meanings for mothers, and these can create a range of experiences. On the one hand, mothers are expected to direct and limit their children's behavior. Many of Brenda's interactions with Becky were from a position of knowledge and authority. When beeped together, both mothers and adolescents more often identified the mother as "the leader."[29] It was the mother who gave advice, drove the car, and supervised a child's performance of chores; in most conflicts we heard about, her will prevailed. When Brenda asked Becky to get off the phone, for example, Becky complied. Another girl said her mother would not let her go over to a boy's house because "she thinks the S thing is going on."

For mothers, caring also means being attentive to their child's inner world. In addition to being directive, mothers are expected to be sensitive to an adolescent's feelings. Historically, mothers have been cast as the one who understands the child more deeply than anyone else does. Thus the mothers in our study reported "worrying about" their adolescents on more beeper sheets than the fathers did. Their attentiveness is also suggested by how well they did when we asked them to guess their child's level of happiness when beeped together. We found that the mothers' guesses were not always right—much of the time, these parents were interacting with a child whose emotions were opaque, or disguised. Nonetheless, the mothers did better than the fathers, who did little better than chance.[30]

But what about *mothers'* moods? How does this combination of directive and attentive caring shape their feelings? Is motherhood as pleasurable and fulfilling as the child-care books of the past would have us believe?

If we look at all times when the mothers in our study were with their adolescent children, their emotions were an even mix of feelings above and below their baseline state. Unlike with their friends and husband, these mothers did not experience elevated mood in the presence of their children. Moments of pride and satisfaction were counterbalanced by the frustration and irritability generated by dealing with indifferent or uncooperative children.

A surprising finding, however, is that mothers' emotional states with their children do not change as children move into the adolescent years, even though teenagers' states, as we just discussed, become less positive (see appendix 6.2). Certainly mothers experience new sources of friction in the relationship: the mother of an eighth grader in our study commented that "she seems to be getting into a pattern of moodiness—she gets a little uppity and doesn't listen to me." Yet this increased friction appears to be balanced by mothers' greater enjoyment of a child who is less whiny, more responsible, and developing the ability to have more adultlike conversations. Several mothers made statements such as, "I enjoy the openness my children sometimes share with me. I enjoy discussions with them." Thus mothers' average emotional states with their adolescent do not decline, nor do mothers feel less warm toward their child.

What this means is that a disparity opens up in how mothers and adolescents experience their time together. Adolescents' moods are worsening, but mothers' are not.

This divergence between mothers' and adolescents' experience of their interactions is evident in Brenda's and Becky's experience of the phone incident. Whereas Becky was enraged that her mother told her to get off the phone, her mother did not even mention it. Becky was angry at her mother, but Brenda reported feeling happy and close to her daughter. Remarkably, parents and adolescents have been found to agree less than half the time on whether a conflict has even occurred.[31]

The same divergence occurred on Saturday when Brenda forced Becky to wake up at 1 in the afternoon. Becky was angry and irritable because she thinks her sleeping hours are none of her mother's business. But Brenda was happy and felt warm toward her daughter because Becky was telling her and her husband all about the field trip. Asked to guess Becky's mood, Brenda guessed that she was "quite happy." Apparently Becky did not let her mother know how upset she was. In fact, later that night Brenda commented on how nice it was that "she didn't yell at us even once today."

Such extreme differences in how mother and child experience the same moments suggest how surreal existence with an adolescent can be. Many studies show that parents and adolescents have widely differing perceptions of family life, and the discrepancies are greater during the child's early adolescence than any other age period.[32] Because parent and child approach their encounters from different vantage points, their emotional experiences differ, sometimes dramatically.[33] What the parent sees as an innocent comment, a teen such as Becky may experience as a major attack on her rights. Even if a teen does not complain right away, her anger may come out unexpectedly at other times.

In our data, and others', the parent usually has a more positive experience of family affairs than the adolescent does.[34] Whereas Becky saw the relationship as getting worse, Brenda felt that though it might be getting worse in some ways, it was getting better in others. Parents are more likely to put things in a favorable light.

But it can go the other way as well. On another occasion, Brenda was angry because Becky forgot to take her money for the book fair to school. Brenda was busy staining the garage and planting flowers on her day off from work; nonetheless, she delivered the money to school. For many women, their obligations to their child are unconditional; thus it is no surprise that mothers get the bad along with the good. Brenda summarized the duality of mothering as she was waiting one day for dinner to cook: "Children—you can't live with them or without them."

Suffering Adolescents' Bumps

The most difficult part of parenting adolescents, according to one sample of mothers, is dealing with their fluctuating moods.[35] Teens come home from school dragging the emotional residue of the day with them and, because of their role, mothers bear the brunt of these feelings.[36] As we have seen, teens swing unpredictably between excitement and despondency, and they swing between feeling warm and cold toward their mothers. Our data suggest that mothers are directly affected by these changing moods (see appendix 6.4), especially their daughters' moods.[37]

When adolescents are happy, their mothers are likely to become happy. For example, when an eighth-grade boy in our study was thrilled by his good performance in a speech for a science fair, his mother was also thrilled. In another case, a mother caught the bubbly mood of her daughter and friend as they chatted about swimsuits while shopping. When we asked mothers in the interview what their child did that made their mood more positive, they emphasized "the child's being in a good mood" and "just being together" (see appendix 6.5). It is not that mothers are so impressionable that they pick up any emotion in the room. Rather, the adolescent's happiness affirms that they have lived up to the high expectations we hold for mothers. One commented, "It makes me feel good because I feel that he feels like he's loved." The child's happiness provides proof that he or she has been well cared for.

Children in positive moods are also likely to be kinder more and cooperative.[38] Thus transmission of positive mood can occur when a child's good mood makes him or her attentive to the mother's reality. One mother said her daughter made her happy when "she acts interested in what I do; when she's interested in me as a person rather than just 'mom.'" Transmission of positive moods also occurs when the child's magnanimous mood simply leads her to do what she is supposed to do. "When she doesn't have the last word to say—when she just does what she's supposed to without sassing." Another said, "When he's happy and doesn't leave any aches and pains."

Adolescents' negative moods get transmitted to mothers for similar reasons. Our expectation that mothers be caring can lead them to adopt an adolescent's negative state as her own. One reported getting upset when her son "doesn't give himself credit for anything, when he 'downs' himself." Mothers pick up negative moods when the child's behavior or mood reflects badly on their success in the maternal role. Often the transmission of negative emotions results from the child's irritable or intransigent behavior. Negative moods make children less compliant. In numerous instances the mothers in our study reported being angry because a child would not do what she was told. For example, "She is asked to do something and she doesn't do it after two or three times." And sometimes mothers get upset because their children resist their attempts to care for them. Thus one mother became angry because her daughter had had a fight with her friend and would not talk about it. "I got mad," this mother said. "I like to talk about problems and she likes to just sit there and be mad for awhile." In a similar situation, an overinvolved mother said: "I could kill her; she gets bothered by the stupidest things. Half the time they are not important."

In most instances, our data suggest, transmission is one-way. Mothers pick up adolescents' emotions; they feel what their teenager feels. But adolescents are less likely to pick up their mothers' emotions. Other research concurs that a mother's daily hassles generally do not affect the adolescent, but the adolescent's hassles do affect her.[39] Having been socialized to see caring as central to their identities, mothers are at once receptive and vulnerable to the emotions of those they care for. The cost of their intense, attentive parenting is susceptibility to the ups and downs in children's lives.

Yet it is not strictly a one-way street. While fluctuations in mothers' immediate emotional states usually do not have an effect on adolescent children, there are larger relationships between a mother's global emotional state and that of the adolescent. Mother and adolescent are interrelated as an emotional system, which sometimes works for the benefit of both and sometimes does not.

MOTHER–ADOLESCENT SYSTEMS

"If Mamma Ain't Happy, Ain't Nobody Happy" reads the T-shirt of one mother we know. The mother is often the "emotional broker" in the family, the person who is most attentive to the emotional needs of others.[40] Though her immediate mood may not affect her child, her underlying emotional buoyancy, her inner reserve of emotional energy, *is* related to the young adolescent's adjustment. As the child changes and puts new demands on the relationship, the mother's emotional well-being is an important determinant of how well the two weather the changes. In some families we see a pattern of irritability and depression in mothers that is related to the child's poorer adjustment; in others we see mothers who seem to be resilient in the face of the stressful daily demands of their life situation, and in these cases their adolescents fare better.

Depressed Mother/Distressed Adolescent

Rob and his mother, Rita, who fought over dinner and cards, are an example of a depressed mother–adolescent system. When together, both reported high irritability, and both reported the relationship to be cold and distant. Rob attributed their difficulty to his mother's depression (as well as to issues with his father that we shall discuss in the next chapter). According to Rob, Rita took an overdose of medication several years ago and subsequently sought psychiatric treatment, which she now was talking about resuming. Indeed, Rita reported many symptoms of depression, low self-esteem, and chronically dysphoric moods.

Our data support Rob's underlying premise: that mothers' depression affects their daily transactions with their children. In the families in our study where the mother was more depressed, mother and teenager reported being together half as often as in other families. They appeared to avoid each other's company. Furthermore, when these mothers and adolescents *were* together, they both frequently felt irritable and angry (see appendix 6.6). In fact, these adolescents showed a drop in mood when entering the presence of their depressed mother.[41]

A substantial body of research indicates that the parenting of depressed women is impaired. They feel less competent, and they are less energetic and less actively engaged in parenting. Whereas the typical mother is emotionally expressive, the depressed mother interacts with less positive feeling, speaks less, exchanges gazes less, and responds more slowly and less often to her child.[42] Much of this follows directly from what we know about negative emotions. Depressed emotions make any parent more self-focused and hypersensitive to negative events. Parents in negative moods expect negative behavior from their child and are more likely to view the child's noncompliance as deliberate.[43] It is not surprising, then, that chronically depressed mothers act in a more irritable manner with their children and are more punitive.[44] Above a certain aggravation threshold, some parents suddenly turn from a kind, caring Dr. Jekyll into an angry and dictatorial Mr. Hyde.

Such parenting can be expected to have a long-term influence on children. One set of authors concludes: "There is no longer any doubt about the deleterious effects of maternal depression on children."[45] This may account for our finding that mothers with chronically low moods have children with significantly lower self-esteem who are themselves more likely to be depressed.[46] Others have also found that school-age children of depressed parents generally show higher levels of behavioral and emotional problems.[47] These findings, then, suggest that mothers' depression leads to poorer parenting, which leads to troubled children.

To blame mothers, however, misses the point. It would be unfair to talk about Rita's depression without considering her total life situation, including the role Rob plays, and may have played since infancy, in making her miserable.

To begin with, motherhood itself has been shown to cause depression in women, beginning with the child's birth. As mothering is structured in our society, depression is an occupational hazard.[48] One study of preschool boys found that their mothers experienced an average of twenty hassles with them per hour, with this rate rising to forty-five per hour for problem boys.[49] In adolescence, the child's inattention, emotionality, and rebelliousness put additional stress on their caretakers,[50] and because mothers assume the most responsibility for children, they bear the brunt of this stress. Mothers' but not fathers' emotional well-being is related to the intensity of daily adolescent–parent conflict.[51]

The evidence further suggests that depression is particularly likely to develop in a mother whose child has an unfavorable temperament. When we look at the young adolescents of depressed mothers in our study, we get clues that these are difficult kids. They reported feeling more irritable and angry not just during interactions with their mothers, but across all contexts (see appendix 6.6). This suggests that their poorer adjustment may be the result of deep-seated personality traits. Rob was hostile to his friends, and to us: halfway through the week he wrote "KISS MY ASS" in his beeper book, then quit filling out our forms. Of course, a counterargument can be made that Rob's hostility may have developed *from* repeated interaction with his depressed mother.

Studies that have attempted to figure out which comes first, depressed mother or difficult child, are not fully conclusive. On the one hand, it is clear that depression is contagious. Following a phone conversation with a depressed person, ordinary research subjects in one study became significantly more depressed, anxious, hostile, and rejecting.[52] College students living with depressed roommates have been found to become gradually more depressed themselves.[53] The neonatal specialist Tiffany Field has found that infants of depressed mothers can acquire a depressed mood style as early as three months.[54] Longitudinal studies, however, have suggested that causality goes both ways. There is a reciprocal process at work: the mother's negative mood and the child's difficult behavior feed off each other.[55]

The most convincing descriptions of how these mother–child systems develop come from the research of the psychologist Gerald Patterson, which shows mothers' depression and boys' antisocial behavior developing together over time. Difficulty often starts in early childhood from multiple origins: a mother's lack of parental skills, her depression, family economic stress, absence of support from the father, and the child's difficult temperament. These initial factors increase the mother's and child's irritable behavior toward each other. As a result, both experience frustration and rejection in the relationship and find that the only way they can get what they want is through coercion. Thus a cycle of coercive interaction gets established, with each alternating in the roles of aggressor and victim. The long-term effects are increased depression in the mother and the boy's use of coercion in other spheres, leading to disruption in schoolwork and peer relations, which may lead to affiliation with deviant peers and ultimately delinquency.[56]

In Rob and Rita we see a well-established cycle of coercive interactions. He acts up, she raises her voice at him, he becomes more intransigent, she pouts. Rita feels too embattled to see beyond Rob's behavior and recognize his needs. Both are too hardened to pay attention to what the other might be thinking or feeling. Given this coercive pattern, it is not surprising that Rob is depressed, achieving poorly in school, and has difficulties with friends, and that two years after the study he reported a pattern of delinquent behavior and worsening school grades. His learned pattern of hostility appeared to have carried over to his life outside the family.

In mothers' relationships with sons, the kind of overt conflict displayed between Rob and Rita is common. In fact, this may explain why we found the amount of time shared between mothers and sons to be related to the sons' well-being: when they have conflicts, they may avoid each other. In relationships between mothers and daughters, we find some of the same elements, but with significant variations.

Living Through One's Daughter

Compared to the mother–son attachment, the mother–daughter attachment is often deeper and more intense. Girls typically have a stronger identification with their mothers than boys do and possess greater interest and capacity for an intimate relationship with her.[57] Girls, our data show, talk more with their mothers than boys do and are more likely to share their inner experience. When relations are good, daughters are capable of feeling empathy for their mother, and they tend to be better adjusted than when relations are not. We reported earlier in this chapter that when daughters felt happy during time with their mothers, their global emotional well-being was higher. When mothers are overinvolved, however, daughters may find themselves caught in a web of emotional dependencies where voicing their own needs and maintaining a sense of inner vitality are difficult.

Eleanor was an empathic full-time mother of three who appeared to have little to fill her time. The first morning she was beeped she reported that she was "not doing anything in particular" and was thinking about cleaning her ring. Another morning she watched *Peggy Sue Got Married* on TV. In the interview she admitted she was "in a rut," and, like Rita, scored high on our depression scale. The interviewer described her as nervous, self-effacing, anxious to please, and overinvolved in her three daughters.

Eleanor felt close to her oldest daughter, Erin, an underachieving seventh grader. Erin, however, did not feel close to her mother. On the beeper forms Erin often did not acknowledge her mother's presence, even when they were watching TV in the same room; when she did report being with Eleanor, Erin's mood was low. Erin was happier away from the home sphere—at school, with friends, and during swimming—although she also found valuable refuge in her bedroom, where she read novels and listened to Madonna and Cyndi Lauper, two rock idols who provided models of defiance and autonomy.

Eleanor's and Erin's realities diverged sharply, as several incidents during the week demonstrated. When Erin learned Wednesday night that her former best friend had been hospitalized for a drug overdose, she was upset, though not so upset she could not make a joke about his acne. Eleanor, in contrast, was profoundly concerned, filling the margins of the beeper page with worries about what she should have done to prevent it and anger at the boys' stepparents, the school, and others involved. Whereas Erin called him "zit-face," her mother said he was "a wonderful young man." Eleanor responded to the situation by feeling closer to her daughter; Erin responded by feeling *closed* to her mother and wrote, "My dad understands me better." Eleanor's attempt to be caring and empathic only alienated her daughter for reasons that became apparent as the week progressed.

The next day there was a swimming meet, and this time their divergence took a more antagonistic form. Before school they had a fight about Erin's clothing. In her words, "Mom was telling me what to wear." Then at the meet, Eleanor reported being "extremely angry" because Erin was "talking instead of concentrating on swimming. I was trying to get her to concentrate on her event. She was distracting others, which was not good for the team." Erin was distressed by her mother's intrusiveness and would have been much happier had her mother not come.

The acrimony between them continued as they rode home with the rest of the family. When beeped, Eleanor was upbraiding her daughter about failing to bring home medical forms for swimming, expressing anger because Erin "doesn't listen." Erin said the topic of conversation was: "that I'm a rotten child." She also wrote, "I hate her," and explained that she felt distant from her mother because "she hates me." In an eerie reminder of the previous day, she added: "I want to kill myself!!"

This conflict is similar to the one between Rita and Rob in that neither seemed to be accurately perceiving the other's point of view. Eleanor claimed, "She deliberately doesn't listen or is inconsiderate." Like Rita's, Eleanor's capacity for empathizing with her child appeared to be exhausted. Rather than trying to understand the circumstances that might have led to Erin's behavior, she attributed it to moral failure in Erin, an attribution that undoubtedly inflamed the conflict.

What is different is that Erin was less able than Rob to speak up for herself and instead turned the conflict inward, threatening her own life. That night she also decided to quit swimming, "because of my mom." Whereas Rob tried to coerce Rita with biting humor, Erin felt she could not directly oppose her mother and thus resorted to these self-destructive gestures, which punished her mother where she was most vulnerable. By hurting herself, Erin threatened Eleanor's main purpose and obsession in life: being a good mother.

Such emotional enmeshment is more common in mother–daughter than mother–son relationships. Compared to boys, girls are found to be more connected with and less emotionally autonomous from their mothers.[58] Because girls are being socialized to become mothers themselves, they find it harder to tell their mothers to back off. For their part, mothers are more critical of adolescent girls than of boys and interrupt them more.[59] As a result of this greater enmeshment, mother–daughter conflicts occur more frequently and last longer than those in other parent–child dyads.[60]

In the case of Eleanor and Erin, the problem stemmed partly from Eleanor's overdependence on her children for gratification. One night, she reported that the happiest event of the day was that "everyone came home safely." Another day, she reported feeling happy because her youngest daughter greeted her with a "big hug and kiss." In an otherwise empty and despondent life, her sole source of meaning was her role as parent. Not surprisingly, we find that depressed mothers are more readily affected by their children's moods.[61]

Asked what Erin did that made her happy, Eleanor said, "If she wants to talk." Eleanor would like nothing more than to be Erin's confidante, but Erin said: "Whenever I think about her I get a chill." Her mother's dependence on her conflicted with her own needs for autonomy, and the neediness stemming from her mother's underlying despondency was deeply threatening to her own sense of well-being.

Healthy mother–daughter relationships are close and caring, but require some measure of mutual autonomy.[62] In cases where mothers and daughters were emotionally symbiotic—both tending to feel the same thing at the same time—we found greater depression in both.[63] Teens seek more emotional autonomy, but some mothers find it painful and difficult to grant because their sense of meaning, their own daily well-being, comes from their children. As another mother said: "She's growing up and I don't want her to. She wants to be more independent and I still want her to be my baby."

Mothers' Well-Being and Adolescents' Well-Being

Rita and Eleanor are victims of what we have called Paradox #1: They are overinvested in a role that does not bring consistent gratification. Although traditional beliefs in our culture hold that homemaking and mothering make a woman happy, in day-to-day life many women do not find them rewarding: they find them frustrating, irritating, and empty. To make matters worse, mothers of adolescents are directly exposed to their fluctuating moods: mothers' commitment to caring requires them to deal with the wide range of strong feelings their children are likely to bring home.

Given that child rearing is inherently stressful, the useful question is not why some mothers are depressed, but rather why all mothers aren't. What happens in the lives of some mothers that allows them to be buoyant and transcend the trap of Paradox #1?

For many women in our study, buoyancy is gained by contact with friends. The chance to share with like-minded souls provides an uplifting experience that gets many mothers through the week. Those mothers who have active relationships with close friends have higher self-esteem, which is in turn related to more positive family relationships and better-adjusted children.[64] When mothers get together with their friends, they often talk about the challenges children create, and, in the process, provide mutual support for the difficult task they have. One mother described how much her mental state improved when she moved back to the neighborhood where she grew up because now many of her friends were right next door.

For some women a similar lift to their morale is provided by paid employment. As we noted in chapter 3, mothers generally feel happier at work than at home. And while they pay the cost of a 6 o'clock crash each evening, employed women feel more accepted, less often weak, and less depressed across the different contexts of their lives. If the job is satisfying, and not too stressful and hurried, if they have a supportive husband, and if they want to be working, employment has a positive effect on women's well-being.

Employment also makes women more resilient to the ups and downs in their adolescents' lives. We found that employed women were less likely to be influenced by their adolescents' moods.[65] Other research also indicates that mothers who are invested in their jobs are less susceptible to being buffeted by events in their adolescents' lives.[66]

Women's experience of employment can have a beneficial influence on their children as well. Contrary to popular belief, our data show that employed mothers do not spend less time with their teenage children, and they report sharing the same activities.[67] One mother said, "You make more use of the time you have with your children."

Coming home from work was one situation in which the mother's emotional state did appear to influence her child's mood, and the effect was usually positive. When the mother had a good day at work, it often raised the child's mood when she got home.[68] In fact, we found that on days when employed mothers went to their jobs, their teens tended to be happier in the evening.[69] Perhaps because of this positive emotional influence, adolescents with employed mothers are sometimes found to be better adjusted than those whose mothers are full-time homemakers.[70]

Whether the influence of a mother's job is beneficial depends, of course, on the mother and on the job. Some jobs can be terribly draining, especially when a mother receives little assistance from her husband at home. We recently overheard a mother rebuke a request from her son, saying, "I've had a really stressful day; I don't need any more stress from you!" In our larger sample we found that young adolescents whose mothers worked part-time reported slightly better emotional adjustment, perhaps because these mothers were less likely to get drained in this way.[71]

Other studies, however, have found that it is mothers who are more satisfied with their constellation of roles, whatever they might be, whose children are better adjusted.[72] What seems to be most important is whether a mother's daily activities, be they communion with friends, volunteer work, or employment, give her a sense of personal meaning and balance.

Rolling with the Changes

Adolescents and mothers, we have said, come to their relationships with disparate tasks, which can set them at odds. Mothers are trying to care for a teenager who, in our society, is often trying not to be cared for. Scholars of adolescence, however, have begun to recognize that parents and teens really have a joint task. Most teenagers do not want total independence from their parents—connection to them continues to be important not only in adolescence, but in adulthood as well. Likewise, while mothers may fantasize about retaining the closeness they had with their baby, most appreciate the need of teenagers to become more separate emotionally. The joint task, then, is to renegotiate their degree of connection/separation in a way that is appropriate to the adolescent's developmental level as well as the parent's well-being.[73]

Easier said than done, of course. It is one thing for detached scholars to set these high expectations. It is another thing for a parent and adolescent to continue to see eye to eye as they endure all the ups and downs of daily life. A few families in our study, however, provide examples of this renegotiation taking place.

Luke and Lorraine, for instance, had their share of disagreements. Luke was a tall, early-maturing seventh grader who was getting interested in girls and seeking new privileges from his parents. Lorraine was a reflective and spiritual full-time homemaker, whom we introduced at the end of chapter 3. Before school on Friday Luke had an argument with her about how late he could stay at a party that night, and he reported feeling angry with her all morning. But after school they talked through his interests and her concerns and agreed that he would be allowed to stay one hour later than his usual curfew. They both felt good about the resolution, and when he was beeped at 9:26 that evening while dancing, he reported an exuberantly positive mood along with warm feelings toward his mother.

Luke and Lorraine also had a disagreement about housework on Sunday afternoon. Along with his new privileges, she believed he should assume some responsibilities as a member of the family. "There are a lot of chores that need to be done and little time." But Luke and his dad wanted to go to a movie. At first they did not take her seriously; she complained, "They don't seem to be listening to my input." Rather than caving in and doing the work herself, however, Lorraine asserted herself. She said, "When I'm angry, people know it. I yell, storm, and slam doors." Father and son went to the movie, but when they got back they reached a consensus that the "guys" would clean out the family room. Rather than letting herself be exploited, Lorraine insisted that Luke carry his weight, and, ultimately, everybody felt good about the solution.

Both Luke and Lorraine saw their relationship getting better, expressing a level of agreement that was rare across the fifty-five families. In separate interviews, Luke said that the relationship had improved, because "I have become more sensitive to her needs"; she said, "I now see him as a person. I don't worry about him anymore." Then she added, "We are much more open with each other and honest about angry and happy feelings," an improvement she attributed to "both of us growing and changing." They had a sense of connectedness—they talked regularly—but they also were learning to respect each other's separate lives.

Why did this relationship seem to be working whereas others were struggling? Obviously there are many, many factors that enter in. Luke was a mature boy who described himself as "helpful, reliable, and responsible." Nonetheless, we think it significant that both Luke and Lorraine had balanced lives, with meaningful activities besides those in the family. Luke, like most adolescents, was absorbed in friends, as well as sports and his schoolwork. Lorraine was deeply involved with a community of friends and was going back to school to get a master's degree. Her school meant that "responsibilities around the house pile up; housework is so much work. But school is so much fun." She felt "stretched and happy." She was fond of her children but appreciated "that I'm not their whole world and they're not my total world." Her base of experience outside the family gave her the emotional autonomy to stand up to her son, without caving in, becoming irritable, or getting overinvolved.

The adolescent psychiatrist Stuart Hauser argues for the importance of "enduring engagement" between parents and teenagers. A parent should be attentive to a child's concerns, while being flexible and emotionally objective.[74] Adolescents, he writes, inevitably provoke strong feelings in their mothers and fathers, but the sign of a mature parent is the ability to contain these feelings, to allow the relationship to be dictated not by the parents' emotions, but by the adolescent's changing needs. Our findings suggest that when mothers have a more balanced life, when they have investments outside the family, they are better able to provide this objectivity.

Chloe's mother, Carol, is another example of this kind of enduring engagement. There was certainly much in Chloe's life that Carol could worry about. It was Chloe's last week of junior high and she and friends were excited about graduation and the graduation party. Boys also occupied Chloe's attention: at one point she was very excited because a boy had signed a note in her yearbook with "Love"; at another she felt happy "because Darrin is in love with me."

But Chloe's daily emotional swings appeared to have little effect on Carol. She helped with the arrangements for the graduation party, but was not overly involved or affected by Chloe's states. Again, we think this has partly to do with the balance in Carol's life. She was not particularly satisfied with her job as a part-time nurses' aide. In fact, at one time she complained: "I hate the way they do things here." But she was invested and the people there were friendly. Carol also gained satisfaction from the two horses the family kept in the stable at the back of their lot. One beep found her happy and cheerful, shoveling horse manure.

Perhaps because of the diverse sources of reward in her life, Carol approached her relationship with Chloe with equanimity. Whereas full-time mothers, such as Eleanor, can experience adolescents' movement toward independence as a threat to their primary role, employed mothers like Carol are more likely to encourage autonomy in their children.[75] Comparing her life now to a period of unemployment, Carol said: "I think I'm a better mother now, because when you are with them all the time, you're not the same. You get tense and grouchy." Mothers like Carol are engaged, but they are able to let their adolescents' ups and downs roll off them.

Carol and Chloe did not spend a lot of time doing things together, but their emotional states when with each other were usually positive. They had occasional disagreements; in fact, once Chloe reported feeling warm toward her parents "because I wasn't getting yelled at." But Chloe nearly always reported feeling "relaxed with" her mother. She appeared to have a feeling that her mother was accessible when she needed her. She was available, but she was not intrusive or emotionally dependent. They had a relationship in which both appeared to be successfully renegotiating their behavior and mutual expectations.

Surprisingly, we find that adolescents enjoy talking with their parents as much as they enjoy talking with their friends.[76] But Hauser finds that some parents discourage their adolescents from conversation by judging, sabotaging, or distracting them from expressing their views. When parents speak in a way that encourages and enables independent opinions, adolescents are more positively engaged. Adolescents like Chloe want to be able to talk to their mothers about events in school and with friends, but on their terms, and when they want to talk—which we found sometimes to be first thing in the morning or late at night.

In early adolescence, the kind of rapport shown between Luke and Lorraine, Carol and Chloe is rare. At this age the developmental changes that allow deep rapport with friends have not yet carried over to interactions with parents. Young adolescents have a limited capacity to empathize with their mothers or understand the relationship from their point of view.

For many kids, however, this begins to happen in middle adolescence. They develop the capacity to be more attuned to their mother's point of view, and as a result interactions become more mutual and the strain that often characterizes relationships between mothers and young adolescents eases. Our data suggest that even by ninth grade, adolescents' emotional experience with their mothers begins to improve.[77] In middle adolescence, kids and their mothers begin to make progress in renegotiating their relationship in a way that allows separateness and togetherness for both of them.

MOTHERHOOD IN THE TRENCHES

From birth, mother and child are cast in a loving, intense, usually warm, and sometimes conflicted drama. The emotional experience of each partner shapes the other's, as the relationship and the two people develop and change. When the child reaches adolescence, this bond between mother and child faces its ultimate test. The child's reality shifts dramatically, requiring the relationship to adjust or suffer the consequences.

What we have seen is that a mother's traditional role can make it harder for her to make this transition. Her uncompromising commitment to caring for her children can lead her to become overinvolved in the hour-to-hour ups and downs of an adolescent's life. The depression related to the dreary, unrewarded tasks of housework can make her more vulnerable to being buffeted by an adolescent's moods and life changes. Our findings suggest that those mothers who have outside interests—in a fulfilling job or other activities—may be better able to weather the storms.

Adolescents demand a measure of independence, yet at the same time they need their parents' steady support as they face the many changes and stresses of growing up. Beneath their quest for separation, most teens still feel a desire to be understood, to maintain the special connection they have known with their mothers. Parents' discerning attention is part of what makes the family a valued arena of comfort.

Adolescents' relationships with their fathers are also important. Yet because of differences in the structure of fathers' lives, these relationships have a different cast. And just as a mother's traditional role can handicap her interactions with adolescent children, so too can a father's traditional role put him at a disadvantage, as we will see in the next chapter.

CHAPTER 7

Adolescents and Fathers:
FUN AND AVOIDANCE

If thirteen-year-old Rob's relationship with his mother was strained, his relationship with his father was in crisis, at least from Rob's point of view. Though his father, Bud, reported feeling warm and close to Rob, Rob felt extremely cold toward and distant from his father. "It's like he doesn't care any more," Rob said. One night Bud, a machinist, angered Rob because he worked late and did not call: "Then he walks in, like nothing happened. I asked him why and he started yelling. He is really starting to get violent." Rob felt alienated from his dad—yet there was also a sense that he really wanted his dad's attention.

Abundant evidence shows that a father's relationship with a child can make an important contribution to the child's growth and development. When fathers are warm, close, and involved, their children demonstrate greater internal control and social maturity.[1] Past research suggests that children in two-parent families do better in school, particularly in quantitative skills, and, on average, have better mental health than children in families where the father is absent.[2] Yet the traditional father, a label that fits many of the men in our study, is often criticized for not being warm or involved. Popular voices lament the "absent father" who, at least in memory, was never there at key moments.[3]

Early adolescence is certainly one of these key times: it is when children are experiencing fundamental changes in their lives. Many fathers, however, are not very tuned in to these changes. Adolescents usually report their fathers to be less sensitive to what's going on in their lives than their mothers are; daughters especially describe their fathers as colder, less nurturant, and less caring.[4] By middle adolescence, most teenagers feel their fathers know them less well than they did earlier, a feeling they do not have about their mothers.[5] To make matters worse, many fathers seem unaware of this distance. There is what might be called a "closeness gap," with many fathers, like Bud, feeling close to adolescents who do not feel close to them.[6] Fathers appear to be the weak link in the companionate family.

But rather than castigating men, we need to understand the factors governing their daily relationships with their children. How does their reality, as family wage earner, shape and constrain their ability to relate to the volatile and vulnerable reality of young adolescents? As we look at our emotional snapshots of daily life, we see that many fathers in these two-parent families are trying to be involved parents—but they are often missing the boat. What opportunities does daily life provide for men to be connected to their adolescents, for this important link in the family to become more vital?

Fathers' Reality and Fathers' Role

Critical portrayals of fathers do them an injustice unless they understand men's behavior within the historical evolution of the father role, one that limited their involvement as parents and discouraged empathy. Colonial fathers were involved, but often from a stern, authoritarian posture. The Puritans believed that fathers were called by God to enforce absolute obedience, with the goal of "breaking the child's will."[7] Agrarian fathers of the nineteenth century had the role of "moral teacher." Children worked under their direction in the fields or as part of the family economy, and it was the father's job to ensure they were prepared to be upstanding adults in the community.[8]

As families left the farm and fathers became the wage earner and family provider, their daily lives became reorganized in a way that greatly restricted their time with children. Fathers' disciplinary role continued: in the 1950s, at the crest of the father-provider family, 77 percent of dads in one survey reported involvement in "teaching children right from wrong."[9] Their participation in daily child care, however, was minimal—the same survey found only 6 percent involved in "seeing that children get dressed in the morning." One parent advice book commented that as far as their children were concerned, many fathers were either "guests or ghosts" in the home—they were either a privileged patriarch who had to be catered to or a shadowy figure who was rarely seen.[10]

Fathers' time and emotion, as we saw in chapter 2, are still structured by this historical breadwinner role. A great majority of couples still see the husband's primary responsibility to be providing a secure income for the family. This is not a task that brings him immediate happiness, but it is a role that he has internalized as his own; men often become addicted to and subsumed by it. Because of this internalized obligation, researchers find, fathers are less willing than mothers to adjust their work schedules to accommodate children's needs.[11]

Men's interactions with their adolescent children, then, occur in the windows of opportunity permitted by their jobs. On weekdays, the typical father in our suburban sample left for work at 6:45 A.M. and did not return home until 5:30 P.M. These hours meant most fathers had little chance for contact with their children in the morning, because their children did not get up until 7, on average. And opportunity for interaction in the evening was limited to a few hours. The largest chance these fathers had to interact with their children was on the weekend. In fact, half (47 percent) of the time they reported being with their adolescent occurred on weekends, with 28 percent on Sunday. Yet even on weekends, unexpected events came up at their jobs that forced some fathers to cancel activities with their families. Although fatherhood is not just the "Sunday institution" it was at the turn of the century, men's interactions with their children are still limited by their jobs.

Within these constraints, however, the amount of time men spend with their children is not inconsequential. Most of the fathers in our study wanted to be involved; they wanted to be good parents. In total, these men reported being in the presence of their adolescent child for 27 percent of their waking hours. This was not dramatically less than the 36 percent reported by mothers, and it was about half of men's time that was not committed to their jobs.[12] Fathers *are* clocking in hours in the vicinity of their adolescent children. Historical data show that contemporary fathers in two-parent families are spending somewhat more time with their children than fathers of the recent past did.[13] But we need to probe further and ask, What happens during this time?

TIME TOGETHER

In chapter 6 we described a scolding that thirteen-year-old Erin received from her mother in the car, which led Erin to write in her booklet, "I want to kill myself!!" Erin's father, Ed, was present and was beeped at that moment—he was driving the car—but he mentioned nothing of this incident when he had the chance to fill out his booklet a few minutes later. During that week, Ed, an accountant at a downtown insurance company, was looking for a new job, so he was preoccupied. Some research has shown that when fathers and adolescents are together in the presence of mothers, the father is often passive and disengaged.[14] Many men still have a "ghost-like" presence in the family.

Much of the time the fathers in our study spent with their adolescents involved this kind of shadowy presence. These fathers did interact directly with their adolescent children, but we found it difficult to sharply define when they were really engaged. For one thing, as with other family relationships, the adolescents and fathers often disagreed on when they were together: they concurred for only half the time that one reported being with the other (see appendix 6.1).[15] For another thing, the mothers were also present for a great majority of the times that the fathers and adolescents were together (77 percent by the adolescents' report), and, as with Ed, Dad may be a marginal presence in such situations. The amount of time these fathers actually spent alone with their adolescent was remarkably small, twelve minutes a day.[16] In short, a father's report of being with or near his child did not necessarily mean he was interacting with or parenting the child. Research by others confirms that fathers see themselves as "available" to children very often (more so than children see them as available), but direct interaction is less common and rarely do fathers see themselves as "responsible."[17]

When we zero in on times that the fathers and teens shared the same activity, leisure was the most common venue. Watching TV, a pastime that may involve little interaction, accounted for 40 percent of this shared time; an additional 6 percent was spent in active recreation (see appendix 7.1). Critics charge that divorced fathers are often "Disneyland dads" who spend much of their parenting time in leisure activities, yet this is a pattern for many married fathers as well.[18] One mother commented that her husband's relationship with their son revolved entirely around sports.

This leisure venue, of course, follows from men's priorities for their homelife: in addition to spending time with the kids, they want to engage in activities that help them relax from the rigors of their breadwinning role. Many men see fathering as a voluntary activity. A father can enjoy playing a game of ping-pong with their child, but if he does not feel like being engaged, he may withdraw behind the newspaper or retire to watch sports or work in the yard. Unlike mothers, fathers face few sanctions if their jobs prevent them from being engaged parents.[19] Even on weekends, during times fathers and mothers are equally available, fathers' participation is often seen as voluntary.[20]

Certainly most fathers engage in activities other than leisure with their children. They spend time together eating, doing household tasks, or doing the teens' homework. On Sunday, Ed reported cleaning up the kitchen with Erin. The pager found another father shopping for a basketball backboard with his daughter and another having his son help with tasks at his lab.

But the activity that was noticeably rare among the fathers and adolescents in our study was personal conversation. Dads and teens reported few occasions when talk was their main activity—it accounted for an average of just three minutes a day—and the content of these conversations was more restricted in scope and less personal than of those between mothers and adolescents.[21] Whereas mothers periodically chatted with their adolescents about personal, family, and peer issues, the most frequent topic of conversation when adolescents and fathers were alone together was, not surprisingly, sports. In the interview, almost half the fathers, compared to 12 percent of the mothers, said their child "rarely" talked with them about their feelings or emotions.

This absence of deep conversation can be partly attributed to fathers' historically evolved role. The legacy of moral teacher and absent wage earner has not provided men with the rich tradition of involvement and nurturant concern that mothers have inherited. Many men do not know how to be emotionally sensitive, such as one father who reported feeling distraught and embarrassed when his eighth-grade daughter started crying at a school spelling bee. For many fathers, empathy and personal conversation with an adolescent are outside their realm of experience. Beginning at the child's birth, many fathers cede this side of parenting to their wives.

To these fathers' credit, at least, the amount of time spent in shared activities does not decline as children move across the volatile early adolescent years covered by our study. Likewise, the small fragment of time spent talking and one on one does not shrink with age for the average father (see figure 6.1). The channel for daily contact does not diminish. Fathers' presence in the adolescents' day-to-day lives—albeit ghostlike sometimes and often recreational—is at least steady in quantity across this age span.

But what is its emotional quality? By fathers' own reports, they are anything but distant and uninvolved with their children.

WHAT DADS EXPERIENCE

Fathers portray themselves differently from how others perceive them. Although Ed seemed unengaged in the conflict in the car between his wife and daughter, he reported feeling quite close to Erin, then and at other times. Fathers experience themselves as engaged parents. In fact, when with their children, the fathers in our study reported feeling greater warmth toward them than the mothers did.[22] Fathers also reported more favorable emotions during these times: they were more likely to feel happy and less likely to feel irritable when with their children than the mothers were.

In these fathers' daily lives, occasions with their children were among their most positive moments. Many of the happiest times occurred when the whole family was together: eating dinner, watching TV, or gathering with friends or relatives. These fathers often described these occasions in warm, glowing terms. "Everyone is good-natured and kidding around," one father wrote. "It is a rare treat to all be together," said another. They reported even higher average emotion when they were alone with their adolescent. One dad, for example, reported ebullient moods when his son accompanied him to buy a motorcycle, then again later when he gave the boy a ride on his purchase.

These fathers sometimes contrasted their pleasure on these occasions with their experience at their jobs. In fact, it is not fully clear whether their positive emotional states are attributable to being with their children or just to being away from work in the more pleasant family sphere.[23] One father explained his happiness watching Walt Disney videos with his family as a great relief after a high-pressure week at work. In comparison to other moments in their lives, fathers felt less competitive at home, stronger and kindlier. With their children, these men were more likely to let go of their combative work self and have fun.

Of course, these fathers' interactions with their children were not all pleasant. A tremendous range of experience underlay this "average," including many moments of tension and anger. "I feel like I want to kill her sometimes," one father remarked. In another case, a father reported getting angry and slapping his son for his misbehavior. But generally, there is less conflict between father and adolescent than between mother and adolescent, partly because fathers are less involved in adolescents' day-to-day lives.[24] And from Dad's point of view, the petty conflicts he has with his children may often seem of little significance compared to the larger battles that sometimes engage him at work.

In general, then, the fathers in our study reported positive experiences with their teenage children. Furthermore, this favorable emotion does not change as the child gets older (see appendix 6.2). Fathers continue to enjoy their children as they move into the adolescent years—they report just as many happy occasions, just as much warmth.

To reconcile the stereotyped image of a cold, distant father with these dads' self-descriptions of being happy and warm requires that we understand these men's interpretation of their parental role. Their way of relating to others, as we have emphasized, is different from their wives'. Intimacy and sharing of personal feelings are less important for these fathers; other things matter more.

Father as Leader

Fathers relate to their children in the way they know how, and the repertoire of most men is limited. In colonial families, the father was the authority and straw boss; even though the sphere of father–child interactions has now shifted from the labor they shared on the farm to the leisure they now share around the TV or ball field, most fathers are still happiest in interactions that cast them in a leadership role. But this role, while rewarding for them, may make it harder for them to cultivate empathic relations with an adolescent.

Fathers, even more so than mothers, approach interactions with adolescents from a position of power, and they are more disposed to use this power.[25] One even quoted Machiavelli to us on the importance of having a single ruler who directs the activities of others. Fathers more often than mothers identified themselves as "the leader" when with their children, and they were more likely to report they were "in control of" the adolescent.

What is striking is that even as children become more mature and move into adolescence, fathers give up little of their authority. With age, adolescents gain in power relative to their mothers, particularly as they go through puberty and reach adult height; in adolescent–father interactions, however, fathers remain dominant.[26] In our data, fathers' reports of being the leader actually *increase* for older children. Fathers are more resistant to yielding their authority.

Fathers' limited repertoire includes several modes of relating to children that maintain this position of power. First, fathers often relish playing the role of *teacher*. An engineer described the enjoyment he gained in teaching his daughter about the pH scale. "I dug it, I felt like I accomplished something." Two fathers mentioned doing homework with their children as the best time of their week. And another father said his daughter made him happy when she asked for his advice or opinion. Fathers have always found easy pleasure in being a sage. But while this role may make them feel close to their child, it does not necessarily make their child feel close to them.

A second of fathers' common and enjoyable modes of relating to children is *booster and promoter*. In the traditional family, the father was the ambassador to the outside world, the person who saw that his sons were prepared for jobs. The fathers in our study often reported playing this inherited role as proud overseer of both sons' and daughters' public accomplishments. Asked what the adolescent did that made them happy, more fathers than mothers mentioned the adolescent's achievements (see appendix 6.5). One father said, "When she brings home a good report card"; another said, "When he does well in basketball"; another said, "Getting A's when she thought she couldn't." As with the role of teacher, this is a mode of relating that may be rewarding for him but does not necessarily promote warmth from the adolescent, especially when her or his desires or behavior diverges from the father's expectations.

Fathers third mode of relating, one that brings less direct pleasure for them, is that of *disciplinarian*. Because the father is often removed from daily interactions, he is sometimes called in as the authority of last resort. Thus when Brenda was exasperated with trying to get her daughter, Becky, to limit her phone use, she asked her husband to speak to the girl. He was not present during the immediate confrontation, but when he got home he laid down the law limiting her calls, and "No, we cannot get call-waiting." Fathers have been found to use a narrower range of strategies for trying to control children's behavior and are often more preemptive. Mothers' most frequent strategy is to ask a child to do something; fathers are more likely to issue an order.[27]

Even in ordinary interactions, fathers adapt less to the adolescent's perspective; they are less likely to seek consensual solutions to problems. When one boy suggested a different way of mounting the basketball net, his dad felt "damn mad, because he's trying to argue with me." Fathers have been found to exercise more verbal dominance than mothers, interrupting children and more often talking simultaneously with them.[28] Whether disciplining or just interacting, many fathers comport themselves in a manner that maintains their authority and can short-circuit empathic understanding.

In sum, fathers do much of the directive parenting that mothers do, but they perform less of the attentive parenting. When we asked fathers to guess their adolescent's mood, they were less accurate than mothers: they repeatedly erred in assuming adolescents were happy at times they were not. In fact, their guesses were closer to their own moods than to the child's. Teenagers confirm that they find their fathers less likely to try to understand them, and as a result, they report hiding their feelings from them.[29] Of course there are exceptions, but most fathers appear to be not very attuned to their adolescents' emotions. Other things, such as maintaining order and authority, are more important to them.

There is one common mode of relating, however, in which dads shed some of this imperiousness.

Father as Playmate

"You want to teach your children to have fun," one father declared. Many men see it as their role to set a positive mood for the family. The beeper found one father playing monster with his younger children and another enacting a "crooked salesman" as he tried to move the children toward bed. Men resolve their dual agenda for their homelife—recovering from the stress of their jobs and spending time with their families—by being a recreational leader, or sometimes a jokester.

One father achieved this by taking his seventh-grade son to a Chicago Bulls basketball game, in which Michael Jordan wowed the crowd by scoring fifty-eight points. Later this father described it as his best time of the week, saying, "I was happy to see Jordan reach his goal and to share the thrill of this sport with my son." He had accomplished both aims of his dual agenda: he had a wonderful night out and he spent time with his son. Indeed, he saw a synergy between the two enterprises: "It's a good experience to share a common interest with your son—whether it be basketball or something else." Throughout the night they admired the Bulls' finesse interchangeably with discussion of the son's upcoming school basketball games.

This father also said that when he is happy, he is a better parent: "I have a softer touch; I am a little more giving." It is important to note, however, that this dad was still the leader; he was the one who planned the event and bought the tickets. Even when watching TV, it was usually Dad who held the remote. But, provided his authority is not challenged, leisure brings out fathers' more compassionate qualities.

Even in nonrecreational activities, fathers often try to connect and create positive moods through humor, like Bill Cosby's Cliff Huxtable. Joking, clowning, and teasing were mentioned in fathers' interactions much more often than in mothers' interactions with children; dads more often described occasions of humor as the best time of the week. Furthermore, more men than women said their children put them in a good mood when they joked with them (see appendix 6.5). Ed, for example, told us that Erin was a good teaser and they enjoyed badgering each other. When he and Erin got into teasing he felt like "the cat that swallowed the mouse."

Joking seems to be almost synonymous with having fun for many men, perhaps because it provides an antidote to the seriousness of their jobs. One father reported having pizza and joking around with the family, "trying to get away from the worry of work." But joking is valued also because it is one of men's limited ways of making emotional contact.

For many fathers, intimacy is not sharing self-revelations, but back-slapping comradely joking and teasing. Fathers, like mothers, appear to use their friendships as the ideal model for their relationship with their teenager. Struggling for words, one father described a high point with his adolescent as like what he felt when he had "a couple of beers with the guys."

Yet while humor is ice-breaking and fun, it can also have costs. If fathers make everything into a joke, their adolescents may start to suspect them of not taking their feelings seriously. Fathers use humor to teach—it can dislodge children from their egocentric perspectives and show them alternative viewpoints. Sarcasm and teasing, however, can easily cross over into hazing, avoidance, and manipulation.

Later we will see problems in relationships where Dad sees creating "fun" as his sole means of relating. But first we need to address the question of how adolescents experience this time. What are their emotions when interacting with a dad who feels warm toward them, but only from a position of authority? How do adolescents respond to a teacher, disciplinarian, and recreational leader who mixes parenting with a priority on relaxing from work?

THE ADOLESCENT'S SIDE OF THE RELATIONSHIP

Between ages ten and fifteen, teenagers are developing a new sense of who they are. They begin spending more time alone, cultivating a nascent, fragile private self. They develop new reasoning powers that increase their self-awareness, alter their experience of friends, and make them more critical of parents' authority. How does this emerging person relate to this father with his limited sensitivity and restricted paternal repertoire?

Adolescents often acknowledge their father's assumption of a dominant position in the relationship. When alone with their dad, the teens in our study reported he was leader for about a quarter of the time, and they reported themselves to be leader for only 8 percent. These reports were not quite so extreme as those of fathers, who saw themselves as the leader for 35 percent of the time and never saw the adolescent as leader. Nonetheless, both agreed that the father was more often in charge. Father and adolescent also concurred in reporting that he was more "in control of" the other when they were together.[30]

Fathers' dominance was apparent in another way, too. Their emotional states influenced their adolescent's states. We found that the moods of teens when they were with their fathers were predicted by their fathers' prior moods, especially right after Dad came home from work. If the father reported a positive or negative state during the day at his job, it predicted the child's mood at home that evening.[31] Fathers exert an emotional leadership in the relationship, which includes both raising and lowering a teenager's mood.

Transmission of positive emotions from father to child is often quite direct and deliberate. When men come home from work in a good mood, children may be the beneficiaries of their largess. Even adolescents are buoyed when their dads take them out for pizza or are in their best comical form. Since the father is often the most powerful person in the family, when he is in a good mood favorable perks flow to other family members.

But fathers' negative emotions also affect their adolescent children. Even though men try to screen out their stress from work, it may nonetheless alter their behavior in ways that influence their families.[32] One father of a fifth-grade girl admitted that when he comes home in a bad mood, "I'm less tolerant and not as affectionate with her." Events other than work may also set fathers off and lead to a chain of contagion. Another man in our study was busily trying to repair the barbecue for a picnic that night and got short with his daughter, causing a crash in her emotional state. When in a negative mood, parents are more likely to see children's actions as intentional misbehavior and respond punitively.[33]

With some fathers, these situations can turn ugly. A ninth-grade girl from the larger study reported that her stepfather came home drunk and angry one night while her mother was at work. "He called me names for no reason and pushed me into the wall. He yelled at me; he hurt me." Recent research suggests that there is a sizable but well-hidden group of fathers for whom negative emotion, often combined with alcohol, turns into physical violence.[34] In our data it was far more common for fathers to communicate their anger verbally, such as a father who yelled at his daughter after she repeatedly interrupted him during a TV show.

A father's leadership in the family, then, is a double-edged instrument. He can use it to raise the moods of his children, or to lower them. But which is more common? We have seen that men often enjoy the time they spend with their children. Do adolescent children usually enjoy their time with him?

Adolescents' Typical Experience with Dad

The seventh-grade boy whose father took him to a Bulls game reported having a great time when beeped in the middle of the game. Michael Jordan's phenomenal performance, his dad's magnanimous mood, and the talk about his own upcoming basketball games all worked to make it an extremely happy occasion for him. Many other teens in our study reported enjoyable times with their fathers. But on average, their experience with their fathers, like that with their mothers, did not stand out from the rest of life. Their typical emotional state with Dad was not better or worse than at other moments—it was average. When we look more closely, however, an age change appears to be taking place.

With entry into adolescence, young people's enjoyment of their time with their father declines. Older kids in our study reported less favorable emotions during their time with their dad (see appendix 6.2). This decline is evident for time alone with their father and time with him in family groups. Just as with mothers, fathers appear to become less pleasurable companions as the adolescent grows older.

What this means is that Dad is often having a good time, but the teenager is not. As children move into adolescence, a gap opens in how they and their fathers experience their time together. One boy recalled a moment when his dad had taken him fishing. The teen was sitting in the boat, feeling bored and wishing he were with his friends, when his dad turned to him with great exuberance and declared, "Isn't this *great!*" Another boy complained that his father always wanted to organize some sporting activity; in fact, it had become a standing joke with his friends that his dad wanted to get them together again to play hockey.

The gap that appeared between adolescents' and fathers' experience of their time together in our study included a larger number of emotional dimensions than the gap with mothers. In addition to feeling less happy during this time, adolescents also felt less strong, less kindly, more competitive, and they perceived the social climate as less "joking" than their fathers did. Adolescent and father may be together, in the same activity, but their experience is different. Dad may be trying to create enjoyment, but his son's or daughter's pleasure lags behind his. This is, of course, partly because for adolescents, friends are where the fun is.

This gap, however, is also due to fathers' imperious position, which may be rewarding for him, but not for the child. A father may enjoy being a teacher, booster, or recreational leader, but these modes of relating are not as enjoyable for the teen at the receiving end. Adolescents increasingly want to be their own person and can resent their father's inattentiveness to their concerns and their agendas. Teens bend to fathers' itinerary, but they do not experience fathers bending to theirs. In one interview study, adolescents claimed that their interactions with their dad consisted largely of his exercise of authority. They often felt ignored by him; they perceived him as more judgmental and closed; and many said their father made little effort to engage himself in their interests.[35] We, too, found numerous situations where adolescents perceived their father to be acting unilaterally, with little weight given to their opinion. In one instance a dismayed boy said "It was like a court," with his dad acting as the judge.

Thus while teens may often accede to their father's leadership, they may also find it annoying. They may laugh as their father cloaks his directiveness in humor, but they may just be appeasing him. The adolescents in our sample reported lower emotions when their father was the leader; as they get older they do not want to be led. Without an open channel of feedback from child to father, it is not surprising that fathers' and adolescents' experience of their time together frequently diverges.

Daughters and Fathers: A "Non-Relationship"?

The divergence in experience takes a different cast for daughters and sons. The gap in emotional state occurs for both genders, but at a lower range for girls: fathers are less happy when with their daughters; their daughters are unhappier when with their dads than at other times (see appendix 7.2). Other research suggests that this is the most difficult and distant family relationship. Some have even called it a "non-relationship," but this misses the fact that much is going on beneath the surface.

One explanation for girls' lower moods with their father is that his brusqueness and attempts at humor do not play as well with adolescent girls, for whom personal understanding is highly valued. Amy, whom we met in chapter 4, complained that when she cried or got upset, her dad did not understand. "He tries to explain but gets mad and says things that hurt me. He says he's sorry, but there is a grudge between us."

Her father admitted as much: "I'm a traditional father. She has feelings I don't understand. We don't really fight. We just don't get along that well."

When asked what his daughter did that made him happy, this man focused not on personal qualities, but on her achievement in school. She wanted a father who would be sensitive to her as a person, but he was more interested in her external behavior. Many adolescent girls feel their father does not try to understand them. The psychologists James Youniss and Jacqueline Smollar found that only 35 percent of the adolescent daughters they surveyed felt their fathers met their emotional needs, as compared to 72 percent for mothers.[36]

Many fathers and daughters lack common interests. For developing adolescent girls, talk about people and feelings is becoming a major part of their lives, yet most dads have limited experience in or enthusiasm for this activity. Even some proponents of the "men's movement" who have much to say about the ancient bond between father and son are strangely quiet about father–daughter relationships.[37] For their part, daughters may have limited interest in sports or other things their dads enjoy.[38] When asked what they like to do best with their fathers, 27 percent of the girls in Youniss and Smollar's study said "nothing."

Sexual feelings between fathers and daughters are another explanation for why this relationship is so often difficult.[39] Beeped while helping his sixth-grade daughter do homework, one father felt comfortable enough to write that she "is very cute and imaginative. She was writing an Easter-bunny story and I was helping her. She was adorable and I responded." With an eighth-grade, post-pubertal daughter, however, expression of such sentiments might be too loaded. The dramatic changes of puberty are rarely discussed or even acknowledged between fathers and daughters.[40] At best—or worst—pubertal change is another topic for dads to tease daughters about.[41] We found that both daughters' and fathers' moods during their shared time dropped as a function of puberty, independent of the girl's age.[42]

Discomfort, censored feelings, uneasiness over a daughter's interest in and attractiveness to teenage boys create a barrier of denial and noncommunication. Our data suggest it is not just a one-way street with fathers dominating daughters. We found that the daughters' emotions had a substantial influence on their fathers' emotional states.[43] It is known that less powerful individuals can readily influence the emotions of those with power through resistance or compliance.[44] The adolescent psychologist John Hill suggested that teenage daughters affect their fathers through these kinds of manipulations.[45] If an adolescent girl is in a bad mood, she may transmit it to her father, for example by disrupting the restorative calm he hopes to find in the home sphere. Not surprisingly, we found transmission from daughters to fathers to be greatest when daughters felt cold toward their dads.

Despite these tensions, some girls in our study had positive experiences with their fathers. One girl said her relationship with her dad had gotten better. "He's been real sensible and not fooling around, not joking as much with me and my friends as before." Although some girls enjoy humor with their dads, she said: "I like it better when he's not joking—we like to be alone and talk." Another girl, comparing her father to her stepmother, said, "I feel like I can talk to him more. He seems more open. My stepmom only worries about my younger brother. My dad worries about me." She added, "I'm more open with him too." Girls who received individual attention from their father felt closer to him; we also found evidence that this kind of warmth between father and daughter shielded her from disturbed attitudes toward her weight and eating.[46] In spite of its difficulties, the father–daughter relationship should not be written off.

Sons and Fathers: Boy to Man or Man to Man?

Fathers' relationships with sons have a more clearly prescribed cultural history. Beginning at birth, men often take more responsibility for boys than for girls and invest more of themselves in the relationship.[47] Their interactions sometimes have a stereotypically masculine script: they may watch sports together or go fishing. And as the boy grows older, this sex-role bonding may increase. One father in our study said, "He's become more of an adolescent, an adult. He's more of a guy. I can talk more man to man, less father to son."

It is not surprising, then, that the boys in our study reported feeling closer to their fathers than the girls did. When with their dads, these boys felt more choice over their actions than the girls did, more wish to be doing what they were doing, and they perceived their dads as friendlier and more joking. Likewise, the fathers felt closer to their sons than to their daughters; they also felt happier with them, and this positive mood increases with the age and pubertal development of the boy.[48]

But, even though interactions between father and son may work better than those between father and daughter, the gap in emotion is still there. Both parties reported more positive states during their time together than we saw in father–daughter interactions, but fathers reported states that were much more positive that their sons did (see appendix 7.2).

Despite the appearance of male comradeship, these boys were treated as the subservient party in the relationship. Whereas the girls occasionally felt that they were the leader with Dad, for the boys it was extremely rare; in fact, when alone with their father, these boys never saw themselves as leader. Furthermore, while the girls' emotions influenced their father's, the boys' did not. The ups and downs these boys reported did not register on their dads' emotions.

Studies have shown that fathers become *more*, not less, assertive after their sons' pubertal development.[49] The same father who enjoyed taking his seventh-grade son to a Bulls game got angry on another evening when his son acted in a manner that threatened his authority: "Washing the car he gets a 'know-it-all' attitude—I told him he had to wash the car before he could go out with his friends—he gets 'smart alecky.'" Another father acknowledged that his son was "scared to argue with me." Dad's authority cannot be directly challenged. It is not surprising, then, that the boys in our study felt less accepted and less strong than average during times with their fathers.[50]

The multiple ways that fathers dominate their sons is illustrated in the times Randy, an eighth-grader, spent with his father during a weekend, illustrated in figure 7.1. They were first beeped together at 10:18 A.M. on Saturday at the club playing racquetball. The father, who was winning, reported that he was having a great time; Randy was less happy. At the next signal, they were still at the club. Dad was enjoying the steam room; Randy was feeling bored watching TV while waiting for his dad so they could go home. These interactions were structured by Dad's agenda and thus less rewarding for Randy. It was only later in the day, when Randy joined his friends, and plotted an assassination of Hitler in a computer game, that his mood rose.

Randy's dad's posture of authority inhibited Randy's enjoyment of their shared time and his feelings of warmth toward him. Sunday morning they were together again, and Dad was yelling at him about how he was dressed. Both reported low moods, but as the recipient of the anger, Randy reported a mood that was again lower than that of his father. At the next beep, we did catch them with equivalent states, again on the racquetball court. Later in the week, however, Randy related an occasion when "I didn't feel like playing racquetball with him and, when I played, I didn't play that good so he got mad at me. He was mad at me all last night." His father's version was: "I was trying to get him a little pumped up. He wasn't paying attention. You have to keep drumming things into him."

Thus while Randy's father felt warm toward him, Randy did not feel warm or close toward his dad. Although there may be an illusion of man-to-man contest on the racquetball court, the not too thinly disguised reality is that Dad maintained dominance, even in recreational pursuits.

A father's relations with both daughters and sons can be compromised by his imperiousness. But is it possible for men to have more vital relationships with their adolescent children? Several of the fathers in our study openly wished their child would stay home more and spend more time with them: 40 percent said they wanted more time with their child. And many adolescents expressed a desire to spend more time with their dads.[51] What can our data tell us about successful father–adolescent relationships?

FATHER–ADOLESCENT SYSTEMS

Enjoyment ≠ Warmth

Our story takes a surprising twist at this point. We have characterized one of fathers' primary parental roles as emotional and recreational leader, and although fathers are not always successful in raising their children's moods, we assumed this goal of "creating fun" to be a worthy one that would increase warmth between father and teenager. We assumed that those dads who were most successful in fostering enjoyment would be closest to their children and that shared happiness and humor would translate into warmth, open communication, and feelings of connectedness. Yet, if anything, exactly the opposite appears to be true.

Fun between father and adolescent, we find, is not associated with warmth and closeness—it may even be associated with greater coldness and distance. In families where adolescents and fathers typically reported positive emotion when together, warmth was not greater (see appendix 7.3).[52] For example, Rob and his dad, Bud, whom we introduced at the beginning of the chapter, both usually reported positive moods during times they were together. These were usually times with other family members in a pleasant activity—eating dinner, watching baseball on TV, playing cards. This positive emotion, however, had little meaning for their relationship: Rob's feelings toward his dad were extremely cold and distant. Happy times did not make for a happy relationship.

If anything, the reverse seems to be true. In our sample, the fathers and adolescents who reported more negative emotion when together were likely to feel warmer toward each other. In instances together when both reported unhappiness, irritability, and anger, they also reported feeling warmer and closer to each other (see appendix 7.3). This finding startled us. We found joint negative emotion to be related to coldness in marital couples, as we noted in chapter 5. In fact, marital research identifies reciprocal negative emotion between husband and wife as a cardinal feature of distressed marriages. Likewise, irritability between mothers and adolescents is related to poorer adolescent adjustment. Yet in father–adolescent relationships, shared negative emotion appears to be associated with a warmer and closer bond.[53]

One father, Victor, a weathered-looking assembly-line foreman, described how his eighth-grade daughter, Vicki, always snapped at him: "In the morning she's one of the crabbiest persons." And her anger usually got him angry. In one situation he yelled at her to shut the radio off, then "she blew her cork, and that made me mad." And yet, in spite of these exchanges of nega-

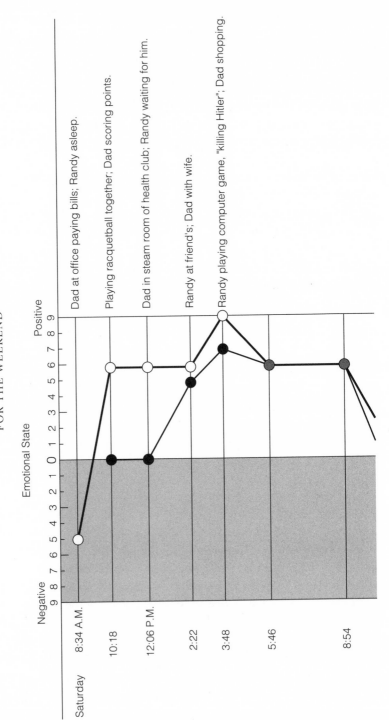

Figure 7.1

RANDY'S AND HIS FATHER'S EMOTIONS
FOR THE WEEKEND

RANDY AND HIS FATHER'S EMOTIONS (continued)

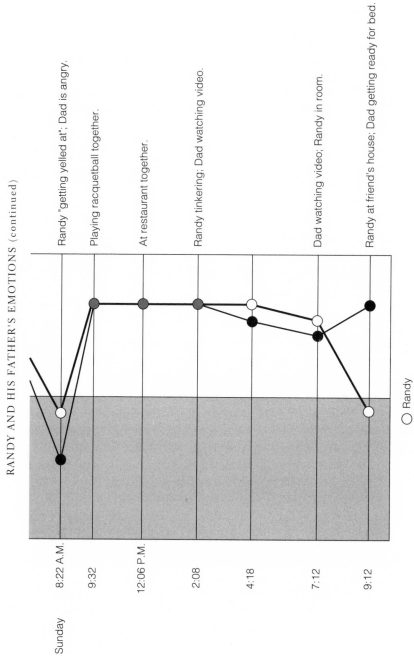

Sunday

8:22 A.M. Randy "getting yelled at"; Dad is angry.

9:32 Playing racquetball together.

12:06 P.M. At restaurant together.

2:08 Randy tinkering; Dad watching video.

4:18

7:12 Dad watching video; Randy in room.

9:12 Randy at friend's house; Dad getting ready for bed.

○ Randy
● Father

tive emotions, Vicki described feeling as close to and warm toward her father as any child in the study, and Victor felt likewise. Our findings suggest that in father–adolescent relationships, shared negative emotion does not appear to be the poison it is in marital relations.

This startling finding is reinforced when we discover that shared negative emotion between fathers and adolescents is also associated with higher well-being in adolescents. Those teens who experienced more negative emotion with their fathers reported higher self-esteem.[54] But how can this be?

The Quick Exit: Avoidance of Feelings

Clues to the puzzling association between negative emotion and warmth are provided by the troubled relationship between Amy and her father. This eighth-grade girl told us that her dad could not deal with her when she cried or was upset. Likewise, her father suggested that she could not handle his negative emotions. We asked him to describe how one dispute between them was resolved, and he said, "We didn't work it out. It went my way. She stomped upstairs." By both accounts, when things were bad, they separated. In this cold relationship, negative emotion led to a quick exit by one or the other.

We found these "quick exits" in other cold father–adolescent relationships as well. The moods these dads and teens reported when together appeared to dictate whether they would still be together the next time they were signaled. If they were in good moods, they were more likely to stay together. If they were in bad moods—especially if the teen was—they were likely to separate (see appendix 7.4).[55]

No wonder they rarely reported joint negative emotion—a selection process was at work. In cold father–adolescent pairs, the two stayed together *only if* they were enjoying themselves. They could not seem to tolerate each other's anger or sadness for very long. The pattern for many fathers is to leave when things get unpleasant. After all, parenting for many men is a voluntary activity carried out during leisure time. If things aren't fun, a father can exercise his "escape clause," turning things over to mom and going off to play the piano or do something else. More often, the teenager becomes so uncomfortable that she or he is the one who leaves.[56]

In some families, this dynamic takes the form of cheery denial. When a sixth-grade girl in our study asked her dad not to root so loudly at her softball game that evening, he responded by asking whether she would prefer that he not go. She said yes, so he stayed home, and according to his wife was really hurt. Then at the game the daughter saw all the other enthusiastic parents and felt terrible that she had told her dad to stay away. She arrived home in tears, and her mother discussed with her how she might try to smooth things over with her dad. But when she tried, he denied that he was hurt, and she felt embarrassed all over again and went to her room.

Such separations are hardly compatible with a healthy and close relationship. By fleeing negative feelings and conflict, fathers and teens sacrifice a critical opportunity to learn about each other. By refusing to work through their negative emotions, they do not get the chance to communicate about deeply felt aspects of their realities.

In other families, such as Rob and Bud's, the dynamic is more overt. Bud described himself as an "easygoing guy," "a kid in a man's body," who often used his humor and joking to put the family in a good mood. But his loud and abrupt manner suggested his underlying explosiveness. Indeed, when he got angry, he became authoritarian. He readily admitted to the interviewer that he had a quick temper, with a tendency toward violence. In an echo of his wife Rita's sentiments, Bud said: "When Rob gets smart with his mouth, I want to kill him." He estimated this occurred about two or three times a week.

The pager just happened to catch Rob and Bud during one of these occasions. They were at the dinner table with the rest of the family, plus grandparents, watching a baseball game on TV, and they were having a shouting match. The argument, they reported, was about the baseball game, but the underlying issues might well have been the family's move to Oregon and Rob's sense that his views did not count for much in the family. Both Bud and Rob used the extremes of the scales to identify how irritable and angry they felt. Rob added, "I wish I could leave town before I go bananas." Rob, you may recall, could be pretty headstrong himself, but his father could be terribly imposing. Thus at the next report, Rob had gone to his bedroom, still fuming at his dad. There was not enough space in one room for Bud and Rob when both were angry, and it was Rob who typically felt compelled to leave.

Men, according to Gottman and Levenson, are less able to control strong emotions. They are more likely to either deny them or let them influence their actions.[57] One father admitted, "I yell and then feel bad." Because men wield so much power in the family, they check their anger less. No wonder Rob left the room.

As with the topic of sex, teens and fathers do not do well with sadness and anger. The script for their relationship is to have fun—or to avoid each other.

Fathers' Well-Being and Adolescents' Well-Being

What we see, then, is that fathers often miss the boat in their attempts to relate to their adolescent children. Adolescents get more fun from their friends—dads cannot, and perhaps should not try to, compete. Teens are more interested in a stable arena of comfort from their father, a relationship in which they can be honest and open about their feelings. Unfortunately, fathers often short-circuit such openness with avoidance or unilateral acts of authority.

To be fair to fathers, we need to understand the emotional quality of their interactions in terms of the constraints of their daily reality. We have seen that Dad's life at home is strongly influenced by his life at work. Negative emotion at the job gets carried over to home. His avoidance and authoritarian parenting often arise from the residual stress of work.[58] Perhaps fathers are doing the best they can do, given the emotional strains of their jobs.

But men's approach to parenting is also due to their socially constructed claim of entitlement over their homelife. We have seen that mothers are less likely to carry home stress from work and less likely to let it get passed to their kids. Fathers, however, assert a "right" to recover from their work—and this feeds their avoidant and preemptive relationship to their children. After work, for example, Bud often dozed on the living room couch and expected others not to wake him with noise. He parented only on his terms and got angry when others did not comply.

Regardless of where you put the blame, fathers' stress at work registers on their adolescents. A father's negative emotions at work create negative emotions in the adolescent that evening; day after day, week after week, these incidents add up. Thus, we find that a father's overall rate of irritability at work predicts distress in his adolescent. The amount of hours a father works and the amount of time he spends with the adolescent are not the critical factors. But when dads, such as Bud, frequently feel upset at their jobs, it appears to affect not only their parental relationships, but also their adolescents' adjustment.[59] Men's stress at their jobs gets carried home and interferes with their ability to have the kind of open and warm relationship that is beneficial for teenagers.

Other studies have also found this connection between fathers' stress at work and their inclination to be more irritable, punitive, and arbitrary toward their children—with negative consequences for the children's physical and mental health.[60] Clearly, fathers' depression can be just as harmful to kids as mothers' depression. Although teens, such as Rob, may try to avoid these emotions, they have their impact. Children growing up with depressed or angry fathers have usually been found to show the same degree of maladjustment as those growing up with depressed and irritable mothers.[61] In particular, fathers' use of verbal and physical aggression has a strong relationship to adolescents' problems.[62]

What's more, fathers who are avoidant or preemptive leave the task of family emotional management to mothers. In some families, mothers even take responsibility for trying to repair the fractures that emerge in relationships between fathers and children. This allocation of emotional management to mothers creates a critical flaw in family organization, one that we take up in the next chapter.

These unhealthy patterns, however, are not followed by all fathers. Not all men miss the boat.

Healthy Father–Adolescent Relationships

Child-care books laud the "authoritative" parent, one who avoids both preemptive authoritarianism and neglectful disengagement. These parents are more child-centered; they use their position of power not to dominate but to provide support and challenge to their adolescents. Research confirms that such authoritative parenting is conducive to children's development, at least in European-American middle- and working-class families.[63] But what we do not know is how fathers achieve the necessary detachment from their own emotional needs. How can fathers structure their day-to-day lives to avoid the twin horns of anger and disengagement?

We find that the nature of daily interactions differs in warm and cold father–adolescent relationships. Being together is not contingent on having fun; negative emotion does not cause parent and child to avoid each other (see appendix 7.4). In one close pair, for example, father and daughter reported anguished feelings watching a TV show about German death camps together; at another time they shared her anxiety and trepidation as they drove to a concert where she was to play a violin solo. These two seemed able to tolerate sadness and worry in each other.

Anger, too, does not cause these fathers and adolescents to disengage. Victor, the assembly-line foreman whose daughter, Vicki, "blew her cork" at him, is one example. He complained, "She's got the idea that everything her parents say is directed right at her." Like other adolescents in the study, Vicki, a tall, early-developing thirteen-year-old, was starting to challenge some of her parents' rules. She could be impatient and bossy. At times Victor got mad because "she starts treating me like her son instead of her father." Yet they seemed to be able to ride out these altercations without disconnecting.

Both Victor and Vicki said the relationship was getting better because of greater mutual understanding. Victor said, "I'm starting to pay attention to what affects her moods." In their separate interviews, both expressed a shared perception that Vicki had a short temper and that when she blew up, the best thing to do was to let her scream and then wait, and she'd feel better soon after that. Vicki added, "I fight with Dad over stupid things. I get mad at him, but I can't stay mad because he makes funny faces." Victor was able to use humor to overcome mutual anger and remain engaged.

But what was different about Victor's life that allowed him to stay engaged? Like other fathers, he experienced foul-ups at his job. One day a machine on his segment of the assembly line broke down and was out of commission for several days. Later in the week, he was called before the labor board about an employee he had fired. But he was able to maintain a positive disposition during these incidents. His anger passed quickly; he was able to keep his emotions at his job under control. Thus he did not bring negative emotions home, and we think this allowed him to be more attentive to Vicki. Rather than just having a series of fragmented "interactions," they genuinely appeared to have a "relationship." Victor had an ongoing sense of her life, and he was slowly helping her understand his.

The critical skills of parenting—patience, caring, attentiveness to a child's needs—are not endowed to one gender. They are learned, for both men and women. This is evident in anthropologists' discovery of cultures where fathers are tender, nurturant, and laugh when their children disobey them.[64] It is also evident in research showing that, when given a chance, fathers are as nurturant with young children as mothers are.[65] By the time their children reach adolescence, most fathers are way behind in knowing them and learning these abilities. Yet studies show that when their lives allow them increased involvement, fathers' skills and self-confidence as a parent improve markedly.[66] We can see this change in a second example.

Thirteen-year-old Luke, the tall, early-maturing son of Lorraine, whom we introduced in the last chapter, also shared a warm and close relationship with his father, John. John was a recovering alcoholic, with a career in sales. A few months before the study, John had held a high-pressure sales job and his drinking was out of control. He related how he used to "come home and fly off the handle." There would always be something in Luke's behavior to provide an excuse to get angry. Because of his drinking and the stress of his job, he was erratic and unpredictable as a parent. He admitted that even at the time of the study, if he was upset or frustrated he tended to withdraw or project it onto others.

In order to get his emotions under control, John quit the job and stopped drinking. When he participated in our study he had a new, less demanding job that he enjoyed, and he had joined Alcoholics Anonymous; in fact, he gave a talk at AA on the Saturday night that he had the pager. John's acknowledgment of his own shortcomings may have set the stage for a more mutual, empathic relationship with his son. He was willing to admit he was mortal, something teens rarely hear from their fathers.

John did play the Disneyland dad. He said he loved buying treats for his kids; he took Luke to the motorcycle shop, and they planned a fishing trip together. But they also talked. John was frequently there when Luke came home from school—they discussed Luke's day; John helped Luke with his homework and checked it. Luke said he often went to his father for advice, even about issues with his friendships. The two clearly had a daily, ongoing personal relationship; both saw it as getting better. In this case it was the adolescent, rather than the father, who said the relationship was getting better because the other was becoming more responsible.

Because of the changes in his life, John was able to be more child-centered. Since his new job was less stressful, he did not bring home urgent personal needs. As a result, he was more emotionally flexible when confronted with Luke's needs and interests. Thus there was more give-and-take in their interactions: Luke argued with his dad over what movie they should see and was successful in convincing him to go to the one he wanted. We found that teens who less often experienced their dads as leader were better adjusted.[67]

But authoritative parenting does not mean that parents abdicate their directive role. When it is not motivated by the father's own needs, his leadership can be used constructively. Stuart Hauser and his colleagues found in a laboratory study that fathers actually did more than mothers to encourage healthy autonomy in adolescents. In a focused family conversation, fathers made a larger number of "enabling statements"—statements that help adolescents solve problems and develop an independent point of view.[68] In real life, however, many fathers may be too distracted by their jobs to play this role. Effective fathers are those like John, who have enough control over their lives that they can be present, attentive, and can parent on behalf of the child.

FATHERS AND THE FAMILY SYSTEM

In many respects, fathers in two-parent families face the same predicament as mothers: maintaining a stable relationship with a young adolescent whose reality is rapidly diverging from theirs. Both fathers and mothers feel close to the child, yet the child's feelings of warmth toward them and enjoyment of time with them decline with entry into adolescence. Both parents face the quandary of how to exercise their authority with a child who increasingly sees their authority to be limited. And both are ultimately judged by the same criterion: regardless of parents' gender, it is their children's experience of a warm, caring relationship that is important to their adjustment and growth.[69]

Yet, while they faced the same challenges, mothers and fathers in our sample went about parenting in different ways. Fathers' parenting has evolved out of a different tradition, one marked by men's detached role as family provider. If the major hazard in mother–child relationships is overenmeshment, the danger in father–child relationship has been the opposite: being unconnected, being nothing more than a gaming partner.[70] The limited repertoire of fatherhood and the needs men bring home from work have made them more preemptive and less able to listen to what adolescents feel. And without open interchange, the relationship cannot grow to accommodate all the changes in the adolescent. Thus just as the mother's traditional role often gets in the way of being a good parent, so does the father's.

Adolescents' relationships with their mothers and fathers, of course, are not isolated from each other, they are interrelated. The fact that Rob had a strained relationship with his depressed mother, Rita, cannot be fully understood without considering the hostile dynamics with his angry father, Bud. Underlying Rob's relationship with both parents was low marital communication *between* them, and Rob's fear that he would soon be a "child of divorce." Between Bud, Rita, and Rob was a complex family system at work that affected everyone's behavior and feelings. Likewise, the fact that Luke had a good relationship with his dad, John, cannot be understood in isolation from their interactions with Lorraine. In the final two chapters we turn to examining these larger family systems.

PART THREE

Families

CHAPTER 8

Troubled Families:

SEPARATE REALITIES

S OME FAMILIES are dysfunctional most of the time. Most families are dysfunctional some of the time. It was one of those Sunday mornings when things were just not working right for the Searle family. Sixth grader Sue Anne was tired of being at home and really wanted to eat out. But her father, Jim, who was experiencing "trying times" at his job, wanted to spend the morning at home. Sue Anne got her way, and when they arrived at the restaurant Jim had accommodated and reported feeling moderately cheerful. However, now Sue Anne felt tense toward her father and could not wait to get out of there, and her mother, Jackie, was upset with both of them.

Family life can be absurdly disjointed. Other family members are never what you want them to be. Parents wish adolescents could be more cooperative. Adolescents feel parents don't understand. One spouse is interested in sex when the other is not. Plato's famous cave allegory might be retold for families incorporating the multiple perspectives of family life. Each family member is chained to their own wall—to their own emotional world—and while they may *think* they comprehend other family members, each sees only shadows of the others' diverging realities.

Once we go inside family life, we find that it is an illusion to talk about "the family," as though it were a single entity. The family is the meeting ground of multiple realities—in a sense, multiple cultures. The two-parent households studied here bring together the divergent worlds of women and men, adults and children. The result is often a cacophony of clashing feelings and wants, such as those within the Searle family on Sunday morning.

This divergence between family realities, as this chapter will demonstrate, provides fertile conditions for dysfunctional processes to grow. Day after day, week after week, when family members have discrepant ways of experiencing their lives, they easily begin relating to one another in a distorted manner. When they do not understand the others' realities, some members often do not get their needs met—or they try to get them met in unhealthy ways. The result is a family system that is not functioning in the best interest of all members.

For the purposes of this chapter and the next we divided the fifty-five families in our study into those we judged to be healthier and those we judged to be less healthy, or distressed. To make this division, we took into account the well-being of all layers of the family system: the mental health of the individuals, the warmth of the dyadic relationships, and how people perceived the climate of the whole family.[1] Of course, such divisions are always fallible—all families contain a mix of healthy elements and distress. Furthermore, since we got information from only three family members, our findings are necessarily incomplete.[2] Nevertheless, even this imperfect division gives us a tool for trying to separate the processes that impair family well-being from those that promote it. The findings we obtained provide clues to how dysfunction emerges from the confluence of family members' daily lives.

EMOTIONAL DOMINANCE

The Thompson Family, Part 1

Much of the dysfunction in the Thompson family seemed to start in the father's life. Russ Thompson was a large and muscular thirty-eight-year-old steelworker, employed in the remnants of Chicago's once prosperous steel mills. His job was hot, dirty, and intense. At work, the beeper found him "forging I-beams" and "getting ready to make steel rods." Though he joked a lot on the job, the social environment could be hostile. One day there was a fistfight, another day a coworker got fired for little reason. Thousands have been laid off over the last twenty years. As a result, like other fathers, Russ often felt irritable and unhappy at work. But he viewed his job as a necessary sacrifice he made for his family.

As a response to this negative work experience, Russ spent a lot of his free time at the track, betting on horses. His gambling, mentioned on thirteen of his forty-five beeper sheets, occurred with the frequency of an addiction. The track was also a place where he talked with old friends and enjoyed meeting new ones. He usually drank there too, and the alcohol may have intensified a process we have seen in other families in our study: the transmission of his emotions to other family members.

Sometimes Russ's gambling had a positive effect on his family. On Thursday night after work, at 7:14, the beeper found him sitting in the car looking at the race program with hopeful anticipation: "I know I am going to get some winners." He bet heavily and indeed he did win, "for a change." At 9:08 he was elated, standing in line collecting $586. Later he wrote that he "had a ball" at the racetrack. Perhaps because of his positive mood, the next day he left work early and got the backyard pool ready for his two children to swim in. That night his wife, Wendy, and his seventh-grade daughter, Roxanne, reported above-average moods and a break in their usually hostile feelings toward him.

Saturday, however, the opposite scenario took place. Russ worked over-time hours at the steel mill in the morning, then went to the track that afternoon. This time he came home unhappy and irritable because "I just lost all my money." At 7:12 P.M. he reported feeling bored, tired, and weak, reading the newspaper in the living room. Roxanne was in the kitchen doing the dishes and reported feeling unhappy and "angry at my dad because I think he's drunk." Wendy was also distressed and said that his drinking and spending money at the track often upset her; she reported that she was talking to Roxanne about him, perhaps trying to soothe her. Whereas Russ's and Wendy's moods improved later that evening, Roxanne remained distressed until midafternoon on Sunday.

The transmission of emotion from one person to another is not, in and of itself, an unhealthy process. It is common in daily life for us to be cheered by talking with someone in a good mood and to have our spirits deflated by interacting with a person in distress. In any close relationship we affect and are affected by each other. But when emotional transmission always goes one way, it suggests an imbalance between two people's realities: that the sender's reality is dominating and the receiver's is being dis-counted.

Dad's Emotions Become the Family's Emotions

Strong emotions, we have seen, most often pass from fathers to other family members. In earlier chapters, we noted that men's emotions are reg-ularly transmitted to their wives and to their children, particularly when the men come home from work.

This one-way transmission is more common in distressed families.[3] In less healthy families, like the Thompsons, the father's emotions regularly overpower everyone else's. The family therapists Michael Kerr and Murray Bowen suggest that the dominant spouse "sprays" his or her anxiety at other family members.[4] Fathers like Russ come home from their jobs with a feeling of having done battle for the family and make it known that they expect others to accommodate their needs.

It was Russ's aggressive and domineering manner, we suspect, that conveyed his negative emotion to others in the family. During several hours in the home, the interviewer observed that Russ was "harsh, stern and yells a lot." After he came home one day Russ wrote, "Son of a bitch, I'm tired," and on another, "I'm fuckin' tired." When Russ came in, everyone knew he was home and what his mood was. If he had a stressful day at work, his back hurt, he became less tolerant of others, and he demanded that his needs take priority.

Russ's wife, Wendy, was a perfect target for Russ's domination. Like that of many women we have introduced in this book, Wendy's identity was centered in caring for her family. When Russ came home drunk and depressed after losing money at the track, Wendy first soothed Roxanne's feelings; then, at the next beep, she was submissively massaging Russ's back. Even though she felt distant from him and bored, she responded to his needs because she believed it was part of her role. No wonder she was so readily susceptible to his moods.[5]

We suspect that Russ had a longer-term effect on Wendy's well-being, too. Murray Bowen writes, "The one who functions for long periods in the adaptive position gradually loses the ability to function and make decisions for self."[6] Perhaps it is for this reason that Wendy reported low self-esteem and many symptoms of depression. In her relationship with Russ, Wendy's feelings—her reality—was being denied.

Russ's daughter, Roxanne, was also susceptible to his emotions, but things with her were more complex. She came home from her teenager's life at school with strong moods of her own, and at times she affected her father's emotions. Russ reported that Roxanne "gets to" him when "she starts getting to be a wise guy." But he also affected her.[7] When he was in a bad mood, she tried to avoid him: she left the room. But it was hard to avoid the pall Russ cast over the house when he came home drunk and irritable.

At its simplest, we might describe the emotional dominance fathers wield in many distressed families as the manifestation of raw power. Social psychologists suggest that emotions are readily transmitted from powerful to less powerful people,[8] and in our society fathers usually have most power in the family. Because of this power, even a small gesture or the threat of anger may sometimes influence others' feelings. One mother said that when her husband is in a bad mood the "kids start to bounce off each other; they don't know how to act." Another said that when her husband is mad or upset about something, "everyone goes into a shell."

A more thorough explanation of this emotional dominance, however, requires understanding it in terms of the family role system: in terms of father's reality and the relationship it sets up for him with other family members.

Fathers' Reality, Fathers' Needs

Men's relationship to their families, the feminist sociologist Jessie Bernard suggests, could be described as that of an "emotional parasite."[9] These are harsh words, but our study provides evidence that they are frequently true. We have seen that men often deplete themselves at their jobs. Some of the fathers in our study got themselves into lawsuits, and fistfights: their "Things to Do Today" lists kept them going into the evening. They got deeply absorbed in a way that increased their vulnerability to frustration and anger, then they depended on their home time to restore them and make them happy. Even when their wife was employed and also came home tired from her job, most men still expected her to keep the family in order. Fathers' enactment of their traditional breadwinning role creates emotional needs that they expect their family time to fulfill.

Moreover, many fathers give little back emotionally, because they are not tuned in to the intrapersonal events going on at home. Their traditional breadwinner role did not encourage fathers to be sensitive, emotionally involved family participants. Indeed, when conflicts occurred, the men in our study often withdrew to watch TV, play piano, or work in the yard, instead of investing energy in finding resolution. Rather than being sensitive to other people's needs, fathers' strategy is often to try to wipe them away through joking or leisure activities. While fathers provide materially for the family, many take more than they give back emotionally.

This "parasitic" pattern appeared to be especially common in the more distressed families we studied. These fathers, like Russ Thompson, had jobs that created more negative emotion than those of other fathers (see appendix 8.1). Whether working a white-collar or blue-collar job, they reported more unhappiness, irritability, and anger at work. What is striking, however, is that these men felt markedly better in the home sphere, showing a larger improvement in mood from their jobs than men in nondistressed families. Fathers like Russ experienced their leisure time at home as a relatively happier part of their lives. This suggests that they exploited the traditional privileges of their role, perhaps more than other men, to ameliorate the distress created by their work.

These fathers also appear to have been more emotionally insulated from the rest of their families. Their wives and adolescent children showed signs of distress when at home (see appendix 8.1), yet these fathers still experienced their home time as a respite from the rigors of their jobs. These men appeared to shield themselves from the unhappiness in the family and make certain that the context was happy for them. Russ's obliviousness is evident in his claim that he and Wendy never disagreed, in spite of Wendy's reports of numerous conflicts with him. Likewise, Roxanne reported that her father did not understand what she was really like, even though he thought their relationship was fine. Russ felt too burned from the stress of work to attend to Wendy's or Roxanne's reality.

Thus dads in these families appeared to draw on their life at home to take care of their emotional needs, but to distance themselves from the emotional needs of other family members. This disengagement of fathers from the inner lives of their families has been found to relate to lower well-being in their wives and children.[10] But while the father's pattern of relating affects other family members, our data suggest that his well-being is not affected by the emotional quality of his relationships with his wife and child.

What our findings indicate, then, is that men's experience of job stress magnifies flaws in the traditional role system. In Bernard's words, fathers have all "their eggs in the basket" of providing for the family and thus develop only limited skills for attending to and nurturing others. Though many contemporary fathers voice a desire to be more involved with their families, when the going gets tough they readily revert to traditional assumptions. Men's distress at work becomes an easy excuse to cut themselves off from the life of the family and focus on their own needs. When they come home tired with a backache, they may have little awareness that their mood is affecting the rest of the family. And when this pattern is repeated again and again, dysfunctional processes become entrenched as part of the family's daily life.

CROSS-GENERATIONAL COALITIONS

The Thompson Family, Part 2

Up to this point, we have focused mainly on Russ and how his emotions often dominated those of Wendy and Roxanne. We have yet to learn how

Wendy and Roxanne adapted to life with this domineering and frequently hostile man.

The interviewer said of Wendy, "There is faded beauty in her plump, worn face—she was once pretty—but the lines around her mouth and eyes make her look bitter." She worked fifteen hours a week for her brother, mostly out of her home, in a job that provided little personal satisfaction. "It is not a real job," she reported. In the absence of meaningful employment and a warm relationship with her husband, Wendy adapted by maintaining what she experienced as a close relationship with her thirteen-year-old daughter, Roxanne.

Roxanne had long blond hair, a good complexion, and a pretty smile—much of the beauty that Wendy must have had at an earlier age. Roxanne's popularity, as well as the many cheerleading awards displayed prominently in the living room, gave her an air of confidence and security. She described herself as someone who gets along easily with other people. Yet her heavy blue eye shadow, combined with a fully developed body, hinted at a pseudo-maturity. Our interviewer speculated that she was "headed for trouble."

The coalition that had formed between Wendy and Roxanne was evident in their constant companionship. When Roxanne was not in school, mother and daughter were nearly always together. In fact, on Wednesday and Friday, Roxanne stayed home from school and the two went shopping. On many of these occasions their relationship resembled a close friendship. One night, Wendy relished the warm time they'd had reading together. Another time, Roxanne said she felt relaxed, "because I can be myself around her."

This coalition, however, was not fully mutual. Wendy reported her most positive moods when with her daughter, but Roxanne's moods with her mother were more variable. On several of their shopping trips when Wendy reported feeling happy, Roxanne felt bored. Wendy also reported much greater warmth toward her daughter than Roxanne felt toward her; in fact, Roxanne rarely reported feelings of warmth toward her mother.

This discrepancy between Wendy's and Roxanne's experience of the relationship begins to suggest the flaw in this coalition. As with Eleanor, who intruded in her daughter's swim team participation (see chapter 6), Wendy's deep involvement with her daughter was a dependency that attempted to fill an emotional void in her life. Except for her job, Wendy had few outside interests. Further, she said she did not like being alone, especially when Russ was at work or the track and the kids were at school. "I get depressed and lonely; I start to worry." No wonder she was so willing to let Roxanne skip school: she needed her.

But Roxanne, like many adolescents, had one foot in the family and one foot out. In particular, Roxanne was obsessed with boys, an interest that provided some vicarious pleasure to her mother, but was also a source of distress because it competed with the mother–daughter relationship. On the first day of the study, during a shopping trip with her mother, Roxanne wrote "I love Andy" on nearly every pager sheet. But late that afternoon, she discovered that Andy was visiting another girl, Kerry, and became very upset. "I hate Kerry!" she wrote.

Wendy, however, was working behind the scenes, and Wendy's sister set Roxanne up with her best friend's son, Leon. That night, in her diary, Roxanne expressed elation that "Leon likes me," and for the rest of the week she wrote "I love Leon" or "I love Leon *forever*" on nearly every beeper sheet—with a regularity that resembled her father's obsession with gambling and suggested how strong her unmet needs for attachment were.

Though Wendy had facilitated Roxanne's romance with Leon, it then became a source of conflict between them. Because Leon lived twenty-five miles away, they had battles in which Roxanne tried to get her mother to drive her to see Leon. And when a rendezvous was arranged, Leon's presence put a wedge between Roxanne and Wendy. Friday night Leon was over and the warmth reported between mother and daughter was lower. At 9:03 Friday night, Roxanne reported that she felt in control of Wendy because "my mom is bugging me to tell her what happened between me and Leon! (HE KISSED ME)."

As a result of Wendy's dependence on her, Roxanne had considerable power over her. She had achieved a role reversal, illustrated in her tone of command, at the end of the study, when the interviewer heard her cajoling Wendy to accompany her to the store, saying, "I want you to go with me, you lazy bum."

Mothers' Reality, Mothers' Needs

The organization of mothers' lives, as we have seen, can leave them emotionally vulnerable. Mothers' traditional role engages them in many hours of unrewarding labor for others without a dependable counterbalancing context of emotional respite and enjoyment. While motherhood is usually the most important part of their lives, on an hour-to-hour basis being a mother is often empty or aggravating. Many long-suffering women are constantly playing "52 Pickup" for the rest of the family; doing dishes, cleaning the floor, keeping track of children do not provide sufficient sustenance to maintain their emotional buoyancy.

In distressed families, we found this imbalance in women's lives to be magnified. Women in less healthy families reported lower emotional states at home: they reported more loneliness, frustration, and unhappiness (see appendix 8.1). They were, in effect, sponges that soaked up family distress. Because of their commitment to caring for others, these women were vulnerable to the unhappiness in the rest of the family. Mothers like Wendy paid the price of the stress their husbands brought home from work and other strains in the family.

In some cases these women were able to partly protect themselves with involvements outside the family sphere. Wendy, however, did not have an outside emotional base: she did not have regular interactions with friends; her job was done at home; and she rarely got out on her own. Wendy's two most positive experiences of the week were watching Roxanne and her son have a good time and buying her son an expensive birthday present.

Limited in their options for fulfilling their needs, some women attempt to deny them, but the result is often that these needs manifest themselves in dysfunctional ways. Under the guise of taking care of Roxanne, Wendy was really taking care of her own needs. The mandate that mothers have to care for their children gets turned around and becomes a vehicle for meeting mothers' needs. Wendy used her daughter in attempts to alleviate the loneliness, depression, and emptiness in her own life. Just as Russ was addicted to gambling and Roxanne to being "in love," Wendy appeared to be deeply dependent on her daughter.

Hapless Alliances

Cross-generational coalitions, such as that between Wendy and Roxanne, reflect efforts of family members to adjust to their realities. Frequently a parent attempts to form an alliance with a child in order to obtain support against difficulties with her or his spouse. This style of adjustment, however, is usually not very successful for those involved.

For Wendy, the coalition with her daughter did not really work. She got temporary relief from her loneliness by shopping and hanging out with Roxanne, but these activities did not reduce her underlying depression. The problem is that adolescents like Roxanne cannot reciprocate very well and often are ambivalent about doing so. They have too many needs of their own. Parents may *perceive* an alliance, but we found that the warmth parents in our study felt toward their child was only weakly correlated with the warmth the child felt toward them.[11] At bottom, children cannot be expected to adequately satisfy the intimacy needs of adults.[12]

Instead of satisfying Wendy's needs, this mother–daughter "friend-ship" opened Wendy to an additional source of pain. Roxanne used the relationship with Leon against her mother. This vulnerability was especially evident at the end of the week when the family learned that a close friend of Roxanne's had just been killed in a boating accident. For the final two days of the study, Wendy reported emotional states that were close to rock bottom because of the death. She wrote on the pager sheet, "This is a very sad and hard time for us. We all miss Tim." She also added, "I am very worried about Roxanne." Yet the death had more of an effect on Wendy's mood than on Roxanne's; she was absorbed by her new romance. In fact, Roxanne felt worried about her mother because "she's very upset; she's taking it hard."

Cross-generational coalitions do not benefit the adolescent either. When a mother is overly involved and dependent on an adolescent, the adolescent does not feel more supported; in fact, there may be increased conflict.[13] Family therapists assert that emotional enmeshment with a parent prevents an adolescent from growing, thinking, feeling, and acting independently. Furthermore, because of the control such coalitions give to the teenager (as expressed in "you lazy bum"), the parent cannot maintain an authoritative position. The adolescent does not get the steady, guiding, objective parenting necessary to deal with his or her changing, tumultuous world.

Our study substantiates the idea that adolescents in cross-generational coalitions are not helped by them. Roxanne attempted to act self-confident and adultlike, but according to our index of emotional health, she was in the most troubled 10 percent of the kids in the study. She reported more symptoms of depression than most other girls her age; in fact, the number and severity of her symptoms placed her in the clinically depressed range. She also reported lower self-esteem and lower average emotional states than most other girls. She was not getting her needs met. Across our sample, we found that when a mother felt closer to her teen than to her husband, the teen's well-being was significantly lower (see appendix 8.2).[14]

Family therapists suggest that because of her traditional role, the mother is usually the parent who seeks a cross-generational coalition;[15] however, we found some fathers who felt warmer toward their adolescent child than to their wife. These families also showed signs of poorer health. Likewise, when the adolescent experienced a strong imbalance in the warmth they felt toward one parent versus the other, family well-being was lower (see appendix 8.2).

Attempts at coalitions with children by either mother or father reflect a dysfunctional family system. We cannot say from these data that cross-generational coalitions are the *cause* of poorer adjustment in an adolescent like Roxanne or her family. Nonetheless, they are a sign that things are not working right.

THE FAMILY SYSTEM: BREAKING THE CIRCLE

Where *do* we place responsibility for the development of these dysfunctional coalitions? Early family-systems theories declared, almost as an article of faith, that all members contribute to family disorder. Theorists such as Murray Bowen, Salvadore Minuchin, and Nathan Ackerman argued that each family member affects every other family member, that dysfunction gets passed around in a circle, with no discernible starting point. Our data, however, challenge this assumption of circularity, suggesting that many problems begin with the father.[16]

In the Thompson family it is apparent that much of the dysfunction started with Russ and his job. Russ reacted to his job as a steelworker with frequent negative emotion, and this got carried home and infected other family members. When he was home he was often abrasive, sometimes drunk, and nearly always insensitive to other family members' feelings. We think it unlikely that the coalition between Wendy and Roxanne emerged in a vacuum. Rather, we suspect they developed it as a defensive barrier against the hostility and insensitivity that Russ frequently directed at the family. Indeed, when Russ came home drunk and angry on Saturday night, their beepers found mother and daughter together, providing emotional reinforcement for each other. Researchers have found that such coalitions between mothers and children are most common when they perceive the father as critical and unsupportive, and especially when he is prone to violence, a tendency Russ showed at times.[17]

Rather than assuming circularity, we should recognize that in cases such as this, the origins of family dysfunction may be unidirectional. The principal elements provoking the Thompson family's dysfunctional patterns, we think, come largely from Russ, his job, and from his enactment of a father's traditional rights and prerogatives.

We have seen the same elements among many families in our study, especially those with greater distress. Russ's carryover of negative emotions from work is a pattern evident in other men as well. His appropriation of his home time for his own needs is the accepted prerogative of the male breadwinner in our culture. Russ's disposition to be perfunctory and

authoritarian is a disposition we have seen in other fathers. And his insensitivity to the feelings of other family members reflects deficits in the socialization of males. Other research has also found that the chain of family distress often leads from the father and his job to the mother and the family
system to the adolescent.[18]

It would be naive, of course, to contend that other family members
contribute nothing to family dysfunction. As with some of the other mothers we have seen, Wendy's lack of activities outside the family and her
inability to acknowledge her own needs exacerbated her vulnerability and
reinforced her enmeshment with her daughter. Roxanne's strong emotions,
her intense disposition to be "in love," and her sexuality were probably
threatening to both her parents and may have magnified other dysfunctional processes. It is also possible that Russ spent so much time at the
track partly *because* he felt shut out by the mother–daughter coalition.
Certainly there are families in which a martyred mother or a strong-willed
child dictates the family's dynamic. But overall, our data suggest that
fathers usually have the most influence over the family's emotional life.

Family dysfunction often emerges, then, from the flaws in the traditional role system. Virginia Goldner argues that the typical dysfunctional
pattern, in which the father is dominant but peripheral and the mother is
overinvolved with the children, is the product of family gender roles that
have evolved over two hundred years.[19] The traditional role structure
between husband and wife sets up and sustains maladaptive patterns of
relating. In the more distressed families we have seen, the asymmetry of
family roles is often magnified: the traditional male position of power allows
these men to be emotionally dominant; mothers' stereotypical role catches
them in a set of paradoxes that limits their options to resist and respond.

In the Perkins family, whom we describe next, the mother is fighting
back against this current, although the conflict that results also has adverse
implications for the family.

DISTRESSED MARRIAGE → DISTRESSED CHILD

For a developing child, the parents' marriage is an important part of
the environment in which she grows up. In order to understand why
Vivian, a quiet, intelligent eighth-grader, was having adjustment difficulties, we need to understand the emotional climate of her parents' relationship.

Kevin Perkins, a lean forty-six-year-old man with a sheepish smile, was
like many traditional fathers we have introduced in this book. He worked

seven days a week as a supervisor at a vending machine firm, a stressful position in which he felt trapped and unsatisfied.

Kevin expected Kim, his wife of twenty-three years, to take responsibility for keeping things together at home, as well as providing support services for his needs. Her performance as cook was a particular concern of his. One day the beeper found him eating his lunch at work and he complained on our form about the sandwiches she had made for him. Another evening, when Kim was off at night school, he groused about what a "rotten supper" she had left for them. Kevin made negative comments about a lot of things in his life, from his coworkers to his daughter Vivian's basketball playing. Like Russ Thompson, he sprayed his hostility around. The difference was that, unlike Wendy Thompson, Kim Perkins did not massage her husband's back. She fought fire with fire.

The domestic snare of Kim's life as a full-time homemaker resembled that of many women in our study; in fact, it was worse. She and Kevin had ten children, ages two to twenty-four, and the labor of taking care of them kept her going continually, just as it required Kevin to work long hours to support them financially. Friday at noon, Kim expressed a fusillade of anger and frustration about her entrapment, explaining: "I feel controlled by my spouse and children because, even if they are not around, they control my day by what I have to do for them."

In addition to performing her homemaking tasks, however, Kim was going to school three evenings a week to get a nursing degree. Kevin was unsupportive: he complained about the cost of her classes, and when the beeper caught him at home taking care of the kids, he griped that "raising a family is *her* job." Yet this time at school was the one consistent bright spot in Kim's life. Monday evening she reported feeling ecstatic that she received an A, that even as a middle-aged housewife she could do as well as the younger students in the class.

Perhaps it was this external base of reinforcement that gave her the confidence to confront Kevin. The first beep, on a Wednesday night, found the couple arguing. The hockey coach had ended practice early and they could not find their sons, who had wandered off somewhere in the high school. Kevin was angry at the boys for not staying put. Kim defended the boys and was angry at the coach for his irresponsibility in not monitoring them.

The hostility between them continued for two days, then on Friday night, when Kevin came home from work, Kim had had enough of his complaining. The pager did not catch them during the fight that ensued, but at 8:56, Kevin reported that he was bedding down in the camper, because "I got thrown out of the house." Although he commented on "how stupid my wife is," she had taken the upper hand. Then Saturday, Kevin worried all day at his job about whether she would let him back in, and in his diary at the end of the day he reported, "Wife let me sleep at home—no supper though."

This conflict appears to have been chronic in their marriage. On the following Wednesday night, the interviewer observed palpable tension between them, with Kim nagging Kevin and Kevin passively resisting by pretending not to hear. Kim admitted that she has an occasional temper tantrum. "I keep my sanity by just holding on," she said. Kevin retaliated with passive, icy hostility and denied he might be making any contribution to their disharmony; for example, he insisted he had no idea why Kim kicked him out of the house. The Perkinses scored the lowest of all the couples in our study on the marital adjustment scale; and the level of warmth between them was nearly at the bottom of the scale.[20] Given the chance to live her life over, Kim said, she would marry a different person; Kevin said he would not marry.

How the Dog Gets Kicked

Many people in our society believe that divorce is "bad" for children, that warring parents should stay together "for the sake of the kids." Young people, it is claimed, need daily relationships with both parents. What is not often asked, however, is how marital conflict affects these daily relationships. What kind of environment does a conflictual marriage, such as the Perkinses, create for developing children?

Husbands' and wives' feelings of hostility toward each other, we found, was regularly followed by their feeling hostile toward their children. Our data show that animosity was passed from the one with most power on to the one with the least power, just as in the classic cartoon sequence that concludes with the youngest child giving the family dog a swift kick.

Not surprisingly, this chain of contagion often starts with Dad. When fathers in our study felt hostile toward their wives at one point in time, they were likely to feel hostile to the adolescent at the next point in time. Furthermore, a father's antagonism toward his wife was also followed by her subsequent antagonism toward the child (see appendix 8.3).

Put simply, anger begets anger. Earlier in the chapter we discussed how negative emotions are transmitted from one family member to another. This finding shows how feelings are transmitted from one *relationship* to another. Anger is passed from the marital relationship to the parent–child relationship. The researchers Andrew Christensen and Gayla Margolin obtained a similar finding when they asked families to keep track of fights. They learned that an argument between father and mother was often followed by an argument between parent and child, as well as between brothers and sisters.[21]

Children such as Vivian, then, are the beneficiaries of marital hostility. On Saturday night, while her parents were still fighting, Vivian tried to get her mother to talk about a private high school she wanted to attend next year. But Kim, preoccupied with her husband, was emotionally unavailable and cold to her daughter. On Sunday morning Vivian finally got her mother to discuss the issue, but Kim, who had "a thousand things on my mind," became annoyed thinking about the costs associated with a private school—and her financial dependence on Kevin. As a result, Kim and Vivian had a fight and at 10:54 Vivian was sitting alone in the family room angry and crying.

After many repetitions, this fallout from marital conflict takes its toll on relationships between adolescents and their parents. Marital distress was associated with greater negative emotion in interactions between mothers and adolescents in our study (see appendix 8.4), as we saw in Vivian and Kim's Sunday morning argument. Vivian reported that she did not go to her mother for advice nor to share inner feelings. She had been burned too many times.

The effect of marital conflict on adolescents' relationships with their mothers can be substantial; the effect on their relationships with their fathers is even greater. Vivian reported feeling very distant from her dad. We found that if the marriage was poor, the adolescents felt less warm toward their fathers, and their fathers felt less warm toward them (see appendix 8.4). They didn't necessarily fight; rather, the relationships were superficial. Vivian and Kevin showed the *low* rate of shared negative emotion that we found to characterize shallow father–adolescent relationships. When they had a disagreement about her basketball, for example, Vivian reported that Kevin left the room rather than talking it out. Instead of being sympathetic, he responded contemptuously and made a quick exit, avoiding engagement.

Many of these superficial father–adolescent relationships may reflect the important part mothers play in fostering this bond. In their traditional role, mothers are often the go-between, promoting relations between adolescents and their fathers. Mothers sometimes even coach fathers on what to do and say.[22] When father and mother are hostile to each other, she may be less likely to play this facilitative role. In fact, Kim's strategy in her battle with Kevin was to punish him by making him unwelcome in the house and restricting his access to their children, whom he dearly loved. The responsibility that fathers give mothers to orchestrate family relations places their own relationship with their children at risk.

A distressed marriage, then, disrupts the web of connections that link mothers, adolescents, and fathers.[23] It interferes with the kinds of daily communications that bind a family together, thus weakening the argument that a couple should continue the marriage in order to maintain vital relationships with their children. From the young adolescent's point of view, however, the negative effects of marital conflict do not stop here.

Adolescents' Reality, Adolescents' Needs

Adolescents' needs in many respects are greater than those of either parent. Many things are changing for them, disrupting their sense of a secure place in the world, and they have had less time than their parents to adapt and habituate their emotional reactions to life changes. As a result, their feelings are often raw, unpredictable, and sometimes out of control.

An adolescent's family experience can be part of the solution. Home life can be a secure base; it can provide a predictable arena of comfort that stabilizes these emotional gyrations. In the presence of his family, we found, the average young adolescent felt more important and calm than in other parts of his or her life, as well as less nervous, embarrassed, and frustrated.

In Vivian's case, however, her family was clearly part of the problem. We have seen that marital conflict has disrupted her relationships with her parents. It has also added a major strain to her life. Young adolescents rate parental fighting as one of the most difficult stressors they experience.[24] Witnessing conflict between parents often makes young people scared and upset,[25] and young adolescents appear to be particularly vulnerable to family stress.[26]

Thus even though Vivian did not see the scene in which her dad was kicked out of the house, she heard the story of the event from her siblings, and the imminent possibility that the fight might flare up again kept her depressed and unable to do homework. At 2:44 P.M. on Saturday she reported feeling angry and worried because of her parents' conflict. That evening, at 6:42, she was anxious because "my dad just came home from work and I'm afraid my parents might have an argument." Figure 8.1 shows Vivian's moods across the week, and we can see how they responded to the state of her parents' relationship. She was consistently happier at school than at home. Even on Thursday, after her team won a volleyball game, her mood dropped when she returned home that evening.[27] She was depressed all weekend, and, after staying home sick Monday morning, her mood improved only when she got out Monday evening and found a friend with whom she discussed her family problems.

The bitter irony for adolescents is that marital conflict simultaneously increases their need for an arena of comfort and robs them of it. Marital conflict adds to the stress in their lives and weakens the relationships with parents that are often their most helpful buffer *against* stress. This irony was vivid for Vivian, who said that her mother and father were each "very important" to her, but reported feeling weak and distant relationships with both of them.

Perhaps because they lacked this arena of comfort, adolescents in the more distressed families in our study reported feeling significantly worse both at home *and* away from home (see appendix 8.1). Compared to those of kids in less distressed families, their emotional states were more dysphoric across all domains of their daily lives. We also found that these adolescents' global well-being was related to the quality of their parents' marriage. When parents reported marital coldness and maladjustment, their young adolescents were likely to have lower self-esteem and be more depressed than other young adolescents (see appendix 8.4).

Research by others reinforces this picture. Studies indicate that the association we have been discussing is at least partly causal: marital distress directly hurts a child's adjustment.[28] They also show that children's and adolescents' adjustment problems are greater in quarrelsome, hostile marriages than in apathetic, indifferent ones.[29] Indeed, the negative effects attributed to divorce may often be a result of the marital conflict that had raged prior to the separation.[30] And while we have used a girl, Vivian, to illustrate these processes, some research suggests that the costs of marital conflict may be even greater for boys.[31]

In Vivian's case, her school grades were adequate, but she was also caught cheating on a test. She was doing well in sports, but Kevin reported that she has had a conflict with the coach because she refused to play the position she was assigned. Most important, she reported low self-esteem and numerous symptoms of depression. She marked that she does not like herself, often has trouble sleeping, is always tired, and feels like crying every day. Obviously, we only scratched the surface of what was going on in her life. Without information from the other nine children in the Perkins fam-

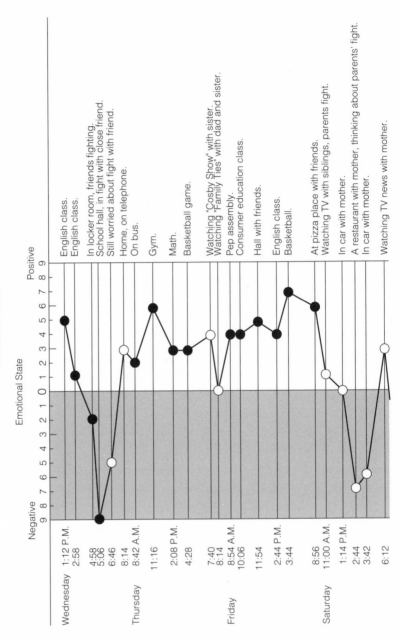

Figure 8.1

VIVIAN'S WEEK

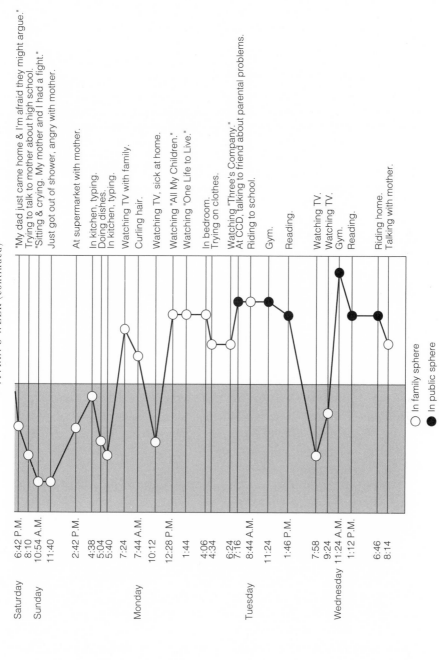

VIVIAN'S WEEK (continued)

"My dad just came home & I'm afraid they might argue."
Trying to talk to mother about high school.
"Sitting & crying. My mother and I had a fight."
Just got out of shower, angry with mother.

At supermarket with mother.

In kitchen, typing.
Doing dishes.
In kitchen, typing.

Watching TV with family.

Curling hair.

Watching TV, sick at home.

Watching "All My Children."
Watching "One Life to Live."

In bedroom.
Trying on clothes.

Watching "Three's Company."
At CCD, talking to friend about parental problems.

Riding to school.

Gym.

Reading.

Watching TV.
Watching TV.
Gym.

Reading.

Riding home.
Talking with mother.

Saturday   6:42 P.M.
  8:10
Sunday   10:54 A.M.
  11:40

  2:42 P.M.

  4:38
  5:04
  5:40

  7:24

Monday   7:44 A.M.

  10:12

  12:28 P.M.

  1:44

  4:06
  4:34

  6:24
  7:16

Tuesday   8:44 A.M.

  11:24

  1:46 P.M.

  7:58
  9:24
Wednesday 11:24 A.M.

  1:12 P.M.

  6:46
  8:14

○ In family sphere
● In public sphere

ily, we cannot pretend to have an adequate understanding of their family system. Nonetheless, it appeared this was a young adolescent whose emotional and developmental needs were not being met, and her parents' chronic state of conflict was a major part of the problem.

A CAULDRON OF NEEDS

Deep down, we all expect the family to be a respite from the other difficulties in our lives, a "haven in a heartless world," as Christopher Lasch put it. Each family member descends on the home each evening with hopes of finding a warm and calm refuge that will be responsive to his or her private needs. Such expectations may be particularly high for magazine-cover, two-parent, European-American, middle-class families, like those we have studied. Yet instead of a refuge, members of many of these families often encounter a cacophony of incompatible realities, competing needs, and interpersonal conflicts. Rather than meeting fellow wayfarers, they come home to unsympathetic rivals.

Because each family member is attending to different priorities, because they all have different needs and stresses, their realities are often out of sync. Even when they want to share a leisure activity they may be at odds. One man reported that his wife liked to shop, his daughter liked playing video games, and he would rather stay home. "When we try to do something together, nobody can agree and we argue." The family is supposed to be a haven, but sometimes no one can get her needs met. Contemporary family life is often like the classic Japanese film *Rashomon*, in which the family members experience conflicting versions of the day's events. Reality is contested; discrepant perceptions are a constant obstacle;[32] conflict or malfunction in one part of the family generates conflict and malfunction elsewhere.

In a way, even the more dysfunctional families in our study still functioned for the fathers. Their home life was still a refuge from the stress they experienced at their jobs and away from the family. In spite of the unhappiness experienced by others in the family, fathers like Russ and Kevin were happier at home because they claimed it as their domain to do what they needed. They shifted into leisure mode and in some cases forced their frustrations and hostility onto their wives and children. But while serving fathers' short-term needs, this pattern of adjustment perpetuates the larger family dysfunction. Other family members are subject to fathers' moods, and the hostility that often emerges between these men and their wives adversely affects their children.

In contrast to fathers, mothers in distressed families exercise less power to get their own needs met at home. Society assigns women responsibility for the well-being of the family; as a result, they are often the recipients of everyone else's emotional laundry. Hence when the family experiences higher distress, it lowers the mother's well-being in this sphere. The mother may feel she must deny her own needs, yet when her needs are not satisfied, she may be less available to her child, as Kim was, or attempt to form a dysfunctional cross-generational alliance with the child, as Wendy did.

Young adolescents have the most profound needs for refuge and are most vulnerable to family dysfunction. Their turbulent, changing lives and limited life skills make an arena of comfort at home crucial. Vivian said her mother and father were very important to her, yet her parents' chronic conflict created an environment in which little energy was available to support her adjustment and growth. When family life is not calm and secure, it handicaps an adolescent both at home and away from home. Without an arena of comfort, her or his entire range of experience is less buoyant.

Why are so many contemporary families unhealthy? We might be wiser to reverse the question and ask why should we expect them to be? Unlike any other institution in our society, the family places people of different ages and genders in close proximity and expects them to live harmoniously together. Should it be a surprise that children and adults, men and women often start relating to each other in distorted ways? Rather than asking why so many families are not functioning, it may be more useful to ask what occurs in other families that allows them to function well? What goes right in some families?

CHAPTER 9

Healthy Families:
TOWARD CONVERGENT REALITIES

In many ways the deck is stacked against contemporary families, including the comparatively privileged two-parent families we studied here. They must struggle to create internal vitality within a society that is massive, fragmented, and often pulls family members in different directions. When a couple gets married and has children, they enter a minefield of problems waiting to happen. Differences between the fast-paced daily realities lived by each family member create endless potential for misunderstanding and conflict.

Against this backdrop, our society has evolved a new ideal for family life: providing warm relationships and a personal haven for all members. Evidence shows that this new gold standard is one we should aspire to. When marital partners are caring toward each other, their well-being is greater, as is their children's. When relations between parent and child are warm, the child grows up to be a healthier adult. Our question has been, What can families do that would allow them to live up to this standard more consistently? How can families maintain internal warmth despite all the daily processes that pull them apart?

Certainly there are no easy answers. One woman said, "If you claim to have gotten through your child's adolescence without problems, you're lying." We have seen that the simplest interactions of daily life can lead family members into discord. Getting haircuts for the children, fixing the humidifier, a phone call between an adolescent and her boyfriend can create individual distress and collective disharmony.

Nonetheless, we feel it useful to look closely at the families in our study that were faring better. Despite the hazards of contemporary life, in some of these families the members usually got through most days feeling

211

warm toward each other and good about themselves. Husbands and wives shared love and mutual respect, most of the time. Their children usually rebounded quickly from setbacks in their lives. Of course, all these families had moments of conflict, stress, and exchange of negative feelings—no one family had solved the Rubik's cube of domestic harmony. But in some families individual members were buoyant and their daily lives were coordinated most of the time.

In this concluding chapter we search for clues to what it was that was working in these healthier families: What daily patterns allowed them to surmount the many challenges of modern life? The conclusions we draw are limited to households sharing the cultural niche of those we studied: European-American, middle- and working-class, two-parent families. Even within this population, our conclusions are tempered by the fallibility of the measures we have used and the restricted size of our sample. Nevertheless, we think these families provide hints about a "wisdom" whereby some households function more smoothly.

DAILY PATTERNS OF HEALTHIER FAMILIES

Equilibrium Between Family and Public Spheres

We have already introduced some of the families that scored high on our index of family well-being: Del and Marlene, whose marital conflict was followed not by cycles of acrimony, but rather by creative thought about how to resolve the underlying source of their misunderstanding; Lorraine and her son, Luke, who appeared to maintain a healthy balance between their lives together and apart; Victor and his daughter, Vicki, who seemed to be more accepting of each other's feelings, including negative feelings, than most fathers and adolescents.

When we examine the daily patterns of these healthier families, a first finding that emerges concerns the equilibrium between the parents' lives at home and away from home. Throughout this book we have noted that both fathers and mothers typically experience an imbalance between these two spheres: men report high rates of distress at work and compensate for it by cultivating happier states at home; women are drained at home and depend on their job or interactions with friends for the happier part of their lives. These imbalances, we observed in the last chapter, make each spouse dependent on a particular part of his or her life for emotional sustenance and, as a result, promote distorted family relationships. In healthier families, however, we find that *fathers and mothers maintain emotional balance between their lives inside and outside the family.* They report comparable levels of emotion at home and away from home (see appendix 8.1).

For fathers, this balance means that they less often burned themselves out at their jobs. Fathers in healthier families reported more favorable moods at their jobs than other fathers did: they were less likely to deplete themselves with frustration and anger. Possibly these fathers have deliberately chosen less stressful jobs. We mentioned one such father, John, who quit a high-pressure job because he was bringing home too much hostility and taking it out on his son. But our data also suggest that the fathers in healthier families took more breaks and paced themselves at work.[1] We suspect they did more to regulate the intensity of their involvement, in order to avoid getting agitated. The important point is that these fathers were less likely to be emotional wrecks when they got home.

A good example of this balance is Erik Schaak, a father of four who worked in a factory as a forklift operator. This affable thirty-eight-year-old man experienced some pressure at work to move so many items a day, and events at the plant could anger him. At one point he got upset and cursed an "SOB." But he was usually able to regain his composure and keep himself from becoming overwrought. Because his wife, Judy, had a stable career, he did not feel as much obligation to be the breadwinning hero for the family as so many other fathers in our study did. The result of Erik's ability to keep stress in check at his job was that he arrived home with less of an emotional debt than many other fathers did and thus felt less need for immediate leisure when he came in the door.

For mothers as well, emotional balance means having sources of buoyancy both away from home and at home. While some mothers are solely invested in activities at home, many of the women in the healthier families in our study had rewarding outside activities: a job, school, volunteer work, or regular contact with friends. At home, they were engaged with their families but also gave themselves permission to relax and take care of their own needs: we found they had more leisure on weekends at home than other mothers did.[2] They described pleasure in family recreation, reading a book by themselves, or taking a long bath, activities that restored their personal well-being.

Judy Schaak, a self-assured first-grade teacher, was a good example of this balance. She encountered stresses both at work and at home, but was able to keep them under control; she also found emotional rewards in both contexts, which she savored. Judy consistently reported looking forward to the next day, emphasizing the value of maintaining a "positive attitude." Because Erik shared responsibility for family work, she was able to disengage at home when she needed to, reporting time on her own for reading and embroidering. Because women in these healthier families had vital lives apart from their family activities, they were less likely to become over-involved.

One result of this balance is that neither spouse felt like a victim at home. Neither brought home a personal agenda of unmet emotional needs. Each was less dependent on the family experience for emotional sustenance—and neither had to leave home to get needs met. Consequently, a couple like Judy and Erik are more flexible to accommodate to each other and negotiate each day according to whatever exigencies arise. When Judy heard on Friday that her job was threatened, she called and got support from Erik, just as he turned to her in other situations.

Another result of this balance is that they were more emotionally available as parents to deal with their children's needs. Fathers who are not preoccupied with work and mothers who have the perspective gained from outside involvements may be better able to provide this even, objective attention. Judy and Erik's sixth-grade son, Calvin, was sometimes angered by the discipline his parents imposed, but he also reported learning from the conversations he had with each of them around these disciplinary incidents. Through steady efforts, Calvin said, his father "finally made me realize that I lose my temper too much," for example. Because Erik's emotions were not continuously raw from events at work, he was better able to maintain an even-keeled dialogue with his son, resulting in an important victory of reason over adolescent passion.

The picturebook image of the happy family is one where everyone feels content when together. Our findings suggest that mothers' and fathers' feelings *away from* home may be nearly as important to a family's well-being.[3] "Part of being a parent," the family educator Michael Popkin writes, "is taking care of the parent."[4] And while this is a complicated topic, evidence throughout this book shows that maintaining a healthy family depends on how members run their lives across all their waking hours.

Containing Emotional Brushfires

We suspect this balance in parents' lives contributes to a second feature we find in healthier families. At various points we have seen that negative emotions can be contagious within families. Most often fathers affect other family members, but it can begin with others as well. In some families this contagion leads to cycles of runaway hostility, such as the quarrel between Jerry and Glenna that went on for three days. Healthier families, we find, show less evidence of this transmission of emotion and fewer of these sustained cycles. *One person's emotional states are less likely to be passed to another.*[5]

The family therapist Robert Beavers reached a similar conclusion from his study of successful families. He found that in such families there are stronger "emotional boundaries" between members: it is easier to distinguish mothers', fathers', and children's feelings. Negative states were less often conveyed through blaming, attacking, or scapegoating.[6]

Rather than spraying negative emotions, members of healthier families seem to find ways to process them. One father tried to get home from work early enough so he could go for a run before dinner to dissipate stress. A mother reported taking thirty minutes to pull herself together before leaving her office, because she knew she would be deluged with demands the minute she stepped in the door at home; and though this meant thirty minutes less with her daughter, she found that the restorative effect this time had on her mood made it worthwhile.

Certainly there were occasions in these families where negative emotions got expressed. Erik Schaak admitted that he was sometimes short-tempered after a hard day's work. But these families seemed to be able to respond to members' emotions without letting one person's emotions dictate or dominate another's, as was demonstrated one evening at the Schaaks'. Events on this evening began much like other conflagrations we have seen that rebounded out of control for hours. At 6:58 P.M. Erik and Judy Schaak both reported intense anger over Calvin's "mouthing off." By 8:52, however, all remaining trace of negative feeling was gone. What happened? First, both parents agreed that Calvin's behavior was unacceptable and presented a united front. They did not allow Calvin to play them off against each other as we have seen in some less healthy families. Second, in a kind of "bad cop, good cop" routine, Erik disciplines Calvin by sending him to his room with a clear explanation of why his behavior is unacceptable, then later, Judy went in and comforted Calvin and discussed what had happened. By communicating about the causes of their negative feelings and listening to each other, these families appeared to keep emotional brushfires from getting out of control. Later Calvin reported feeling respectful of how his parents handled the situation.

At heart, members of these families seemed to have greater understanding and acceptance of their own and each other's emotional patterns. Mothers, fathers, and even some adolescents were able to tell us that, yes, they got irritable in certain situations and those feelings could alter their behavior, but they realized it was a pattern they could work on. Parents of one eighth-grade girl characterized their daughter as emotional, but were aware that her emotions passed quickly. Thus rather than fixating and ruminating on her transgressions, they accepted that she was "a moody adolescent" and avoided being pulled in by her hour-to-hour emotional oscillations.

It was fathers in these healthier families who showed the biggest deviation from typical norms for their gender, more often shedding the cloak of patriarchal authority and relating to their wives and children as equals. They were more aware of their own feelings and thus were less likely to dump their negative emotions onto others. They also appeared less likely to withdraw from difficult situations: we found examples of these fathers sustaining engagement with their wives about marital issues and staying with their children even when emotions were painful.

While such attentiveness is customary for mothers, it is rare among fathers. Yet when it exists, it does much to stop the cycles of negative exchange and create a more favorable environment for all family members. Our findings suggest that the art of family life resides in all members being able to attend to, communicate, and contain negative emotions in ways that do not transmit and perpetuate them.

Averting the 6 O'Clock Crash

The volatility of many of the families in our study and the calm of others lie in what happens during the dicey period around six o'clock on weekday evenings. This is a time when lines are most often crossed, when negative emotions are frequently exchanged. It is during this period that we saw a mother's harsh words lead one girl to thoughts of suicide, an angry stepfather push his daughter against the wall, and a dispute between one husband and wife escalate into the husband being kicked out of the house.

Better-functioning families found ways to get through this crunch period with fewer negative emotions. In healthier families, *everyone's mood during this period was more favorable.*[7] Irrespective of mothers' and fathers' employment situations, they avoided the hostile and explosive feelings that are rife in other families.

Part of the problem, as we have discussed, is that fathers bring home emotional stress from work. The other part of the problem is that, in most families, everything that needs to be done during this period hinges on the mother. This can be especially problematic in dual-earner families, where the mother is coming home tired from work herself. In these families the father often flops down in front of the TV, while the mother, who is equally tired, is forced into labor. The result is often negative feelings all around.

So how did healthier families get through this difficult time? In the Schaak family, it was simply understood that Erik, who usually got home from work around 3:30 P.M., was jointly responsible for the urgent tasks of this period. He reported folding clothes with his wife one late afternoon and changing the baby's diaper on another. On yet another, he cooked dinner for Judy, who had had a particularly rough day.

Unlike most fathers, Erik Schaak refused to see his tiredness as more debilitating than his wife's, and Judy was unambivalent about sharing responsibilities with him. Before the school year started, Judy reported, they "sat down and figured out menus for the week and what days laundry and other housework would be done." Now, whatever needed to be done, Erik pitched right in. At times he would lose his cool with the children— late afternoon could still be a stressful period for all. But the fact that both Erik and Judy were involved made them more flexible to handle whatever combination of pressing needs people brought home.

The Schaak family's solution to the 6 o'clock crunch is more the exception than the rule. Some other families reduced the amount of labor required by making microwave dinners or ordering takeout food. Other families have relaxed the expectation that they share a hot meal at 6 each day; in one, different combinations of family members went to exercise during this time, an activity that was effective in both dissipating the day's stress and giving them a chance to check in with each other. In another, each ate separately; the daily family time was not at 6 over supper, but at 10 when all shared a snack and discussed events of the day.

These findings suggest that the art of cultivating a healthy family resides in finding creative solutions for household work, particularly during the 6 o'clock crunch. Each evening produced its unique vortex of urgencies, but through communication, flexibility, and engagement of all members, these healthier families were *usually* able to get through this challenging period with less conflict and transmission of negative emotion.

In Search of Quality Time

Healthy families, according to some family advocates, require not just the avoidance of destructive emotional exchanges, they require renewing ones. Eating meals or spending other time together is thought to provide the opportunity for a family to replenish themselves and affirm their experience of "we-ness."[8]

But defining what makes for this "quality time" is elusive. Some dysfunctional families eat every breakfast and dinner together and spend enormous amounts of time with each other, as we saw in the enmeshed relationship between Wendy Thompson and her daughter Roxanne (chapter

8). Spending time in a dysfunctional family may only make members more dysfunctional. "Togetherness is a grand and wonderful thing," the family therapist Nathan Ackerman has written, "but . . . mere physical togetherness may be worse than none at all."[9]

Clearly, just clocking in hours with each other does not automatically reinvigorate the family. We reported earlier that the amount of time husband and wife spent together is related to better marital adjustment, but the same is not true of shared time between parents and adolescents.[10] You may remember that adolescents often experience family time as slow, boring, and constrained; it is thus easy to see why an increase of this kind of time does not enhance family health. But what kind of time do healthier families share? Is there anything unique about their daily contact that might provide hints about improving families' functioning?

First, we found that *members of these families reported fewer negative states when they were together.* Mothers, fathers, and adolescents in the healthier families we studied reported fewer occasions of feeling irritable and angry in each other's presence.[11] This follows from what we have just discussed above: These families find ways to minimize situations that create and perpetuate negative feelings. They maintain a comfortable, relaxed climate in which sustained anger, hurt, and unhappiness cannot thrive.

Second, we found that *the healthier families spent more time in leisure together.* They were more likely than distressed families to go to the zoo, visit relatives, or, as the Schaaks did frequently, just watch TV together.[12] Part of the reason they had more time for each other is that they apparently limited the net hours of work that family members performed. Families who spent most of their time working were less likely to be healthy; this was true irrespective of family social class or mother's employment, suggesting the pattern is not merely a result of financial pressures.[13] Rather than tying up their weekends working overtime or doing household work, members of healthier families are more likely to be available for shared recreational activities.

The third characteristic is that *these families experienced their time together as more egalitarian.* Fewer of them reported a unilateral power structure among members. For times they were together, they reported no one to be the leader twice as often.[14] This mutuality is evident, for example, on a Sunday night when one family was planning a fishing trip together, and all contributed ideas. It is evident in another when they went out for ice cream cones and shared a calm, low-key mood. In many other instances this mutuality was reported when doing chores together or even watching TV. Parents were able to set aside their impulse to control things.

These families appeared more able to relax traditional authority structures and find islands of time when they could interact as equals.

What, then, is quality family time? To define it by any rigid criteria would be mistaken. The activities, topics of conversations, and emotional spirit that rekindle family élan may vary from household to household, occasion to occasion, and even from person to person within a family. The elements we have discussed—shared leisure, egalitarian relationships, and avoidance of negative emotion—are important, but there is surely no simple formula. For some families, quality time might even include fathers and adolescents openly airing negative feelings. What is important, we suspect, is not any singular group activity or mystical state, but a climate of attunement between family members, interactions in which each is able to listen and respond to what others are thinking and feeling, even when there is conflict.

In this and the other properties of healthier families, we see a pattern of relating in which fathers, mothers, and adolescents transcend traditional prescriptions for their behavior. This leads us to step beyond our specific findings and discuss the broader conclusion we have drawn from our study.

BEYOND ROLES: TOWARD A NEW FAMILY ETHIC

The traditional family established its order from a fixed structure of role assignments: the father did this, the mother did that; all family members followed a script that dictated their behavior. The foundation of this order was a Hobbesian belief that without strict norms, behavior degenerates into chaos. Yet we discarded this dark view of human nature in the political and other arenas as much as two hundred years ago.[15]

Over the last century, we have been gradually substituting a view of family order that puts value not just on members' behavior, but also on the family's internal life. We have slowly realized that the traditional role assignments often have harsh emotional costs to individuals' well-being. Sequestered housewives, solo breadwinners, and compliant children can suffer from the isolation of their fixed roles. Furthermore, we have recognized that when family members are chronically stressed, unhappy, or exhausted, it affects those around them; it generates anger and conflict within the family.

What the findings of this book suggest is that collective family well-being depends not on fixed role assignments, but rather on flexible *processes* that allow the family to adjust and adapt. In healthier families, fathers are able to talk with their wives about the cause of a misunderstanding and tolerate the anguish their adolescent children feel over a violin solo or a falling-out with friends. In healthier families, mothers' family relationships are less likely to be dictated by the emptiness of housework, and both parents are able to roll with the changes in their adolescents' lives. The key to promoting a positive internal family life, we believe, lies not in rigid prescriptions, but in the wisdom behind a family's daily practices.

There is no one "right" way to create family health, just as there is no "correct" family structure. Whether we are talking about a two-parent family, such as those studied here, or a one-parent or other family form, what is important is how well family members adapt their daily lives to their joint situation. Some households deal with more difficult economic circumstances than others, which may make family life harder. Each family also has its own unique constellation of personalities to accommodate and draw from. Maintaining a family's internal balance is the art of honestly struggling with ongoing circumstances, whatever they might be.

The foundation of these practices, we believe, should be their underlying attentiveness to both individual and group needs. The starting place for interpersonal ethics, according to the theologian Carter Heyward, should be the "needs, values, obligations, and visions" of each individual.[16] Within families this means adapting to the unique vulnerabilities of children. It also may mean recognizing the distinct traditions that have shaped the lives of women and men. Families should not let one person's reality dominate others': all realities need to be acknowledged and respected.

At the same time, the needs of the group must be attended to. We have seen that for individuals to thrive, they must have caring, supportive, and enjoyable interactions with those around them. Families should develop an internal ethos that encourages each person to develop in his or her own way but also affirms the connections between individuals. Families should acknowledge individual difference and change, but strive for mutuality. The critical ingredient, Heyward says, is the capacity for continuous renegotiation of interpersonal boundaries—the flexibility to grow both together and apart.

Let us try to discuss this more concretely.

Parenting for the Twenty-first Century

The loudest argument one hears against the fading of fixed roles in the family concerns its effects on children. Respecting children as equals, traditionalists assert, only feeds their narcissism. Relaxing parental authority, many people worry, gives adolescents license to talk back and run wild.[17]

But to focus on parental strictness versus leniency misses the critical issue, which is the quality of the relationships an adolescent experiences in the family: Is there trust and open communication between parent and child? Is there encouragement and support for the adolescent to mature?

In earlier times, it may well have been that obedience was the most important lesson a child could learn from his or her family. Much of adult life in the past involved authoritarian relationships—at work, in marriage, in the public domain—and, regardless of their suffocating effects on morale, people had to learn to live with them. Yet much of contemporary adult life in our society involves interactions with putative equals, and it has become clear that much of the distress people experience in life comes from their inability to control and manage such interactions. Adolescents and adults are unable to protect themselves from manipulation, are seduced into exploitive relationships, or find it too easy to exploit others. Families could bequeath their children no more important lesson than the ability to avoid unhealthy relationships and create and maintain healthy ones.

A large body of research indicates that children and adolescents in our society develop maturity when they receive a combination of *support* and *challenge* from their parents.[18] Support means that parents respect and pay attention to adolescents' feelings, needs, and the organization of their emotional lives. In the healthier families we studied, the parents were more often available to their children to discuss the breaking events of the day, whether in person or by phone. Many parents spoke not of solving problems for their adolescents, but of helping them think about alternative courses of action. One mother said, "Occasionally we've even switched roles and taken the other person's point of view in role playing." These parents engaged with their teens and helped them see the big picture. At the same time, they possessed the very difficult ability to let go; they recognized that teens need time apart from their parents.

Challenging an adolescent means that parents push the child to the edge of (but not beyond) his or her capabilities. This includes encouraging the adolescent to see parents' and siblings' sides of interactions. Children need to be given the language to talk about their feelings and other people's feelings at an early age.[19] Adolescents should not be allowed to dump their problems on their parents, nor let others take household responsibilities that should be theirs. When parents set limits, they should explain them and help teens understand their reasoning. In healthier parent–child relationships there is an ongoing dialogue about what is reasonable, healthy, and safe for all parties involved.

The combination of support and challenge to adolescents has visible payoffs. The psychologist Catherine Cooper has found that when families engage adolescents in negotiation of parent–child differences, not only does family life run more smoothly, adolescents solve problems in a more mature manner with their peers as well.[20] Give-and-take between parent and child that strives for intelligent regulation of behavior becomes a template for adolescents' other relationships.

In an atmosphere of flexible engagement between parents and adolescents, teens often prove to be quite worthy of defining their own limits. We were stirred by one mother's description of talking her eighth-grade daughter through a romantic involvement with a boy whose father had AIDS. Instead of giving advice and peremptory opinions, this mother helped her daughter reflect as she went through a long sequence of events, including the man's funeral. As a result of this dialogue, the daughter made the important discovery that feeling sorry for a boy is not a good reason to continue a romantic relationship with him.

Parents discover, of course, that it is anything but easy to maintain one's poise with an adolescent who oscillates between being cantankerous and profoundly needy, especially when numerous other pressures exist in one's life. Many parents who belong to the "me generation" are simply unprepared for how demanding children can be. Even when mothers and fathers maintain a balanced life and have a good marital relationship, it is inevitable that adolescents will tax their time and well-being, and that moments will occur when they feel they have said exactly the wrong thing. But it is hardly a fatal flaw for parents to acknowledge their own shortcomings and recognize that they too have room for growth.

Making the Democratic Family Work

The family, it is useful to recognize, is the ultimate experiment in human relations. It brings together individuals of different ages and genders—people with much different emotional worlds—and expects them to live together and harmoniously negotiate the numerous hazards of daily life. A couple is mistaken to assume that having children magically results in a "family." Families do not just happen, they are what their members make them. Each family must struggle with its own internal dynamics.

Sustaining warm family relations is a difficult, creative accomplishment. If any aspect of family life needs to be institutionalized, it is not fixed roles, but rather processes of communication that allow this creativity to occur. Families need to routinize procedures for family members to express their changing needs, be accountable for their actions, and jointly adjust and adapt to each other.

For the adults in a family, this means finding opportunities apart from the daily grind to discuss and reflect on their lives as parents and partners. Given their busy lives, just finding this time can be difficult. Some parents in our study found that the only way to get time to talk was to call each other at work; one couple met regularly in the factory lot. Men in particular need to learn to recognize their impact on the family and develop skills for this kind of communication. A marriage built on listening to each other's concerns and sharing of important decisions is ultimately more empowering for both partners.

Regular family meetings are becoming an increasingly common vehicle for fostering communication among the family as a whole. Structured weekly councils of family members offer a forum for all voices to be expressed and family responsibility to be shared.[21] Family meetings provide an opportunity to talk about joint issues. These may also be a time for each member to work on his or her own issues: for fathers to discuss ways of dealing with their stress from work, for mothers to stand up for their own needs, and for adolescents to examine what their membership in the family means.

The agenda for these regular marital and family communications has been suggested by the findings of this book. Families need to analyze the structure of their week: When do conflicts usually occur? Are one person's emotional states repeatedly dominating others'? When do their schedules allow for shared time?

Clearly, a major issue that every family needs to keep on the front burner is responsibility for family work. Housework is depressing, not only because it is repetitious and unchallenging but because it is often experienced as invisible and menial work being performed by one person for another.[22] Change needs to come from all family members.

With increasing numbers of women employed full-time, men can no longer assume carte blanche to do what they wish at home. Whatever basis there once was for dads' exclusive "right" to relax is outmoded. Fathers need not only to "help out," but to internalize the executive responsibility for seeing that family needs are met. They need to learn to clean, cook, and share the burden of care for children at the end of the day in the way they once learned to shave and brush their teeth—with a change of mental set so that what may now feel involuntary becomes routine and automatic.

Adolescents, as well, should be required to do their part. Parents often feel it takes more labor to motivate and monitor adolescents' contribution to family work than to do it themselves. But adolescents, especially boys, need to grow up recognizing their shared responsibility for the family's day-to-day operation. Neither fathers nor children have the right to be a leisure class within the family.

Mothers also need to be willing to cede some of the control over household matters that many are now ambivalent about sharing. One father complained that he often had to spend long periods searching for diaper pins, phone numbers, and kitchen utensils that his wife seemed to think were her dominion to leave wherever she wanted. Without a shared commitment to communicating, no one can feel empowered within the household sphere. The objective is to strive toward a system where all feel mutually responsible and no one person has to ride herd over the others. The solution is not detailed negotiation of every activity, but rather mutual investment and recognition.[23]

Just as family work is important, so too are people's needs for renewal and enjoyment of life. Family communications should focus on creating practices that allow individuals to recover from their harried work and school lives. For a family to function smoothly, everyone may require the opportunity when they come in the door to discharge the demons they bring home, even if it means others must eat later or the family eats without one person. Mothers, in particular, should work on voicing their own needs. Giving everyone the opportunity to get his or her needs met is important in its own right, but also in preventing these needs from being manifest in dysfunctional ways.

Families should also negotiate occasions when they can have shared, comfortable time together. In Germany it is just understood that Sunday is family time;[24] in the United States more strenuous effort is often needed to create shared leisure time.

In order to regulate their daily patterns of time and emotion, some families develop charts on the refrigerator door. Some even write contracts that lay out rights and designate tasks that dads, moms, and children will do, with contingencies for nonperformance and rewards for consistent compliance.[25] Other families have institutionalized a regular cleaning time on the weekend, when all work side by side until tasks are completed, as well as a regular family leisure time, when they do something fun together.

Each family, of course, is different and will find its own solutions. In a study of egalitarian couples, one researcher found that some were very casual, easy going, and low-key: whoever felt like doing a task did it. Others were more structured, with specific divisions of tasks and financial responsibilities and set times for talking, doing work, and enjoying leisure.[26] Some families may need to recognize that they need professional or pastoral help to get communication going and overcome entrenched patterns. The common core that needs to be institutionalized is a commitment to processes of mutual negotiation, a pursuit of solutions that accommodate both the individuals' and the family's well-being.

The Family in Society

In this book we have focused on the internal lives of families, yet it is an illusion to see their internal world as isolated from the many other worlds in which family members participate. Regardless of a family's wisdom and balance, it is deeply influenced by the many other institutions that shape its members' lives each day, and currently this wider society is more likely to work against, rather than for, the family's well-being.

For families to be more consistently successful, they need more synergistic relationships with the other institutions their members are involved in. We have seen that employers have a major influence on the daily emotional course of parents' lives: jobs often create distress which is brought home and sometimes propagated within the family. Most businesses seem to assume their employees have a family support system that can put them back together each night, but the cost of this assumption to families is great. Employers need to deliberately create an internal culture that is supportive of employees' lives as parents.[27] And men, who have proven so adept at saying no and setting limits at home, need to do better at exercising this ability at their jobs.

Likewise, schools can do more to create synergy between their world and the lives of their students at home.[28] Schools for young adolescents, in particular, need to find ways to help them manage the stress of this challenging age period. It is an unfortunate irony that just at an age when young people are going through a host of life changes, they also must make the transition to large, alienating junior highs or middle schools. Many seventh and eighth graders find themselves in a situation where teachers know little more than their names, yet, if anything, children of this age need relationships with adults that are more, not less, supportive. In our society, we have conveniently accepted the falsehood that adolescents want to have minimal contact with their elders, yet our data show that when it happens, adolescents enjoy and value talking with their parents and other adults. If we were to flood kids with opportunities for quality relationships with caring grown-ups—through well-funded school and other activities—it could make a remarkable difference in reducing the current plague of adolescent problems.

Local communities also play a vital role in the well-being of families. In the traditional close-knit community there were links between institutions that made for greater synergy with the family. We need to look for this kind of constructive community in new ways: through schools, religious groups, community centers, even computer networks. In one junior high the parents have banded together with the explicit purpose of creating a stronger consensus about the appropriate norms for adolescents' behavior. We also need to create more community spaces—indoor parks, libraries, family centers—where families can enjoy themselves together.[29] And we need to provide more opportunities for joint family activities, as is done by a synagogue that encourages families to work together in their soup kitchen, and a nature center that arranges family "moon walks."

National and local governments also shape the conditions in which families live and, thus, their internal lives.[30] The working- and middle-class households in our study do not face the economic deprivation that challenges many families today, nor do their teenagers confront the violence experienced daily by many urban youth. Had we studied a different set of U.S. families, we would have seen that these are added sources of daily and hourly stress. Nonetheless, in less striking ways, we saw the effects in our sample of the absence of government policies in this country on health care, family leave, and youth development.

The helping and counseling professions also have a role to play in teaching families to adapt to their changing circumstances. We find it remarkable how many young adults enter marriage with little awareness of what they are getting into.[31] Dizzied by a mythology of romantic love, many couples never discuss what type of relationship they want, how tasks will be allocated, nor how they will deal with the hard realities of daily life.[32] We need workbooks, films, and classes that help couples think through what their values are, what kind of a contract they want to have, and we need more ways of helping families make mid-course corrections when their daily practices are not working. In addition, fathers could benefit from more parental-support programs that address their specific needs and blind spots. One program that was successful in getting men to contribute more to family labor found that after a short-term period of unhappiness, many men accommodated themselves to and were pleased with the change.[33] Imaginative energy is also needed to break down the barriers we have seen in father–adolescent, especially father–daughter, relationships.

The media could also try to project more accurate images of families into our homes. Rather than imposing a fixed, Norman Rockwell portrait of the ideal, happy family, magazine covers of the future could laud *processes* in which negotiations occur between family members. Television and other media could also do much to create an "ethos of fatherhood" in the way that an ethos of motherhood was so successfully marketed in the nineteenth century and the early half of this century. And the media have a role to play in releasing women from 1950s norms that hold them to inordinately high expectations.

Finally, families and family professionals could benefit from a richer glossary of knowledge from scholars about the complex emotional dynamics of family life. While much research is available on family disorder, we lack open, creative study and discussion on the diverse ways families maintain daily health. The findings of this study are only suggestive and apply to a limited population of families. Research on families outside the mainstream in our society may ultimately prove more fruitful in helping us move beyond our outdated traditional conceptions of how a family should function. Research on the day-to-day lives of African-American families, single-parent families, multiple-resident families, and gay and lesbian families, among other types, is important, not only in its own right but also in broadening our collective knowledge about the variety of elements that can make a household function smoothly.[34]

The bottom line is that family success depends on a collaborative relationship between families and other institutions in society. In this postmodern world, all of us live lives that are a collection of fragments. As we pass between settings each day, as we pass between the spheres of life defined by these disparate institutions, we inhabit multiple selves that do not easily fit together. Yet in these passages, negative emotions get conveyed between spheres. When things are going wrong at work or at school, it affects life at home, and vice versa. Society needs to provide a set of institutions that helps weave individuals' and families' divergent realities together rather than split them apart.

The final goal should not be a melding of different realities—our complex society is too diverse for this to happen. The goal should be communication and understanding between realities. What families need is internal commitment, with community support, for their members to listen to and repeatedly reorganize their daily patterns in ways that allow them to negotiate the hazardous challenges of daily family life with warmth and resiliency.

Appendixes

Appendix 1.1

PARENT BEEPER SHEET

Day: _____   Time Signalled: _____ AM/PM   Time Filled Out: _____

JUST BEFORE YOU WERE SIGNALLED:

What were you thinking about? _____

Where were you? _____

What were you doing? _____

Name of TV show, book, record or tape; topic of conversation: (*circle one*)

	NOT AT ALL	SOME- WHAT	QUITE	VERY
How much choice did you have about doing this activity?	+ — + — + — + — + — + — + — +
Do you wish you had been doing something else?	+ — + — + — + — + — + — + — +
How well were you paying attention?	+ — + — + — + — + — + — + — +
How skilled are you at this activity?	+ — + — + — + — + — + — + — +

              1   2   3   4   5   6   7   8   9   10

☆ ☆

Appendix 1.1 (continued)

How were you feeling before you were signalled?*

	VERY MUCH	KIND OF	A LITTLE BIT	NOT AT ALL
Accepted	+++	++	+	•
Awkward	+++	++	+	•
Calm	+++	++	+	•
Competitive	+++	++	+	•
Cooperative	+++	++	+	•
Disappointed	+++	++	+	•
Embarrassed	+++	++	+	•
Free	+++	++	+	•
Frustrated	+++	++	+	•
Great	+++	++	+	•
Guilty	+++	++	+	•
Hard-working	+++	++	+	•
Hurried	+++	++	+	•
Hyper	+++	++	+	•
Ignored	+++	++	+	•
Important	+++	++	+	•
In control	+++	++	+	•
In love	+++	++	+	•
Interested	+++	++	+	•
Kindly	+++	++	+	•
Lonely	+++	++	+	•
Nervous	+++	++	+	•
Proud	+++	++	+	•
Rowdy	+++	++	+	•
Self-conscious	+++	++	+	•
Sorry	+++	++	+	•
Tired	+++	++	+	•
Worried	+++	++	+	•

✳✳

Overall, how were you feeling?

	VERY	QUITE	SOME	NEITHER	SOME	QUITE	VERY	
Cheerful	•	•	•	-	•	•	•	Irritable (grouchy)
Bored	•	•	•	-	•	•	•	Excited
Unhappy	•	•	•	-	•	•	•	Happy
Alert	•	•	•	-	•	•	•	Drowsy
Angry	•	•	•	-	•	•	•	Friendly
Strong	•	•	•	-	•	•	•	Weak

✳✳

Appendix 1.1 (continued)

If you were feeling a lot of something, *why* did you feel that way?

I felt: _____   Because: _____

_____

☆ ☆

Who were you with (or talking to on the phone)? (*Check all that apply*)

Alone, other people nearby .... ( )   Other relatives _____

Alone, no one around .... ( )   A friend or friends .... ( )

Spouse .... ( )   Coworkers .... ( )

Your children _____   Other: _____

Would you rather have been: Alone .... ( )   With people ...... ( )

☆ ☆

If you were with people, were they:

	VERY	QUITE	SOME	NEITHER	SOME	QUITE	VERY	
Friendly	•	•	•	-	•	•	•	Unfriendly
Serious	•	•	•	-	•	•	•	Joking

☆ ☆

Describe how you feel right now about:

THE CHILD IN THE STUDY		YOUR SPOUSE	
Close to	Distant from	Close to	Distant from
• • • - • • •		• • • - • • •	
Friendly toward	Angry with	Friendly toward	Angry with
• • • - • • •		• • • - • • •	
Worried about	Not worried at all	Worried about	Not worried at all
• • • - • • •		• • • - • • •	
Relaxed with	Tense toward	Relaxed with	Tense toward
• • • - • • •		• • • - • • •	
In control of	Controlled by	In control of	Controlled by
• • • - • • •		• • • - • • •	

If you feel better/worse towards your child/spouse, why? _____

_____

☆ ☆

If you are with your child, how would you describe his or her mood?

	VERY	QUITE	SOME	NEITHER	SOME	QUITE	VERY	
Drowsy	•	•	•	-	•	•	•	Alert
Happy	•	•	•	-	•	•	•	Unhappy

☆ ☆

Other thoughts:

---

*Items in this section rotated, with only nine of these items occurring on each ESM form. All other parts of the form were constant.

Appendix 2.1

FREQUENCY OF DIFFERENT SUBJECTIVE STATES REPORTED BY FAMILY MEMBERS

Subjective State Items	Item Range	Mothers Mean %[1]	Fathers Mean %[1]	Significance of Difference: Mother vs. Father p	Young Adolescents Mean %[1]	Significance of Difference: Child vs. Same Sex Parent p
INVESTMENT						
Attention ("How well were you paying attention?")	1 to 10	26.5	37.1	.027	47.8	.000
Choice ("How much choice did you have about doing this activity?")	1 to 10	26.5	37.4	.607	52.3	.000
Wish ("Do you wish you had been doing something else?")	1 to 10	9.9	10.3	.810	19.7	.000
Skill ("How skilled are you at this activity?")	1 to 10	46.6	47.7	.821	56.9	.014
Excited/Bored Excited	−3 to +3	9.3	13.9	.105	34.4	.000
Bored		2.2	2.5	.766	20.2	.000
Interested	1 to 4	57.5	59.2	.908	47.8	.085

[1]For items on a scale from 1 to 10, we computed the percent of time each person reported a score of 9 or 10, then computed means of these values. For items on a scale of 1 to 4, we computed percentages for values of 3 and 4. For items on a scale of −3 to +3, we computed percentages at or above +2 for the positive pole (e.g., excited, alert, happy) and percentages at or below −2 for the negative pole (e.g., bored, drowsy, unhappy).

Appendix 2.1 (continued)

INVESTMENT (continued)							
Hardworking		1 to 4	34.8	39.3	.560	31.0	.189
Competitive		1 to 4	10.9	20.5	.006	27.8	.005
Cooperative		1 to 4	54.3	56.7	.900	43.4	.054
AROUSAL							
Alert/Drowsy	Alert	−3 to +3	38.6	44.8	.223	38.8	.882
	Drowsy		7.5	5.6	.172	17.7	.001
Strong/Weak	Strong	−3 to +3	10.2	21.4	.012	36.0	.002
	Weak		4.4	1.5	.016	6.6	.051
Tired		1 to 4	27.9	19.0	.024	34.2	.062
Hurried		1 to 4	29.9	24.8	.248	19.7	.012
Calm		1 to 4	60.5	61.5	.674	53.0	.553
Rowdy		1 to 4	3.7	5.2	.603	17.9	.000
Hyper		1 to 4	8.7	9.6	.827	12.0	.780
In control		1 to 4	67.8	71.5	.804	43.7	.000
POSITIVE EMOTIONS							
Happy		−3 to +3	30.6	34.7	.347	49.1	.000
Cheerful		−3 to +3	35.5	39.0	.459	59.6	.000

Appendix 2.1 (*continued*)

Positive Emotions (*continued*)

Friendly	-3 to +3	34.1	37.0	.446	51.0	.000
Proud	1 to 4	29.2	28.6	.640	42.0	.326
Great	1 to 4	31.2	36.8	.153	48.1	.155
In love	1 to 4	42.3	33.0	.024	26.9	.103
Kindly	1 to 4	45.7	42.9	.473	43.6	.269
Accepted	1 to 4	56.4	55.9	.611	46.9	.111
Free	1 to 4	41.9	41.3	.745	48.8	.432

Negative Emotions

Unhappy	-3 to +3	2.6	2.6	.066	8.2	.001
Irritable	-3 to +3	3.7	4.1	.759	4.5	.793
Angry	-3 to +3	5.4	4.6	.396	7.6	.001
Sorry	1 to 4	5.1	5.9	.786	5.4	.557
Frustrated	1 to 4	17.5	17.1	.359	15.8	.580
Nervous	1 to 4	7.2	9.2	.379	12.6	.018
Disappointed	1 to 4	9.4	9.9	.692	14.2	.830
Worried	1 to 4	15.3	12.1	.120	14.9	.635
Guilty	1 to 4	3.5	3.5	.468	6.6	.112

Appendix 2.1 (continued)

NEGATIVE EMOTIONS (continued)						
Awkward	1 to 4	2.0	5.6	.038	8.9	.022
Lonely	1 to 4	4.8	7.1	.863	11.2	.084
Self-conscious	1 to 4	2.5	10.1	.002	22.7	.000
Embarrassed	1 to 4	1.3	1.5	.673	5.0	.001
Ignored	1 to 4	3.4	3.3	.669	8.8	.000
PERCEIVED SOCIAL SITUATION						
"If you were with people, were they . . ." Friendly	−3 to +3	69.5	78.1	.024	76.1	.821
Unfriendly		1.4	.5	.090	3.9	.001
Joking	−3 to +3	20.7	21.9	.725	33.2	.004
Serious		17.0	22.6	.127	25.8	.610

Appendix 2.2

HOW FAMILY MEMBERS SPEND THEIR TIME

	Mothers	Fathers	Young Adolescents
HOUSEHOLD SPHERE			
Housework	21.9	8.6	3.9
Child care	4.1	2.5	.3
Family transport	4.4	3.4	3.3
Homework[1]	—	—	3.8
Personal care	6.1	3.2	5.6
Eating	4.9	4.8	4.5
Resting, idling	5.4	2.9	4.5
Family talk	12.1	5.8	5.9
Media	11.6	13.2	15.0
Active recreation	3.2	2.9	7.0
Household Total	73.8	47.4	53.8
PUBLIC SPHERE			
Working at job/school	14.8	30.6	21.9
Other activities at job/school	3.8	8.9	14.0
Personal transport	2.9	5.5	1.4
Public, personal	4.7	7.6	8.9
Public Total	26.2	52.6	46.2

Note: Table gives the average percentage of time people reported being in each activity.

[1]This category was used only with the adolescents.

Appendix 2.3

HOW OFTEN FATHERS EXPERIENCE DIFFERENT STATES
IN THE JOB AND HOUSEHOLD SPHERES

	Work (mean %)	Family (mean %)	p
INVESTMENT			
Attention	41.2	30.6	.003
Choice	22.9	43.5	.000
Wish (doing something else)	15.3	5.7	.002
Skill	51.4	40.7	.000
Bored	4.2	1.4	.015
Hardworking	61.1	27.6	.000
Competitive	29.2	11.2	.000
AROUSAL			
Alert	48.9	37.6	.001
Drowsy	3.8	6.1	.051
Strong	22.1	15.8	.030
Hurried	37.4	12.7	.000
Hyper	13.9	4.1	.025
In control	73.3	63.7	.014

This table shows only the states that were different between the two spheres at $p < .10$.

Appendix 2.3 (continued)

NEGATIVE EMOTIONS			
Angry	5.3	3.6	.071
Frustrated	20.9	14.1	.043
Awkward	8.4	4.6	.082
POSITIVE EMOTIONS			
Cheerful	32.4	39.9	.015
Happy	28.6	39.2	.000
Great	29.4	41.4	.005
Friendly	33.5	40.4	.007
In love	25.7	40.0	.002
Kindly	32.6	50.6	.000
PERCEIVED SOCIAL SITUATION			
Serious	34.3	15.5	.000

Appendix 2.4

CORRELATES OF FATHERS' AND MOTHERS' AVERAGE ATTENTION
LEVEL AT THEIR JOBS

	Fathers	Mothers
Choice	.37**	.30
Excited	.47***	.38*
Interested	.35*	.27
Alert	.42**	.40*
Strong	.35*	−.02
Tired	−.27†	−.17
Hurried	.24†	−.16
Frustrated	.28*	.18
Competitive	.46***	.30†
How often the leader (percent)	.35*	.27
Amount of time spent at job (percent)	.38**	.02

Note: For each person we computed his or her average attention and his or her average score for the other subjective state variables when at the job, based on z-scores. Correlations were then computed between these values.

†$p < .10$; *$p < .05$; **$p < .01$; ***$p < .001$

Appendix 2.5

FATHERS' AND MOTHERS' EMOTION
DURING ACTIVITIES PERFORMED AT WORK

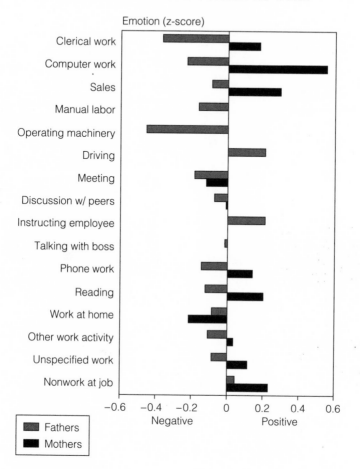

Appendix 2.6

FAMILY MEMBERS' RATES OF TELEVISION
VIEWING BY TIME OF DAY

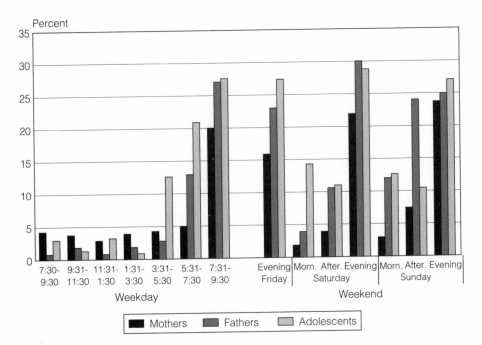

Appendix 2.7

FATHERS' AND MOTHERS' AVERAGE EMOTION AND CHOICE DURING FAMILY WORK

Activity	Number of Reports		Emotion		Choice	
	Fathers	Mothers	Fathers	Mothers	Fathers	Mothers
Cooking and food preparation	18	40	−.05	−.07	.09	−.26
Kitchen cleanup	18	28	−.01	−.31	.02	−.56
Laundry	12	14	−.07	−.44	.40	−.52
Housecleaning	20	24	−.41	−.36	−.18	−.12
Shopping	16	16	.46	−.09	.17	−.03
Outdoor work	71	4	−.04	.14	.21	.28
Maintaining possessions	78	6	−.02	−.68	.00	.10
Money-related	27	8	−.95	−.25	.27	−.28
Direct child care	37	24	.06	−.08	.10	−.29
Child's activities	44	10	.61	.04	.49	.08
Family transport	46	20	−.20	.17	−.04	−.13

Appendix 2.8

FATHERS' EMOTION BEFORE, DURING, AND
AFTER ACTIVE RECREATION

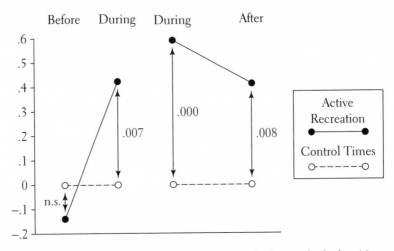

Explanation: This graph shows two analyses. In the first we looked at 46 occasions when there were two beeps in a row in which the second one occurred during active recreation. These two were compared to similar control pairs (N = 1,203) when the second beep did not occur during active recreation. Numbers in the figure give the p value for the significance tests. In the second analyses we looked at 30 occasions when the first beep was during active leisure and the second was not and compared them to control times (N = 1,209). For both analyses we restricted the data base for both the target and controls to beeps that were within $2\frac{1}{2}$ hours of each other. The important finding here is that emotion prior to active leisure is not significantly different from baseline, and emotion after active leisure is.

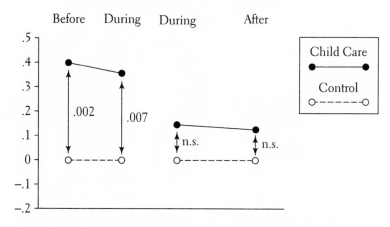

Appendix 2.9

FATHERS' EMOTION BEFORE, DURING, AND
AFTER CHILD-CARE ACTIVITIES

Note: The Before→During pairs have an N of 33 (1,223 for the controls).
The During→After pairs have an N of 30 (1,209 for controls).

Appendix 3.1

WHERE FAMILY MEMBERS FEEL "HURRIED"

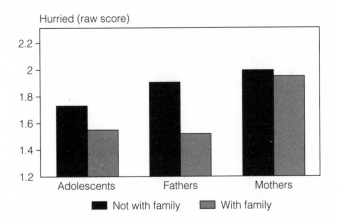

Appendix 3.2

GENDER DIFFERENCES IN FEELING COOPERATIVE
AND COMPETITIVE DURING ONE'S JOB

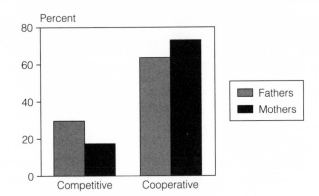

Appendix 3.3

MOTHERS' EMOTION AFTER GOOD AND
BAD DAYS AT THEIR JOBS

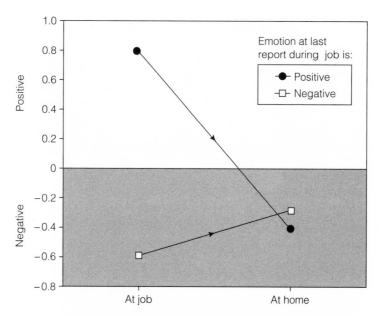

Note: Figure shows emotion for last report at job and first report at home.
The two lines show emotions for days when the last-reported emotion at
work was in the top third (z>.37) and bottom third (z<−.07).

Appendix 4.1

ADOLESCENTS' EMOTION DURING
ACTIVITIES IN THE HOUSEHOLD SPHERE

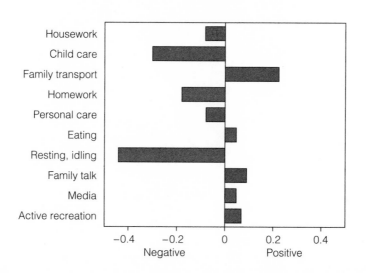

Appendix 5.1

HUSBANDS' AND WIVES' EMOTION DURING DIFFERENT
CATEGORIES OF TOGETHERNESS

Narrowing Categories of Time Together	N^1	Wife's Emotion		Husband's Emotion	
		Average Z-Score	With Activity Controlled	Average Z-Score	With Activity Controlled
Unmutual togetherness[2]	220	−.11	−.08	−.00	−.09
Both say they are together	388	.15**	.14**	.09*	−.01
Both report same activity	203	.20**	.15*	.14*	.04
Together in conversation or active recreation	39	.63***	.46***	.51***	.15
Alone together in conversation or active recreation	14	.57*	.40	.41	.06

Note: Significance tests evaluate difference from z = .00.

*p < .05; **p < .01; ***p < .001

[1]Categories are not mutually exclusive.

[2]This includes times when only one spouse reports being with the other. Emotions do not differ by whether it is the husband or wife who reports togetherness.

Appendix 5.2

EMOTIONAL TRANSMISSION BETWEEN HUSBAND AND WIFE

a. ALL TIMES

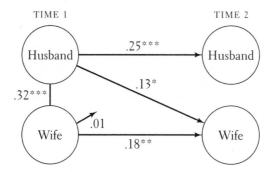

Note: Figure displays beta weights for predicting Time 2 emotions, based on times that both say they are together at Time 1 or Time 2; N = 253. Regressions were computed on values of emotion with activity controlled. Only occasions when reports occurred within four hours of each other are included (median time difference = 1.67 hours).

b. WHEN HUSBAND COMES HOME FROM WORK

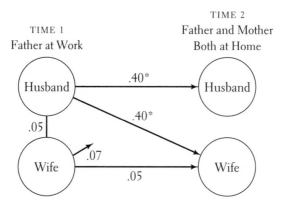

Note: Figure displays beta weights for regressions predicting Time 2 emotions (N = 33). Similar analyses examining occasions when employed women came home did not yield strong or significant paths.

Appendix 5.3

CORRELATIONS BETWEEN MARITAL QUALITY AND
CATEGORIES OF SHARED AND SEPARATE TIME

	Warmth		Marital Adjustment	
	Wife to Husband	Husband to Wife	Wife	Husband
AMOUNT OF TIME SPENT TOGETHER[1]				
Total (both say they are together)	.35**	.26[†]	.19	.28*
In same activity	.23	.28*	.19	.34*
In conversation or active recreation	.39**	.23	.34*	.22
AMOUNT OF TIME SPENT APART				
Unmutual togetherness[2]	−.19	−.26[†]	−.23†	−.28*
Wife's separate leisure[3]	−.32*	−.34*	−.17	−.29*
Husband's separate leisure[3]	−.25[†]	−.29*	−.26[†]	−.23†
Time when one but not other is in home sphere	−.27*	−.30*	−.20	−.24[†]
Rate of not being together at home[4]	−.29*	−.37**	−.40***	−.42**
FREQUENCY OF EMOTION WHEN TOGETHER[5]				
Joint negative emotions	−.35*	−.50***	−.22	−.27[†]
Joint positive emotions	−.05	−.02	.03	−.00

Note: Table displays person-level correlations. [†]p < .10; *p < .05; **p < .01; ***p < .001

[1]Correlations based on percentage of all reports that each couple reported designated category of togetherness. These percentages were normalized with a square root transformation.

[2]As a proportion of all times either said they were together.

[3]As a proportion of all of person's leisure.

[4]As a proportion of all times both are in home sphere.

[5]Proportion of times when together that both husband and wife reported emotions below −.33 or above .33.

Appendix 6.1

PARENTS' AND ADOLESCENTS' TIME TOGETHER AND APART

	Percent of Time	
	Mother–Adolescent	Father–Adolescent
Not together	56.5	66.6
Child says together, parent not	7.0	6.3
Parent says together, child not	16.1	10.9
Both say they are together	20.3	16.2
Both report same activity[1]	5.9	5.8
Both together in conversation or active recreation[1]	1.0	.8

Note: Table gives percentages based on all reports.

[1]These are subcategories of the category listed above each.

Appendix 6.2

EMOTION DURING ADOLESCENT–MOTHER AND
ADOLESCENT–FATHER INTERACTIONS AS A
FUNCTION OF GRADE

Mother–Adolescent Interactions

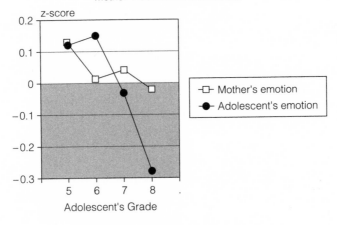

Father–Adolescent Interactions

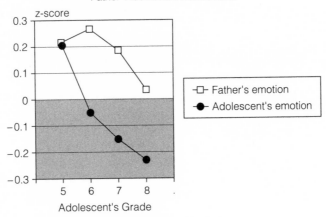

Appendix 6.3

CORRELATIONS BETWEEN AN ADOLESCENT'S EXPERIENCE WITH HIS OR HER MOTHER
AND THE ADOLESCENT'S ADJUSTMENT

	Adolescent's Reported Closeness to Mother	Teachers' Rating of Adolescent's Adjustment	Adolescent's Reported Depression	Adolescent's Weight and Eating Concerns	Adolescent's Average Emotional State
Boys (N = 133)					
Total time together	.04	.17†	.17†	−.11	.15†
Time alone together	.17†	.23**	−.05	−.07	.24**
Time talking	.02	.16†	−.15	−.07	.13
Adolescent's emotions with mother[1]	.05	−.03	−.07	.00	−.04
Girls (N = 138)					
Total time together	−.02	−.08	.01	.13	.21*
Time alone together	.08	−.01	−.02	.15†	.17*
Time talking	−.12	.06	.05	.01	−.02
Adolescent's emotions with mother[1]	.07	−.12	−.21*	−.16*	.15†

Note: Table reports partial correlations with grade controlled. Data are from two-parent families from the larger, young adolescent sample.

†p < .10; *p < .05; **p < .01; ***p < .001

[1]These scores are an adolescent's average emotional state (z-score); thus they represent the adolescent's state with the mother relative to other times.

Appendix 6.4

EMOTIONAL TRANSMISSION BETWEEN ADOLESCENT AND MOTHER

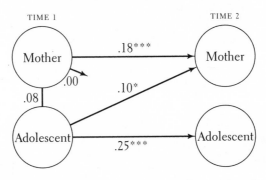

Note: Figure displays beta weights for regressions predicting Time 2 emotions from Time 1 emotions (N = 436).

Appendix 6.5

"WHAT DOES YOUR CHILD DO THAT
PUTS YOU IN A GOOD MOOD?"

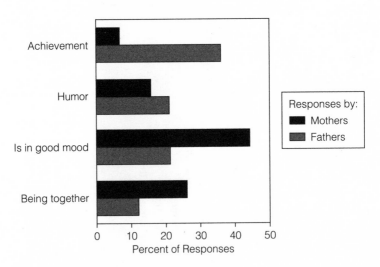

Overall differences are significant at p = .007.

Appendix 6.6

FREQUENCY OF IRRITABILITY WHEN MOTHER IS DEPRESSED

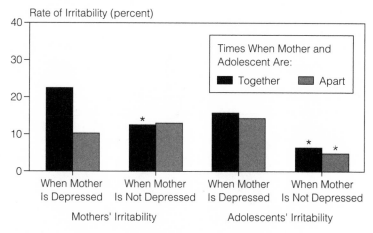

Mothers' Irritability   Adolescents' Irritability

*Significantly different from when mother is depressed, p < .05.

Appendix 7.1

THE ACTIVITIES ADOLESCENTS SHARE WITH THEIR MOTHERS
AND WITH THEIR FATHERS

| | Percent of Time ||
	With Mother (N = 108)	With Father (N = 97)
Housework	16	9
Child care	0	1
Family transport	11	11
Child's homework	3	5
Personal care	2	1
Eating	17	20
Resting, idling	1	1
Talking	14	6
Media	33	40
Active recreation	3	6
	100	100

Note: Table is based on times that the adolescent and the parent reported being together and doing the same activity.

Appendix 7.2

EMOTIONS DURING INTERACTIONS BETWEEN
FATHERS AND ADOLESCENT BOYS AND GIRLS

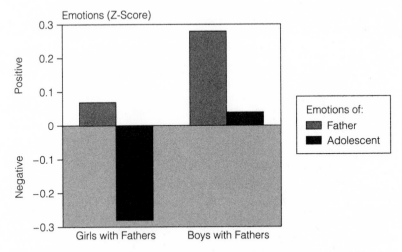

Note: The difference between girls and their fathers is significant at the .05 level;
the difference between boys and their fathers is significant at the .10 level.

Appendix 7.3

HOW SHARED TIME BETWEEN FATHER AND ADOLESCENT IS CORRELATED WITH THE QUALITY OF THEIR RELATIONSHIP

	Warmth		Closeness	
	Adolescent to Father	Father to Adolescent	Adolescent to Father	Father to Adolescent
AMOUNT OF TIME SPENT TOGETHER				
Total (both say they are together)	.07	−.09	.01	.04
In same activity	−.01	−.03	−.07	.15
In conversation or active recreation	−.13	.16	.04	.06
EMOTION WHEN TOGETHER				
Adolescent's mean (z-score)	−.19	−.32*	−.18	.15
Father's mean (z-score)	−.14	−.16	.00	.04
Rate of joint negative emotions	.25	.33*	.26†	−.13
Rate of joint positive emotions	.11	−.03	.17	.18

Note: Table displays partial correlations, controlling for grade. Separate analyses by gender indicate that the trends suggested in this table are evident for both boys and girls.

†$p < .10$; *$p < .05$

Appendix 7.4

PREDICTING WHEN ADOLESCENTS AND FATHERS
WILL SEPARATE OR STAY TOGETHER

FAMILY WHERE ADOLESCENT DOES NOT FEEL WARM TOWARD FATHER

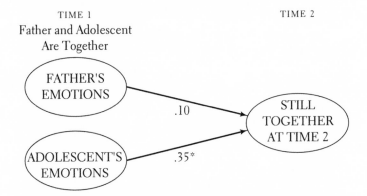

FAMILY WHERE ADOLESCENT DOES FEEL WARM TOWARD FATHER

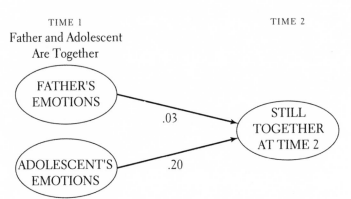

Table displays point-biserial correlations.
Being together is defined by both saying they are together.

* p < .05

Appendix 8.1

EMOTION OF FAMILY MEMBERS IN HEALTHIER AND
LESS HEALTHY FAMILIES IN PUBLIC AND AT HOME

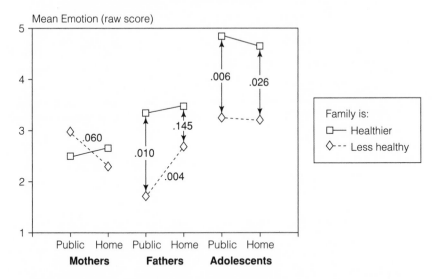

The numbers in the figure give the p-values for tests of significance between the designated means.

Appendix 8.2

CORRELATIONS BETWEEN PERCEIVED ALLIANCES AND FAMILY WELL-BEING

| | Family Well-Being | | | | | | Family Environment[1] | | | |
| | Mother's Well-Being | | Father's Well-Being | | Child's Well-Being | | Rated by Mother | | Rated by Father | |
Perceived Alliances	Depression (−)	Self-Esteem	Depression (−)	Self-Esteem	Depression (−)	Self-Esteem	Cohesion	Conflict (−)	Cohesion	Conflict (−)
Mother feels warmer toward child than toward father[2]	−.19	−.14	−.09	−.10	−.40**	−.40**	−.21	.02	−.41**	−.41**
Father feels warmer toward child than toward mother[2]	−.23	−.32*	−.14	−.01	−.25†	−.29*	−.02	.01	−.44***	−.33*
Child feels warmer toward mother than toward father[2]	−.12	−.15	−.30*	−.16	−.04	−.12	−.30*	.05	−.35**	−.06
Child feels warmer toward either parent[3]	.01	−.07	−.15	−.15	−.20	−.27†	−.22†	−.13	−.12	−.13

†p < .10; *p < .05; **p < .01; ***p < .001

[1]Rated on the Moos Family Environment Scale.

[2]Difference scores computed by subtracting warmth reported toward one family member from that reported toward the other.

[3]This variable is the square of the variable in the row above it.

´Appendix 8.3

CONTAGION OF HOSTILITY BETWEEN RELATIONSHIPS

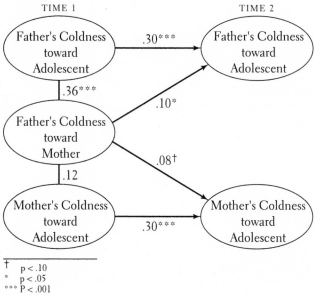

†   p < .10
*   p < .05
*** P < .001

Appendix 8.4

CORRELATIONS OF MARITAL QUALITY WITH ADOLESCENT–PARENT
RELATIONSHIPS AND ADOLESCENT'S WELL-BEING

| | Marital Adjustment | | Marital Warmth | |
	Mother	Father	Mother	Father
ADOLESCENT'S RELATIONSHIP				
WITH PARENTS				
Feels close to mother	−.04	.11	−.04	.00
Warmth felt toward				
mother	.08	.01	.17	.09
Shared negative				
emotions with				
mother	−.39**	−.30*	−.34*	−.52***
Warmth felt by mother	.08	.08	.62***	.19
Feels close to father	.43*	.27†	.28*	.38**
Warmth felt toward				
father	.25†	.02	.19	.14
Shared negative				
emotions with				
father	.22	.33*	.28†	.32*
Warmth felt by father	.34*	.33*	.39**	.66***
ADOLESCENT'S WELL-BEING				
Depression	−.33*	−.16	−.14	−.36**
Self-esteem	.43***	.48***	.21	.35**
Average emotions:	.30*	.31*	.16	.26†
in household sphere	.30*	.29*	.14	.29*
in public sphere	.29*	.31*	.14	.21

†p < .10; *p < .05; **p < .01; ***p < .001

Notes

Chapter 1. The Family: A Brew of Emotions

1. Numerous authors have demonstrated that income loss has a direct adverse effect on families (Conger et al., 1992, 1993; Elder, 1974; McLoyd, 1989). Bronfenbrenner (1986) demonstrates that much of the government and community support for families that is present in other Western countries, but absent in the United States, has a major beneficial effect on children and families. Zimmerman (1992) also shows a direct relationship between government programs and family well-being. It should be noted that some of the increase in rates of divorce is attributable to what we see as a positive change: to women's (and sometimes men's) lesser willingness to endure physical or emotional abuse.

2. Bellah et al., 1985; Cancian, 1987.

3. Inglehart, 1990; Skolnick, 1991; Veroff, Douvan, and Kulka, 1981.

4. Mellman, Lazarus, and Rivlin, 1990, p. 83.

5. Skolnick, 1991, p. 189.

6. Orthner and Mancini, 1990; Skolnick, 1991.

7. Gadlin, 1978.

8. Wolfenstein, 1955.

9. The relationship between marriage and psychological health was found by Gove, Style, and Hughes (1990), among others. Small and Eastman (1991) review the literature on the connection between the parenting relationship and adolescents' well-being.

10. See Mellman et al. (1990). Another survey finds that eight of ten Americans say spending time with their families is "very important" (United Media Enterprises, 1983).

11. Montemayor, 1983; Steinberg, 1987.

12. Gecas and Seff, 1990; Paikoff, 1991.

13. Poor relations between parent and adolescent are related to delinquency and disturbed mental health in the adolescent (Ryan and Lynch, 1989) and psychological distress in parents (Silverberg and Steinberg, 1990).

14. Silverberg and Steinberg, 1990.

15. The decline in wages and effects on parents' time are documented by Robinson (1990) and Schor (1991). Since 1960, the amount of time parents spend with children is estimated to have declined by ten hours a week (Demo, 1992; Schor, 1991).

16. In current research we are now studying adolescents in African-American and Mexican-American families. Rather than including a fractional representation of these families in this book, we felt it important to concentrate on the patterns within each cultural group.

17. Yankelovich, 1981.

18. *Paging Schedule.* Families began the procedure in the middle of the week, almost always on a Tuesday, Wednesday, or Thursday. Participants were beeped at a random moment within every two-hour block of time between 7:30 A.M. and 3:30 P.M. and within every ninety-minute block between 3:30 and 9:30 P.M. This greater density of signals during the evening hours was designed to obtain a more thorough sampling of *family* experience. For many analyses in this book, where we intend to portray participants' representative experience across all waking hours, we down-weighted reports from these evening hours to adjust for their greater density.

19. The experience sampling method has been used successfully for a number of years in psychological studies of individuals, including adolescents, elderly people, and psychiatric patients in the United States and other countries (for example, Csikszentmihalyi and Larson, 1984; deVries, 1987, 1992; Mannell, Zuzanek, and Larson, 1988). Four methodological papers have demonstrated that the procedure generates reliable and valid data (Csikszentmihalyi and Larson, 1987; Hormuth, 1986; Larson, 1989a; Larson and Csikszentmihalyi, 1983).

20. Fitzpatrick, 1988; Gottman, 1979; Reiss, 1981.

21. Bernard, Killworth, Kronenfeld, and Sailer, 1984; Thomas and Diener, 1990.

22. *The Interview and Questionnaires.* The interview included a protocol of semi-structured questions about best and worst times during the week, family relationships during the week, and the family's participation in the study.

The packet of questionnaires included established measures of individual well-being and family functioning. Adolescents provided information on their well-being by completing the Children's Depression Inventory (Kovacs, 1985), a measure of self-esteem (Rosenberg, 1965), and a measure of disturbed attitudes toward eating and weight (Richards, Casper, and Larson, 1990). We also obtained their school grades for the past year from their schools, and their parents completed a measure of their psychological symptoms, the Child Behavior Checklist (Achenbach and Edelbrock, 1986). Parents provided information on their own well-being by completing the same measure of self-esteem and the short form of the Beck Depression Inventory (Beck and Beck, 1972).

Measures of family functioning included the Cohesion and Conflict scales of the Family Environment Scale (Moos and Moos, 1986), the Locke-Wallace Marital

Adjustment Scale (Locke and Wallace, 1959), and a measure of closeness in relationships between adolescents and parents (Blyth, 1982).

23. *How Adequately the Study Sampled People's Daily Activities.* Participants in the family study provided a total of 7,073 reports. We calculated that the adolescents responded to a median of 85 percent of the signals we sent them, fathers responded to 82 percent, and mothers 86 percent. Since about 6 percent of the signals we sent were not received because of pager failure (Larson, 1989a), we estimate that our participants provided reports for approximately 90 percent of the signals they could have received.

These missed signals introduce only slight distortion into the sample of ESM reports. At the end of the week, participants were asked to identify times when they turned the pager off or were "out of touch." They reported missing signals during a wide range of activities: during sleep (31 percent), work at a job (19 percent), schoolwork (14 percent), sports (12 percent), socializing (6 percent), church (4 percent), transportation (4 percent), personal care (3 percent), personal maintenance (3 percent), art or hobby (3 percent), thinking (3 percent), and eating (1 percent). Since we told participants to turn the pagers off when sleeping, we were not concerned about loss during this activity. The rates of missed beeps during schoolwork, job, sports, and church are somewhat above the frequencies of these activities; thus these activities may be slightly underrepresented. Comparisons of the ESM with traditional time-diary research methods suggest that the ESM may underrepresent activities taking place away from home, because people occasionally forget the pager, but it is more effective at sampling short, undefined activities, such as idling and telephone calls (Csikszentmihalyi and Graef, 1980; Robinson, 1985).

Of course, we also missed people's experience before 7:30 A.M. and after 9:30 P.M. Three mothers and two fathers worked nights, so we missed large segments of their waking time. For the others, comparatively little early morning or "after-hour" time was missed. The adolescents' average wake-up time was 7:30, mothers' 7:12, and fathers' 6:27. Average bedtime was 10:17 for the teens, 11:17 for mothers, and 11:15 for fathers.

24. Dix, 1991; Wessman and Ricks, 1966.

25. *Measurement of Activities and Presence in the Household versus Public Spheres.* A person's activity at the time of each signal was identified by his or her response to the open-ended question "What were you doing?" Responses were coded into 110 mutually exclusive categories, with inter-rater agreement maintained above 94 percent. Location was identified by responses to the question "Where were you?" coded into 68 categories (inter-rater agreement 99 percent). Companionship was identified by responses to an item asking, "Who were you with (or talking to on the phone)?", for which fixed response categories were provided. For purposes of analysis, all these codes have been collapsed into smaller numbers of categories.

These codes were also used to define when a person was in the family versus the public sphere (Larson, Richards, and Perry-Jenkins, in press). Presence in the family sphere was defined as times a person was either: (a) at home, (b) with at least one other family member, or (c) carrying out a household task for the family (such as grocery shopping). These conditions, we reasoned, approximately define times a person is cast in a family role (mother, father, spouse). Presence in the public sphere was then defined as all times a person was away from home, not with a family member, and not undertaking a household task. This included time at one's job and time in public locations devoted to personal business or leisure.

26. *Measurement of Emotional State.* The scale of mood or emotion was computed from responses to three semantic differential items (happy–unhappy, cheerful–irritable, friendly–angry). Raw values ranged from –9 to +9, with positive values corresponding to positive moods. For many analyses we employed z-scored values for this scale. To do this, raw emotion scores were standardized so that each person's mean score was 0.0 and standard deviation was 1.0. This transformation adjusts for differences in individuals' means and standard deviations and thus allows us to consider differences across situations that are not confounded by person effects (Larson and Delespaul, 1992).

Analyses indicate that this emotion scale is reliable. First, the internal consistency of these items is high (alpha = .81). Second, the stability of the scale over time is indicated by the finding that individuals' mean scores for the first half of the week and the second half of the week were highly correlated (mothers: r = .60; fathers: r = .69; adolescents: r = .71).

The construct validity of the emotion scale is suggested by its correlation with other related constructs. For the adolescents, average emotion was significantly correlated with depression (r = –.29), self-esteem (r = .31), and parents' ratings of their internalizing symptoms on the Child Behavior Checklist (r = –.37). Curiously, it had stronger correlations with indicators measured two years after the original study: with adolescents' rates of self-reported delinquency (r= –.35), depression (r = –.42), school grades (r = .38), extracurricular activity participation (r = .44), and psychosomatic symptoms (r = –.30). Likewise, average emotion on the ESM sheets was strongly correlated with these two-year variables for parents: with fathers' depression (r = –.39), mothers' depression (r = –.47), mothers' self-esteem (r = .48). Further substantiation of the construct validity of this scale has been reported in other publications (Csikszentmihalyi and Larson, 1987; Larson, 1989a, 1989b).

27. Throughout the book we use the term "young adolescents" and sometimes just "adolescents" or "teenagers" to refer to the young people we studied, even though many people might view fifth graders as children or "preadolescents." While large differences exist between the experience of the youngest and oldest students in our sample, there are also many similarities, and we find it necessary at times to employ a single label in order to contrast these young people with their parents.

28. Larson and Richards, 1989.

29. The comparison to the larger sample is important because we know the larger sample to be closely representative of the suburban working- and middle-

class population from which it was drawn (Larson, 1989a). Analyses show that the fifty-five families did not differ significantly from families in the larger study in most criteria we considered, such as family cohesion and conflict as rated on the Family Environment Scale, parents' occupational status, fathers' educational level, mothers' and fathers' role satisfaction, and children's age, sex, grade, and depression level. However, mothers in the family study were somewhat more educated, somewhat less likely to be employed full-time, and the children reported slightly higher mean emotion.

30. *Sample Description.* Approximately equal numbers of families participated in the autumn of 1986, the winter of 1987, and the spring of 1987. Adolescents were paid $10 for their participation; parents were paid $12.50 each.

The sample represents a range of working-class and middle-class families with European and Eastern European ethnic backgrounds. The median household size for these families was 4.00 (range 3–10). Only eight of the families had preschool children in the 0–5 age range. Mothers ranged in age from 29 to 52 (mean = 38.3, SD = 4.6); fathers from 29 to 53 (M = 39.3, SD = 5.2). Nearly all mothers had completed high school (96 percent); 22 percent had completed college. All but one father had completed high school and 38 percent had completed college.

The conditions of parents' employment varied across families. Twenty-two mothers were employed part-time (eight through thirty-four hours a week) and fourteen were employed full-time. All but one of the fathers, a man who was recovering from an accident at work, were employed at the time of the study. The social prestige of these jobs was assessed using Featherman and Stevens's (1982) adaptation of the Duncan scale, which adjusts for sex bias in the original scale. Fathers' jobs had a mean score of 44.8 (SD = 21.4), which is comparable to other suburban samples. About half the fathers worked in professional or managerial jobs, half in blue-collar, technical, or sales jobs. Mothers' jobs had a mean Featherman–Stevens score of 43.0 (SD = 16.0), and while this did not differ significantly from the fathers' mean, the variance was less: Mothers had fewer low-status, blue-collar jobs, but also fewer higher-status, professional or managerial jobs. Most of their jobs were in sales, clerical work, lower-level management, or in lower-status traditional feminine professions, such as nursing and teaching.

Since we used mothers' employment as a moderating variable, it is important to note that these demographic characteristics did not differ by mothers' employment status. Using a liberal p-value of .10, family size, age of youngest child, education levels of father and mother, and Featherman–Stevens ratings of fathers' jobs all did not differ significantly across the maternal employment groups. The one exception is that women who worked full-time had higher-status jobs than those who worked part-time.

31. *Experimental Effects of the Study.* Psychologists have learned to ask whether a research procedure alters the phenomena it attempts to assess. To answer this question, first we asked some of the parents, "Do you think the family's week was different because of the study?" On a five-point scale, 54 percent responded "not at all," 31 percent said "a little," 7 percent said "some," 8 percent

said "quite a bit," and no one said "very much." Those who reported effects said that the pagers made them more aware and self-conscious: for example, "We realized some of the things we hadn't been doing together, like talking and listening to feelings"; "It brought us together a little"; "It felt like someone was looking over your shoulder."

A second test of experimental effects involved looking for changes in mood states across the week of the study. We reasoned that if the study had an effect on people, their emotional states would change over the week as these effects intensified or wore off. These analyses showed no significant change in people's average emotional state from the first to the second half of their week of participation, although the standard deviations of their scores did shrink slightly (the mean SD changed from 2.88 to 2.60; see also Csikszentmihalyi and Larson, 1987; Larson, 1989a). Our conclusion is that the effects of the study on people's lives were, at most, minor.

Respondents' Honesty. A related question that we are asked is whether our participants told the truth. Anticipating this query, we asked them directly whether there were any times they "did not tell the truth or changed what was going on." Seventy-eight percent said "never," 16 percent "not more than once," and 4 percent "not more than several times." In follow-up questions they reported that they had been most likely to disguise a thought or a feeling state, rather than an activity. We also asked the participants whether they thought other participants in the study were telling the truth. In response to this question, 96.4 percent endorsed the statement "Most people told the truth most of the time." These responses suggest that nearly all participants made a sincere attempt to represent their experience accurately.

Chapter 2. Fathers: Cycles of Work and Leisure

1. Demos, 1982; J. Pleck, 1987.
2. Levenson and Gottman, 1985; Gottman and Levenson, 1988.
3. In another ESM study of couples, LeFevre, Hedricks, Church, and McClintock (1991) also found that men and women did not differ in the variability of their reported emotional states.
4. J. Pleck, 1985.
5. E. Pleck, 1976.
6. Hareven, 1982.
7. Ehrenreich, 1983.
8. Morawski, 1984.
9. Demos, 1982; Rotundo, 1985.
10. Hood, 1986.
11. E. Pleck, 1976, p. 181.
12. In one study 86 percent of married men reported that their wives had provided direct assistance to their careers (Menaghan and Parcel, 1990).
13. Rybczynski, 1991.

14. Elder, 1974; Jahoda, 1982.

15. Parsons, 1942, p. 608. It should be noted that this distancing of men from the family was fueled by other factors as well. Fathers brought home not only a paycheck, but prestige. The social standing of the wife and the family in the community was determined in part by what job the father held. Research in the 1950s and 1960s shows that wives' marital satisfaction and their conduct of housework were also affected by the status of this job (Scanzoni, 1970). Such contingencies almost certainly impelled many fathers to work longer and harder hours in hopes of improving the family's social rank (Gould, 1974).

16. Cited by Demos, 1982, p. 442.

17. Bloom-Feshbach, 1981; Demos, 1982; J. Pleck, 1987.

18. Bernard, 1981; Brenton, 1966; Ferree, 1990; Hood, 1986; Lein, 1979; J. Pleck, 1985.

19. Perry-Jenkins and Crouter, 1990.

20. Wilson, 1987.

21. J. Pleck, 1986; Stafford and Duncan, 1985.

22. Day and Mackey, 1986.

23. The amount of time men spend at their jobs has continued to decline even in the last twenty years (Schor, 1991).

24. This distribution of fathers' time is remarkably consistent with time budget figures obtained from time diary studies. Martha Hill (1985), for example, reported that employed American men spent an average of forty-eight hours a week in job-related activities. If we include driving to work, as they did, this is nearly identical to the estimate of forty-six hours per week that we get when we convert our percentage to hours. In fact, the difference of about two hours might be attributable to our decision to exclude going out for lunch from job time.

25. Csikszentmihalyi, 1975, 1982, 1990.

26. Csikszentmihalyi and LeFevre, 1989.

27. Men in blue-collar jobs reported high attention for 37 percent of their reports at work, technical and sales workers for 47 percent, and professional/managerial men for 43 percent.

28. Differences in level of absorption by job type and activity might well be found if we had a larger sample with more people in each job category and were able to more closely control the type of job activity. It should also be noted that many of our employed women work only part-time, or have been at their current job for only a few years, so they have had less opportunity to get invested.

29. Weiss, 1990, p. 3.

30. Ibid., p. 10.

31. Longitudinal research shows that investment in work is passed from father to son (Mortimer, Lorence, and Kumka, 1986), and while investment fluctuates considerably during early adulthood (Lorence and Mortimer, 1985), our culture currently provides limited reinforcement for men's identities outside the work role.

32. Csikszentmihalyi and LeFevre, 1989, p. 821.

33. Men were significantly more likely than women to feel nervous at their jobs (13 percent of men's work reports versus 5 percent for women), lonely (6 percent versus 1 percent), and self-conscious (11 percent versus 1 percent). Although the disparity is not quite significant, men reported more frequent anger (5 percent versus 2 percent), irritability (4 percent versus 2 percent), and frustration (20 percent versus 16 percent). Men did not differ from women in the frequency of these states when at home.

34. In an analysis of variance, sex but not activity emerges as a predictor of a parent's immediate emotion at work. Parent's sex is highly significant ($F = 12.9$, $p < .001$), activity is not ($F = 1.42$, $p = .21$), nor is the interaction of gender and activity ($F = 1.36$, $p = .23$).

35. Martin and Wall, 1989.

36. Weiss, 1990, p. 45.

37. A telling finding is that men tend to think the work they contribute is worth more than that of women, irrespective of its objective value (Heimovics and Herman, 1988).

38. Cohler and Boxer, 1984.

39. Waldron, 1976.

40. Osherson, 1986.

41. Rybczynski, 1991; Thompson, 1963.

42. Reis, 1986.

43. Brown, 1981.

44. Men's average tiredness for the first report at home was $z = .33$, which is significantly above their average level of tiredness, $p < .05$.

45. Weiss, 1990, p. 95.

46. Ferree, 1990.

47. E. Pleck, 1976.

48. Samdahl, 1991; Shaw, 1985.

49. Neulinger, 1974, p. xi.

50. de Grazia, 1962, p. 416.

51. Pieper, 1963.

52. M. Hill, 1985.

53. Novak, 1976.

54. Messner, 1987.

55. Kubey and Csikszentmihalyi, 1990.

56. The proportion of time a man spent in media use was correlated with his rate at work of feeling competitive ($r = .35$, $p = .014$), frustrated ($r = 32$, $p = .023$), and worried ($r = .35$, $p = .014$).

57. Kubey, 1990; Rosenblatt and Cunningham, 1976.

58. These men's active leisure included: playing games (33 percent), sport and exercise (20 percent), family outings (19 percent), creative activities (18 percent), recreational shopping (15 percent), and participation in organizations with family members (5 percent). Half of it occurred away from home; the other half occurred at home.

59. Among all activities, active recreation ranked highest in rates of choice, excitement, happiness, cheerfulness, friendliness, and lowest in rates of boredom and unhappiness.

60. J. Pleck, 1985.

61. Researchers have sometimes found that fathers of young children, working-class fathers, and husbands who work fewer hours at their job devote a slightly larger share of home time to family work, especially to child care, but the differences are small (J. Pleck, 1985; Stafford and Duncan, 1985; Thompson and Walker, 1989). We, like other researchers, find that these proportions vary little by father's age, type of job, or his wife's employment (Berk, 1985; L. Hoffman, 1989; Walker and Woods, 1976).

62. Perry-Jenkins and Crouter, 1990.

63. Friedan, 1963.

64. de Beauvoir, 1968, p. 451.

65. In separate beeper studies, Csikszentmihalyi and Graef (1980) and Zuzanek and Smale (1991) also found that men experience family work as more voluntary and less unpleasant than women.

66. Shaw (1984) also found that men perceive family work as a leisure activity.

67. Barnett and Baruch, 1987; Hood, 1986; Lamb, 1986. Our data confirm that fathers' thoughts are less often focused on family issues than mothers' are. The fathers we studied reported thinking about their families for 23 percent of their time in the home sphere (versus 30 percent for mothers); housework was the topic of 15 percent of their thoughts (versus 22 percent for mothers). Five percent of fathers' thoughts specifically involved care, concern, and worry about children (versus 9 percent for mothers).

68. Crouter, Perry-Jenkins, Huston, and Crawford, 1989; Repetti, 1989.

69. Men's average emotion during occasions of talking with family was $z = .27$. Emotion when talking with a combination of family and friends was $z = .84$ (as compared to $z = .34$ for their wives), and their mean rating of how "joking" (versus "serious") people were during these times was $z = 1.14$ (as compared to $z = .44$ for their wives).

70. Larson, Richards, and Perry-Jenkins, in press.

71. Repetti (1989, 1993a) also shows that after a stressful day at work these men reported more health complaints and negative moods at home in the evening.

72. The correlation between men's emotion on their last report at work and their first report at home was $r = .45$, $p < .001$. The correlation between their average emotional state for the day at work and for the evening at home was $r = .28$, $p < .001$. Numerous other researchers have observed this emotional "carryover" (Bolger, DeLongis, Kessler, and Wethington, 1989; Crouter et al., 1989; Piotrkowski, 1979; Repetti, 1989).

73. Tait, Padgett, and Baldwin, 1989.

74. Fathers who reported higher average "choice" at home (relative to elsewhere) reported higher self-esteem ($r = .25$, $p = .072$), as did fathers who reported higher relative average emotion at home ($r = .37$, $p = .009$).

75. Epstein, 1984; Harré, 1984; Hochschild, 1979; Lutz, 1988.
76. Robinson, 1977.

Chapter 3: Mothers: Interweaving Work and Relationships

1. Rosaldo, 1974.
2. Friedan, 1963, p. 256.
3. Greer, 1971, p. 278.
4. Goldner, 1985.
5. Anderson, Finn, and Leider, 1981; Bernard, 1981; E. Pleck, 1976.
6. Filene, 1975; Welter, 1966.
7. Morawski, 1984; Welter, 1966.
8. Weitzman, 1981, p. 62.
9. Ferree, 1990; Gerson, 1985; Hareven, 1982.
10. Gerson, 1985.
11. Rainwater (1979), cited by Ferree, 1988, p. 8.
12. Chafe, 1972; Peterson, 1965.
13. Hewlett, 1986, p. 248.
14. Parsons and Bales, 1955, p. 14.
15. Gerson, 1985; Matthews and Rodin, 1989.
16. Mellman, Lazarus, and Rivlin, 1990.
17. We report the differences between employed mothers and full-time homemakers in Lauren, Richards, and Perry-Jenkins, in press. See also Michelson, 1985; Robinson, 1977; Walker and Woods, 1976.
18. In reality, the imbalance of effort between employed wives and their husbands is probably worse than these figures suggest. First, remember that our data cover only the hours from 7:30 A.M. until 9:30 P.M., so we may be missing some additional housework by women "after hours." Other research indicates that working mothers sleep a half hour less than working fathers, in part to accommodate more housework (Szalai, 1972; Walker and Woods, 1976).
19. Our findings here are reported in Larson, Richards, and Perry-Jenkins, in press; see also Ferree, 1991; Spitze, 1988.
20. Hochschild, 1989.
21. See also Michelson, 1985; Robinson, 1977.
22. Friedan, 1963.
23. Duckett, Raffaelli, and Richards, 1989.
24. This statement is relative to a woman's overall average, which is typically slightly above a neutral mood. During child care, women reported a wide variance of ups and downs, and for every occasion that was above their overall average, there was one below it.
25. Wells's (1988) research is with mothers of infants, but we will show in chapter 6 that the same is often true for mothers of adolescents.
26. Skolnick, 1991.
27. Mothers do more directive child care activities, such as getting the child

to take a bath, clean his or her room, or do chores, than fathers do (Russell and Russell, 1987).

28. During housework, women reported less frequent happiness than men at their jobs (23 percent versus 27 percent, p = .10) and less frequent cheerfulness (25 percent versus 32 percent, p = .02). They felt strong less often (8 percent versus 24 percent, p < .001) and tired more often (29 percent versus 15 percent, p < .001).

29. We found very few significant differences between how full-time employed women, part-time-employed women, and housewives experienced any of the activities at home or in the public sphere. Our ability to detect such differences, however, is limited by the small number of women represented in each group.

30. During housework, women reported less than half the rate of deep attention than men at their jobs (17 percent versus 41 percent, p < .001), much less frequent interest (37 percent versus 64 percent, p < .001) and less feeling of skill (47 percent versus 58 percent, p = .009).

31. Berheide, 1984.

32. Ibid.; Robinson, 1977.

33. Allison and Duncan, 1987; Berheide, 1984.

34. Ferree, 1990.

35. Shaw, 1988; Thompson and Walker, 1989.

36. Another factor that adds to the noxiousness of housework for women is that it is often done alone. Numerous commentators have lamented the solitariness of women's housework, citing loneliness as an "occupational hazard" of housewives (Berheide, 1984; Berk, 1985; Shaw, 1988). The housewives in our study reported being alone for 58 percent of housework, the full-time employed women 44 percent, and indeed their emotion during housework was lower when it was done alone. And yet for the men, 54 percent of housework was also done alone, so loneliness does not totally account for women's more negative emotion during housework, only the greater depression they feel from doing more of it.

37. Research demonstrates that attractive women are viewed as more feminine (Gillen, 1981); they are more likely to be promoted in female-oriented professions, but less likely to be promoted in high-prestige, male-oriented professions (Croxton, Van-Rensselaer, Dutton, and Ellis, 1989); they have higher self-esteem (Striegel-Moore, Silberstein, and Rodin, 1986). Slim female bodies are associated with intelligence and professional success (Silverstein and Perdue, 1988). One study found that declines in a wife's physical attractiveness, but not a husband's, negatively affected the quality of marital sexuality (Margolin and White, 1987).

38. Women's TV watching included less sports than men's (9 percent versus 29 percent of viewing time) and more dramatic series (10 percent versus 3 percent), soap operas (11 percent versus 3 percent), and exercise shows (3 percent versus 0 percent), but the experience of TV differed little by content. Women reported less frequent happiness and unhappiness during TV viewing than men.

39. Whereas the men reported reading newspapers, magazines, and manuals,

the women in our study were more likely to read novels (37 percent of reading time versus 12 percent for men).

40. Hunter and Whitson, 1991.

41. This quote is from a woman interviewed by Shank (1986). In our data, women were more likely to be thinking about family or housework tasks during leisure activities (28 percent) than men were (22 percent).

42. The frequency of women reporting two times of home leisure in a row is much lower than for men (30 percent versus 50 percent). See also Chambers (1986) and Deem (1982).

43. Another explanation for these women's lower emotional state during household leisure is that they were more often alone during this time than the men were, and being alone is associated with lower moods. Full-time homemakers, in particular, were more often alone during their leisure—they watched soap operas alone during the day, or took time out from housework to play with the dog. Nonetheless, in an ANOVA with aloneness, maternal employment, and activity controlled, women's emotion during leisure was still lower, although the difference was not quite significant ($p = .08$).

44. Bialeschki and Henderson, 1986.

45. Henderson and Dialeschki, 1991; Shank, 1986.

46. Robinson, 1977.

47. Mothers' average emotion in the household sphere was 2.6, which was significantly below their average of 3.0 for the public sphere (Larson, Richards, and Perry-Jenkins, in press). Women also reported significantly higher rates of feeling irritable and weak in the home sphere, and higher rates of feeling in control, accepted, skilled, cheerful, and excited away from the household sphere.

48. Women reported feeling most hurried during housework (54 percent versus 25 percent for men), but also felt hurried across other home activities. Surprisingly, rates of feeling hurried at home were actually greater among full-time homemakers.

49. Depression is related both to number of hours spent at home ($r = .27$, $p = .05$, with number of work hours controlled) and to number of hours in family-related work ($r = .32$, $p = .022$, with work hours controlled).

50. Ferree, 1990.

51. Robinson, 1977.

52. Juster, 1985; J. Pleck, 1985; Schor, 1991.

53. Ferree, 1991; J. Pleck, 1985.

54. Ferree, 1988.

55. Homemakers reported being "alone, no one else nearby" for 21 percent of their reports, as compared to 12 percent for full-time employed women ($p = .033$).

56. Lopata, 1971.

57. Scarr, Phillips, and McCartney, 1989.

58. Ibid.

59. This finding is replicated by Robinson (1977).

60. Martocchio and O'Leary, 1989.

61. At work they were significantly less likely to feel unhappy (a mean of .8 percent of work beeps versus 3.7 percent at home), drowsy (2 percent versus 8 percent), lonely (.7 percent versus 5.7 percent), and guilty (0 percent versus 4 percent).

62. Thompson and Walker, 1989.

63. Karasek, cited by Hochschild (1989), p. 137.

64. Of course, as we reported in chapter 2, women also experience themselves as "the leader" less often at work, and the absence of this responsibility for others may partly account for their lesser frequency of negative emotions. We cannot say for certain whether women in exactly the same jobs as men might not experience equivalent levels of distress. All we can say is that, in their current jobs, the women we studied did not.

65. The correlation between a woman's average emotion at her job and the friendliness she experienced from others at the job was $r = .61$, $p < .001$. For men this correlation was $r = -.20$, n.s.

66. England and McCreary, 1987; Repetti, Matthews, and Waldron, 1989.

67. Women's tiredness on their first report after coming home from work in the evening was $z = .23$; this was not significantly different from the level of $z = .33$ reported by men.

68. Rosenblatt and Meyer, 1992.

69. Using different methods, other researchers have also found that women's jobs are more compartmentalized from home than men's are (Duxbury and Higgins, 1991).

70. These emotional plunges were also evident for the part-time-employed women in the study, but less severe; they did not occur for full-time homemakers. From 7:30 in the morning until 4:30 in the afternoon, the homemakers' moods were somewhat lower than average, because they were often alone and often doing housework. But in the evening and on weekends their moods were higher. They had completed many of the home-related tasks, so evenings and weekends allowed more time to relax. The homemakers were also not as tired as full-time-employed mothers during the evenings and weekends.

71. Ferree, 1988.

72. Greenglass, Pantony, and Burke, 1989; Pittman and Orthner, 1989.

73. Menaghan and Parcel, 1990.

74. Ibid.; J. Pleck, 1985; Spitze, 1988; Verbrugge, 1987.

75. Repetti et al., 1989.

76. Women who felt less "hurried" at work reported greater happiness; for men, exactly the opposite was the case. The average emotion a woman reported at work was negatively correlated with how "hurried" she felt at work ($r = -.32$, $P < .10$), whereas for men this correlation was positive ($r = .34$, $p < .05$).

77. Schultz, Chung, and Henderson, 1989.

78. Greenhaus and Beutell, 1985; Menaghan and Parcel, 1990; Ross, Mirowsky, and Huber, 1983; Scarr et al., 1989; Ulbrich, 1988. We should also note that the women in our study who had part-time employment did not stand out as

having better or worse well-being than other women. Given the structure of the labor market, part-time employment is rarely compatible with maintaining a career, so while these women may have had more flexible hours, they have had more limited job choices.

79. Joebgen and Richards, 1990; Ross et al., 1983.

80. The partial correlation between the amount of time a woman spent in the public personal domain and depression, with hours of employment controlled, was $r = -.29$, $p = .03$.

81. Tannen, 1990, p. 25.

82. Bateson, 1990, p. 13.

83. Ross et al., 1983.

Chapter 4. Adolescents: Lives of Emotional Flux

1. Hess and Goldblatt, 1957; Musgrove, 1963.

2. Cited by Fox, 1977.

3. Carnegie Council, 1989.

4. A complete chart of Selman's week is provided in Larson (1988).

5. To evaluate the possibility that adolescents are just more liberal in what they consider to be a feeling of extreme happiness and unhappiness, we had the adolescents and their parents use the same seven-point scales to rate the level of happiness they perceived in six pictures of faces, drawn to express a range of emotions. If there is a difference in how adults and adolescents calibrate the scale, we would expect the adults to be more restrained in how they rated these faces. Yet they were not. Adults and adolescents rated the happy faces at about the same level of happiness on the scale and rated the distressed faces as equally unhappy. This suggests that the scales have the same calibration for children and parents and, therefore, that the differences in ratings of their own states reflect real, not artifactual, differences.

6. Most of these findings replicate a prior ESM study in which we compared the daily subjective states of 75 high-school-age adolescents to those of 107 unrelated adults. The adolescents were found to report more extreme high and low emotional states, less feeling of control, less desire to be doing what they were doing, and more frequent states of drowsiness, weakness, and boredom (Larson, Csikszentmihalyi, and Graef, 1980).

7. Kett, 1977; Modell and Goodman, 1990.

8. Nearly all the findings reported in this chapter are based on the larger sample of 483 adolescents and thus are more robust. The older students in this large sample reported both more day-to-day hassles within the week of the study (Ham and Larson, 1990) and more major events within the last six months (Larson and Ham, 1993).

9. Larson and Ham, 1993; Simmons, Blyth, Van Cleave, and Bush, 1979; Simmons, Burgeson, Carlton-Ford, and Blyth, 1987.

10. Larson and Asmussen, 1991.

11. The ratings younger and older kids made of the drawings of faces (see note 5) did not differ, indicating that this worsening of emotional experience is not simply a "response set," but rather reflects real perceived differences (Larson and Lampman-Petraitis, 1989).

12. This decline in average moods with age occurs for both boys and girls (Larson and Lampman-Petraitis, 1989); however, girls show the most marked increase in sad and depressive affect. Gender differences between boys and girls are generally small. In our large sample, the boys reported slightly lower average emotion than the girls did, with slightly less variability (Greene and Larson, 1991). The girls were somewhat more likely than boys to feel nervous (16 percent versus 12 percent of reports), embarrassed (7 percent versus 5 percent), kindly (40 percent versus 30 percent), worried (16 percent versus 13 percent), tired (16 percent versus 13 percent), very excited (18 percent versus 14 percent), weak (18 percent versus 14 percent), and ugly (11 percent versus 5 percent). The boys were somewhat more likely to feel very strong (18 percent versus 13 percent). All these differences are significant at the .05 level.

13. Larson, Ham, and Raffaelli, 1989.

14. Our findings are reported in Richards and Larson (1993). Similar findings based on different research techniques are reported in Buchanan, Eccles, and Becker (1992), Brooks-Gunn and Warren (1989), and Inoff-Germain et al. (1988). In our data, physically mature teens reported feeling "in love" more often, which makes sense, given that sexuality and mating are the biological agenda of puberty. Also, early-maturing boys reported more *positive* emotion, suggesting that bigger, more muscular boys enjoy certain social rewards less available among other boys. Thus, if anything, it is not the hormonal changes of puberty but the social evaluation of the teen's new body that affects his or her emotional experience (Tobin-Richards, Boxer, and Petersen, 1983).

It should be emphasized, however, that these analyses do not involve hormonal measures, only self-reports of pubertal level using established instruments. It is possible that there are yet-to-be-discovered complex relationships between adolescents' hormones and their subjective feelings.

15. The correlation between negative emotion and daily hassles is reported in Larson and Ham (1989). The correlation between negative emotion and major negative life events is reported in Larson and Ham (1993). The latter paper reports significant correlations between negative emotion and both adolescents' and parents' reports of events in the adolescents' life. It also demonstrates that the effect occurs for events across all domains of adolescents' lives: family, friends, school. Longitudinal research suggests that this relationship is at least partly causal. Stressful events have a negative effect on adolescents' well-being (Compas, 1987; Simmons et al., 1987).

16. During this same period, adolescents' understanding of emotional processes also deepens (Nannis and Cowan, 1987); they make greater differentiations of the emotions suited to different situations (Harter, 1980; Schwartz and Trabasso, 1984; Weiner and Graham, 1984), and they more often consider internal

processes in their emotions (P. Harris, Olthof, and Terwogt, 1981; Wolman, Lewis, and King, 1971). Although in early adolescence these cognitive changes lower emotional states, we suspect that in the long run for most adolescents they probably lead to better emotional adjustment (Greene and Larson, 1991).

17. Larson and Asmussen, 1991; Larson and Ham, 1993.

18. Elkind, 1980.

19. Larson, Raffaelli et al., 1990; Leone, 1989; Richards, Casper, and Larson, 1990. Our data do not prove that negative emotion causes these problems, only that they are correlated. It is likely that the problems also feed the negative emotion.

20. Simmons and Blyth, 1987.

21. Larson, Kubey, and Colletti, 1989.

22. Larson and Asmussen, 1991.

23. Eccles and Midgley, 1990.

24. Larson, 1988.

25. Lee, 1991; Rohlen, 1983; Won, 1989.

26. The students also reported positive experiences during extracurricular activities (Larson and Kleiber, 1993). Their least positive experience was in academic classes, such as social studies, reading, and science. The difference is partly attributable to the fact that their academic classes relied more on traditional lecture and deskwork methods, which elicit especially low motivation and emotion (Larson, Ham, and Raffaelli, 1989; Larson and Richards, 1991b). Students reported higher motivation and attention during projectlike activities (Larson and Kleiber, 1993) and interactive activities, like group work and discussion, as well as field trips. This profile of subjective states during classroom experience is closely similar to our findings for high-school-age students in our prior ESM study (Csikszentmihalyi and Larson, 1984).

27. Larson and Kleiber, 1993; Leone and Richards, 1989.

28. We report extensive analyses of these students' boredom in school and outside of school in Larson and Richards (1991b).

29. The average adolescent reported feeling less skilled during class than his or her father during work ($z = -.31$ versus .17, $p < .001$); adolescents' interest was less ($z = -.15$ versus .11, $p = .014$); and they report greater desire to be doing something else ($z = .16$ versus $-.07$, $p = .002$). They also reported feeling greater boredom ($z = .31$ versus .07, $p = .002$) and feeling less in control ($z = -.03$ versus .17, $p = .10$).

30. We find that the pattern of moods during drug use is the mirror opposite of classroom moods, a finding that suggests teens use drugs to counteract the experience of school (Larson and Kleiber, 1993).

31. A student's average emotion during class was correlated with scores two years later for delinquency ($r = -.29$, $p = .001$), depression ($r = -.18$, $p = .003$), self-esteem ($r = .16$, $p = .008$), and school grades ($r = .14$, $p = .02$).

32. Farrell, 1988; Kirsch, 1986.

33. Savin-Williams and Berndt, 1990. We provide a detailed account of age differences in the daily companionship of fifth to ninth graders in Larson

and Richards (1991a). We found that the younger students spent more time with neighborhood friends and older students spent more time with friends known through school or organizations. Within the 7:30 A.M.–9:30 P.M. period covered by the study, there was no age difference for boys in amount of time spent with friends. Girls showed a slight increase in the ninth grade, largely because they talked to friends on the phone more and spent more of their time in public with friends rather than family members. We also suspect that the older students, who went to bed later, spent some additional time with friends after 9:30 P.M.

34. Average emotional state with friends increases with age, relative to other parts of their lives (Larson and Richards, 1991a).

35. Larson, Ham, and Raffaelli, 1989.

36. Selman, 1980.

37. Buhrmester and Furman (1987) demonstrate this increase.

38. Savin-Williams and Berndt, 1990.

39. Raffaelli and Duckett, 1989. Schwartz, Fisher, Tolan, and Thomas (1993) also find this gender difference in amount of time spent talking for a sample of urban Latino and African-American adolescents.

40. Larson, 1983.

41. Richards and Larson, 1990.

42. Larson and Asmussen, 1991.

43. Larson, 1988.

44. Berndt, 1990; Brown, Eicher, and Petrie, 1986.

45. Shantz and Hobart, 1989.

46. Larson and Asmussen, 1991.

47. Richards and Larson, 1990.

48. Research on this topic is summarized by Savin-Williams and Berndt (1990). Data from our large sample suggest similar patterns, particularly for boys. We found that the amount of time a boy spent with friends was positively correlated with average emotion ($r = .25$, $p < .001$); with school GPA ($r = .14$, $p = .029$); and with teachers' ratings of adjustment ($r = .21$, $p = .004$); and correlated negatively with parents' ratings on Achenbach and Edelbrock's (1986) scales of internalizing behavior ($r = -.19$, $p = .004$), and externalizing behavior ($r = -.15$, $p = .023$). Girls' spending more time with friends was correlated with lower internalizing scores ($r = -.15$, $p = .017$), and also with greater mood variability ($r = .16$, $p = .014$) and lower GPA ($r = .18$, $p = .005$).

49. Our data suggest that the amount of time adolescents spend on chores does not vary by maternal employment (Richards and Duckett, 1994) nor parents' marital status (Asmussen and Larson, 1991). Unlike in other studies, the girls in ours reported no more time in chores than boys did. But there was a striking sex difference in types of chores reported, with girls doing more indoor chores and boys more outdoor chores (Duckett, Raffaelli, and Richards, 1989). This finding suggests that the next generation of adults may be as sex-typed in their performance of housework as are the mothers and fathers in our study.

The contrast between U.S. adolescents and others is reported by Munroe et al. (1983).

50. Duckett et al., 1989; Kirshnit, Ham, and Richards, 1989; Larson, Kubey, and Colletti, 1989; Raffaelli and Duckett, 1989; see also Timmer, Eccles, and O'Brien, 1985.

51. Asmussen and Larson, 1991.

52. Boys reported little choice when doing housework and a strong desire to be doing something else; older girls reported less of this pattern. This suggests that girls more often accept some responsibility for the family's needs, perhaps because they identify more with their mother's strain. See Goodnow (1988) for a helpful discussion of adolescents and household work.

53. Raffaelli, 1992.

54. Offer and Offer, 1975; Offer, Ostrov, and Howard, 1981.

55. Compas and Wagner (1991) compared effects of different types of stress on young, middle, and older adolescents and found that family stress was particularly consequential for young adolescents. We also found that stress at home had more effect on adolescents' well-being than stress in other domains (Larson and Ham, 1993).

Others have confirmed that an adolescent's positive family life is related to better performance of schoolwork (Entwisle, 1990), healthier peer relationships (Ryan and Lynch, 1989; Savin-Williams and Berndt, 1990), and higher self-esteem (Hoffman, Ushpiz, and Levy-Shiff, 1988), among other things. We found that those in our large young-adolescent sample who experienced a cohesive family, as measured by the Family Environment Scale, reported more positive average emotion, both with the family and away from the family (O'Donnell, 1993). They also reported fewer symptoms of depression ($r = -.54$, $p < .001$), and had higher GPAs at school ($r = .20$, $p < .001$). Among girls, a cohesive family environment was related to less variability in emotion ($r = -.26$, $p < .001$), a sign that healthy families stabilize some of adolescents' gyrating moods.

56. For the students in the family study, the correlation between their emotion during school hours and at home that evening was $r = .38$, $p < .001$.

57. Larson and Richards, 1991a.

58. The number of children in our sample who had their own bedroom rises from 56 percent for the fifth graders to 73 percent for the ninth graders. Controlling for grade, those with their own bedroom spent only about 3 percent more of their waking hours alone.

Even more so than time with family and friends, we assume that the meaning these teens give to solitude is shaped by unique values of European-American culture (Larson, 1990; Malik, 1981). Nonetheless, Schwartz, Fisher, Tolan, and Thomas (1993) have found that Latino and African-American inner-city teens spend comparable amounts of time alone.

59. Parke and Sawin, 1979.

60. Larson, 1990.

61. We find that amount of time spent alone shows only a slight relationship

to family conflict. Other research showing age changes in the experience of solitude is reported in Coleman (1974); Larson (1990); Marcoen, Goossens, and Caes
(1987).

62. A subset of students in the larger study were asked on the beeper sheets to
explain their reason for being alone. These students reported proactive explanations
most often, particularly with age. Nineteen percent in fifth and sixth grade and 30
percent in seventh and eighth grade checked "I want to be alone to concentrate on
what I am doing." "I enjoy being alone" was checked 9 percent and 18 percent by
the two age groups, and "I want to be alone to think about things and get myself
together" was checked by 3 percent and 5 percent. Forty-eight percent versus 36
percent reported that they were alone because no one else was at home.

63. Larson, Csikszentmihalyi, and Graef, 1982.

64. Kurdek, 1987.

65. Markus and Nurius, 1986.

66. Larson, 1990, 1992.

67. Nolen-Hoeksema, Girgus, and Seligman, 1991; Nolen-Hoeksema, Morrow, and Fredrickson, 1993.

68. Controlling for grade, amount of time spent alone at home was negatively correlated with average emotion ($r = -.15$, $p = .002$); however, the quadratic term was also significant ($r = -.18$, $p < .001$), indicating that only those
adolescents who spent an extreme amount of time by themselves showed lower
emotion. For parents' ratings of the child's well-being (Achenbach and Edelbrock,
1986), teachers' ratings of the child's adjustment, and school GPA, there is no lin-
ear effect; however, the quadratic effect is significant. Adolescents who spent an
optimal, intermediate amount of time alone (10 percent to 25 percent of waking
time) were better adjusted. These findings replicate two previous studies (Larson
and Csikszentmihalyi, 1978, 1980).

Chapter 5. Fathers and Mothers: Marriage in the Trenches

1. Fromm, 1956, pp. 4–5.

2. Glenn, 1990.

3. Orthner and Mancini, 1990; Rubin, 1976.

4. Huston, Robins, Atkinson, and McHale (1987) report declines in shared
activities during the first year of marriage. Belsky (1990) reports that time spent
talking, exchanging ideas, and sharing joint projects further declines after couples
have children.

5. Goffman, 1971.

6. Our estimates of the hours and minutes people spent in given situations
are based on a simple conversion formula. Because we sampled ninety-eight hours of
people's time for the week, 1 percent of their beeps can be estimated to approxi-
mate one hour a week.

7. Pooling all conversations between husband and wife, the most frequent
topic was family (31 percent), leisure activities (16 percent), and maintenance (14
percent).

8.   Because our data included only contact between 7:30 A.M. and 9:30 P.M., we missed the important nighttime phase of relations between husbands and wives, when sexual interaction is more likely. But other research suggests that after fifteen years of marriage, sexual intercourse typically occurs about once a week (Blumstein and Schwartz, 1983) and that the quality of sexual relations tends to reflect other aspects of the relationships. Therefore we suspect that our picture of these couples' marriages is not terribly distorted by omission of these nighttime hours.

9.   Berscheid, 1983.

10.   For the report prior to being together, husbands' emotional state was $z = -.12$, then jumped to $z = .14$ when they were together; wives' emotional state increased from $z = .09$ to $z = .17$. Both changes are significant at $p < .01$.

11.   Huston, McHale, and Crouter (1986) find that the amount of pleasurable and affectionate interchange between partners declines substantially in the first year of marriage.

12.   For both husbands and wives, we tested the effect of spouse's presence on emotional state during times in the home sphere, including activity and the presence of others as additional independent variables in the ANOVA. For husbands, the main effect for presence of spouse was not significant, but the interaction with activity was ($p = .018$). For wives, the main effect for spouse's presence was significant ($p = .026$), and the interaction was not. Additional analyses including presence of others, location, and maternal employment did not alter this basic pattern, but did suggest that the presence of spouse had a greater effect on employed women than on housewives (interaction: $p = .021$), especially during times alone together.

The interaction for men is interesting. When men were eating or talking, the wife's presence was associated with higher emotional state. This suggests that men do enjoy interaction with their wives when it is direct and unencumbered. However, when engaged in child-related activities, family transportation, and active leisure, her presence was associated with less positive moods. Why the opposite effect? One possibility is that the latter are activities in which the wife's presence constrained the husband's enjoyment. Research with younger children suggests that the mother's presence can inhibit the father's involvement (Russell and Radin, 1983), and perhaps that was happening here.

13.   See note 12. The time wives spent with husbands was somewhat more likely to be devoted to leisure and events away from home; nonetheless, when we control for these contextual factors, including location and the presence or absence of children, the company of their husband still raised their mood.

14.   When with their husband during the 5:30–7:30 P.M. period, employed women's emotion was $z = -.36$. When with their husbands on Saturday afternoon, it was $z = .00$.

15.   The presence of a woman's husband is related to her feeling less hurried than usual ($z = -.28$). In an ANOVA, including her activity and the presence (versus absence) of children, husband's presence is associated with mothers feeling less hurried ($p = .055$).

16. Fitzpatrick, 1988.

17. Holman and Jacquart, 1988; Williams, 1988.

18. Bernard, 1982.

19. Ibid. In the same vein, others have found that wives' marital satisfaction is more responsive to shared activities and affectional behavior from their spouse, while husbands' is affected by their wives' household labor (Thompson and Walker, 1989; Wills, Weiss, and Patterson, 1974).

20. Gottman, 1991.

21. In marital interactions observed in a lab, wives were more likely to respond in kind to positive and negative emotions displayed by their husbands than vice versa (Notarius and Johnson, 1982). Likewise, in an examination of how stress in people's lives affects their spouse's emotional well-being, three studies have found much stronger transmission from husband to wife than the reverse (Compas, Howell, Phares, Williams, and Ledoux, 1989; Galambos and Silbereisen, 1989; Rook, Dooley, and Catalano, 1991).

22. Other research has shown that men's stress level at the end of the work-day increases conflictual marital interactions (Crouter et al., 1989). If a man has an argument at work, there is increased probability of an argument with his wife that night (Bolger et al., 1989). In our data, transmission to both full-time homemakers and employed women was evident.

23. Weiss, 1990.

24. Rook et al., 1991.

25. Gottman, 1991; Guthrie and Noller, 1988; Tannen, 1990.

26. For two much different discussions of husbands' and wives' power, see Polatnick (1973–74) and Szinovacz (1987).

27. *Measures of Happy vs. Distressed Marriages.* The Locke-Wallace Short Marital Adjustment Test (Locke and Wallace, 1959) is one of the most frequently used and well validated measures of marital adjustment (Sabatelli, 1988). While one set of researchers is highly satisfied with this measure (for example, Gottman and Levenson, 1984, 1988), others have argued that this and similar mainstream measures blur together a host of different dimensions, which may often be confounded with other variables of interest (Fincham and Bradbury, 1990 Huston et al., 1986). It requires respondents to sum across all their affective experience, yet, as Berscheid (1983) points out, we have no idea how such summations are made and whether they might be distorted.

Our measure of "marital warmth" circumvents some of these concerns. It assesses a singular dimension (beep-level alphas = .83, fathers; .85, mothers; person-level alphas = .98, .97); and, because we obtained measures at many random moments, we can compute our own average score, without relying on people's mental summations of their experience. We should note that, although Jerry and Glenna demonstrated enormous variability on this measure across the week as a result of their fight (figure 5.2), most individuals show a stable range of feelings toward their spouses, and this range is quite similar whether they are together or apart. While this measure deals with a narrower construct, its limitation is that it is new and thus has not been scrutinized over time.

Nonetheless, values for the two measures are strongly correlated with each other (wives: $r = .57$, $p < .001$; husbands: $r = .57$, $p < .001$). For both measures, wives' and husbands' scores are also highly correlated (adjustment: $r = .62$, $p < .001$; warmth: $r = .60$ $p < .001$). In our sample, neither is associated with social class, and correlates are generally similar across social-class groupings.

28. See also Kirchler, 1989; Orthner, 1975; Orthner and Mancini, 1990.

29. The greater importance of talk and interaction to wives is consistent with findings by two other studies: Holman and Jacquart, 1988; Smith, Snyder, Trull, and Monsma, 1988.

30. Rosenblatt, Titus, Nevaldine, and Cunningham, 1979.

31. See appendix 5.3; see also Holman and Jacquart, 1988; Orthner, 1975; Orthner and Mancini, 1990.

32. M. Hill, 1988. In analysis of another set of longitudinal data, Zuo (1992) also shows that the amount of time together predicts subsequent marital happiness.

33. We defined shared positive emotion as times when both partners reported an emotional state with a value of $z > .33$. Partners in cool marriages reported joint positive emotion for 21 percent of the times they were together; those in warm marriages reported it for 23 percent. The difference is not significant. It should be noted, however, that because warm couples spent more time together, the absolute frequency of their positive experiences was significantly greater.

We also want to note that neither husbands' nor wives' average emotion when together was a stronger predictor of marital well-being in our sample.

34. Baucom and Mehlman, 1984; Hahlweg and Jacobson, 1984; Margolin and Wampold, 1981.

35. Cool couples reported joint negative emotion, defined as both having values with $z < -.33$, for 23 percent of the times they were together; warm couples for 12 percent. The difference is significant at the $p < .05$ level.

36. In lab studies, distressed couples express far more negative affect to one another than nondistressed couples (Gottman and Levenson, 1984; Schaap, 1984). Levenson and Gottman (1983, 1985) find that unhappy couples respond to discussion of difficult topics with more physiological arousal than nondistressed couples do.

37. Gottman and Levenson, 1986.

38. Bradbury and Fincham, 1990; Guthrie and Noller, 1988.

39. In cool marriages, husbands' emotions predict wives' subsequent emotions with a *beta* of .28, $p = .009$. In warm marriages this value is *beta* = .09, n.s. Lab findings, too, have shown that distressed husbands' emotions are more likely to be transmitted to wives' emotions (Gottman and Levenson, 1984; Guthrie and Noller, 1988).

40. Lewis and Spanier (1979) review evidence regarding effects of financial strains, community disorder, and numerous other variables on marital well-being. Larsen and Olson (1989) demonstrate that attitudes and personality traits prior to marriage affect marital quality.

41. Wives' global average emotion was correlated with the amount of time husbands reported in child care activities ($r = .42$, $p = .002$) and family transportation ($r = .28$, $p = .002$). The amount of time husbands reported doing housework was correlated with husbands' ($r = .36$, $p = .044$) and wives' ($r = .45$, $p = .006$) increase in marital adjustment scores in the two years after the study.

42. Gottman, 1991; Leslie and Anderson, 1988; Ross et al., 1983; Suitor, 1991; Yogev and Brett, 1985.

43. The correlation between mothers' hours of employment and shared time together was $r = -.25$, $p < .05$. The distribution of this shared time across activities did not vary as a function of mothers' employment. Other studies have generally found little or no relationship between wife's employment and amount of shared time (Holman and Epperson, 1984; Kingston and Nock, 1987; White, 1983).

44. This lack of association is evident in our data and others' (Barling, 1990; Spitze, 1988).

45. When the employed women in our study were at home on weekdays between 5:30 and 7:30 P.M., their rate of housework was 49 percent in cool marriages versus 34 percent in warm marriages ($p = .067$). Their mean emotional state when at home during this time was $z = -.55$ in cool marriages, as compared to $z = .01$ in warm marriages ($p = .007$ in ANOVA with activity controlled). If we narrow this to women who were employed full-time, these figures were $z = -.99$ and $z = -.17$ ($p = .026$).

46. Orthner, 1975.

47. Berger and Kellner, 1970; Kingston and Nock, 1987.

48. Gottman, 1991.

49. Jacobson, Follette, and McDonald, 1982.

50. Gottman, 1991; Margolin and Wampold, 1981; Schaap, 1984.

51. Gottman, 1979.

52. Noller and Gallois, 1988.

53. We found that wives' and especially husbands' feelings of being "in control of" his or her spouse (as opposed to feeling "controlled by") was related to marital warmth.

54. Prigogine, 1980.

55. Mace, 1983.

56. Montemayor, 1982, p. 86.

Chapter 6. Mothers and Adolescents: Love and Conflict

1. Marshall, 1991; Wollett and Phoenix, 1991.

2. Collins, 1990.

3. Collins and Russell, 1991.

4. LaRossa, 1986.

5. Hewlett, 1986; Vinovskis, 1987.

6. Slater, 1970, p. 64, cited in Hewlett, 1986, p. 263.

7.   In fact, many researchers, even more recently, ignore other factors that affect a child and begin from the assumption that a child's mother bears the blame if the adolescent develops psychological or behavioral problems (Caplan and Hall-McCorquodale, 1985; Wollett and Phoenix, 1991).

8.   Gadlin, 1978; Youniss and Smollar, 1989.

9.   Thompson and Walker, 1989.

10. Cooper and Baker, 1991.

11. For the period from 7:30 to 8:30 on weekday mornings, adolescents or their mothers reported being with the other for 42 percent of the time; the equivalent rate for fathers was 19 percent. For the period from 3:30 to 5:30 on weekday afternoons, adolescents or their mothers reported being with the other for 54 percent of the time; for fathers this rate was 37 percent.

12. Mothers' employment had relatively little relationship to the amount of time they spent with their teenage children, since the children were in school much of the time the mothers were at work. The median employed mother in our family sample left for work at 8:15 A.M. and returned at 4:00 P.M. In a careful analysis of the data from our larger young-adolescent study, Richards and Duckett (1994) found that the full-time employed mothers spent no less time with their children. Our family study data suggest that they may have had slightly less peripheral time (times when mother and child didn't agree they were together and times when they agreed but were doing separate activities) but did not differ in time spent in shared activities. Employing a larger data set, Nock and Kingston (1988) also found that the main difference in contact time between school-age children and employed versus nonemployed mothers was in peripheral time when mother and child were not engaged.

13. See also Youniss and Smollar, 1985.

14. In the family sample, mothers and adolescents reported talking to each other for .85 percent of all times, or about 8.6 minutes a day; for fathers this figure was .40 percent, or 3.1 minutes a day. These figures primarily reflect "social" talk and do not include times when a parent was disciplining a child, helping with homework, or when either party reported talk as secondary to some other activity, like eating or driving. In the larger adolescent sample, the girls reported slightly, but significantly, more time talking with their mother than the boys did.

15. See also Collins and Russell, 1991; Noller and Bagi, 1985; Youniss and Smollar, 1985.

16. Collins and Russell, 1991; Wright and Keple, 1981.

17. Youniss and Smollar, 1985.

18. Larson and Richards, 1991a; Raffaelli and Duckett, 1989.

19. The time mothers and adolescents reported being together but in different activities fell from 17 percent to 10 percent between the fifth and eighth grade. Time spent in the same activity edged down from 7 percent to 6 percent across the same period.

20. Smetana, 1988a.

21. These findings are based on occasions within the family study data when

both child and mother reported being together. Fifth graders reported feeling "very happy" for 56 percent of these times; eighth graders never reported feeling "very happy." Fifth graders reported feeling "very," "quite," or "somewhat unhappy" for 2 percent of these times, compared to 33 percent for eighth graders. The decline in the child's emotional state was evident during time alone with either parent and during time with both parents together.

A study by Flannery, Montemayor and Eberly (1991) in which adolescents were observed during interactions with their parents in a lab provides validation of this age trend. Teens' expression of positive emotion was found to decrease and expression of negative emotion to increase as a function of age and pubertal stage. In that study the effect was curvilinear, with expression becoming more positive at later ages. Our data show a similar curvilinear trend, with emotion improving in middle adolescence, especially for boys (Larson and Richards, 1991a).

22. Steinberg, 1991.

23. Montemayor, 1983; Steinberg, 1987.

24. Smetana, 1988b.

25. Ibid.

26. *Measures of Closeness and Warmth Between Adolescents and Mothers.* To evaluate the quality of the parent–adolescent bond, we used indexes similar to those used to evaluate husband–wife relationships. We employed the same measure of hour-to-hour warmth, obtained from the beeper sheets (used for the family study only). And we employed a commonly used questionnaire measure of closeness, which asks about satisfaction, sharing, and respect within the relationship, adopted from Blyth (1982).

Both these measures of the mother–adolescent relationship were related to the mental health of the adolescent. Students in the larger study who felt close to their mother were less depressed ($r = -.33$, $p < .001$) and reported higher self-esteem, ($r = .27$, $p < .001$); boys were rated as better adjusted by their teachers ($r = .23$, $p = .004$), and girls' parents reported fewer psychological symptoms ($r = -.21$, $p = .003$). Kids who felt warm and close to their mother were much less depressed and reported higher overall emotional states. Warmth toward their mother was correlated with depression for both boys ($r = -.28$) and girls ($r = -.42$, $p < .05$). It was also related to a child's overall emotional state ($r = .61$, $p < .001$). Both these measures showed that adolescents' feelings toward their mother became less favorable with age. Neither was related to the family's socioeconomic status.

In an extensive set of analyses, we found negligible relationships between either of these measures and the amount of time these adolescents spent with their mother, irrespective of child's age. Likewise, they were not related to the teens' emotional states when with their mother.

27. Montemayor (1982) also did not find a correlation between time spent with the mother and conflict with her.

28. Leone and Richards, 1989.

29. When they were together, mothers reported themselves to be the leader

for 29 percent of the time and the teen to be the leader for 1 percent of the time. Adolescents reported their mother to be the leader for 18 percent and themselves for 3 percent.

30. The correlation between adolescents' ratings of their state on a seven-point scale from "very happy" to "very unhappy" and mothers' estimates of their child's state was $r = .25$, $p < .001$, based on 444 occasions. For fathers this correlation was $r = .02$, $p = .683$, $N = 323$.

31. Montemayor and Hanson, 1985.

32. Collins, 1990; Jessop, 1981; Paikoff, 1991.

33. The correlation between the mothers' and adolescents' emotions when together was not significant for girls and $r = .31$, $p < .001$, for boys. See Larson and Richards (in press).

34. Feldman, Wentzel and Gehring, 1989; Larson and Ham, 1993; Noller and Callan, 1986.

35. Ballenski and Cook, 1982.

36. Repetti (1993b) shows that negative events in a child's life during the day, such as failure experiences in school or fights with friends, are often followed by negative parent–child interactions that evening.

37. Larson and Richards, in press.

38. A study of four-year-olds indicates that kids in positive moods are more compliant (Lay, Waters, and Park, 1989). We suspect this is equally true of teenagers.

39. Compas et al., 1989.

40. Cassidy, Parke, Butkovsky, and Braungart, 1992; Hampson and Beavers, 1987.

41. Mothers' depression was correlated with the proportion of time that mother and adolescent reported being together ($r = -.23$, $p = .095$), with mothers' rate of irritability ($r = .34$, $p = .050$), and with anger ($r = .38$, $p = .030$) during these interactions, and with change in adolescents' emotion when entering their mother's presence ($r = -.42$, $p = .005$). The last finding is attributable to an upward change in emotion for children of nondepressed mothers and a downward trend for those of depressed mothers. Mothers' depression was also correlated with overall average emotion in the adolescent ($r = -.44$, $p < .001$), with the adolescent feeling lower warmth toward her ($r = -.44$, $p < .001$), and with the mother reporting greater conflict in the relationship ($r = -.40$, $p = .002$).

42. A large volume of research has focused on the effects of mothers' depression, a focus that reflects researchers' too willing acceptance of society's assumption that mothers are solely responsible for their children's mental health. Yet our findings, reported in the next chapter, and findings by others indicate that fathers' emotional states are equally responsible (Downey and Coyne, 1990).

43. Dix, 1991; Dix, Reinhold, and Zambarano, 1990.

44. Hops, Sherman, and Biglan, 1990; Patterson and Dishion, 1988.

45. Hops et al., 1990, p. 185.

46. Duckett and Richards, 1992.

47. Downey and Coyne, 1990.

48. Ibid.; Forehand, McCombs, and Brody, 1987.

49. Patterson, 1980.

50. Small, Eastman, and Cornelius, 1988.

51. Steinberg and Silverberg, 1986.

52. Coyne, 1976.

53. Howes, Hokanson, and Loewenstein, 1985.

54. Field, 1992.

55. Downey and Coyne, 1990.

56. Patterson, 1986; Patterson and Bank, 1989.

57. Boyd, 1989; Chodorow, 1978.

58. Frank, Avery, and Laman, 1988.

59. Bronstein, Duncan, Frankowski, Pieniadz, and D'Ari, 1992; Smith and Forehand, 1986.

60. Montemayor, 1982, 1986; Smetana, 1988a, 1988b.

61. For more-depressed mothers, the beta coefficient between the child's emotion at one beep and the mother's emotion at the next beep was *beta* = .17, p = .04. It did not approach significance for less depressed mothers.

62. Boyd, 1989.

63. The degree of association between mothers' and daughters' fluctuations in emotion was correlated with greater depression in mothers ($r = .47$, $p < .05$), and the degree of association between a mother's and daughter's positive emotion was correlated with greater depression in the daughter ($r = .43$, $p < .05$).

64. Daniels and Moos, 1989.

65. For full-time homemakers, the beta coefficient between the adolescent's emotion at one beep and the mother's emotion at the next was *beta* = .13, p = .10. For employed women, it did not approach significance.

66. Silverberg and Steinberg, 1990.

67. Richards and Duckett, 1994.

68. On days that mothers' last-reported emotion at work was most positive (see appendix 3.3), adolescents' emotion rose from $z = -.35$ to $z = .37$ when their mother came home. A dramatic example is a businesswoman who landed a $100,000 contract during the day and came home and shared her sense of excitement with the family at dinner. Negative carryover is also possible—for example, a boy reported that his fight with his mother was due to her being "tired and crabby" from work—but this scenario was less common. On days that mothers' emotion at work was most negative, adolescents' emotion did not change substantially when their mother came home. The irony, of course, is that a mother's positive or negative mood at work had no consistent effect on *her* mood when she got home: she experienced a crash regardless of what happened at work (see appendix 3.3).

69. At first, it seemed the teens' positive mood on the days their mother worked might be explained by the extra freedom they potentially had after school when their mother was not around. An examination of the child's emotional states during the day, however, showed no difference. Thus it appears there is something

about the child's experience of the mother when she returned from work that influenced the child's state.

70. Hoffman, 1989; Silverberg and Steinberg, 1990. Furthermore, when a mother has a job with greater "substantive complexity" (less routine, high autonomy and control, abstract, requires verbal skills, lower supervision), it appears to improve the verbal intelligence of the child (Parcel and Menaghan, 1990).

We also find evidence that children in single-parent families benefit when their mothers are employed. Duckett and Richards (submitted) find that when the mothers are employed for more hours, adolescents in these families report higher self-esteem and daily emotional states. These teens also spend more time with their mothers and feel greater closeness to them than similar teens whose mothers are not employed or are employed for fewer hours. These findings hold up with controls for socioeconomic status, suggesting they are not attributable to economic factors.

71. Richards and Duckett, 1994. In our smaller sample of fifty-five families, things were even more complex: children of mothers who were better educated and employed *or* less educated and unemployed reported more positive daily emotion (Joebgen and Richards, 1990).

72. Lerner and Galambos, 1985.

73. Grotevant and Cooper, 1985, 1986.

74. Hauser, 1991. Adams, Dyk, and Bennion (1990) also find the maturity of parents to be an important factor.

75. Hoffman, 1989.

76. Raffaelli and Duckett, 1989; see also Youniss and Smollar, 1985.

77. After bottoming out in the seventh grade, our data show, teens' emotion with their mothers became more favorable in ninth grade. Likewise, after a low point in seventh grade, mothers were experienced as more friendly in the ninth grade, especially by boys.

Chapter 7. Adolescents and Fathers: Fun and Avoidance

1. Hoffman, 1989; Lamb, 1987.

2. Radin, 1988. It might also be noted that children in two-parent gay and lesbian families are as well adjusted as children in traditional husband–wife families (C. Patterson, 1992).

3. Osherson, 1986.

4. Collins and Russell, 1991; Wright and Keple, 1981; Youniss and Smollar, 1985.

5. Youniss and Ketterlinus, 1987.

6. See Paulson, Hill, and Holmbeck, 1991, for example.

7. Gadlin, 1978.

8. J. Pleck, 1987.

9. Johannis, 1957.

10. B. Katz, 1953.

11. Bernard, 1982.

12. The total amount of time the fathers in our study reported being with their adolescents varied between 0 and 46 percent of their time samples. Some studies have found that fathers and mothers spend comparatively more time with same-sex children (see, for example, Lamb, 1981); this trend, however, was only marginally significant in our data, even within our larger sample. Our data also suggest that the amount of time spent with their children may be somewhat greater for younger fathers, having jobs of lower socioeconomic status, in families with no preschoolers. Other researchers have found that the amount of hours a man works at his job correlates inversely with contact time with his child (Lamb, 1986). In the larger data set, we found that husbands with employed wives spent slightly more time with their adolescent (Richards and Duckett, in press).

13. Lamb, 1987; J. Pleck, 1985.

14. Gjerde, 1986.

15. Unlike with mothers, rates of disagreement were about equal between fathers and children (see appendix 6.1), although a sex difference was noted. Girls and fathers had a substantially higher rate of disagreeing about either's presence (56 percent) than boys did (40 percent). Among girls, the disagreements were not attributable to overperception of togetherness by either party. Both fathers and daughters acknowledged each other's presence at equal rates. But boys acknowledged the presence of their father less often than fathers reported the presence of their son.

16. See also Crouter and Crowley, 1990.

17. Barnett and Baruch, 1987.

18. Other studies confirm that fathers are more recreational than mothers in their interactions with children and adolescents, both in the United States (Montemayor and Brownlee, 1987; Parke and Tinsley, 1984; Russell and Russell, 1987; Youniss and Smollar, 1985) and elsewhere (Malik, 1990). Data from our larger study show that resident fathers spent a greater proportion of their time with their children in nonrecreational activities than nonresident, divorced fathers did (Asmussen and Larson, 1991).

19. Harris and Morgan, 1991.

20. Backett, 1987.

21. Our estimate of time spent talking was computed from times when both said they were together and both said they were talking, and included times when the mother was also present. For the content of talk, see also Collins and Russell (1991) and Youniss and Smollar (1985).

22. On a scale from 0 to 21, fathers' average warmth toward the child was 18.95 and mothers' was 17.85 (t = 3.53, p < .001).

23. Across all occasions, the presence versus absence of children was not related to fathers' emotional state once we controlled for fathers' activity. However, if we look just at times when the fathers were alone with their child, their emotion was more positive than would be predicted by their activity.

24. Montemayor and Hanson, 1985.

25. Youniss, 1980.
26. Paikoff and Brooks-Gunn, 1991.
27. Gecas, 1976; Lamb, 1981; Youniss and Smollar, 1985.
28. Bronstein, 1988.
29. Youniss and Smollar, 1985.
30. In addition, the adolescents reported feeling more controlled by their fathers than by their mothers, although the difference was not quite significant (p = .082).
31. The father's emotion prior to being with the adolescent predicted the adolescent's subsequent mood (*beta* = .19, p = .051). Likewise, the father's aggregate emotion at work during the day predicted the adolescent's aggregate emotion in the evening after father got home (*beta* = .26, p = .007).
32. Weiss (1990) described men's attempts to screen work stress from their families. Repetti (submitted), however, found that after distressing social interactions at work, a group of male air traffic controllers reported more expression of anger at their children and greater use of discipline.
33. Dix, 1991.
34. Steinmetz, 1987.
35. Youniss and Smollar, 1985.
36. Youniss and Smollar, 1985.
37. See, for example, Bly, 1990.
38. The girls in our study also reported low mood in the presence of boys during this time (as did boys in the presence of girls). So it is not just fathers but males in general whom girls are uncomfortable with at this age (Richards and Larson, 1990).
39. Collins and Russell, 1991.
40. Paikoff and Brooks-Gunn, 1991.
41. Brooks-Gunn, 1984.
42. We assessed girl's pubertal development with a self-report measure of pubic hair growth and breast development (Morris and Udry, 1980). With grade controlled, pubic hair growth was negatively correlated with the emotions of both fathers (r = −.38, p = .085) and daughters (r = −.41, p = .058) when they were together. Breast development was correlated with daughters' emotions when they were together (r = −.41, p = .056).
43. Larson and Richards (in press).
44. Hsee, Hatfield, Carlson, and Chemtob, 1990.
45. J. Hill, 1988.
46. Crouter and Crowley, 1990; Swarr and Richards, 1993.
47. Gecas, 1976; Lamb, 1981.
48. The emotions of these fathers with their children showed different trends with age for boys and girls. Dads were happier with older boys and less happy with older girls (this interaction is significant, p = .05). Likewise, whereas these fathers' emotion with their daughters declined as a function of her pubertal development, their emotion with their sons became more positive. With grade controlled, the

correlation between fathers' emotional state when with their son and the son's pubic hair growth was r = .51, p = .035, and it was r = .41, p = .099 with the son's penis and testes growth. However, sons' emotion with their father was not correlated with these measures of pubertal development.

49. Paikoff and Brooks-Gunn, 1991.

50. With their fathers, boys reported lower than average acceptance (z = −.29, p < .05) and strength (z = −.23, p < .05). We also found that as boys get older, both fathers and sons report feeling more competitive during their time together.

51. In one survey, 32 percent of teens felt their dads spent too little time with them (Martin, 1985).

52. *Measures of Closeness and Warmth Between Adolescents and Fathers.* We employed the same measures here that we used to evaluate the quality of relationships between adolescents and mothers (see notes for chapter 6). As with mother–child relationships, we found these measures to be correlated with the mental health of the adolescent. For example, the adolescents' closeness to their father was correlated with the adolescents' depression (r = −.31, p < .001), self-esteem (r = .30, p < .001), and parents' reports of the adolescents' psychological symptoms (r = −.16, p < .05). Likewise, the adolescents' ratings of warmth toward their father were correlated with the adolescents' depression (r = −.44, p < .001) and self-esteem (r = .25, p < .10).

53. This inverse relationship between enjoyment and warmth is also evident when we look at divorced, noncustodial fathers and their children. Young adolescents report having a lot of fun with these dads—their emotions with these fathers are higher than those experienced by teens in intact families. But these young adolescents feel less close to their fathers than teens in two-parent families do (Asmussen and Larson, 1991).

54. Rate of shared negative emotion between these fathers and adolescents was correlated with adolescents' self-esteem (r = .46, p = .002; r = .41, p = .023 when warmth scores are controlled).

55. The analyses reported in appendix 7.4 show only that the adolescents' moods predict separation, but other analyses suggest that fathers' moods are also predictive. This finding is also discussed in Larson (in press).

56. After a separation related to a negative mood, children in our study quite often reported being in their bedrooms.

57. Gottman and Levenson, 1988.

58. Repetti, submitted.

59. Fathers' rate of irritability at work was correlated with teens' daily experience of warmth toward Dad (r = −.42, p = .003), teens' global feeling of closeness toward Dad (r = −.28, p = .058), teens' depression (r = .33, p = .023), and teens' self-esteem (r = −.26, p = .078). Of course, rates of irritability at home also tended to be correlated with these measures, but since we have seen that emotions are carried over from work to home, we feel it reasonable to suggest that the chain of causality started at men's jobs.

In our sample the number of hours a father worked and his degree of absorption were not related to his child's well-being. The amount of time fathers and adolescents were together was not related to the quality of the father–child relationship (see appendix 7.3). For boys only, we found a modest relationship between amount of time spent alone with their father and teachers' ratings of adjustment (r = .18, p < .05).

60. Compas et al., 1989; McLoyd, 1989.

61. Compelling evidence on this point is provided by Downey and Coyne (1990) and Phares and Compas (1992). Our data showed little relationship between fathers' depression and the daily interactions between fathers and adolescents. Amount of time together, emotion with each other, and warmth and closeness were not correlated with fathers' depression, partly because the fathers in our sample reported very little depression. However, fathers' depression was correlated with the child's GPA (r = −.34, p < .05).

62. Kempton, Thomas, and Forehand, 1989.

63. Baumrind, 1971; Steinberg, 1991.

64. O. Harris, 1983; M. Katz and Konner, 1981.

65. Parke and Tinsley, 1984.

66. Russell and Radin, 1983.

67. In the larger study, boys who frequently identified their fathers as leaders reported greater depression (r = .20, p = .028), and were rated as less well adjusted by their teachers (r = −.18, p = .035) and by their parents (r = −.20, p = .020).

68. Hauser and colleagues (1987) also found that in families where fathers did this often, adolescents demonstrated greater ego development—suggesting that these enabling statements may help the teen's development of maturity. Of course, it is also likely that the maturity of the teenager, such as Luke, allows his father to be more enabling.

69. Lamb, 1987.

70. Grotevant and Cooper (1986) found that adolescents showed more healthy identity exploration when mothers were lower on "permeability" and fathers were higher on "mutuality." See also Rubin (1983).

Chapter 8. Troubled Families: Separate Realities

1. *Index of Healthier and Less Healthy Families.* We divided the families at the median on an index of family well-being. This index was created by summing standardized scores for sixteen variables: mothers', fathers', and adolescents' self-esteem and depression, the warmth felt by each toward the two other members, and mothers' and fathers' evaluation of the family environment on the scale of family cohesion and conflict from the Moos Family Environment Scale. Scores for this index were not related to our measures of a family's socioeconomic status. We also made sure that our key findings were not simply a result of the contribution of one family member to the index. It should be emphasized, nonetheless, that findings based on this index should be seen as "suggestive" and certainly limited to the European-American population studied here.

2.   Given the limits of our sample, we have not been able to consider sibling dynamics here. Research indicates that children in the same family often have very different experiences of that family (Dunn and Plomin, 1990). Each child can be expected to contribute something unique to family processes.

3.   In the distressed families we studied, wives' emotions were more strongly correlated with husbands' emotions ($r = .45$) than in nondistressed families ($r = .24$; the difference was significant, $t = 2.78$, $p < .01$). Likewise, adolescents' emotions were more strongly correlated with their fathers' emotions in distressed than in nondistressed families ($r = .34$ versus .26, although this difference was not significant). L. Katz, Kramer, and Gottman (1992) also report findings suggesting stronger emotion transmission in distressed families.

4.   Kerr and Bowen, 1988, p. 182.

5.   Russ's emotions predicted Wendy's subsequent emotions (*beta* $= .38$), but Wendy's emotions did not predict Russ's emotions (*beta* $= -.18$).

6.   Bowen, 1976, p. 80.

7.   Roxanne's emotions predicted Russ's subsequent emotions (beta $= .27$), and Russ's emotions appeared to predict Roxanne's (beta $= .31$). However, because they came into contact rarely ($N = 11$), these values are not significant.

8.   Hatfield, Cacioppo, and Rapson, 1992.

9.   Bernard (1981a) also states that the traditional "pampered" housewife in an affluent household could be described as an "economic parasite" (p. 10).

10. Hoffman, 1983.

11. The correlation between mothers' and children's warmth toward each other was $r = .31$, $p = .022$. The correlation between fathers' and children's warmth was $r = .24$, $p = .086$.

12. Johnston, 1993; Sroufe and Fleeson, 1988.

13. Christensen and Margolin, 1988; Teyber, 1983a, 1983b.

14. We use comparative warmth here as a rough measure of cross-generational coalitions, but other and better measures might be conceived. Employing a different measure of coalitions, Bell and Bell (1982) also showed that cross-generational alliances were associated with poorer adjustment, in a sample of adolescent girls.

15. Bowen, 1976; Haley, 1988.

16. The assumption that family dysfunction is circular is also being challenged by other family theorists such as Goldner (1988) and Burck and Daniel (1990).

17. Teyber, 1983a.

18. Elder, Van Nguyen, and Caspi, 1985; McLoyd, 1989; Skinner, Elder, and Conger, 1992.

19. Goldner, 1985. The emotional dominance that fathers exert in the family might also be traced to the historic role system in which both children and wife were considered legally and morally subordinate to him (Schnucker, 1990).

20. Scores on the Locke-Wallace Marital Adjustment Scale were 43 for Kevin (as compared to a sample average of 102 for men) and 52 for Kim (as compared to an average of 106 for women).

21. Christensen and Margolin, 1988.

22. Weiss, 1990.

23. The link between marital conflict and poor parent–child relationships is further documented by Grych and Fincham (1990). Another set of researchers has found evidence that the depression of children in families with distressed marriages might be entirely due to the effect on the parent–child relationship—in other words, these children are depressed not because of the conflictual marriage, but because of the effect the conflictual marriage has on their relations with their parents (Fauber, Forehand, Thomas, and Wierson, 1990).

It should be noted that there is also evidence that conflict between adolescents and parents can affect parents' marital satisfaction (Steinberg and Silverberg, 1987). The unhappiness adolescents experience at school and with friends may be a contributing factor to the family's distress.

24. Kanner, Feldman, Weinberger, and Ford, 1987.

25. Cummings, 1987.

26. Compas and Wagner (1991) show that young adolescents are more vulnerable to family stress than older adolescents are.

27. On a scale of −9 to +9, Vivian's average emotional state was −.43 at home, 3.62 at school. This difference is highly significant.

28. Easterbrooks and Emde, 1988; Grych and Fincham, 1990.

29. Children's perception of intense, frequent, and poorly resolved marital conflict has been found to increase the negative effect on their psychological well-being (Grych and Fincham, 1990; Grych, Seid, and Fincham, 1992).

30. Amato, 1993.

31. Some studies have found boys to be more vulnerable to distressed marital relations (O'Leary and Emery, 1984), others have found girls to be more vulnerable (Grych and Fincham, 1990; Teyber, 1983a).

32. The greater the discrepancy between members' perceptions of the family, the lower the well-being of the individuals and the family (Paikoff, 1991; Reiss, 1981).

Chapter 9. Healthy Families: Toward Convergent Realities

1. Fathers in healthier families reported more time at their jobs when they were not working (r = .26, p = .06).

2. In the healthier families, mothers reported more recreational and personal activities on weekends (61 percent) than in distressed families (53 percent), p = .013. The same difference was evident in dual-earner families: 62 percent versus 47 percent (p < .001).

3. Other researchers have also found that healthier families are characterized by the balance members maintain between the shared and separate parts of their lives (Beavers, 1982; Larsen and Olson, 1989).

4. Popkin, 1987, p. 67.

5. In chapter 8, note 3, we reported that the correlations of men's emotions

with those of their wives and their children were greater in distressed families. We also found that the correlation between the emotional states of children and their mothers was greater in distressed families ($r = .25$) than in nondistressed families ($r = .05$; the difference is significant, $t = 2.02$, $p < .05$).

6. Beavers, 1982.

7. During the 5:30–7:30 period on weekdays, adolescents in healthier families reported more favorable emotions ($z = .17$) than those in less healthy families ($z = -.17$, $p < .05$). The same difference is suggested for fathers ($z = .19$ versus $z = -.05$, $p = .16$), and mothers ($z = -.05$ versus $z = .16$, n.s.). These differences were evident irrespective of mothers' employment status.

8. Holoman and Epperson, 1984.

9. Ackerman, 1958, p. 112.

10. Others have also concluded that the amount of time parents spend interacting with their children (beyond a minimal amount) has very little effect on the quality of their relationship (Lamb, 1986; Lewis, Feiring, and Weinraub, 1981).

11. Rates of irritability when all were together, for example, were correlated with our scale of family well-being for mothers ($r = -.36$, $p < .01$), fathers ($r = -.35$, $p < .01$), and adolescents ($r = -.41$, $p < .01$). Similar correlations occurred for rates of feeling angry and rowdy. Mothers in these families also reported fewer occasions of feeling weak and out of control, and adolescents reported fewer occasions of feeling worried and ignored. These correlations remained even when we removed a family member's own contribution to family well-being scores.

12. Of course, we do not know for certain whether this greater shared time was a cause or an effect of these families' better adjustment, but evidence that shared outdoor recreation has a causal relationship to family cohesion comes from a longitudinal study by West and Merriam (1970).

13. We found family well-being scores to be significantly greater in families in which the net amount of time spent in family, job, and school labor was high, as compared to those in which this quantity of time was low or medium. This relationship is independent of mother's employment and the SES ratings of parents' jobs.

14. All three family members reporting no leader occurred for 44 percent of shared time among healthier families as compared to 21 percent of occasions among less healthy families ($p = .013$).

15. Scanzoni, 1983.

16. Heyward, 1989, p. 124.

17. Yankelovich, 1981.

18. Baumrind, 1971; Maccoby and Martin, 1983.

19. Dunn, Brown, and Beardsall (1991) found that when parents engaged their children in talk about their feelings at thirty-six months, these children are better able to talk about feelings, causes of feelings, and the nature of disputes in later childhood.

20. Cooper, 1988.

21. Popkin, 1987.

22. Ross et al., 1983.

23. Arlie Hochschild (1989) found that conflicts over family division of labor often stem not from its distribution, but from its lack of acknowledgment.

24. Oswald and Suess, 1990.

25. Kimball, 1983.

26. Ibid.

27. Hochschild (1992) reports that many businesses deliberately create an internal culture that is typically hostile to families. Numerous studies, however, demonstrate the payoffs of "family-friendly" business practices (for example, Hewlett, 1990; Rodgers and Rodgers, 1989).

28. There is increasing evidence of the advantages that accrue when schools work closely with families (Bronfenbrenner, 1986).

29. See Low, 1990.

30. Longitudinal comparisons between states in the U.S. indicate that those that institute family-friendly policies show improvements in individual and family well-being relative to those that do not (Zimmerman, 1992).

31. J. Larson, 1988.

32. Kimball, 1983.

33. Roberts, Hawkins, and Marshall, 1992. For descriptions of other programs for fathers, see Hawkins and Roberts, 1992; McBride, 1990, 1991.

34. See, for example, Billingsley, 1992; Crosbie-Burnett and Lewis, 1993; McAdoo, 1993.

Bibliography

Achenbach, Thomas M., and Edelbrock, Craig (1986). *Manual for the teacher's report form and teacher version of the child behavior profile.* Burlington: University of Vermont, Department of Psychiatry.

Ackerman, Nathan W. (1958). *The psychodynamics of family life: Diagnosis and treatment of family relationships.* New York: Basic Books.

Adams, Gerald, Dyk, Patricia, and Bennion, Layne (1990). Parent–adolescent relationships and identity formation. In Brian Barber and Boyd Rollins (Eds.), *Parent–adolescent relationships* (pp. 1–16). New York: Lanham.

Allison, Maria T., and Duncan, Margaret C. (1987). Women, work, and leisure: The days of our lives. *Leisure Sciences, 9,* 143–162.

Amato, Paul R. (1993). Children's adjustment to divorce: Theories, hypotheses, and empirical support. *Journal of Marriage and the Family, 55,* 23–38.

Anderson, Lynn R., Finn, Martha, and Leider, Sandra (1981). Leadership style and leader title. *Psychology of Women Quarterly, 5,* 661–669.

Asmussen, Linda, and Larson, Reed W. (1991). The quality of family time among young adolescents in single-parent and married-parent families. *Journal of Marriage and the Family, 53,* 1021–1030.

Backett, Katheryn (1987). The negotiation of fatherhood. In Charlie Lewis and Margaret O'Brien (Eds.), *Reassessing fatherhood: New observations on fathers and the modern family* (pp. 73–90). New Delhi: Sage Publications.

Ballenski, Catherine Brackett, and Cook, Alicia A. (1992). Mothers' perceptions of their competence in managing selected parenting tasks. *Family Relations, 31,* 489–494.

Barling, Julian (1990). Employment and marital functioning. In Frank D. Fincham and Thomas N. Bradbury (Eds.), *The psychology of marriage: Basic issues and applications* (pp. 201–225). New York: Guilford Press.

Barnett, Rosalind C., and Baruch, Grace K. (1987). Determinants of fathers' participation in family work. *Journal of Marriage and the Family, 49,* 29–40.

Bateson, Mary C. (1990). *Composing a life.* New York: Plume.

Baucom, Donald H., and Mehlman, Susan K. (1984). Predicting marital status following behavioral marital therapy: A comparison of models of marital relationships. In Kurt Hahlweg and Neil S. Jacobson (Eds.), *Marital interaction: Analysis and modification* (pp. 89–104). New York: Guilford Press.

Baumrind, Diana (1971). Current patterns of parental authority. *Developmental Psychology Monographs, 4*(1).

Beavers, W. Robert (1982). Healthy, midrange, and severely dysfunctional families. In Froma Walsh (Ed.), *Normal family processes* (pp. 45–53). New York: Guilford Press.

Beck, Aaron T., and Beck, Roy W. (1972). Screening depressed patients in family practice: A rapid technic. *Postgraduate Medicine, 52,* 81–85.

Bell, Linda G., and Bell, David C. (1982). Family climate and the role of the female adolescent: Determinants of adolescent functioning. *Family Relations, 31,* 519–527.

Bellah, Robert N., Madsen, Richard, Sullivan, William M., Swidler, Ann, and Tipton, Steven M. (1985). *Habits of the heart: Individualism and commitment in American life.* Berkeley: University of California Press.

Belsky, Jay (1990). Children and marriage. In Frank D. Fincham and Thomas N. Bradbury (Eds.), *The psychology of marriage: Basic issues and applications* (pp. 172–201). New York: Guilford Press.

Berger, Peter, and Kellner, Hansfried (1970). Marriage and the construction of reality: An exercise in the microsociology of knowledge. In Hans P. Drestzel (Ed.), *Patterns of communicative behavior* (pp. 50–73). London: MacMillan.

Berheide, Catherine W. (1984). Women's work in the home: Seems like old times. *Marriage and Family Review, 7*(3/4), 37–55.

Berk, Sarah F. (1985). *The gender factory: The apportionment of work in American households.* New York: Plenum Press.

Bernard, Jessie (1981). The good-provider role. *American Psychologist, 36,* 1–12.

Bernard, Jessie (1982). *The future of marriage.* New Haven: Yale University Press.

Bernard, Russel, Killworth, Peter, Kronenfeld, David, and Sailer, Lee (1984). On the validity of retrospective data: The problem of informant accuracy. *Annual Review of Anthropology, 13,* 495–517.

Berscheid, Ellen (1983). Emotion. In H. H. Kelley, E. Berscheid, A. Christensen, J. H. Harvey, T. L. Huston, G. Levinger, E. McClintock, L. A. Peplau, and D. R. Peterson (Eds.), *Close relationships* (pp. 110–168). New York: W. H. Freeman.

Bialeschki, M. Deborah, and Henderson, Karla (1986). Leisure in the common world of women. *Leisure Studies, 5,* 299–308.

Billingsley, Andrew (1992). *Climbing Jacob's Ladder: The enduring legacy of African-American families.* New York: Simon & Schuster.

Bloom-Feshbach, Jonathan (1981). Historical perspectives on the father's role. In Michael E. Lamb (Ed.), *The role of the father in child development* (pp. 71–112). New York: Wiley.

Blumstein, Phillip, and Schwartz, Pepper (1983). *American couples: Money, work, sex.* New York: Morrow.

Bly, Robert (1990). *Iron John: A book about men.* Reading, MA: Addison-Wesley.

Blyth, Dale A. (1982). Mapping the social world of adolescents: Issues, techniques, and problems. In Felicisima Serafica (Ed.), *Social cognition, context, and social behavior: A developmental perspective* (pp. 240–272). New York: Guilford Press.

Bolger, Niall, DeLongis, Anita, Kessler, Ronald C., and Wethington, Elaine (1989). The contagion of stress across multiple roles. *Journal of Marriage and the Family, 51,* 175–183.

Bowen, Murray (1976). Theory in the practice of psychotherapy. In Philip J. Guerin (Ed.), *Family therapy: Theory and practice* (pp. 42–90). New York: Wiley.

Boyd, Carol J. (1989). Mothers and daughters: A discussion of theory and research. *Journal of Marriage and the Family, 51,* 291–301.

Bradbury, Thomas N., and Fincham, Frank D. (1990). Attributions in marriage: Review and critique. *Psychological Bulletin, 107,* 3–33.

Brenton, Myron (1966). *The American male.* New York: Coward, McCann and Geoghegan.

Bronfenbrenner, Urie (1986). Alienation and the four worlds of childhood. *Phi Delta Kappan, 67,* 430–436.

Bronstein, Phyllis (1988). Father–child interaction: Implications for gender-role socialization. In Phyllis Bronstein and Carolyn P. Cowan (Eds.), *Fatherhood today: Men's changing role in the family* (pp. 107–124). New York: Wiley.

Bronstein, Phyllis, Duncan, P., Frankowski, B., Pieniadz, J., and D'Ari, A. (1992, March). *Differences in mothers' and fathers' involvement and interactions with girls and boys: Implications for gender role socialization.* Paper presented at the biennial meeting of the Society for Research on Adolescence, Washington, DC.

Brooks-Gunn, Jeanne (1984). The psychological significance of different pubertal events to young girls. *Journal of Early Adolescence, 4,* 315–327.

Brooks-Gunn, Jeanne, and Warren, Michelle P. (1989). Biological and social contributions to negative affect in young adolescent girls. *Child Development, 60,* 40–55.

Brown, B. Bradford (1981). A life-span approach to friendship: Age-related dimensions of an ageless relationships. In Helena Lopata and David Maines (Eds.), *Research on the interweave of social roles. Vol 2.: Friendship* (pp. 23–50). Greenwich, CT: JAI Press.

Brown, B. Bradford, Eicher, Sue Ann, and Petrie, Sandra (1986). The importance of peer group ("crowd") affiliation in adolescence. *Journal of Adolescence, 9,* 73–96.

Buchanan, Christy M., Eccles, Jacquelynne S., and Becker, Jill B. (1992). Are adolescents the victims of raging hormones: Evidence for activational effects of hormones on moods and behavior at adolescence. *Psychological Bulletin, 111,* 62–107.

Buhrmester, Duane, and Furman, Wyndol (1987). The development of companionship and intimacy. *Child Development, 58,* 1101–1113.

Burck, Charlotte, and Daniel, Gwyn (1990). Feminism and strategic therapy:

Contradiction or complementarity? In Rosine Josef Perelberg and Ann C. Miller (Eds.), *Gender and power in families* (pp. 82–103). New York: Tavistock/Routledge.

Cancian, Francesca M. (1987). *Love in America: Gender and self-development.* Cambridge: Cambridge University Press.

Caplan, Paula J., and Hall-McCorquodale, I. (1985). The scapegoating of mothers: A call for change. *American Journal of Orthopsychiatrics, 55,* 610–613.

Carnegie Council on Adolescent Development (1989). *Turning points: Preparing American youth for the 21st Century.* New York: Carnegie Corporation.

Cassidy, Jude, Parke, Ross D., Butkovsky, Laura, and Braungart, Julia M. (1992). Family–peer connections: The roles of emotional expressiveness within the family and children's understanding of emotions. *Child Development, 63,* 603–618.

Chafe, William H. (1972). *The American woman: Her changing social, economic, and political roles, 1920–1970.* New York: Oxford University Press.

Chambers, David A. (1986). The constraints of work and domestic schedules on women's leisure. *Leisure Studies, 5,* 309–325.

Chodorow, Nancy (1978). *The reproduction of mothering: Psychoanalysis and the sociology of gender.* Berkeley: University of California Press.

Christensen, Andrew, and Margolin, Gayla (1988). Conflict and alliance in distressed and non-distressed families. In Robert A. Hinde and Joan Stevenson-Hinde (Eds.), *Relationships within families: Mutual influences* (pp. 263–282). Oxford: Clarendon Press.

Cohler, Bertram J., and Boxer, Andrew M. (1984). Settling into the world: Person, time and context in the middle adult years. In Daniel Offer and Melvin Sabshin (Eds.), *Normality and the life cycle* (pp. 145–203). New York: Basic Books.

Coleman, James C. (1974). *Relationships in adolescence.* London: Routledge and Kegan Paul.

Collins, W. Andrew (1990). Parent–child relationships in the transition to adolescence: Continuity and change in interaction, affect, and cognition. In Raymond Montemayor, Gerard R. Adams, and Thomas P. Gullotta (Eds.), *From childhood to adolescence: A transitional period?* (pp. 85–106). Beverly Hills: Sage.

Collins, W. Andrew, and Russell, Graeme (1991). Mother–child and father–child relationships in middle childhood and adolescence: A developmental analysis. *Developmental Review, 11,* 99–136.

Compas, Bruce E. (1987). Stress and life events during childhood and adolescence. *Clinical Psychology Review, 7,* 275–302.

Compas, Bruce E., Howell, David C., Phares, Vicky, Williams, Rebecca A., and Ledoux, Normand (1989). Parent and child stress and symptoms: An integrative analysis. *Developmental Psychology, 25,* 550–559.

Compas, Bruce E., and Wagner, Barry M. (1991). Psychosocial stress during adolescence: Intrapersonal and interpersonal processes. In Susan Gore and Mary E. Colton (Eds.), *Adolescence, stress and coping* (pp. 67–85). New York: Aldine de Gruyter.

Conger, Rand D., Conger, Katherine J., Elder, Glen H. Jr., Lorenz, Frederick O., Simons, Ronald L., and Whitbeck, Les B. (1992). A family process model of economic hardship and adjustment of early adolescent boys. *Child Development, 63,* 526–541.

Conger, Rand D., Conger, Katherine J., Elder, Glen H. Jr., Lorenz, Frederick O., Simons, Ronald L., and Whitbeck, Les B. (1993). Family economic stress and adjustment of early adolescent girls. *Developmental Psychology, 29,* 206–219.

Cooper, Catherine R. (1988). Commentary: The role of conflict in adolescent–parent relationships. In Megan R. Gunnar and W. Andrew Collins (Eds.), *21st Annual Minnesota Symposium on Child Psychology: Development during the transition to adolescence* (pp. 181–187). Hillsdale, NJ: Lawrence Erlbaum.

Cooper, Catherine R., and Baker, H. (1991, July). *Ethnic perspectives on individuality and connectedness in adolescents' relationships with family and peers.* International Society for the Study of Behavioral Development, Minneapolis, MN.

Coyne, James C. (1976). Depression and the response of others. *Journal of Abnormal Psychology, 85,* 186–193.

Crosbie-Burnett, Margaret, and Lewis, Edith A. (1993). Use of African-American family structures and functioning to address the challenges of European-American postdivorce families. *Family Relations, 42,* 243–248.

Crouter, Ann C., and Crowley, M. Sue (1990). School-age children's time alone with fathers in single- and dual-earner families: Implications for the father-child relationship. *Journal of Early Adolescence, 10,* 296–312.

Crouter, Ann C., Perry-Jenkins, Maureen, Huston, Ted L., and Crawford, Duane W. (1989). The influence of work-induced psychological states on behavior at home. *Basic and Applied Social Psychology, 10,* 273–292.

Croxton, Jack S., Van-Rensselaer, Barbara A., Dutton, Dawn L., and Ellis, James W. (1989). Mediating effect of prestige on occupational stereotypes. *Psychological Reports, 64,* 723–732.

Csikszentmihalyi, Mihaly (1975). *Beyond boredom and anxiety.* San Francisco: Jossey-Bass.

Csikszentmihalyi, Mihaly (1982). Towards a psychology of optimal experience. In Ladd Wheeler (Ed.), *Review of personality and social psychology* (pp. 13–36). Beverly Hills: Sage.

Csikszentmihalyi, Mihaly (1990). *Flow: The psychology of optimal experience.* New York: Harper & Row.

Csikszentmihalyi, Mihaly, and Graef, Ronald (1980). The experience of freedom in daily life. *American Journal of Community Psychology, 8,* 401–414.

Csikszentmihalyi, Mihaly, and Larson, Reed (1984). *Being adolescent: Conflict and growth in the teenage years.* New York: Basic Books.

Csikszentmihalyi, Mihaly, and Larson, Reed (1987). The experience sampling method. *Journal of Nervous and Mental Disease, 175,* 526–536.

Csikszentmihalyi, Mihaly, and LeFevre, Judith (1989). Optimal experience in work and leisure. *Journal of Personality and Social Psychology, 56,* 815–822.

Cummings, E. Mark (1987). Coping with background anger in early childhood. *Child Development, 58,* 976–984.

Daniels, Denise, and Moos, Rudolf H. (1989). Ecosystem influences on family and child functioning. In Elizabeth B. Goldsmith (Ed.), *Work and family: Theory, research, and applications* (pp. 113–133). Newbury Park, CA: Sage.

Day, Randal D., and Mackey, Wade C. (1986). The role image of the American father: An examination of a media myth. *Journal of Comparative Family Studies, 17,* 371–388.

de Beauvoir, Simone (1968). *The second sex.* New York: Modern Library.

Deem, Rosemary (1982). Women, leisure and inequality. *Leisure Studies, 1,* 29–46.

de Grazia, Sebastian (1962). *Of time, work, and leisure.* Garden City, NY: Doubleday.

Demo, David H. (1992). Parent–child relations: Assessing recent changes. *Journal of Marriage and the Family, 54*(1), 104–117.

Demos, John (1982). The changing faces of fatherhood: A new exploration in American family history. In Stephen H. Cath, Alan R. Gurwith, and John M. Ross (Eds.), *Father and child* (pp. 41–67). Boston: Little, Brown.

DeVault, Marjorie L. (1991). *Feeding the family: The social organization of caring as gendered work.* Chicago: University of Chicago Press.

deVries, Marten (1987). Investigating mental disorders in their natural settings. *Journal of Nervous and Mental Disease, 175,* 509–513.

deVries, Marten (Ed.). (1992). *The experience of psychopathology.* Cambridge: Cambridge University Press.

Dix, Theodore (1991). The affective organization of parenting: Adaptive and maladaptive processes. *Psychological Bulletin, 110,* 3–25.

Dix, Theodore, Reinhold, Dana P., and Zambarano, Robert J. (1990). Mothers' judgement in moments of anger. *Merrill-Palmer Quarterly, 36,* 465–486.

Downey, Geraldine, and Coyne, James C. (1990). Children of depressed parents: An integrative review. *Psychological Bulletin, 108,* 50–76.

Duckett, Elena, Raffaelli, Marcela, and Richards, Maryse H. (1989). "Taking care": Maintaining the self and the home in early adolescence. *Journal of Youth and Adolescence, 18,* 549–565.

Duckett, Elena, and Richards, Maryse H. (1992, March). *Maternal employment, family relations, and young adolescents' emotional adjustment.* Washington, DC.: Society for Research on Adolescence.

Duckett, Elena, and Richards, Maryse H. (submitted). Maternal employment and the quality of daily experience for young adolescents of single mothers.

Dunn, Judy, Brown, Jane, and Beardsall, Lynn (1991). Family talk about feeling states and children's later understanding of others' emotions. *Developmental Psychology, 27*(3), 448–455.

Dunn, Judy, and Plomin, Robert (1990). *Separate lives: Why siblings are so different.* New York: Basic Books.

Duxbury, Linda E., and Higgins, Christopher A. (1991). Gender differences in work–family conflict. *Journal of Applied Psychology, 76,* 60–74.

Easterbrooks, M. Ann, and Emde, Robert N. (1988). Marital and parent–child relationships: The role of affect in the family system. In Robert A. Hinde and Joan

Stevenson-Hinde (Eds.), *Relationships within families: Mutual influences* (pp. 83–103). Oxford: Clarendon Press.

Eccles, Jacquelynne S., and Midgley, Carol (1990). Changes in academic motivation and self-perception during early adolescence. In Raymond Montemayor, Gerard R. Adams, and Thomas P. Gullotta (Eds.), *From childhood to adolescence* (pp. 134–155). Newbury Park, CA: Sage.

Ehrenreich, Barbara (1983). *The hearts of men: American dreams and the flight from commitment.* New York: Anchor Press.

Elder, Glen H. Jr. (1974). *Children of the Great Depression.* Chicago: University of Chicago Press.

Elder, Glen H. Jr., Van Nguyen, Tri, and Caspi, Avshalom (1985). Linking family hardship to children's lives. *Child Development, 56,* 361–375.

Elkind, David (1980). Strategic interactions in early adolescence. In Joseph Adelson (Ed.), *Handbook of adolescent psychology* (pp. 432–444). New York: Wiley.

England, Paula, and McCreary, Lori (1987). Gender inequality in paid employment. In Myra M. Ferree and Beth B. Hess (Eds.), *Analyzing gender* (pp. 286–320). Newbury Park, CA: Sage.

Entwisle, Doris R. (1990). Schools and the adolescent. In Shirley Feldman and Glenn R. Elliott (Eds.), *At the threshold: The developing adolescent* (pp. 197–224). Cambridge, MA, and London: Harvard University Press.

Epstein, Seymour (1984). Controversial issues in emotion theory. In Phillip Shaver (Ed.), *Review of personality and social psychology: Emotions, relationships, and health* (pp. 64–88). Beverly Hills, CA: Sage.

Farrell, Edwin (1988). Giving voice to high school students: Pressures and boredom, Ya know what I'm sayin'? *American Educational Research Journal, 4,* 489–502.

Fauber, Robert, Forehand, Rex, Thomas, Amanda, and Wierson, Michelle (1990). A mediational model of the impact of marital conflict on adolescent adjustment in intact and divorced families: The role of disrupted parenting. *Child Development, 61,* 1112–1123.

Featherman, David L., and Stevens, Gillian (1982). A revised socioeconomic index of occupational status: Application in analysis of sex differences in attainment. In Robert Hauser, David Mechanic, Archibald Haller, and Taissa S. Hanser (Eds.), *Social structure and behavior: Essays in honor of William Hamilton Senell* (pp. 141–182). New York: Academic.

Feldman, Shirley S., Wentzel, Kathryn R., and Gehring, Thomas M. (1989). A comparison of the views of mothers, fathers, and pre-adolescents about family cohesion and power. *Journal of Family Psychology, 3,* 39–60.

Ferree, Myra M. (1988, November). *Negotiating household roles and responsibilities: Resistance, conflict and change.* National Council on Family Relations Annual Meeting, Philadelphia.

Ferree, Myra M. (1990). Beyond separate spheres: Feminism and family research. *Journal of Marriage and the Family, 52,* 866–884.

Ferree, Myra M. (1991). The gender division of labor in two-earner marriages:

Dimensions of variability and change. *Journal of Family Issues, 12,* 158–180.

Field, Tiffany (1992). Infants of depressed mothers. *Development and Psychopathology, 4,* 49–66.

Filene, Peter G. (1975). *Him/her/self: Sex roles in modern America.* New York: Harcourt Brace Jovanovich.

Fincham, Frank D., and Bradbury, Thomas N. (1990). Psychology and the study of marriage. In Frank D. Fincham and Thomas N. Bradbury (Eds.), *The psychology of marriage: Basic issues and applications.* New York: Guilford Press.

Fitzpatrick, Mary Anne (1988). *Between husbands and wives: Communication in marriage.* Newbury Park, CA: Sage.

Flannery, Daniel J., Montemayor, Raymond, and Eberly, Mary (1991, November). *Impact of puberty versus chronological age on affective expression in adolescence.* National Council on Family Relations, Denver, CO.

Forehand, Rex, McCombs, Amanda, and Brody, Gene H. (1987). The relationship between parental depressive mood states and child functioning. *Advances in Behaviour Research and Therapy, 9,* 1–20.

Fox, Vivian (1977). Is adolescence a phenomenon of modern times? *Journal of Psychohistory, 1,* 271–290.

Frank, Susan J., Avery, Catherine B., and Laman, Mark S. (1988). Young adults' perceptions of their relationships with their parents: Individual differences in connectedness, competence, and emotional autonomy. *Developmental Psychology, 24,* 729–737.

Friedan, Betty (1963). *The feminine mystique.* New York: W. W. Norton.

Fromm, Erich (1956). *The art of loving.* New York: Harper and Brothers.

Gadlin, Howard (1978). Child discipline and the pursuit of self: An historical interpretation. In Hayne W. Reese and Lewis P. Lipsitt (Eds.), *Advances in child development and behavior* (pp. 231–265). New York: Academic Press.

Galambos, Nancy L., and Silbereisen, Rainer K. (1989). Role strain in West German dual-earner households. *Journal of Marriage and the Family, 51,* 385–389.

Gecas, Victor (1976). The socialization and child care roles. In F. Ivan Nye (Ed.), *Role structure and analysis of the family* (pp. 33–60). Beverly Hills, CA: Sage.

Gecas, Victor, and Seff, Monica A. (1990). Families and adolescents: A review of the 1980s. *Journal of Marriage and the Family, 52,* 941–958.

Gerson, Kathleen (1985). *Hard choices* (pp. 1–190). Berkeley: University of California Press.

Gillen, Barry (1981). Physical attractiveness: A determinant of two types of goodness. *Personality and Social Psychology Bulletin, 7,* 277–281.

Gjerde, Per F. (1986). The interpersonal structure of family interaction settings: Parent-adolescent relations in dyads and triads. *Developmental Psychology, 22,* 297–304.

Glenn, Norval (1990). Quantitative research on marital quality in the 1980s: A critical review. *Journal of Marriage and the Family, 52,* 818–831.

Goffman, Erving (1971). *Relations in public: Microstudies of the public order.* New York: Harper & Row.

Goldner, Virginia (1985). Feminism and family therapy. *Family Process, 24,* 31–47.

Goldner, Virginia (1988). Generation and gender: Normative and covert hierarchies. *Family Process, 27,* 17–31.

Goodnow, Jacqueline J. (1988). Children's household work: Its nature and functions. *Psychological Bulletin, 103,* 5–26.

Gottman, John M. (1979). *Marital interaction: Experimental investigations.* New York: Academic Press.

Gottman, John M. (1991). Predicting the longitudinal course of marriages. *Journal of Marital and Family Therapy, 17*(1), 3–7.

Gottman, John M., and Levenson, Robert W. (1984). Why marriages fail: Affective and physiological patterns in marital interaction. In John C. Masters and Kerry Yarkin-Levin (Eds.), *Boundary areas in social and developmental psychology* (pp. 67–106). Orlando, FL: Academic Press.

Gottman, John M., and Levenson, Robert W. (1986). Assessing the role of emotion in marriage. *Behavioral Assessment, 8,* 31–48.

Gottman, John M., and Levenson, Robert W. (1988). The social psychophysiology of marriage. In Patricia Nollen and Mary Anne Fitzpatrick (Eds.), *Perspectives on marital interaction* (pp. 182–202). Philadelphia: Multilingual Matters.

Gould, Robert E. (1974). Measuring masculinity by the size of a paycheck. In Joseph H. Pleck and Jack Sawyer (Eds.), *Men and masculinity* (pp. 96–106). Englewood Cliffs, NJ: Prentice-Hall.

Gove, Walter R., Style, Carolyn B., and Hughes, Michael (1990). The effect of marriage on the well-being of adults: A theoretical analysis. *Journal of Family Issues, 11,* 4–35.

Greene, Anita L., and Larson, Reed (1991). Variations in stress activity during adolescence. In E. Mark Cummings, Anita L. Greene, and Katherine H. Karraker (Eds.), *Life span perspectives on stress and coping* (pp. 195–209). Hillsdale, NJ: Lawrence Erlbaum.

Greenglass, Esther R., Pantony, Kaye-Lee, and Burke, Ronald J. (1989). A gender-role perspective on role conflict, work stress and social support. In Elizabeth B. Goldsmith (Ed.), *Work and family: Theory, research, and application* (pp. 317–328). Newbury Park, CA: Sage.

Greenhaus, Jeffrey H., and Beutell, Nicholas J. (1985). Sources of conflict between work and family roles. *Academy of Management Review, 10,* 76–88.

Greer, Germaine (1971). *The female eunuch.* London: Paladin.

Grotevant, Harold D., and Cooper, Catherine R. (1985). Patterns of interaction in family relationships and the development of identity exploration in adolescence. *Child Development, 56,* 415–428.

Grotevant, Harold D., and Cooper, Catherine R. (1986). Individuation in family relationships: A perspective on individual differences in the development of identity and role-taking skill in adolescence. *Human Development, 29,* 82–100.

Grych, John H., and Fincham, Frank D. (1990). Marital conflict and children's adjustment: A cognitive-contextual framework. *Psychological Bulletin, 108,* 267–290.

Grych, John H., Seid, Michael, and Fincham, Frank D. (1992). Assessing marital conflict from the child's perspective: The children's perception of interparental conflict scale. *Child Development, 63*, 558–572.

Guthrie, David M., and Noller, Patricia (1988). Spouses' perceptions of one another in emotional situations. In Patricia Noller and Mary Anne Fitzpatrick (Eds.), *Perspectives on marital interaction* (pp. 153–181). Philadelphia: Multilingual Matters.

Hahlweg, Kurt, and Jacobson, Neil S. (1984). *Marital interaction: Analysis and modification.* New York: Guilford Press.

Haley, Jay (1988). *Problem-solving therapy.* San Francisco: Jossey-Bass.

Ham, Mark, and Larson, Reed (1990). The cognitive moderation of daily stress in early adolescence. *American Journal of Community Psychology, 18*, 567–585.

Hampson, Robert B., and Beaver, W. Robert (1987). Comparing males' and females' perspectives through family self-report. *Psychiatry, 50*, 24–30.

Hareven, Tamara (1982). *Family time and industrial time.* New York: Cambridge University Press.

Harré, Rom (1984). *Personal being: A theory for individual psychology.* Cambridge, MA: Harvard University Press.

Harris, Kathleen M., and Morgan, S. Phillip (1991). Fathers, sons, and daughters: Differential paternal involvement in parenting. *Journal of Marriage and the Family, 53*, 531–544.

Harris, Olivia (1983). Heavenly fathers. In Ursula Owen (Ed.), *Fathers: Reflections by daughters* (pp. 46–60). New York: Pantheon.

Harris, Paul L., Olthof, Tjeert, and Terwogt, Mark M. (1981). Children's knowledge of emotion. *Journal of Child Psychology, 22*, 247–261.

Harter, Susan (1980). A cognitive-developmental approach to children's understanding of affect and trait labels. In Felicisima Serafica (Ed.), *Social-cognitive development in context* (pp. 27–61). New York: Guilford Press.

Hatfield, Elaine, Cacioppo, John T., and Rapson, Richard (1992). Primitive emotional contagion. In M. S. Clark (Ed.), *Review of personality and social psychology* (Vol. 14). Newbury Park, CA: Sage.

Hauser, Stuart T. (with Powers, Sally I., and Noam, Gil G.) (1991). *Adolescents and their families: Paths of ego development* (pp. 231–243). New York: Free Press.

Hauser, Stuart T., Powers, Sally I., Noam, Gill G., Jacobson, Ann M., Weiss, Bedonna, and Follansbee, Donna J. (1984). Familial contexts of adolescent ego development. *Child Development, 55*, 195–213.

Hawkins, Alan J., and Roberts, Tomi Ann (1992). Designing a primary intervention to help dual-earner couples share housework and child care. *Family Relations, 41*(5), 169–177.

Heimovics, Richard D., and Herman, Robert D. (1988). Gender and the attributions of chief executive responsibility for successful or unsuccessful organizational outcomes. *Sex Roles, 18*, 623–635.

Henderson, Karla A., and Dialeschki, M. Deborah (1991). A sense of entitlement to leisure as constraint and empowerment for women. *Leisure Sciences, 13*, 51–65.

Hess, Robert, and Goldblatt, Irene (1957). The status of adolescence in American society: A problem in social identity. *Child Development, 28,* 459–468.

Hewlett, Sylvia A. (1986). *A lesser life: The myth of women's liberation in America.* New York: Morrow.

Hewlett, Sylvia A. (1990). Good news? The private sector and win-win scenarios. In David Blankenhorn, Steven Bayme, and Jean B. Elshtain (Eds.), *Rebuilding the nest* (pp. 207–226). Milwaukee, WI: Family Service America.

Heyward, Carter (1989). *Touching our strength: The erotic as power and the love of God.* New York: Harper & Row.

Hill, John P. (1988). Adapting to menarche: Familial control and conflict. In Megan Gunnar and W. Andrew Collins (Eds.), *21st Minnesota Symposium on Child Psychology: Development during the transition to adolescence* (pp. 43–77). Hillsdale, N.J.: Lawrence Erlbaum.

Hill, Martha S. (1985). Patterns of time use. In F. Thomas Juster and Frank P. Stafford (Eds.), *Time, goods, and well-being* (pp. 133–176). Ann Arbor, MI: Institute for Social Research.

Hill, Martha S. (1988). Marital stability and spouses' shared time. *Journal of Family Issues, 9*(4), 427–451.

Hochschild, Arlie R. (1979). Emotion work, feeling rules, and social stratification. *American Journal of Sociology, 85,* 551–575.

Hochschild, Arlie R. (1989). *The second shift.* New York: Avon.

Hochschild, Arlie R. (1992, November). *Beyond the second shift: Denying needs at home and contesting rules at work?* Paper presented at the meetings of the National Council on Family Relations, Orlando, FL.

Hoffman, Lois W. (1983). Increase fathering: Effects on the mother. In Michael E. Lamb and Abraham Sagi (Eds.), *Fatherhood and family policy* (pp. 167–190). Hillsdale, NJ: Lawrence Erlbaum.

Hoffman, Lois W. (1989). Effects of maternal employment in the two-parent family. *American Psychology, 44,* 283–292.

Hoffman, Michael A., Ushpiz, Verda, and Levy-Shiff, Rachel (1988). Social support and self-esteem in adolescence. *Journal of Youth and Adolescence, 17,* 307–316.

Holman, Thomas B., and Epperson, Arlin (1984). Family and leisure: A review of the literature with research recommendations. *Journal of Leisure Research, 16*(4), 277–294.

Holman, Thomas B., and Jacquart, Mary (1988). Leisure-activity patterns and marital satisfaction: A further test. *Journal of Marriage and the Family, 50,* 69–77.

Hood, Jane C. (1986). The provider role: Its meaning and measurement. *Journal of Marriage and the Family, 48,* 349–359.

Hops, Hyman, Sherman, Linda, and Biglan, Anthony (1990). Maternal depression, marital discord and children's behavior: A developmental perspective. In Gerald R. Patterson (Ed.), *Depression and aggression in family interaction* (pp. 185–208). Hillsdale, NJ: Lawrence Erlbaum.

Hormuth, Stefan E. (1986). The sampling of experiences *in situ. Journal of Personality, 54,* 262–293.

Howes, Mary J., Hokanson, Jack E., and Loewenstein, David A. (1985). Induction of depressive affect after prolonged exposure to a mildly depressed individual. *Journal of Personality and Social Psychology, 49,* 1110–1113.

Hsee, Christopher K., Hatfield, Elaine, Carlson, John G., and Chemtob, Claude (1990). The effect of power on susceptibility to emotional contagion. *Cognition and Emotion, 4,* 327–340.

Hunter, Patricia L., and Whitson, David J. (1991). Women, leisure and familism: Relationships and isolation in small-town Canada. *Leisure Studies, 10,* 219–233.

Huston, Ted L., McHale, Susan M., and Crouter, Ann C. (1986). When the honeymoon's over: Changes in the marriage relationship over the first year. In Robin Gilmour and Steve Duck (Eds.), *The emerging field of personal relationships* (pp. 109–132). Hillsdale, NJ: Lawrence Erlbaum.

Huston, Ted L., Robins, Elliot, Atkinson, Jean, and McHale, Susan M. (1987). Surveying the landscape of marital behavior: A behavioral self-report approach to studying marriage. In Stuart Oskamp (Ed.), *Family processes and problems: Social psychological aspects* (pp. 45–72). Newbury Park, CA: Sage.

Inglehart, Ronald (1990). *Culture shift in advanced industrial society.* Princeton, NJ: Princeton University Press.

Inoff-Germain, Gale, Arnold, Gina S., Nottelmann, Edith D., Susman, Elizabeth J., Cutler, G. B., and Chrousos, George P. (1988). Relations between hormone levels and observational measures of aggressive behavior of young adolescents in family interactions. *Developmental Psychology, 24,* 129–139.

Jacobson, Neil S., Follette, William C., and McDonald, Debbie W. (1982). Reactivity to positive and negative behavior in distressed and nondistressed married couples. *Journal of Consulting and Clinical Psychology, 50,* 706–714.

Jahoda, Marie (1982). *Employment and unemployment.* Cambridge: Cambridge University Press.

Jessop, Dorothy J. (1981). Family relationships as viewed by parents and adolescents: A specification. *Journal of Marriage and the Family, 43,* 95–106.

Joebgen, Alicia, and Richards, Maryse H. (1990). Maternal education and employment: Mediating maternal and adolescent emotional adjustment. *Journal of Early Adolescence, 10,* 329–343.

Johannis, Theodore B. Jr. (1957). Participation by fathers, others and teenage sons and daughters in selected child care and control activity. *Coordinator, 6*(2), 31–32.

Johnston, Janet R. (1993). Family transitions and children's functioning: The case of parental conflict and divorce. In Philip A. Cowan, Dorothy Field, Donald A. Hansen, Arlene Skolnick, and Guy E. Swanson (Eds.), *Family, self, and society: Toward a new agenda for family research* (pp. 197–234). Hillsdale, NJ: Lawrence Erlbaum.

Juster, F. Thomas (1985). A note on recent changes in time use. In F. Thomas Juster and Frank P. Stafford (Eds.), *Time, goods, and well-being* (pp. 313–332). Ann Arbor: Survey Research Center, Institute for Social Research, University of Michigan.

Kanner, Allen D., Feldman, Shirley S., Weinberger, Daniel A., and Ford, Martin E. (1987). Uplifts, hassles, and adaptational outcomes in early adolescents. *Journal of Early Adolescence, 7,* 371–394.

Katz, Barney (1953). *How to be a better parent.* New York: Ronald Press.

Katz, Lynn F., Kramer, Laurie, and Gottman, John M. (1992). Conflict and emotions in marital, sibling, and peer relationships. In Carolyn U. Shantz and Willard W. Hartup (Eds.), *Conflict in child and adolescent development* (pp. 122–149). New York: Cambridge University Press.

Katz, Mary M., and Konner, Melvin J. (1981). The role of the father: An anthropological perspective. In Michael E. Lamb (Ed.), *The role of the father in child development* (pp. 155–185). New York: Wiley.

Kempton, Tracy, Thomas, Amanda M., and Forehand, Rex (1989). Dimensions of interparental conflict and adolescent functioning. *Journal of Family Violence, 4,* 297–307.

Kerr, Michael E., and Bowen, Murray (1988). *Family evaluation.* New York: W. W. Norton.

Kett, Joseph F. (1977). *Rites of passage: Adolescence in America 1790 to the present.* New York: Basic Books.

Kimball, Gayle (1983). *The 50–50 marriage.* Boston: Beacon Press.

Kingston, Paul W., and Nock, Steven L. (1987). Time together among dual-earner couples. *American Sociological Review, 52,* 391–400.

Kirchler, Erick (1989). Everyday life experiences at home: An interaction diary approach to assess marital relationships. *Journal of Family Psychology, 2,* 311–336.

Kirsch, Irwin S. (1986). *Literacy: Profiles of America's young adults.* Princeton, NJ: Educational Testing Service.

Kirshnit, Carol, Ham, Mark, and Richards, Maryse H. (1989). The sporting life. *Journal of Youth and Adolescence, 18,* 601–616.

Kovacs, Maria (1985). The Children's Depression Inventory. *Psychopharmacology Bulletin, 21,* 995–998.

Kubey, Robert (1990). Television and family harmony among children, adolescents, and adults: Results from the experience sampling method. In Jennings Bryant (Ed.), *Television and the American family* (pp. 73–88). Hillsdale, NJ: Lawrence Erlbaum.

Kubey, Robert, and Csikszentmihalyi, Mihaly (1990). *Television and the quality of life: How viewing shapes everyday experience.* Hillsdale, NJ: Lawrence Erlbaum.

Kurdek, Lawrence (1987). Gender differences in the psychological symptomalogy and coping strategies of young adolescents. *Journal of Early Adolescence, 7,* 395–410.

Lamb, Michael E. (1981). Fathers and child development: An integrative overview. In Michael E. Lamb (Ed.), *The role of the father in child development* (pp. 1–70). New York: Wiley.

Lamb, Michael E. (1986). The changing roles of fathers. In Michael E. Lamb (Ed.), *The father role: Applied perspectives* (pp. 3–27). New York: Wiley.

Lamb, Michael E. (1987). Introduction: The emergent American father. In

Michael E. Lamb (Ed.), *The father's role: Cross-cultural perspectives* (pp. 3–25). Hillsdale, NJ: Lawrence Earlbaum.

LaRossa, Ralph (1986). *Becoming a parent.* Beverly Hills, CA: Sage.

Larsen, Andrea S., and Olson, David H. (1989). Predicting marital satisfaction using PREPARE: A replication study. *Journal of Marital and Family Therapy, 15,* 311–322.

Larson, Jeffry H. (1988). The marriage quiz: College students' beliefs in selected myths about marriage. *Family Relations, 37,* 3–11.

Larson, Reed W. (1983). Adolescents' daily experience with family and friends: Contrasting opportunity systems. *Journal of Marriage and the Family, 45,* 739–750.

Larson, Reed W. (1988). Social contexts of adolescents: A world unto themselves. *Illinois Research, 30,* 6–9.

Larson, Reed W. (1989a). Beeping children and adolescents: A method for studying time use and daily experience. *Journal of Youth and Adolescence, 18,* 511–530.

Larson, Reed W. (1989b). *The factor structure of moods and emotions in a sample of young adolescents.* Unpublished manuscript, University of Illinois, Urbana-Champaign.

Larson, Reed W. (1990). The solitary side of life: An examination of the time people spend alone from childhood to old age. *Developmental Review, 10,* 155–183.

Larson, Reed W. (1992, April). *Private selves/public media in early adolescence.* Paper presented at the conference "Are the Kids All Right? Early Adolescence and the Media," Pennsylvania State University.

Larson, Reed W. (in press). Finding time for fatherhood: The emotional ecology of adolescent–father interactions. To be published in Shumel Shulman and W. Andrew Collins (Eds.), *Father–adolescent relationships: New directions.* San Francisco: Jossey-Bass.

Larson, Reed W., and Asmussen, Linda (1991). Anger, worry, and hurt in early adolescence: An enlarging world of negative emotions. In Mary Ellen Colton and Susan Gore (Eds.), *Adolescent stress, social relationships, and mental health* (pp. 21–41). New York: Aldine de Gruyter.

Larson, Reed W., and Csikszentmihalyi, Mihaly (1978). Experiential correlates of time alone in adolescence. *Journal of Personality, 46,* 677–693.

Larson, Reed W., and Csikszentmihalyi, Mihaly (1980). The significance of time alone in adolescent development. *Journal of Current Adolescent Medicine, 2,* 33–40.

Larson, Reed W., and Csikszentmihalyi, Mihaly (1983). The experience sampling method. In Harry T. Reis (Ed.), *Naturalistic approaches to studying social interaction* (pp. 41–56). San Francisco: Jossey-Bass.

Larson, Reed W., Csikszentmihalyi, Mihaly, and Graef, Ronald (1980). Mood variability and the psycho-social adjustment of adolescents. *Journal of Youth and Adolescence, 9,* 469–940.

Larson, Reed W., Csikszentmihalyi, Mihaly, and Graef, Ronald (1982). Time alone in daily experience: Loneliness or renewal? In L. Anne Peplau and Daniel Perlman (Eds.), *Loneliness: A sourcebook of research and theory* (pp. 40–53). New York: Wiley Interscience.

Larson, Reed W., and Delespaul, Philippe A. E. G. (1992). Analyzing experience sampling data: A guidebook for the perplexed. In Marten deVries (Ed.), *The experience of psychopathology: Investigating mental disorders in their natural setting* (pp. 58–78). Cambridge: Cambridge University Press.

Larson, Reed W., and Ham, Mark (1989, April). *Stressful events and adolescents' mood states.* Society for Research on Child Development.

Larson, Reed W., and Ham, Mark (1993). Stress and "storm and stress" in early adolescence: The relationship of negative events with dysphoric affect. *Developmental Psychology, 29,* 130–140.

Larson, Reed W., Ham, Mark, and Raffaelli, Marcela (1989). The nurturance of motivation and attention in the daily lives of adolescents. In Carol Ames and Martin Maehr (Eds.), *Advances in motivation and achievement, Vol. 6,* (pp. 45–80). Greenwich, CT: JAI Press.

Larson, Reed W., and Kleiber, Douglas (1993). Daily experience of adolescents. In Patrick Tolan and Bertram Cohler (Eds.), *Handbook of clinical research and practice with adolescents* (pp. 125–145). New York: Wiley.

Larson, Reed W., Kubey, Robert, and Colletti, Joseph (1989). Changing channels: Early adolescent media choices and shifting investments in family and friends. *Journal of Youth and Adolescence, 18,* 583–600.

Larson, Reed W., and Lampman-Petraitis, Claudia (1989). Daily emotional states as reported by children and adolescents. *Child Development, 60,* 1250–1260.

Larson, Reed W., Raffaelli, Marcela, Richards, Maryse H., Ham, Mark, and Jewell, Lisa (1990). Ecology of depression in late childhood and early adolescence: A profile of daily states and activities. *Journal of Abnormal Psychology, 99,* 92–102.

Larson, Reed W., and Richards, Maryse H. (Eds.) (1989). The changing life space of early adolescence (special issue). *Journal of Youth and Adolescence, 18* (6), 501–626.

Larson, Reed W., and Richards, Maryse H. (1991a). Daily companionship in late childhood and early adolescence: Changing developmental contexts. *Child Development, 62,* 284–300.

Larson, Reed W., and Richards, Maryse H. (1991b). Boredom in the middle school years: Blaming schools versus blaming students. *American Journal of Education, 91,* 418–443.

Larson, Reed, and Richards, Maryse H. (in press). Family emotions: Do young adolescents and their parents experience the same states? *Journal of Research on Adolescence.*

Larson, Reed W., Richards, Maryse H., and Perry-Jenkins, Maureen (in press). Divergent worlds: The daily emotional experience of mothers and fathers in the domestic and public spheres. *Journal of Personality and Social Psychology.*

Lay, KengLing, Waters, Everett, and Park, Kathryn A. (1989). Maternal responsiveness and child compliance: The role of mood as a mediator. *Child Develop-ment, 60,* 1405–1411.

Lee, Meery (1991). *Effectiveness of coping in adolescence: The case of Korean exami-nation stress.* Master's thesis submitted to the University of Illinois, Urbana-Champaign.

LeFevre, Judith, Hedricks, Cynthia, Church, R. Breckinridge, and McClintock, Martha K. (1991). Psychological and social behavior of couples over a men-strual cycle: "On-the-spot" sampling from everyday life. In Alice Dan and Linda Lewis, (Eds.), *Menstrual health research.* Chicago: University of Illinois Press.

Lein, Laura (1979). Male participation in home life: Impact of social supports and breadwinner responsibility on the allocation of tasks. *Family Coordinator, 28,* 489–495.

Leone, Carla M. (1989). *The influence of family relationships and mood states on academic achievement.* Unpublished doctoral dissertation, Loyola University of Chicago.

Leone, Carla M., and Richards, Maryse H. (1989). Classwork and homework in early adolescence: The ecology of achievement. *Journal of Youth and Adoles-cence, 18,* 531–548.

Lerner, Jacqueline V., and Galambos, Nancy L. (1985). Maternal role satisfaction, mother–child interaction, and child temperament: A process model. *Develop-mental Psychology, 21,* 1157–1164.

Leslie, Leigh A., and Anderson, Elaine A. (1988). Men's and women's participation in domestic roles: Impact on quality of life and marital adjustment. *Journal of Family Psychology, 2,* 212–226.

Levenson, Robert W., and Gottman, John M. (1983). Marital interaction: Physio-logical linkage and affective exchange. *Journal of Personality and Social Psy-chology, 45,* 587–597.

Levenson, Robert W., and Gottman, John M. (1985). Physiological and affective predictors of change in relationship satisfaction. *Journal of Personality and Social Psychology, 49,* 85–94.

Levinson, Daniel J. (1978). *The seasons of a man's life.* New York: Ballantine.

Lewis, Michael, Feiring, Candice, and Weinraub, Marsha (1981). The father as a member of the child's social network. In Michael E. Lamb (Ed.), *The role of the father in child development* (pp. 259–294). New York: Wiley.

Lewis, Robert A., and Spanier, Graham B. (1979). Theorizing about the quality and stability of marriage. In Wesley R. Burr, Reuben Hill, F. Ivan Nye, and Ira L. Reiss (Eds.), *Contemporary theories about the family: Research-based theo-ries* (vol. 1) (pp. 268–294). New York: Free Press.

Locke, Harvey J., and Wallace, Karl M. (1959). Short marital-adjustment and pre-dictor tests: Their reliability and validity. *Marriage and Family Living, 21,* 251–255.

Lopata, Helena Z. (1971). *Occupation: Housewife.* New York: Oxford University Press.

Lorence, Jon, and Mortimer, Jeylan T. (1985). Job involvement through the life course: A panel study of three age groups. *American Sociological Review, 50,* 618–638.

Low, Richard (1990). *Childhood's future.* Boston: Houghton Mifflin.

Lutz, Catherine A. (1988). *Unnatural emotions: Everyday sentiments on a Micronesian atoll and their challenge to western theory.* Chicago: University of Chicago Press.

Maccoby, Eleanor E., and Martin, John A. (1983). Socialization in the context of the family: Parent–child interaction. In Paul H. Mussen (Ed.), *Handbook of child psychology: Socialization, personality, and social development,* vol. 4 (pp. 1–101). New York: Wiley.

Mace, David R. (1983). The marriage enrichment movement. In David R. Mace (Ed.), *Prevention in family services* (pp. 98–109). Beverly Hills: Sage.

Malik, S. M. (1981). *Psychological modernity: A comparative study of some African and American graduate students.* Unpublished doctoral dissertation, University of Chicago.

Malik, S. M. (1990, March). *Time use and juvenile delinquency in the Kingdom of Saudi Arabia.* Society for Research on Adolescence, Atlanta, GA.

Mannell, Roger C., Zuzanek, Jiri, and Larson, Reed W. (1988). Leisure states and "flow" experiences: Testing perceived freedom and intrinsic motivation hypotheses. *Journal of Leisure Research, 20,* 289–304.

Marcoen, Alfons, Goossens, Luc, and Caes, Paul (1987). Loneliness in pre- through late adolescence: Exploring the contributions of a multidimensional approach. *Journal of Youth and Adolescence, 16,* 561–578.

Margolin, Gayla, and Wampold, Bruce E. (1981). Sequential analysis of conflict and accord in distressed and nondistressed marital partners. *Journal of Consulting and Clinical Psychology, 49,* 554–567.

Margolin, Leslie, and White, Lyon (1987). The continuing role of physical attractiveness and other demographic characteristics on promotion decisions. *Journal of Management, 16,* 723–736.

Markus, Hazel, and Nurius, Paula (1986). Possible selves. *American Psychologist, 41,* 954–969.

Marshall, Harriette (1991). The social construction of motherhood: An analysis of childcare and parenting manuals. In Ann Phoenix, Anne Woollett, and Eva Lloyd (Eds.), *Motherhood: Meaning, practices and ideologies* (pp. 66–85). Newbury Park, CA: Sage.

Martin, Dorothy H. (1985). Fathers and adolescents. In S. M. H. Hanson and F. W. Bozett (Eds.), *Dimensions of fatherhood* (pp. 170–195). Beverly Hills: Sage.

Martin, Robin, and Wall, Toby D. (1989). Attentional demand and cost responsibility as stressors in shopfloor jobs. *Academy of Management Journal, 32,* 69–86.

Martocchio, Joseph J., and O'Leary, Anne M. (1989). Sex differences in occupational stress: A meta-analytic review. *Journal of Applied Psychology, 74,* 495–501.

Matthews, Karen A., and Rodin, Judith (1989). Women's changing work roles: Impact on health, family, and public policy. *American Psychologist, 44,* 1389–1393.

McAdoo, Harriette P. (1993). *Family ethnicity: Strength in diversity.* Thousand Oaks, CA: Sage.

McBride, Brent A. (1990). The effects of a parent education/play group program on father involvement in child rearing. *Family Relations, 39,* 250–256.

McBride, Brent A. (1991). Parental support programs and paternal stress: An exploratory study. *Early Childhood Research Quarterly, 6,* 137–149.

McLoyd, Vonnie C. (1989). Socialization and development in a changing economy: The effects of paternal job and income loss on children. *American Psychologist, 44,* 293–302.

Mellman, Mark, Lazarus, Edward, and Rivlin, Allan (1990). Family time, family values. In David Blankenhorn, Steven Bayme, and Jean B. Elshtain (Eds.), *Rebuilding the nest: A new commitment to the American family* (pp. 73–92). Milwaukee: Family Service America.

Menaghan, Elizabeth G., and Parcel, Toby L. (1990). Parental employment and family life: Research in the 1980s. *Journal of Marriage and the Family, 52,* 1079–1098.

Messner, Michael (1987). The life of a man's seasons: Male identity in the life course of the jock. In Michael S. Kimmel (Ed.), *Changing men* (pp. 53–67). Newbury Park, CA: Sage.

Michelson, William M. (1985). *From sun to sun: Daily obligations and community structure in the lives of employed women and their families.* Totowa, NJ: Rowman and Allanheld.

Modell, John, and Goodman, Madeline (1990). Historical perspectives. In S. Shirley Feldman and Glen R. Elliott (Eds.), *At the threshold: The developing adolescent* (pp. 93–122). Cambridge, MA: Harvard University Press.

Montemayor, Raymond (1982). The relationship between parent–adolescent conflict and the amount of time adolescents spend alone and with parents and peers. *Child Development, 53,* 1512–1519.

Montemayor, Raymond (1983). Parents and adolescents in conflict: All families some of the time and some families most of the time. *Journal of Early Adolescence, 3,* 83–103.

Montemayor, Raymond (1986). Family variation in parent–adolescent storm and stress. *Journal of Adolescent Research, 1,* 15–31.

Montemayor, Raymond, and Brownlee, John R. (1987). Fathers, mothers, and adolescents: Gender-based differences in parental roles during adolescence. *Journal of Youth and Adolescence, 16,* 281–291.

Montemayor, Raymond, and Hanson, Eric (1985). A naturalistic view of conflict between adolescents and their parents and siblings. *Journal of Early Adolescence, 5,* 23–30.

Moos, Rudolf H., and Moos, Bernice S. (1986). *Family environment scales manual* (2nd ed.). Palo Alto, CA: Consulting Psychologists Press.

Morawski, Jill G. (1984). Not quite new worlds: Psychologists' conceptions of the ideal family in the twenties. In Miriam Lewin (Ed.), *In the shadow of the past: Psychology portrays the sexes* (pp. 97–125). New York: Columbia University Press.

Morris, Naomi M., and Udry, J. Richard (1980). Validation of self-administered instrument to assess stage of adolescent development. *Journal of Youth and Adolescence, 9,* 271–280.

Mortimer, Jeylan T., Lorence, Jon, and Kumka, Donald S. (1986). *Work, family and personality.* Norwood, NJ: Ablex.

Munroe, Ruth H., Munroe, Robert L., Michelson, Carol, Koel, Amy, Bolton, Ralph, and Bolton, Charlene (1983). Time allocation in four societies. *Ethnology, 22,* 355–370.

Musgrove, Frank (1963). Intergenerational attitudes. *British Journal of Social Clinical Psychology, 2,* 209–223.

Nannis, Ellen D., and Cowan, Philip A. (1987). Emotional understanding: A matter of age, dimension, and point of view. *Journal of Applied Developmental Psychology, 8,* 289–304.

Neulinger, John (1974). *The psychology of leisure.* Springfield, IL: Charles C. Thomas.

Nock, Steven L., and Kingston, Paul W. (1988). Time with children: The impact of couples' work-time commitments. *Social Forces, 67,* 59–85.

Nolen-Hoeksema, Susan, Morrow, Jannay, and Fredrickson, Barbara L. (1993). Response styles and the duration of episodes of depressed mood. *Journal of Abnormal Psychology, 102,* 20–28.

Noller, Patricia, and Bagi, Stephen (1985). Parent–adolescent communication. *Journal of Adolescence, 8,* 125–144.

Noller, Patricia, and Callan, Victor J. (1986). Adolescent and parent perceptions of family cohesion and adaptability. *Journal of Adolescence, 9,* 97–106.

Noller, Patricia, and Gallois, Cynthia (1988). Understanding and misunderstanding in marriage: Sex and marital adjustment differences in structured and free interaction. In Patricia Noller and Mary Anne Fitzpatrick (Eds.), *Perspectives on marital interaction* (pp. 53–77). Philadelphia: Multilingual Matters.

Notarius, Clifford I., and Johnson, Jennifer S. (1982). Emotional expression in husbands and wives. *Journal of Marriage and the Family, 44,* 483–490.

Novak, Michael (1976). *The joy of sports: End zones, bases, baskets, balls, and the consecration of the American spirit.* New York: Basic Books.

O'Donnell, Kathleen A. (1993). *"Quality time" during adolescence: The relationship between family-time experience and positive family adjustment.* Master's thesis, University of Minnesota.

Offer, David, and Offer, Judith B. (1975). *Teenage to young manhood: A psychological study.* New York: Basic Books.

Offer, David, Ostrov, Eric, and Howard, Kenneth I. (1981). *The adolescent.* New York: Basic Books.

O'Leary, K. Daniel, and Emery, Robert E. (1984). Marital discord and child behavior problems. In Melvin D. Levine and Paul Satz (Eds.), *Middle childhood: Development and dysfunction* (pp. 345–364). Baltimore, MD: University Park Press.

Orthner, Dennis K. (1975). Leisure activity patterns and marital satisfaction over the marital career. *Journal of Marriage and the Family, 37,* 91–102.

Orthner, Dennis K., and Mancini, Jay A. (1990). Leisure impacts on family interaction and cohesion. *Journal of Leisure Research, 22,* 125–137.

Osherson, Samuel (1986). *Finding our fathers.* New York: Fawcett Columbine.

Oswald, Hans, and Suess, Klaus U. (1990, March). *German teenagers' time distribution between parents and peers.* Society for Research on Adolescence, Atlanta, GA.

Paikoff, Roberta L. (Ed.) (1991). *Shared views in the family during adolescence: New directions for child development,* (vol. 51). San Francisco: Jossey-Bass.

Paikoff, Roberta L., and Brooks-Gunn, Jeanne (1991). Do parent–child relationships change during puberty? *Psychological Bulletin, 110,* 47–66.

Parcel, Toby L., and Menaghan, Elizabeth G. (1990). Maternal working conditions and children's verbal facility: Studying the intergenerational transmission of inequality from mothers to young children. *Social Psychology Quarterly, 53,* 132–147.

Parke, Ross D., and Sawin, Douglas B. (1979). Children's privacy in the home: Developmental, ecological, and child-rearing determinants. *Environment and Behavior, 11,* 87–104.

Parke, Ross D., and Tinsley, Barbara R. (1984). Fatherhood: Historical and contemporary perspectives. In Kathleen A. McCluskey and Hayne W. Reese (Eds.), *Life-span developmental psychology: Historical and generational effects* (pp. 203–248). Orlando, FL: Academic Press.

Parsons, Talcott (1942). Age and sex in the social structure of the United States. *American Sociological Review, 7,* 604–616.

Parsons, Talcott, and Bales, Robert F. (1955). *Family, socialization and interaction process.* Glencoe, IL: Free Press.

Patterson, Charlotte J. (1992). Children of lesbian and gay parents. *Child Development, 63,* 1026–1042.

Patterson, Gerald R. (1980). Mothers: The unacknowledged victims. *Monographs of the Society for Research in Child Development, 45,* 42–49.

Patterson, Gerald R. (1986). Performance models for antisocial boys. *American Psychologist, 41,* 432–444.

Patterson, Gerald R., and Bank, Lorita (1989). Some amplifying mechanisms for pathologic processes in families. In Megan R. Gunnar and Esther Thelen (Eds.), *22nd Minnesota symposia on child psychology: Systems and development* (pp. 167–209). Hillsdale, NJ: Lawrence Erlbaum.

Patterson, Gerald R., and Dishion, Thomas J. (1988). Multilevel family process models: Traits, interactions, and relationships. In Robert A. Hinde and Joan Stevenson-Hinde (Eds.), *Relationships within families: Mutual influences* (pp. 283–310). Oxford: Clarendon Press.

Paulson, Sharon E., Hill, John P., and Holmbeck, Grayson (1991). Distinguishing between perceived closeness and parental warmth in families with seventh grade boys and girls. *Journal of Early Adolescence, 11,* 276–293.

Perry-Jenkins, Maureen, and Crouter, Ann C. (1990). Men's provider-role attitudes: Implications for household work and marital satisfaction. *Journal of Family Issues, 11,* 136-156.

Peterson, Eric (1965). Working women. In Robert J. Lifton (Ed.), *The woman in America* (pp. 144–172). Boston: Houghton Mifflin.

Phares, Vicky, and Compas, Bruce E. (1992). The role of fathers in child and adolescent psychopathology: Make room for daddy. *Psychological Bulletin, 111,* 387–412.

Pieper, Joseph (1963). *Leisure: The basis of culture.* New York: New American Library.

Piotrkowski, Chaya S. (1979). *Work and the family system: A naturalistic study of working-class and lower-middle-class families.* New York: Free Press.

Pittman, Joe F., and Orthner, David K. (1989). Gender differences in the prediction of job commitment. In Elizabeth B. Goldsmith (Ed.), *Work and family: Theory, research, and application* (pp. 227–248). Newbury Park, CA: Sage.

Pleck, Elizabeth H. (1976). Two worlds in one. *Journal of Social History, 10,* 178–195.

Pleck, Joseph H. (1985). *Working wives/working husbands.* Newbury Park, CA: Sage.

Pleck, Joseph H. (1986). Employment and fatherhood: Issues and innovative policies. In Michael E. Lamb (Ed.), *The father role: Applied perspectives* (pp. 385–412). New York: Wiley.

Pleck, Joseph H. (1987). Men in domestic settings: American fathering in historical perspective. In Michael S. Kimmel (Ed.), *Changing men* (pp. 83–97). Newbury Park, CA: Sage.

Polatnick, Margaret (1973–74). Why men don't rear children: A power analysis. *Berkeley Journal of Sociology, 18,* 45–86.

Popkin, Michael (1987). *Active parenting: Teaching cooperation, courage, and responsibility.* New York: HarperCollins.

Prigogine, Ilya (1980). *From being to becoming: Time and complexity in the physical sciences.* San Francisco: W. H. Freeman.

Radin, Norma (1988). Primary caregiving fathers of long duration. In Phyllis Bronstein and Carolyn P. Cowan (Eds.), *Fatherhood today: Men's changing role in the family* (pp. 127–165). New York: Wiley.

Raffaelli, Marcela (1992). Sibling conflict in early adolescence. *Journal of Marriage and the Family, 54,* 652–663.

Raffaelli, Marcela, and Duckett, Elena (1989). "We were just talking . . . ": Conversations in early adolescence. *Journal of Youth and Adolescence, 18,* 567–582.

Reis, Harry (1986). Gender effects in social participation: Intimacy, loneliness, and conduct of social interaction. In Robin Gilmour and Steve Duck (Eds.), *The emergent field of personal relationships* (pp. 91–105). Hillsdale, NJ: Lawrence Erlbaum.

Reiss, David (1981). *The family's construction of reality.* Cambridge, MA: Harvard University Press.

Repetti, Rena L. (1989). Effects of daily workload on subsequent behavior during marital interaction: The roles of social withdrawal and spouse support. *Journal of Personality and Social Psychology, 57,* 651–659.

Repetti, Rena L. (1993a). Short-term effects of occupational stressors on daily mood and health complaints. *Health Psychology, 12,* 125–131.

Repetti, Rena L. (1993b, March). *The effects of daily social and academic failure experiences on children's subsequent interactions with parents.* Society of Research in Child Development, New Orleans, LA.

Repetti, Rena L. (submitted). Short-term and long-term processes linking perceived job stressors to father–child interaction.

Repetti, Rena L., Matthews, Karen A., and Waldron, Ingrid (1989). Employment and women's health. *American Psychologist, 44,* 1394–1401.

Richards, Maryse H., Casper, Regina C., and Larson, Reed W. (1990). Weight and eating concerns among pre- and young adolescent boys and girls. *Journal of Adolescent Health Care, 11,* 203–209.

Richards, Maryse H., and Duckett, Elena (1994). The relationship of maternal employment to the daily experiences of young adolescents with and without parents. *Child Development, 65,* 225–236.

Richards, Maryse H., and Larson, Reed W. (1990). *Romantic relations in early adolescence.* International Conference on Personal Relations, Oxford, England.

Richards, Maryse H., and Larson, Reed W. (1993). Pubertal development and the daily subjective states of young adolescents. *Journal of Research on Adolescence, 3*(2), 145–169.

Roberts, Tomi Ann, Hawkins, Alan J., and Marshall, Christina (1992, November). *A multi-method evaluation of a program to help dual-earner couples share housework and child care.* National Council on Family Relations, Orlando, FL.

Robinson, John P. (1977). *How Americans use time: A social-psychological analysis of everyday behavior.* New York: Praeger.

Robinson, John P. (1985). The validity and reliability of diaries versus alternative time use measures. In F. Thomas Juster and Frank P. Stafford (Eds.), *Time, goods, and well-being* (pp. 63–92). Ann Arbor: Institute for Social Research.

Robinson, John P. (1990). The time squeeze. *American Demographics, 12,* 30–33.

Rodgers, Fran S., and Rodgers, Charles (1989). Business and the facts of family life. *Harvard Business Review, 67,* 121–129.

Rohlen, Thomas P. (1983). *Japan's high schools.* Berkeley and Los Angeles, CA: University of California Press.

Rook, Karen, Dooley, David, and Catalano, Ralph (1991). Stress transmission: The effects of husbands' job stressors on the emotional health of their wives. *Journal of Marriage and the Family, 53,* 165–177.

Rosaldo, Michelle Z. (1974). Woman, culture, and society: A theoretical overview. In Michelle Z. Rosaldo and Louise Lamphere (Eds.), *Woman, culture, and society* (pp. 17–42). Stanford, CA: Stanford University Press.

Rosenberg, Morris (1965). *Society and the adolescent self-image.* Princeton, NJ: Princeton University Press.

Rosenblatt, Paul C., and Cunningham, Michael (1976). Television watching and family tensions. *Journal of Marriage and the Family, 31,* 105–111.

Rosenblatt, Paul C., Titus, Sandra L., Nevaldine, Anne, and Cunningham, Michael R. (1979). Marital system differences and summer-long vacations: Togetherness–apartness and tension. *American Journal of Family Therapy, 7,* 77–84.

Ross, Catherine E., Mirowsky, John, and Huber, Joan (1983). Dividing work, sharing work, and in-between: Marriage patterns and depression. *American Sociological Review, 48,* 809–823.

Rotundo, E. Anthony (1985). American fatherhood: A historical perspective. *American Behavioral Scientist, 29,* 7–25.

Rubin, Lilian B. (1976). *Worlds of pain: Life in the working-class family.* New York: Basic Books.

Rubin, Lilian B. (1983). *Intimate strangers: Men and women together.* New York: Harper & Row.

Russell, Graeme, and Radin, Norma (1983). Increased paternal participation: The fathers' perspective. In Michael E. Lamb and Abraham Sagi (Eds.), *Fatherhood and family policy* (pp. 139–165). Hillsdale, NJ: Lawrence Erlbaum.

Russell, Graeme, and Russell, Alan (1987). Mother–child and father–child relationships in middle childhood. *Child Development, 58,* 1573–1585.

Ryan, Richard M., and Lynch, John H. (1989). Emotional autonomy versus detachment: Revisiting the vicissitudes of adolescence and young adulthood. *Child Development, 60,* 340–356.

Rybczynski, Witold (1991). Waiting for the weekend. *Atlantic Monthly, 268*(2), 35–52.

Sabatelli, Ronald M. (1988). Measurement issues in marital research: A review and critique of contemporary survey instruments. *Journal of Marriage and the Family, 50,* 891–915.

Samdahl, Diane M. (1991). Issues in the measurement of leisure: A comparison of theoretical and connotative meanings. *Leisure Sciences, 13,* 33–49.

Savin-Williams, Ritch C., and Berndt, Thomas J. (1990). Friendship and peer relations. In Shirley S. Feldman and Glenn R. Elliott (Eds.), *At the threshold: The developing adolescent* (pp. 277–309). Cambridge, MA: Harvard University Press.

Scanzoni, John (1970). *Opportunity and the family.* New York: Free Press.

Scanzoni, John (1983). *Shaping tomorrow's family: Theory and policy for the 21st century.* Beverly Hills, CA: Sage.

Scarr, Sandra, Phillips, Deborah, and McCartney, Kathleen (1989). Working mothers and their families. *American Psychologist, 44,* 1402–1409.

Schaap, Cas (1984). A comparison of the interaction of distressed and nondistressed married couples in a laboratory situation: Literature survey, methodological issues, and an empirical investigation. In Kurt Hahlweg and Neil S.

Jacobson (Eds.), *Marital interaction: Analysis and modification* (pp. 133–158). New York: Guilford Press.

Schnucker, Robert V. (1990). Puritan attitudes towards childhood discipline, 1560–1634. In Valerie Fildes (Ed.), *Women as mothers in pre-industrial England* (pp. 108–121). New York: Routledge.

Schor, Juliet B. (1991). *The overworked American: The unexpected decline of leisure.* New York: Basic Books.

Schultz, Jerelyn B., Chung, Yonsuk L., and Henderson, Chinella G. (1989). Work/family concerns of university faculty. In Elizabeth B. Goldsmith (Ed.), *Work and family: Theory, research, and application* (pp. 249–264). Newbury Park, CA: Sage.

Schwartz, Linda D., Fisher, Alban, Tolan, Patrick, and Thomas, Peter (1993). *Daily experience of urban minority adolescents: Gender patterns in activity across companion groups.* Unpublished manuscript, University of Illinois at Chicago.

Schwartz, Reid M., and Trabasso, Thomas (1984). Children's understanding of emotions. In Carroll E. Izard, Jerome Kagan, and Robert B. Zajonc (Eds.), *Emotions, cognitions, and behavior* (pp. 409–437). Cambridge: Cambridge University Press.

Selman, Robert (1980). *The growth of interpersonal understanding.* New York: Academic Press.

Shank, John W. (1986). An exploration of leisure in the lives of dual career women. *Journal of Leisure Research, 18,* 300–319.

Shantz, Carolyn U., and Hobart, Cathy J. (1989). Social conflict and development: Peers and siblings. In Thomas J. Berndt and Gary W. Ladd (Eds.), *Peer relationships in child development* (pp. 71–94). New York: Wiley.

Shaw, Susan M. (1984). The measurement of leisure: A quality of life issue. *Society and Leisure, 7,* 91–107.

Shaw, Susan M. (1985). The meaning of leisure in everyday life. *Leisure Sciences, 7,* 1–24.

Shaw, Susan M. (1988). Gender differences in the definition and perception of household labor. *Family Relations, 37,* 333–337.

Silverberg, Susan B., and Steinberg, Laurence (1990). Psychological well-being of parents with early adolescent children. *Developmental Psychology, 26,* 658–666.

Silverstein, Brett, and Perdue, Lauren (1988). The relationship between role concerns, preferences for slimness, and symptoms of eating problems among college women. *Sex Roles, 18,* 101–106.

Simmons, Roberta G., and Blyth, Dale A. (1987). *Moving into adolescence: The impact of pubertal change and school context.* Hawthorne, NY: Aldine de Gruyter.

Simmons, Roberta G., Blyth, Dale A., Van Cleave, Edward F., and Bush, Diane M. (1979). Entry into early adolescence: The impact of school structure, puberty, and early dating on self-esteem. *American Sociological Review, 44,* 948–967.

Simmons, Roberta G., Burgeson, Richard, Carlton-Ford, Steven, and Blyth, Dale A.

(1987). The impact of cumulative change in early adolescence. *Child Development*, 58, 1220–1234.

Skinner, Martie L., Elder, Glen H. Jr., and Conger, Rand D. (1992). Linking economic hardship to adolescent aggression. *Journal of Youth and Adolescence*, 21(3), 259–276.

Skolnick, Arlene (1991). *Embattled paradise: The American family in an age of uncertainty*. New York: Basic Books.

Small, Stephen A., and Eastman, Gay (1991). Rearing adolescents in contemporary society: A conceptual framework for understanding the responsibilities and needs of parents. *Family Relations, 40*, 455–462.

Small, Stephen A., Eastman, Gay, and Cornelius, Steven (1988). Adolescent autonomy and parental stress. *Journal of Youth and Adolescence, 17*, 377–391.

Smetana, Judith G. (1988a). Adolescents' and parents' conceptions of parental authority. *Child Development, 59*, 321–335.

Smetana, Judith G. (1988b). Concepts of self and social convention: Adolescents' and parents' reasoning about hypothetical and actual family conflicts. In Megan R. Gunnar and W. Andrew Collins (Eds.), *21st Minnesota Symposium on Child Psychology: Development during the transition to adolescence* (pp. 79–122). Hillsdale, NJ: Lawrence Erlbaum.

Smith, Gregory T., Snyder, Douglas K., Trull, Timothy J., and Monsma, Brian R. (1988). Predicting relationship satisfaction from couples' use of leisure time. *American Journal of Family Therapy, 16*, 3–13.

Smith, Karen A., and Forehand, Rex (1986). Parent–adolescent conflict: Comparison and prediction of the perceptions of mothers, fathers, and daughters. *Journal of Early Adolescence, 6*, 353–367.

Spitze, Glenna (1988). Women's employment and family relations: A review. *Journal of Marriage and the Family, 50*, 595–618.

Sroufe, L. Alan, and Fleeson, June (1988). The coherence of family relationships. In Robert A. Hinde and Joan Stevenson-Hinde (Eds.), *Relationships within families: Mutual influences* (pp. 27–47). Oxford: Oxford University Press.

Stafford, Frank P., and Duncan, Greg J. (1985). The use of time and technology by households in the United States. In F. Thomas Juster and Frank P. Stafford (Eds.), *Time, goods, and well-being* (pp. 245–288). Ann Arbor: Institute for Social Research.

Steinberg, Laurence (1987). The impact of puberty on family relations: Effects of pubertal status and pubertal timing. *Developmental Psychology, 23*, 451–460.

Steinberg, Laurence (1991). Autonomy, conflict, and harmony in the family relationship. In Shirley S. Feldman and Glenn R. Elliot (Eds.), *At the threshold: The developing adolescent* (pp. 255–276). Cambridge, MA: Harvard University Press.

Steinberg, Laurence, and Silverberg, Susan B. (1986). The vicissitudes of autonomy in early adolescence. *Child Development, 57*, 841–851.

Steinberg, Laurence, and Silverberg, Susan B. (1987). Influences on marital satisfaction during the middle stages of the family life cycle. *Journal of Marriage and the Family, 49*, 751–760.

Steinmetz, Susan K. (1987). Family violence: Past, present, and future. In Marvin B. Sussman and Susan K. Steinmetz (Eds.), *Handbook of marriage and the family* (pp. 725–765). New York: Plenum.

Striegel-Moore, Ruth H., Silberstein, Lisa R., and Rodin, Judith (1986). Toward an understanding of risk factors for bulimia. *American Psychologist, 41,* 246–263.

Suitor, J. Jill (1991). Marital quality and satisfaction with the division of household labor across the family life cycle. *Journal of Marriage and the Family, 53,* 221–230.

Swarr, Amy, and Richards, Maryse H. (1993, March). *The longitudinal effects of pubertal timing and relationship with parents on eating problems in adolescent girls.* Society for Research in Child Development, New Orleans.

Szalai, Alexander (1972). *The use of time: Daily activities of urban and suburban populations in twelve countries.* The Hague: Mouton.

Szinovacz, Maximiliane E. (1987). Family power. In Marvin B. Sussman and Susan K. Steinmetz (Eds.), *Handbook of marriage and the family* (pp. 651–693). New York: Plenum.

Tait, Marianne, Padgett, Margaret Y., and Baldwin, Timothy T. (1989). Job and life satisfaction: A reevaluation of the strength of the relationship and gender effects as a function of the date of the study. *Journal of Applied Psychology, 74,* 502–507.

Tannen, Deborah (1990). *You just don't understand: Women and men in conversation.* New York: Ballantine.

Teyber, Edward (1983a). Effects of the parental coalition on adolescent emancipation from the family. *Journal of Marital and Family Therapy, 9,* 305–310.

Teyber, Edward (1983b). Structural family relations: Primary dyadic alliances and adolescent adjustment. *Journal of Marital and Family Therapy, 9,* 89–99.

Thomas, David L., and Diener, Ed (1990). Memory accuracy in the recall of emotions. *Journal of Personality and Social Psychology, 59,* 291–297.

Thompson, E. P. (1963). *The making of the English working class.* New York: Vintage.

Thompson, Linda, and Walker, Alexis J. (1989). Gender in families: Women and men in marriage, work, and parenthood. *Journal of Marriage and the Family, 51,* 845–871.

Timmer, Susan G., Eccles, Jacquelynne, and O'Brien, Kevin (1985). How children use time. In F. Thomas Juster and Frank P. Stafford (Eds.), *Time, goods, and well-being* (pp. 353–382). Ann Arbor: Institute for Social Research.

Tobin-Richards, Maryse H., Boxer, Andrew M., and Petersen, Anne C. (1983). The psychological significance of pubertal change: Sex differences in perceptions of self during early adolescence. In J. Brooks-Gunn and Anne C. Petersen (Eds.), *Girls at puberty: Biological and psychosocial perspectives* (pp. 127–154). New York: Plenum.

Ulbrich, Patricia M. (1988). The determinants of depression in two-income marriages. *Journal of Marriage and the Family, 50,* 121–131.

United Media Enterprises (1983). *Where does the time go? The United Media Enter-*

prises report on leisure in America. New York: Newspaper Enterprise Association.

Verbrugge, Lois M. (1987). Role responsibilities, role burdens, and physical health. In Faye J. Crosby (Ed.), *Spouse, parent, worker: On gender and multiple roles* (pp. 154–166). New Haven: Yale University Press.

Veroff, Joseph, Douvan, Elizabeth, and Kulka, Richard A. (1981). *The inner American: A self-portrait from 1957–1976*. New York: Basic Books.

Vinovskis, Maris A. (1987). Historical perspectives on development of the family and parent–child interactions. In. Jane B. Lancaster, Jeanne Altmann, Alice S. Rossi, and Lonnie R. Sherrod (Eds.), *Parenting across the life span: Biosocial dimensions* (pp. 295–312). New York: Gruyter.

Waldron, Ingrid (1976). Why do women live longer than men? *Journal of Human Stress, 2,* 2–13.

Walker, Kathryn E., and Woods, Margaret E. (1976). *Time use: A measure of household production of family goods and services*. Washington, DC: Center for the Family of the American Home Economics Association.

Weiner, Bernard, and Graham, Sandra (1984). An attributional approach to emotional development. In Carroll E. Izard, Jerome Kagan, and Robert B. Zajonc (Eds.), *Emotions, cognition, and behavior* (pp. 167–191). Cambridge: Cambridge University Press.

Weiss, Robert S. (1990). *Staying the course: The emotional and social lives of men who do well at work*. New York: Fawcett Columbine.

Weitzman, Lenore J. (1981). *The marriage contract: Spouses, lovers, and the law*. New York: Free Press.

Wells, Anne J. (1988). Variations in mothers' self-esteem in daily life. *Journal of Personality and Social Psychology, 55,* 661–668.

Welter, Barbara (1966). The cult of true womanhood: 1820–1860. *American Quarterly, 18*(66), 151–174.

Wessman, Alden E., and Ricks, David F. (1966). *Mood and personality*. New York: Holt, Rinehart and Winston.

West, Patrick C., and Merriam, L. C. Jr. (1970). Outdoor recreation and family cohesiveness: A research approach. *Journal of Leisure Research, 2,* 251–259.

White, Lynn K. (1983). Determinants of spousal interaction: Marital structure or marital happiness. *Journal of Marriage and the Family, 45,* 511–519.

Williams, Dorie G. (1988). Gender, marriage, and psychosocial well-being. *Journal of Family Issues, 9,* 452–468.

Wills, Thomas A., Weiss, Robert L., and Patterson, Gerald R. (1974). A behavioral analysis of the determinants of marital satisfaction. *Journal of Consulting and Clinical Psychology, 42,* 802–811.

Wilson, William J. (1987). *The truly disadvantaged: The inner city, the underclass and public policy*. Chicago: University of Chicago Press.

Wolfenstein, Martha (1955). Fun morality: An analysis of recent American child-training literature. In Margaret Mead and Martha Wolfenstein (Eds.), *Childhood in contemporary cultures* (pp. 168–178). Chicago: University of Chicago Press.

Wolman, Richard, Lewis, William C., and King, Muriel (1971). The development of the language of emotions: Conditions of emotional arousal. _Child Development, 42_, 1288–1293.

Won, Hyung-Joong (1989). _The daily leisure of Korean school adolescents and its relationship to subjective well-being and leisure functioning._ Unpublished doctoral dissertation, University of Oregon.

Wollett, Anne, and Phoenix, Ann (1991). Afterword: Issues related to motherhood. In Ann Phoenix, Anne Woollett, and Eva Lloyd (Eds.), _Motherhood: Meaning, practices and ideologies_ (pp. 216–231). Newbury Park, CA: Sage.

Wright, Paul H., and Keple, Timothy W. (1981). Friends and parents of a sample of high school juniors: An exploratory study of relationship intensity and interpersonal rewards. _Journal of Marriage and the Family, 43_, 559–570.

Yankelovich, Daniel (1981). _New rules: Searching for self-fulfillment in a world turned upside down._ New York: Random House.

Yogev, Sara, and Brett, Jeanne (1985). Perceptions of the division of housework and child care and marital satisfaction. _Journal of Marriage and the Family, 47_, 609–618.

Youniss, James (1980). _Parents and peers in social development._ Chicago: University of Chicago Press.

Youniss, James, and Ketterlinus, Robert D. (1987). Communication and connectedness in mother– and father–adolescent relationships. _Journal of Youth and Adolescence, 16_, 265–280.

Youniss, James, and Smollar, Jacqueline (1985). _Adolescent relations with mothers, fathers, and friends._ Chicago: University of Chicago Press.

Younnis, James, and Smollar, Jacqueline (1989). Adolescents' interpersonal relationships in social context. In. Thomas J. Berndt and Gary W. Ladd (Eds.), _Peer relationships in child development_ (pp. 300–316). New York: Wiley.

Zimmerman, Shirley L. (1992). _Family policies and family well-being: The role of political culture._ Newbury Park, CA: Sage.

Zuo, Jiping (1992). The reciprocal relationship between marital interation and marital happiness: A three-wave study. _Journal of Marriage and the Family, 54_, 870–878.

Zuzanek, Jiri, and Smale, Bryan (1991, June). Life cycle variations in across-the-week allocation of time to selected daily activities. International Society for the Study of Behavioral Development, Minneapolis, MN.

Index